AF901553

Legal Writing Made Simple

Legal Writing Made Simple

A Step-by-Step Approach

Melissa Shultz
PROFESSOR OF LAW
ASSISTANT DEAN OF LEGAL WRITING
ST. MARY'S UNIVERSITY SCHOOL OF LAW

Christine Tamer
ASSOCIATE PROFESSOR &
DIRECTOR OF LEGAL WRITING
UNIVERSITY OF NORTH TEXAS AT DALLAS
COLLEGE OF LAW

CAROLINA ACADEMIC PRESS
Durham, North Carolina

Library of Congress Cataloging-in-Publication Data

Names: Shultz, Melissa (Writer on legal writing), author. | Tamer, Christine, author.
Title: Legal writing made simple : a step-by-step approach / Melissa Shultz, Christine Tamer.
Description: Durham, North Carolina : Carolina Academic Press, 2024. | Includes bibliographical references and index.
Identifiers: LCCN 2024006459 | ISBN 9781531028817 (paperback) | ISBN 9781531028824 (ebook)
Subjects: LCSH: Legal composition. | Law--United States--Language.
Classification: LCC KF250 .S5257 2024 | DDC 808.06/634--dc23/eng/20240209
LC record available at https://lccn.loc.gov/2024006459

Carolina Academic Press
700 Kent Street
Durham, North Carolina 27701
Telephone (919) 489-7486
www.cap-press.com

Printed in the United States of America
2026 Printing

Table of Contents

Acknowledgments

As you can imagine, we have a handful of shout-outs we need to make to acknowledge the key people who made the drafting of this book possible. Very clearly, and always primarily, thanks go to our children—Reagan, Bennett, Palmer, Camille, Tennyson, and Austen—who all deserve serious accolades for understanding weeks of abbreviated bedtime reading and longer than usual work hours. Related to that, we also want to deeply thank our husbands for taking care of the children while we were editing or writing and for (probably more importantly) tolerating our incessant moaning (and necessary procrastinating) while we finalized this second book.

In addition, we owe a huge thank you to the deadline-compliant research assistants who helped finalize this book: Adam Devitt, Amy Gustafson, and Grace Hoffman. Their pages and pages of editorial marks are proof that one—no matter how great an editor—cannot catch her own errors.

We also want to thank our academic colleagues for their unending support, additions, and critiques. In addition, thanks to the editorial staff at Carolina Academic Press, who helped and shepherded us through the process of writing our second book. Their input and edits converted our words and teaching ideas into an easy to follow, well-formatted "real" book that will reach a wider audience than we could have imagined alone.

Finally, thank you to our students—past and present—who have, each year, made us better teachers. Your stories, your grit, and your perseverance amaze us. You were the inspiration for our first book. And, because of that book's success, you too inspired us to write this book for our future students—a book we hope is even better than the first because of what <u>you</u> taught us while using it in the classroom.

Introduction and How to Use This Book

Let's begin with an admission: despite the title of this book, legal writing is not simple. It is difficult. And, it is difficult for innumerable reasons, just a couple of which are worth mentioning here.

The first reason legal writing is difficult is because all law students have written in some form or another since they turned probably about five years old. Given this reality, all law students know how to write at least in the very basic sense of the word (and have known how to do so for quite some time). Moreover, many—top college graduates, English or journalism majors, prior novelists—excel in at least one form of writing. Yet, despite any past experience or success as a writer, no first-year law student comes into law school as a strong ***legal writer***. This is because legal writing requires not only good writing (good grammar, good sentence structure, and good style) but also good legal analysis. How to conduct legal analysis is a new skill. Good legal analysis requires an understanding of what the law is, how the law works, and how the law is communicated by lawyers. Learning the law (and, specifically, learning how to write using it) is a bit like learning a foreign language. Mastery—especially mastery of writing in a new language—takes time, patience, and practice. Law students—especially those who have excelled in other areas of writing—struggle to appreciate the reality that legal writing is much like writing in a new language. Learning to write like a lawyer requires time, patience, and—most importantly—lots of practice in order to become an expert in it.

The second reason legal writing is difficult (and confusing) for students is because legal writing is more like math with words than like quintessential excellent writing, such as poetry. Often students with backgrounds in science or engineering—which are not normally thought of as synonymous with strong writing—excel in legal writing. This is because scientists and engineers are familiar with carefully plotting out the steps they took to reach their result in a logical and methodical fashion. Scientists and engineers are used to formulas and formulaic writing. In legal writing, to conduct sound legal analysis, you also must "show your work"—that is, show the reader step by step how you derived your conclusion from applying the law to the facts of your case. The way you "show your work" in legal writing is formulaic like scientific writing. Courts reach and write decisions in a methodical way and pursuant to an accepted formula, and lawyers must do the same. This can be frustrating to students (especially to students who have their own "style" of writing that has suited them well in the past). As a beginning legal writer, you must set your style aside and first master the math-like content required for excellent legal analysis (and, thus, excellent legal writing).

Given the reality that legal writing is difficult for most new law students, this book aims to demystify the legal writing process by providing concrete formulas—both "macro" formulas and "micro" formulas—for mastering the content required for objective and persuasive legal analysis. The "macro" formula we start with in this book is CRAC, which stands for Conclusion ("C"), Rule ("R"), Analysis ("A"), and Conclusion ("C"). Within this macro formula, we use "micro" formulas to help you draft the different parts of CRAC. This book also breaks down different parts of legal work product, such as the introduction to a motion or the question presented of an objective memo, into smaller components so that you can see how they are constructed. Put simply, at each juncture of your legal writing journey, this book will give you a roadmap to follow (and a step-by-step list of directions). Our goal is that you will never find yourself lost—that is, facing an entirely blank page without directions as to how to start filling it.

Remember those paint-by-numbers kits you received as a gift for your eighth birthday? A bigger picture was broken up into numerous small parts, each with a number indicating which color you were to paint it. Going number by number, following the directions, even the most inexperienced artist could create a beautiful and complex picture. Those paint-by-numbers kits were the inspiration for our method of teaching first-year legal writing and for this book. After working with law students from unique backgrounds, of all different ages, with varied educational experiences, and with diverse core writing abilities, we have learned that the best way to teach beginning legal writing to a diverse set of students is to employ a step-by-step or paint-by-number approach. First, break down the "picture" into small, bite-sized parts. Then, like assigning colors to the numbers in a paint-by-numbers kit, provide formulas and explicit instructions to law students to help them populate their legal product (the picture) with the necessary content (the color). The result is the same: just like the novice artist colored in the small parts in the painting-by-numbers kit to generate a beautiful and complex picture, beginning law students can put the small pieces of legal analysis (CRAC) together to create larger and excellent pieces of legal writing.

Also, just like those paint-by-number kits do not confuse the novice artist with a bunch of choices but instead tell the novice artist that "anything with a number eight should be painted blue," this book aims to not confuse novice law students with a bunch of choices. We have found that, in teaching beginning legal writing, giving a lot of choices to novice legal writers can paralyze them from putting pen to paper (or fingers to keyboard) and writing. If we say, "Here are nine ways to write a case illustration," students think, "I literally just learned what a case illustration is. I have never written a case illustration before. How do I know which of the nine ways I should use to illustrate my case?"

So, in this book, instead of giving you multiple choices for how to—for example—write a rule statement, we show you one way to write a rule statement that works. We then give you an example of that same rule statement in the context of objective writing and persuasive writing (and, in persuasive writing, how the same rule could be written by both sides). In this way, you will not be paralyzed by choices, but, instead, you will be equipped, from the outset, to write your own rule statements by following the instructions, the formulas, and the examples provided.

That said, just like an experienced artist would scoff at a paint-by-numbers kit, an experienced legal writer may scoff at the lack of choices in this book and its strict formulaic approach. But you must learn to crawl before you can walk. You must learn to walk before you can run. Once you master the basics taught in this book, you will have the confidence and skills to take your legal writing to an advanced level and to stray from the strict formulaic approach in this book. That is, once you have learned to talk, you can then learn to make your legal writing sing.

This book is organized into seven parts that can be categorized into three groups. Part One is the longest part of the book. It provides you with an overview of foundational, basic skills that apply to both objective and persuasive writing. Part One discusses (i) the overview of the federal and state legal systems; (ii) the hierarchy of authority; (iii) introductory legal research; (iv) how to read the law; and (v) basic grammar rules. Part One also introduces you to formulaic writing (and its backbone, CRAC—Conclusion, Rule, Analysis, and Conclusion) and why it is important.

Parts Two and Three explicitly address how to draft key legal documents. Part Two dives into objective writing and discusses, in detail, two of the more popular vehicles for objective writing: the formal objective memorandum and the e-mail memorandum. Part and parcel to its discussion of how to draft a formal objective memo, Part Two explains how to use the CRAC formula in the context of objective writing. Part Three discusses persuasive writing and, specifically, persuasive writing to the audience of a trial court via a motion or opposition to a motion. Part Three teaches you to apply the drafting techniques you learned in objective writing and make those techniques persuasive. Part Three builds upon the CRAC formula used in objective writing and shows you how to use it in the context of persuasive writing.

Parts Four through Six expand on the core skills discussed in Parts Two and Three. Part Four, which applies equally to objective writing and persuasive writing, discusses how you edit and polish your written work product (the work product that you so tirelessly drafted according to Part Two or Part Three). Part Five discusses how to take your written work and convert it into an oral presentation, specifically how to convert a motion or opposition into an oral argument. Part Six discusses how the skills at the center of legal writing—Parts One through Four—translate to success on bar-style law-school essay exams, on actual bar essay questions, and on the bar's Performance Tasks.

The last part—Part Seven—is the appendix, which consists of sample objective and persuasive written documents. What makes the appendix unique is that it includes, among other documents, an objective memo, a persuasive motion for summary judgment, and a persuasive opposition to the motion for summary judgment—all of which are written from the same problem and set of facts (although the facts are more developed for the motion and opposition than the memo because those would have been written well after the memo in the life cycle of the case). You will be able to use these documents as examples of not only objective legal writing and persuasive legal writing but also of how each compare to one another. For example, you will be able to see how an objective rule statement for an element compares side by side with a persuasive rule statement for the same element. In addition, you will be able to see how a persuasive rule statement for the same element compares when written by two different sides (the plaintiff and the defendant). The appendix also includes the underlying assigning memo for the objective memo and the factual record for the motion and opposition. You will see how the facts were taken from the assigning memo and transformed into a statement of facts for the objective memo. You will also see how the more complete factual record was transformed into statements of facts that tell two sides of the same story in the motion and the opposition.

Learning how to write—specifically how to write like a lawyer—will be critical to your success both in law school and in your practice as a lawyer. Legal writing is a different kind of writing than any type of writing you have ever done. So buckle up, get comfortable, and get ready to take off into the strange and new world of legal writing!

Note on Permissions

The Westlaw screenshots in Part One and the cases reprinted in the book are reprinted with permission from Thomson Reuters.

Part I | Basic Skills of Legal Writing

In this part of the book, you will learn the basic skills you need to become a proficient—if not an excellent—legal writer. Interestingly, many of these basic skills involve competency in areas different than what may first come to mind when you think of writing. These areas include understanding the state and federal judicial systems, grasping the different types of legal authority and which type of authority is the best to use, finding legal authority using Westlaw and LexisNexis, and reading and comprehending the legal texts you find. Skills in these areas, even though they do not involve putting pen to paper, are critical to your ability to formulate (and then ultimately write) legal analysis and, thus, are critical to your ability to become an excellent legal writer. For example, if you do not know how to read and comprehend a judicial opinion, how will you be able to find the legal rules housed in that judicial opinion that you will need to include in your memo, motion, or brief?

In addition to these "pre-writing skills," this part of the book will introduce you to a number of skills that are more obviously tied to writing, such as ordering your legal analysis the way lawyers expect analysis to be ordered (Conclusion, Rule, Analysis, Conclusion—CRAC), placing and formatting legal citations, and demonstrating competency in basic rules of grammar.

Part One of the book will serve as the backbone of your legal writing course. Although sections of it will be assigned as reading early in the year, you will often find yourself referring back to these lessons.

Chapter 1 | The U.S. and State Legal Systems

As they navigate reading, analyzing, and writing about the law, law students often struggle with the constant requirement to "zoom in" to grasp the specifics and then to "zoom out" to see where those specifics fit into a larger picture. In order to engage in thoughtful legal analysis, however, you, as a law student, must grapple with and understand both the details of the area being studied as well as how the particular area of study relates to the bigger picture. For example, when "zooming in" to analyze whether an act constitutes a battery, you should also "zoom out" to understand the requirements for battery, how battery relates to other intentional torts, and how that analysis fits into the larger legal system. Given the importance of understanding the larger picture, even when studying a limited area of law, we will begin by reviewing the organization of the U.S. legal system so that you can grasp how the cases you read in law school relate to and affect each other and the larger system of government.

The U.S. Constitution divides the U.S. government into three branches—the judicial branch, the legislative branch, and the executive branch.[1] At first blush, it might seem like only the judicial and legislative branches of government are relevant to the study of law, but, in fact, all three branches of government affect the creation and enforcement of law in this country. In brief, the legislative branch makes the laws, the executive branch carries out and enforces the laws, and the judicial

1. U.S. CONST. art. I (legislative branch), art. II (executive branch), and art. III (judicial branch).

branch interprets the laws. As part of a carefully created system of checks and balances among the three branches of government, each branch can impact actions taken by the other branches. For example, the president can veto legislation created and passed by Congress; Congress can remove the president from office under certain circumstances or override the president's vetoes; and the Supreme Court of the United States (also referred to as the U.S. Supreme Court or SCOTUS) can overturn laws passed by Congress that it deems unconstitutional. Given that this is law school, the next section will provide more detail about the judicial branch of government, which includes the Supreme Court of the United States and any inferior courts that Congress or state constitutions establish.

A. Hierarchy of authority: hierarchy of courts

The judicial branch of government—in both the state and federal systems—interprets the meaning of laws, applies laws to individual cases, and decides the legality of laws (under the state and federal constitutions). There are three basic levels of court: trial, intermediate appellate, and appellate court of last resort. These courts are hierarchical in nature, meaning that cases proceed through the three levels of courts in a set order, from lowest to highest. The trial court is the lowest court and a court of original jurisdiction. As such, the trial court is the court where an action is first filed. The intermediate appellate court ("appellate court") and the appellate court of last resort are generally not courts of original jurisdiction. That means, as a general matter, cases are not filed originally in those courts. Instead, appellate courts and courts of last resort review cases from courts below them. The appellate court is the next level up from the trial court—it is the court where the party losing its case (or an aspect of its case) can seek review of ("appeal") the trial court's decision in hopes of achieving a different result. The losing party in the appellate court can then appeal the appellate court's decision to the appellate court of last resort, which is often called a supreme court.

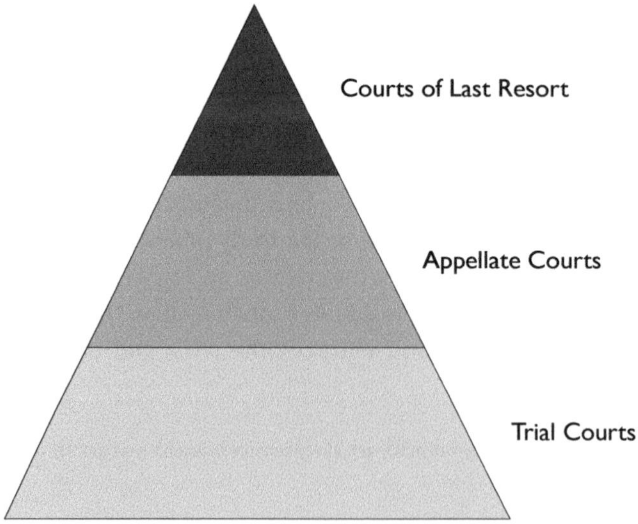

To make things more complicated, however, each state (geographically speaking) houses two distinct court systems—the state judicial system and the federal judicial system.[2] These two systems operate separately from one another, are organized differently, and employ different naming conventions for their courts. Although there is some overlap,[3] generally speaking, the hierarchical structures of the federal and state judicial systems remain distinct. More specifically, what separates the federal and state systems is the types of cases they hear, because each of the 50 states and the federal government retain their own sovereignty, set their own laws, and have their own constitutions.

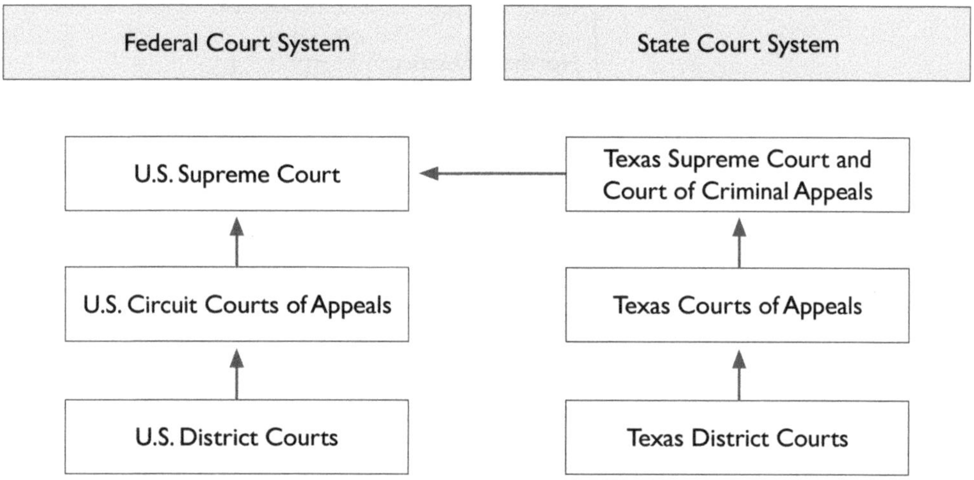

Courts in the federal system apply and interpret federal law. In the federal system, the trial level courts are called district courts, the appellate level courts are called circuit courts of appeals, and the appellate court of last resort is called the Supreme Court of the United States. Federal district courts handle trials—both civil and criminal—within the federal system. There are 94 federal districts that house more than 670 district

2. Tribal court systems comprise a third judicial system that you should keep in mind as you begin to familiarize yourself with the U.S. legal system and hierarchy of authority within that system. There are 574 federally recognized tribal nations. Each tribal nation has a sovereign (nation-to-nation) relationship with the U.S. government. As such, each tribal nation retains inherent powers of self-governance, including the right to determine its own government structure, to pass laws, and to enforce laws through police departments and tribal courts. We encourage you to read more about this interesting and complex area of our legal system, and we encourage you to dedicate some time to exploring this area more deeply during law school.

3. In certain circumstances, state courts can hear cases brought under federal law and federal courts can hear cases brought under state law. For example, and as you will study in first-year Civil Procedure, federal courts can have jurisdiction over cases involving questions of state law when the parties on opposite sides are from different states and the amount in controversy exceeds $75,000.00. This exception to the separation of the state and federal systems is called "diversity jurisdiction."

judges nationwide.[4] Every state, plus the District of Columbia, houses at least one federal district court. Larger states, such as New York, California, and Texas, contain more than one. For example, in Texas, there are four federal district courts: United States District Court for the Northern District of Texas, United States District Court for the Eastern District of Texas, United States District Court for the Western District of Texas, and United States District Court for the Southern District of Texas.

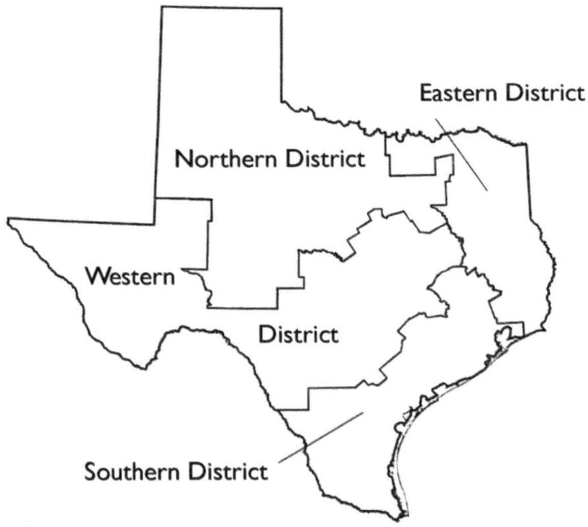

Other states, like Minnesota and Connecticut, only have one federal district court.

Once a federal district court has decided a case, the case can be appealed to the federal circuit court of appeals in which the district court sits. There are a total of thirteen federal circuit courts of appeals, as set forth in the picture below:[5]

4. Congress sets the number of district judges and the number can change. 28 U.S.C. §133.

5. In addition to the 12 location-based circuit courts, the Federal Circuit Court of Appeals, in Washington, D.C., is a nationwide circuit court that has appellate jurisdiction over very specific issues, such as patents.

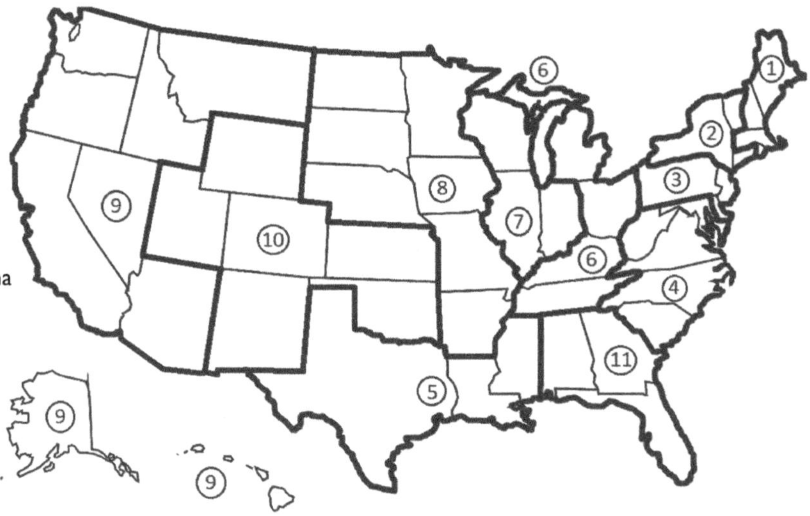

For example, all of the federal district courts located in Texas are in the Fifth Circuit. In addition to Texas, the Fifth Circuit also includes the federal courts in the states of Louisiana and Mississippi. Cases from the federal district courts in all three of those states are appealed to the United States Court of Appeals for the Fifth Circuit, which is headquartered in New Orleans, Louisiana.[6]

The U.S. Supreme Court is the highest court in the federal judicial system. In addition, the U.S. Supreme Court is the ultimate decision-maker when it comes to interpreting federal law as well as interpreting the U.S. Constitution and determining whether either the federal government or a state government has violated rights granted under the U.S. Constitution. The limit on the U.S. Supreme Court's jurisdiction can be confusing for law students—on one hand, the U.S. Supreme Court does **not** have the power to hear cases involving only questions of state law (did the plaintiff commit a battery), but it **can** hear cases that involve whether a state law violates rights granted under the U.S. Constitution (does Texas's battery statute somehow violate the U.S. Constitution). Not all cases that are appealed to the U.S. Supreme Court are heard because it is a court of discretionary review. The U.S. Supreme Court hears only about one percent of the cases that it is asked to hear.

---

6. This description of the federal system is a bit over-simplified. In reality, in addition to the federal districts there are also a few specialty "district" courts, including the U.S.Tax Court, the U.S. Court of International Trade, and the U.S. Court of Federal Claims. Similarly, in addition to the 11 numbered U.S. Courts of Appeals, there are two additional courts of appeals—the District of Columbia Circuit and the Federal Circuit. The hierarchical structure for these specialty courts is a bit different. Decisions from cases heard in the U.S. Tax Courts are appealed to one of the U.S. Court of Appeals. However, decisions from the U.S. Court of International Trade and the U.S. Court of Federal Appeals are appealed in the U.S. Court of Appeals for the Federal Circuit, which was created in 1982 to review decisions of these specialty courts as well as some administrative decisions.

In the state judicial system, the names for each type of court—whether trial, appellate, or last resort—vary from state to state. Let's look at a few examples.

In Texas, there are several different types of trial courts—state-level district courts, county-level courts (which include constitutional county courts, statutory county courts, and statutory probate courts), justice courts, and municipal courts. These trial-level Texas state courts are under the court of appeals in the geographical area where the trial-level court is located. Texas has 14 districts, where 14 courts of appeals are located:

Amarillo	Tyler	Eastland
Beaumont	Houston (2)	Waco
Dallas	Corpus Christi—Edinburgh	Texarkana
El Paso	Austin	
San Antonio	Fort Worth	

In this way, a state district court located in Dallas falls hierarchically under the court of appeals in Dallas. The Texas state system has two appellate courts of last resort: the Court of Criminal Appeals and the Texas Supreme Court. The Court of Criminal Appeals has final appellate jurisdiction over Texas criminal cases. The Supreme Court has statewide, final appellate jurisdiction over most Texas state civil and juvenile cases. Like the U.S. Supreme Court, these two courts are courts of discretionary review.

In contrast, Minnesota—smaller than Texas both in terms of population and geographic size—naturally has a more modestly sized state judicial system. Like the Texas state judiciary, the Minnesota judicial system is comprised of multiple districts. In total, Minnesota has ten judicial districts located throughout the state and each district houses its own district court with original jurisdiction over both civil and criminal cases. Some of these district courts are divided into departments, such as criminal, probate, family, or juvenile departments. Unlike in Texas where there are multiple courts of appeals, Minnesota has only a single intermediary court of appeals, the Minnesota Court of Appeals. This appellate court, created in 1983, hears appeals from all ten of the state's district courts.[7] Although a few cases are appealed directly to the state's highest court, the Minnesota Supreme Court, is tasked with hearing appeals of cases previously decided by the Minnesota Court of Appeals.

Why does judicial hierarchy matter? Understanding the hierarchical structure of the federal and state judicial systems is important because where a case is within that structure dictates whether a decision from a particular court is mandatory or persuasive on the court you are before. If a particular decision is mandatory (also referred to as binding), it means that the lower court must follow that decision with respect to the issue that has been decided by the court or courts above it. On the other hand, decisions issued out of a lower court will not be mandatory or binding on a court higher in the

---

7. Section 3 of Article VI of the Minnesota Constitution also allows district courts to have appellate jurisdiction as "prescribed by law."

judicial hierarchy in the same system; instead, such decisions will merely be persuasive. Similarly, more often than not, decisions from federal courts are not binding on state courts and vice versa.[8]

Determining whether a particular statute or case is mandatory or persuasive requires you to engage in a two-step process. First, you must determine which jurisdiction's law applies: is it federal or state law, and which state or federal circuit are you in? Second, you must determine which of that jurisdiction's cases or statutes will be binding on the court that will be deciding your case.

Let's look at an example. You are an attorney handling a case in Texas related to whether termination of your client's parental rights is in her child's best interest—purely a state law question. The statute implicated by your client's issue is in the Texas Family Code—a Texas law. Your case is being heard by Judge Moyé in the 14th District Court in Dallas County. In support of your motion for summary judgment, you need to cite a case for the standard for summary judgment in Texas. Which cases would be mandatory authority for the 14th District Court?

Step one: Determine what jurisdiction's law applies.

Here, you are dealing with a Texas state statute and are in a Texas state court.

Step two: Determine which of that jurisdiction's cases or statutes will be mandatory or binding on the court you are in.

Here, you are in the 14th District Court in Dallas County. This is a state, trial-level court. Federal courts (in Texas and elsewhere) and other state courts (e.g., Oklahoma or Arkansas) would—at most—be persuasive. Texas state courts "above" the court you are in (the 14th District Court in Dallas County)—the Court of Appeals for the Fifth District of Dallas (not to be confused the federal Fifth Circuit Court of Appeals) and the Texas Supreme Court—would be mandatory. All other Texas state courts (those courts at your same level and those courts above you but overseeing different districts) would be merely persuasive.

Take a look at the chart below. There are two courts that are mandatory or binding on your state, trial-level court in Dallas.

8. Generally, the federal court system hears cases involving federal law and the state court systems hear cases involving state law. There are a few areas—such as criminal law—where state and federal jurisdiction overlaps. In such instances, federal law preempts (i.e. controls) state law when the two laws conflict, when Congress expressly or implicitly says so, or when federal laws are so pervasive that they occupy the entire field of law.

COURT	FEDERAL OR STATE COURT	MANDATORY OR PERSUASIVE
44th District Court in Dallas County	State	Persuasive
Oklahoma Supreme Court	State	Persuasive
14th District Court in Dallas County	State	Persuasive
Court of Appeals for the Fifth District of Texas at Dallas	State	Mandatory
Texas Supreme Court	State	Mandatory
Court of Appeals for the 14th District of Texas at Houston	State	Persuasive
U.S. Supreme Court	Federal	Persuasive
United States Court of Appeals for the Fifth Circuit	Federal	Persuasive

Put in the simplest terms, cases which are both (1) in the same jurisdiction, and (2) from a higher court are considered mandatory or binding authority.

On top of all of this, sometimes mandatory authority conflicts with other mandatory authority and you have to figure out which of the mandatory authority is likely to have more weight. The "weight" a court gives to the conflicting authority may turn on a number of factors, including prestige of the issuing court, the date of the opinion, the strength of the opinion's reasoning, the subsequent treatment of that authority by other authorities, whether the issue you are using the case for is dicta or part of the court's holding, the factual similarity to your case, whether the opinion is published, the number of judges subscribing to the opinion, or the reputation of the judge who drafted the case opinion. Similarly, some persuasive authority is more persuasive than other persuasive authority. Again, the weight given to a certain piece of persuasive authority will turn on the same factors.

Chapter 2 | **Types of Legal Authority**

In addition to assessing how a judicial opinion fits within the judicial hierarchy to determine whether it is mandatory or persuasive, you must also determine whether the source relied on is primary or secondary authority.

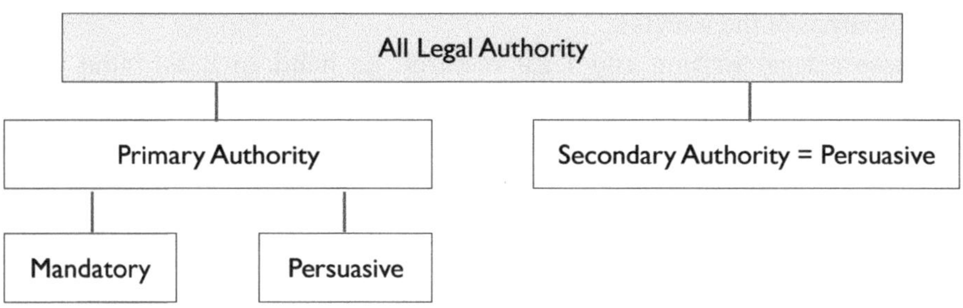

Primary authority includes cases (judicial decisions) and enacted law, such as constitutions, statutes, and regulations. Depending on which jurisdiction the case you are handling is in, primary authority may be, as explained above, either mandatory or persuasive.

Secondary authority, on the other hand, takes a variety of forms. Secondary authority includes such sources as treatises, legal encyclopedias, law review articles, and summaries of the law. Typically, secondary sources seek to explain or comment on primary authority. Secondary authority is always persuasive. To the extent secondary authority conflicts with primary authority, the primary authority will control.

For law students and lawyers, secondary authority sources serve as helpful resources to understand the context and background of an area of the law. Secondary sources can also help you locate relevant primary authority. Secondary sources, however, are not themselves law and, as such, should be used only where primary authority is absent or as background for giving context to primary authority.

A. How to find the law

Now that you have a general overview of how the legal system is organized, let's discuss how you, as a law student, will find the law. In most first-year legal writing programs, during the first semester, students' first big writing assignment is a "closed-packet" objective memorandum. "Closed-packet" means that students are not supposed to do legal research. Instead, all legal authority (statutes, cases, secondary sources, etc.) is provided. The reason for using a closed-packet problem to start off students' legal education is to allow students to focus solely on legal writing, which is a new and difficult skill in and of itself. However, in real life, when given a legal "problem"—whether that be an issue from a client, a memorandum to write for a partner, a motion to draft, or a brief to which you must respond—lawyers are not given an accompanying "closed-packet" of legal authority upon which to rely. Instead, after understanding the problem, in whatever form it takes, a lawyer's first step is usually to find the legal authority or, in other words, to conduct legal research. By conducting that legal research, a lawyer will find the legal authority upon which she will rely to write analysis of the issue(s).

Because legal writing and legal research go hand in hand, after successfully completing a closed-packet problem, most law schools switch to an "open" problem. This means that students must do their own legal research to find the legal authority upon which they will rely for the arguments they will include in their objective memorandum or their persuasive motion, opposition, or brief. Legal research, however, is a varied and expansive skill. It is one that you will continue to refine throughout law school and well into your post-graduate legal practice.

1. Introduction to research

How to do legal research is well beyond the scope of this book. Indeed, there are numerous books devoted solely to teaching you how to conduct legal research in general and how to adjust your legal research process depending on the area of law you are researching. Hopefully, during your tenure at law school you will elect (or be required) to take an entire class devoted to legal research.

For purposes of this book, we will provide you with only a brief overview of how lawyers conduct legal research. And, given that the world is rapidly moving online, we will focus on online legal research. This is not to say that there is not value in conducting research in books; but, truth be told, today most lawyers are doing their research online, especially when it comes to searching for primary authority like statutes and cases. Moreover, many secondary sources—treatises, periodicals, reports, restatements, and so forth—are now, in addition to being in print, available online. Sometimes, it is more efficient to navigate these sources online because you can, with the click of a button, immediately search within them. Also, from online secondary sources, you can click on internal links that will take you directly to the primary authority (cases, statutes, regulations, etc.) that these secondary sources summarize or discuss.

The most commonly used online legal research services are Westlaw® and LexisNexis®. For the sake of simplicity, the quick tips below use Westlaw as an example. Note that, while Lexis is similar, there are a few small differences, such that what is below will not perfectly translate to searching on Lexis.

2. *Quick tips for researching online*

When you first begin researching online using either Westlaw or Lexis, you may feel overwhelmed. Unlike when you were given a closed-packet problem with a set of legal authorities, you now have a whole world of legal authority at your fingertips. You are no longer in a closed universe but are instead in what seems like an endless universe of information. How do you get started? There are lots of theories on how to conduct legal research and discussing each of them (or any of them) is beyond the scope of this book. However, we have set forth some general principles tailored to the problem accompanying this book to help give you an overview of one way to approach researching.

Tip #1: Make your universe smaller.

Although there are tens of thousands of databases on Lexis and Westlaw, most of them will be entirely irrelevant to the problem you are researching. Therefore, after you understand your problem, before researching, you must narrow your universe so that you will look only in databases that are relevant to your problem. For example, if you look at the problem accompanying this book, you will see that it involves a religious discrimination cause of action in the U.S. District Court for the Northern District of Texas. Therefore, the problem (1) is set in a federal trial-level court and (2) involves the legal issue of Title VII religious discrimination (a federal, statutory claim). From this, you can narrow your universe of potentially relevant legal authority considerably. Because the problem is in a federal district court in Texas and involves an issue solely involving federal law, you need to figure out what primary legal authority will be mandatory and persuasive to the court you are before.

As noted, the issue (Title VII religious discrimination) involves a federal statutory claim. Statutory claims come from statutes, whereas common law claims come from caselaw. This means the primary authority upon which you will rely for your rules (law) that govern the issue will come from both the Title VII statute itself and caselaw interpreting it. This narrows your universe even more.

First, we know from the problem that the applicable statute is Title VII, which is found at 42 U.S.C.A. section 2000e-2(a)(1) and provides: "It shall be an unlawful employment practice for an employer—(1) to fail or refuse to hire or to discharge any individual, or otherwise to discriminate against any individual with respect to his compensation, terms, conditions, or privileges of employment, because of such individual's race, color, religion, sex, or national origin ...." The language of the statute itself is not very helpful in determining what exactly is required in a religious discrimination cause of action. Therefore, what we ultimately need to find are cases interpreting this statute.

Now that you know you are ultimately looking for cases, next, ask, where should the cases be from? To answer this question, you need to look at where your problem is set; that is, what court you are before. Here, you are in the U.S. District Court for the Northern District of Texas. This is a federal, trial-level court in the federal Fifth Circuit. The only mandatory authority to a federal trial-level court on an issue of federal law will be the federal intermediate appellate court (Fifth Circuit Court of Appeals) above it and the federal appellate court of last resort (U.S. Supreme Court). Does this mean you are only looking for cases from these two courts? No! Other primary authority may be persuasive, especially cases from other federal courts of appeals and other district courts in the Fifth Circuit (for example, the U.S. District Court for the Northern District of Texas, Southern District of Texas, Eastern District of Texas, or Western District of Texas). Therefore, your universe, in order of priority, should be:

MANDATORY:
Supreme Court of the United States
Fifth Circuit Court of Appeals

PERSUASIVE:
Other Federal Circuit Courts of Appeal
Federal District Court cases (especially from the district courts in the Fifth Circuit)

Do you need to be searching for legal authority from other countries? No, a federal district court in Dallas does not care what Canada does. Do you need to be searching for legal authority from other state courts? No, a federal district court in Dallas will not care what a Maryland state court does because the issue is one of federal law—not Maryland state law. What about legal authority from Texas state courts? The answer is the same as above. Because it is an issue of federal law, a federal district court will not be that persuaded by a state court's interpretation.

As you can see, your universe continues to get smaller. Let's start with what will be most persuasive to our federal district court in Dallas: federal cases from the circuit we are in, which is the Fifth Circuit. To capture searching only federal cases in the Fifth Circuit, you tailor your search. On Westlaw, your beginning screen will look similar to the below image. If you simply type into the search bar, you will be searching **all content types** from **all state and federal jurisdictions** ("All State & Federal"). This is not only an expensive search from a cost standpoint (yes, in practice, searches cost money), but it is also way too broad.

First, you do not want to search all content types; you need to narrow your search to caselaw (not trial court orders, statutes, rules, secondary sources, forms, briefs, etc.). Therefore, you should click on the "Cases" link under "Content types." This will limit your search to only cases, as you can see on the left side of the search bar.

Second, you do not want to search all cases, but only Fifth Circuit cases. To do this, you click on the right grey box in the tool bar and change it to "5th Circuit."

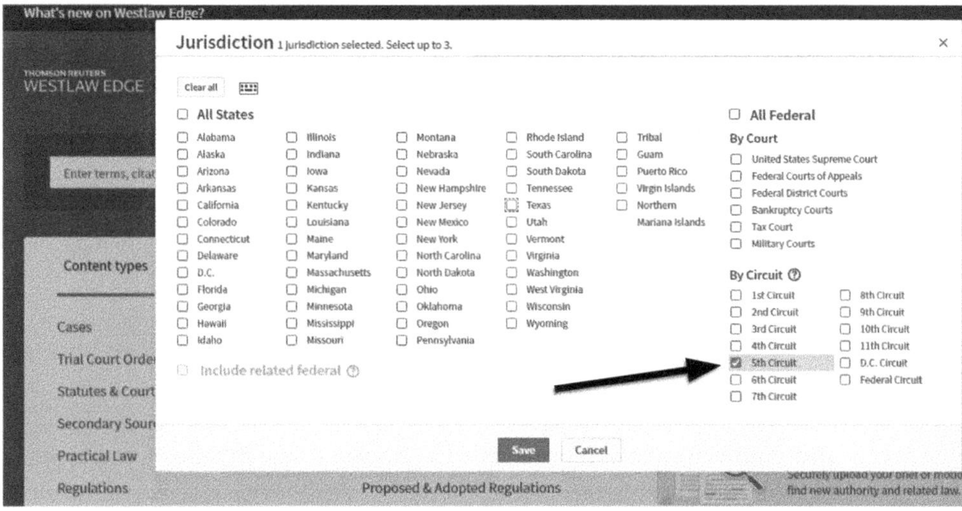

This will capture only cases in the Fifth Circuit, which includes the Supreme Court of the United States (which is in every federal circuit), the Fifth Circuit Court of Appeals, and the federal district courts from the states of Texas, Louisiana, and Mississippi. Now your search will be limited to only cases and only cases from the "Fifth Circuit" (as defined above).

Tip #2: Craft your search terms.

What kinds of Fifth Circuit cases do you want to find? Certainly, you are looking for cases that discuss religious discrimination under Title VII. If a case does not discuss religious discrimination under Title VII, it is probably not going to be very helpful to you.

Therefore, you need to conduct a search within your "Fifth Circuit" cases universe for the term "**Title VII religious discrimination.**" One way to do this is by simply typing the words **Title VII religious discrimination** (without quotations) into the search bar like you would on Google. This is called a "natural language" search. While this natural language search feels comfortable and easy, it is less exacting and does not provide the same strong results as the other type of search—a "terms-and-connectors" search. As you can see, the natural language search of **Title VII religious discrimination** yielded almost 600 results when we ran it (and probably yields even more now if you ran it today).

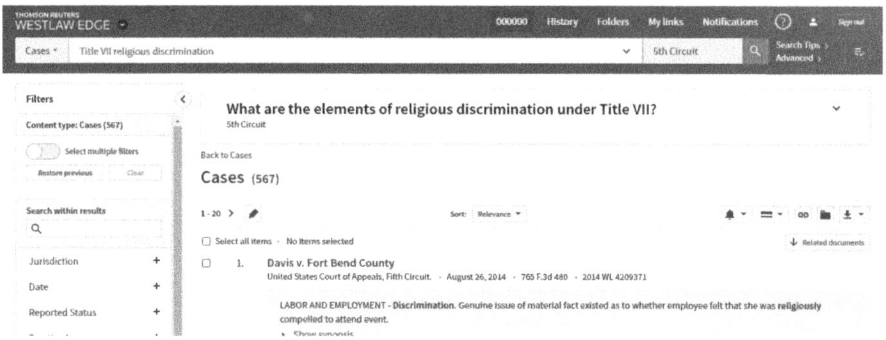

A terms-and-connectors search (also called a "Boolean" search) allows you to specify relationships between search terms and, therefore, allows your searches to be more precise. There are lots of terms and connectors you can use when crafting a search. We will discuss our favorite ones, but a more complete list can be found on both Westlaw and Lexis, which offer free, online quick guides for researching. The favorite term-and-connector we use is /#, which specifies that terms must be within a certain number of words from each other. For example, we do not want cases that simply have the word "religious" and the word "discrimination" anywhere in them, rather we want the words to be either right next to each other or close to each other. We also don't just want the word "Title" and "VII"—we want them together like "Title VII." To capture this, we could search **"Title VII"** in quotations, which would return only cases that have "Title VII" as reflected in the quotation marks. Then, we also want religious discrimination. Therefore, we would use the connector **AND or &** to add those words. We could also put "**religious discrimination**" in quotations, which would return only cases that have the term "religious discrimination" as reflected in the quotation marks. However, if that search turned out to be too narrow or was not capturing the results we needed, we could use the term and connector /# and search **religious /4 discrimination**, which would return cases with the word **religious** within four words of the word **discrimination**. The search we enter could look like this: **"Title VII" & religious /4 discrimination**. When we ran this search, it narrowed the results some (to 496), but not nearly enough.

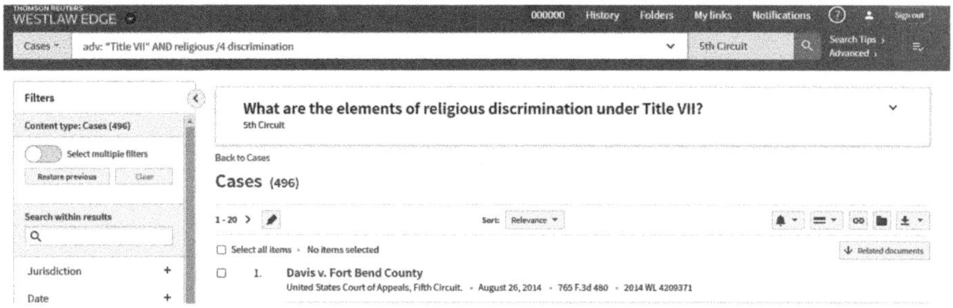

One of the issues is whether the employee held a bona fide religious belief. We could search: **"Title VII" AND religious /4 discrimination /30 bona /4 fide.**

This search will capture cases that include the exact phrase **"Title VII"** and include **religious** within four words of **discrimination** within 30 words of **bona** and within four words of **fide.** By using the /# with respect to these far words (religious, discrimination, bona, and fide), the search will find cases with not only those four words, but cases with those four words in close proximity to one another.

This narrows the results to 102 cases, which is still a lot, but it is much less than the original almost 600 case results.

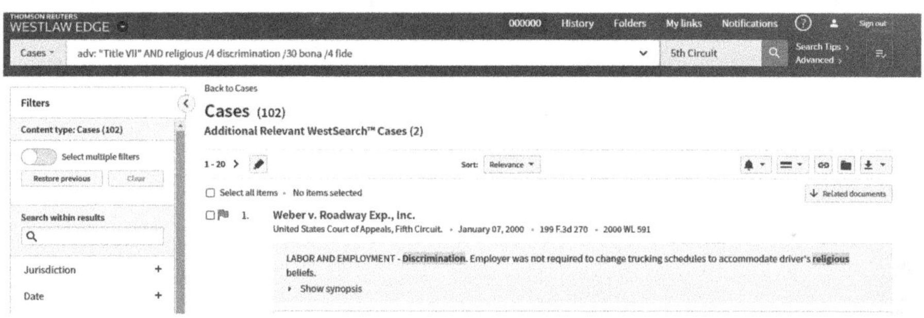

Note, if we wanted to capture not only "discrimination" but also variations of the word (discriminate, discriminating, discriminator, etc.), we could use an explanation mark [!], which is a root expander. So, for example, **"Title VII" AND religious /4 discrimin! /30 bona /4 fide.**

Using terms and connectors is a bit of a science and bit of an art. Play around with it. If you are getting too many results (or too few), you can change the terms, change up the connectors, or do a combo.

Tip #3: Narrow and refine.

When searching, it is best to start broad and then refine or narrow the results. For example, let's say we ran the search **"Title VII" & religious /4 discrimination**, which yielded about 500 results. We can narrow this search by searching within those results using the search box ("Search within results") in the left panel.

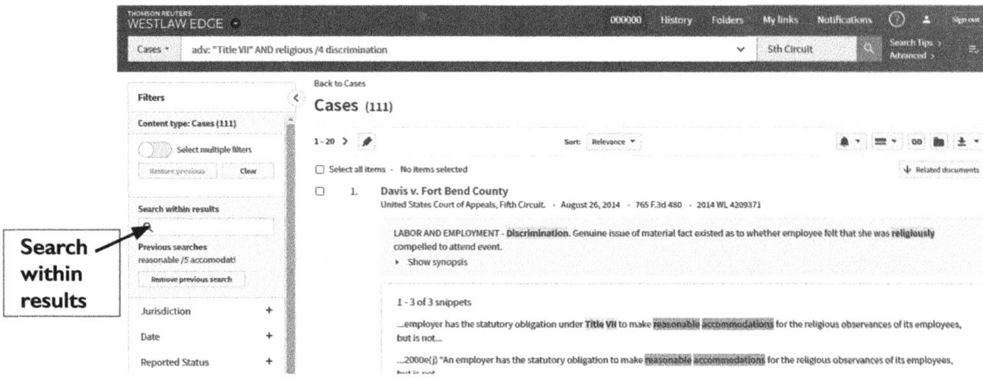

Let's say we searched within the left search bar, **reasonable /5 accommodat!**. This search translates to the following: **reasonable** within five words of all variations of the word **accommodate**. Now, the initial almost 500 results are limited to 111, which is a much more manageable number. Note that we could make this number even smaller by filtering the results using the options on the left panel. You can see under the "Jurisdiction" heading to the left of the 111 case results that eight cases are from the Supreme Court of the United States and 20 are from the Fifth Circuit Court of Appeals, and 88 are from federal district courts. If we wanted to narrow it down to mandatory, binding authority only, we could select only the cases from the Supreme Court and the Fifth Circuit Court of Appeals, which would be 28 cases.

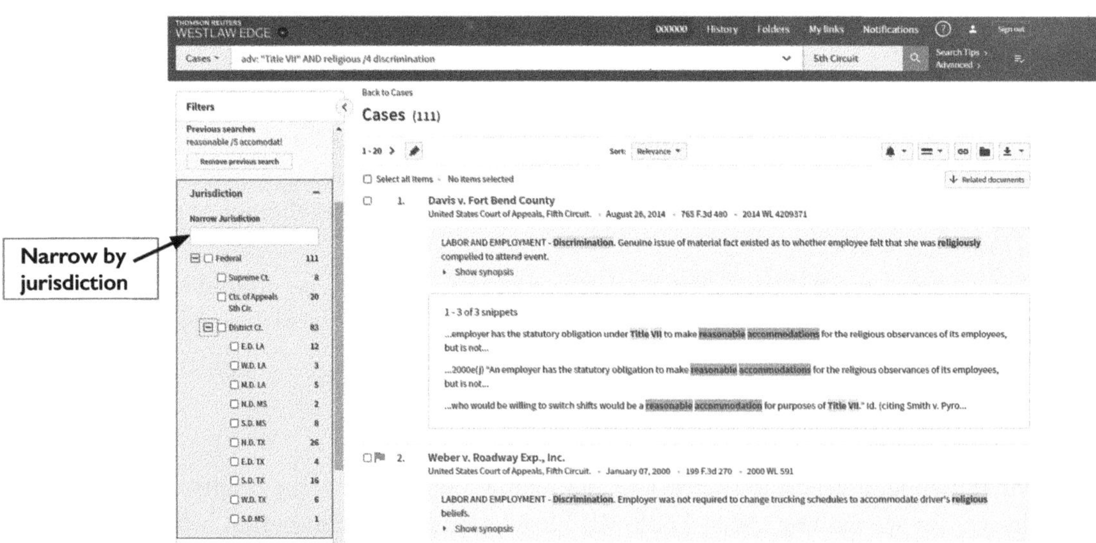

Tip #4: Use good cases to find other good cases.

From the above results, the first case listed is *Davis v. Ford Bend County*. If we were to read this case, we would realize that this Fifth Circuit case (mandatory, binding) is on point because it involves whether an employee suffered religious discrimination by her employer when she wanted to attend a church event and did not report to work. The *Davis* facts are at least somewhat analogous to the facts in the problem. Put another way, it is a "good" case. We can use this "good" case to find other "good" cases in a couple of ways. First, we can see which cases *Davis* cites and read those cases by clicking the link to them from within *Davis*. Second, we can click "Citing References" to see which cases cite to *Davis*. Given that *Davis* is on point, it is likely that many of the cases it cites or many cases that cite to it will be on point and useful as well.

Tip #5: Secondary sources = your friend.

We should refer to secondary sources to refine our understanding of the law. Secondary sources are very helpful in understanding an area of law and leading you to relevant primary authority. Oftentimes, it is wise to start looking in secondary sources before conducting a search of primary authority like caselaw. You can find secondary sources on Westlaw by clicking "Secondary Sources" under "Content types." On the next screen, you will be able to narrow your secondary sources search by type and/or by state.

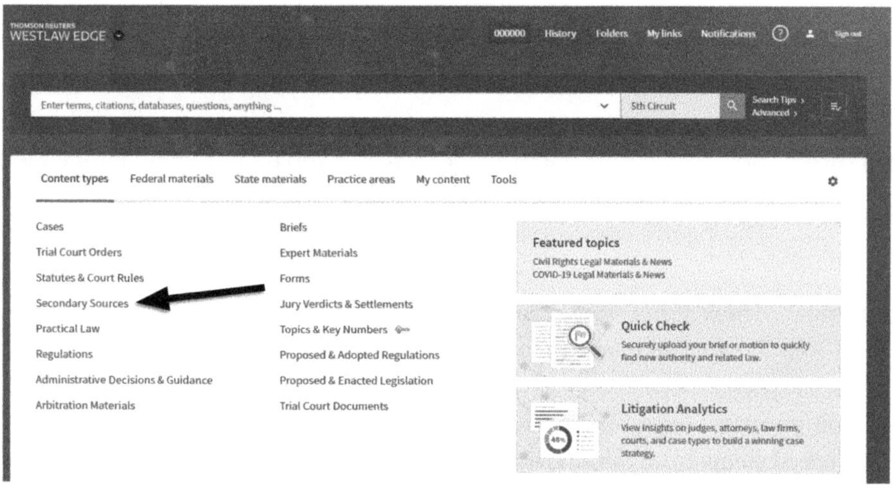

Another place to find secondary sources is in a law school's library. While we find it easier to search for cases online rather than in print, the same is not true of secondary sources, and it can be easier to navigate secondary sources in book form. Much like you probably enjoy having your textbooks in hard copy, flipping through a secondary source in hard copy is, simply put, easier than navigating its contents online (with the caveat that you will not have the ease of following the linked references as discussed above).

B. How to read the law

Reading for law school and reading for the practice of law are different from other types of reading law students have been asked to complete before law school. Law school reading is different in terms of sheer quantity;[1] but, more importantly, it is different in terms of the skills required to parse the text and the depth and breadth of the takeaways that a legal reader is expected to glean from the readings. Instead of assigned readings that are descriptive and tell the reader what she needs to learn from the text, law school readings are nuanced, contextual, and evaluative. This difference means that the popular techniques—such as "speed reading" and "power-browsing"—that are taught and valued in other reading-heavy contexts can end up being a disservice, rather than a tool, for law students trying to understand the law by reading cases and statutes.

Instead of powering through a text with the purpose of capturing the highlights and key terms, students reading legal texts must take a slower, multi-step approach to reading.

Step one: Identify the purpose for which you are reading the source. What part of the law are you trying to understand?

Step two: Skim the source, paying attention to any headings and any conclusions, to get the source's context. Do not use a highlighter or take notes during this step. Sit on your hands.

Step three: Slowly read the source. Look up terms you do not know, interact with the text, and note what is said, as well as what is not said, in the text. During this step, you may take notes and highlight key parts of the text.

Step four: Think about how this source relates to others you have read and/or how it helps you resolve client problems.

As you progress, legal reading will become—and must become—faster. This increased speed stems from familiarity with terms and with the structure of legal sources. It also comes from an appreciation for the fact that some parts of a case can be

1. Law students are assigned on average three to four hours of reading daily. Law School Numbers, *How to Determine if the Law Is for You*, available at http://lawschoolnumbers.com/application-prep/is-law-for-you (last visited April 28, 2024). Such extensive reading, however, does not end in law school because a central part of practicing lawyers' work involves reading. In fact, most lawyers read "at least ten hours per week," and younger lawyers read closer to "thirty hours" a week. *Id.*

skimmed, while others must be more carefully parsed, depending on the issue with which you are grappling. For example, you may be doing research for a case that involves a potential battery. The judicial opinion that you are reviewing may address the requisite elements of battery, but it may also resolve procedural issues or even the presence or absence of other related torts. When you first begin reading cases, you will need to deeply read the entire case to discern which parts of the opinion are relevant to your assigned issue. As you fine-tune your legal reading skills, however, you will be able to focus on the parts of the opinion relevant to your precise issue and skim (or skip) those parts that involve, for example, other torts irrelevant to your research. Again, when you first begin navigating legal texts, you need to read texts in their entirety to begin to build your legal vocabulary and to develop your ability to discern what is (or is not) relevant.

Given this reality, law students are best served by setting aside their preconceptions of how to successfully complete reading assignments from their prior educational or vocational experiences. Instead, you should treat being a legal reader as a new skill that must be practiced and learned. Moreover, different types of legal texts require unique skills in order to successfully parse them. This section aims to identify the key skills and processes lawyers need to read the two most common legal texts: statutes and caselaw.

1. How to read a statute

Statutes are formal written laws enacted by legislative bodies, such as the U.S. Congress, a state legislature, or a city council. Unfortunately, statutes are complex, and because they are often the result of "group thinking" and extensive compromise, they can be dense and difficult to understand (even when they are only a single paragraph long). Sometimes statutes are even—dare we say—poorly drafted.

As a result, it is important for new law students to appreciate that reading a statute is an art as much as it is a science. As such, it is critical for new law students to approach statutory reading slowly and deliberately with a multi-step plan and a significant amount of time allotted for the task. When given an assignment to read a statute, one of the most common mistakes that new law students make is they do simply that: they take five minutes to read the words of the statute. Reading a statute like an article, a chapter from a book, or even a case, will not likely yield a meaningful understanding of the statute, much less how it may or may not apply to a particular context. Thus, you should read a statute like you would read Ikea assembly instructions for a bunkbed: slowly, closely, and with attention to detail.

A legal reader faced with the task of grappling with a new statute should, generally speaking, use the same basic steps set forth above for how to read the law. In an effort to provide you with a bit more guidance, the table below fine-tunes the four steps recommended for general legal reading to conform to the nuances of statutory reading, which requires extra care.

Step one: Identify the purpose for which you are reading the statute. What part of the law are you trying to understand and how does the specific statute you are reading fit into the larger context of the law?

Step two: Skim the statute, paying attention to any headings and any conclusions, to get the statute's context. Make an effort to decipher how the statute operates and to whom or to what it applies. Do not use a highlighter or take notes during this step. Sit on your hands.

Step three: Slowly read the statute with painful particularity. Look up terms you do not know, interact with the text, and note what is said, as well as what is not said, in the text. Pay close attention to "watchwords" and grammatical construction. During this step, you may take notes and highlight key parts of the text.

Step four: Think about how this particular statute relates to other statutes or other pieces of law (cases possibly) that you have read and/or how it helps you resolve client problems.

To better understand the process you should use when you read a statute, let's try reading a statute together. Imagine this scenario in your not so distant future:

> Congratulations, after three years of law school and after successfully passing the Bar Exam, you are a family law attorney in the great state of Texas! One afternoon, a client calls your office and says she has been served with divorce papers by her long-time boyfriend. She explains that they were never formally married. Trying to figure out the basis for the divorce filing, she asks you what the requirements are for an informal marriage in Texas. You set up a meeting to review the law with her tomorrow. You pull up section 2.401 of the Texas Family Code and read it by engaging in each of the four steps above. Below is the text of the relevant statute as it appears in the Texas Family Code.

SUBCHAPTER E. MARRIAGE WITHOUT FORMALITIES

Sec. 2.401. PROOF OF INFORMAL MARRIAGE. (a) In a judicial, administrative, or other proceeding, the marriage of a man and woman may be proved by evidence that:

(1) a declaration of their marriage has been signed as provided by this subchapter; or

(2) the man and woman agreed to be married and after

the agreement they lived together in this state as husband and wife and there represented to others that they were married.

(b) If a proceeding in which a marriage is to be proved as provided by Subsection (a)(2) is not commenced before the second anniversary of the date on which the parties separated and ceased living together, it is rebuttably presumed that the parties did not enter into an agreement to be married.

(c) A person under 18 years of age may not:

(1) be a party to an informal marriage; or

(2) execute a declaration of informal marriage under Section 2.402.

(d) A person may not be a party to an informal marriage or execute a declaration of an informal marriage if the person is presently married to a person who is not the other party to the informal marriage or declaration of an informal marriage, as applicable.

Added by Acts 1997, 75th Leg., ch. 7, Sec. 1, eff. April 17, 1997. Amended by Acts 1997, 75th Leg., ch. 1362, Sec. 1, eff. Sept. 1, 1997.

Amended by:

Acts 2005, 79th Leg., Ch. 268 (S.B. 6), Sec. 4.12, eff. September 1, 2005.

Step one: Identify the purpose for which you are reading the statute. What part of the law are you trying to understand and how does the specific statute you are reading fit into the larger context of the law?

The first step you should take when reading a statute is really a two-part step: first, identify the purpose for reading the statute; and, second, determine how the statute you are reading fits into the larger, statutory context.

In our hypothetical situation, your purpose for reading the statute is relatively straightforward: your client, who was not formally married but has a long-time boyfriend who served her with divorce papers, wants to know the requirements of an informal marriage to determine whether she and her boyfriend were, in fact, ever married. In other words, you are reading the statute to discern the requirements for an informal marriage.

Next, with this in mind, you must figure out how the statute you are reading fits into the overall statutory scheme to determine whether the section you are reading will give a complete answer to your client's question or whether you need to review additional statutory sections. To do this, you must "zoom out" a bit, so you can see beyond the particular statute in front of you. This requires that you understand how statutes are organized and how the statute you are reading fits into that larger organizational structure.

a. Organization and structure of state statutes

Like many other states, Texas statutes are—for the most part—organized by subject matter. Each "code" or book of Texas statutes includes the state laws—statutes—on a particular topic. For example, Texas has the Alcoholic Beverage Code, Election Code, Estates Code, Family Code, Penal Code, etc. Each subject matter code is then broken up into multiple titles, chapters, subchapters, and sections. In our hypothetical, you are tasked with finding out what is required to prove an informal marriage. In which subject matter code do you think you would find this information? Below is a list of Texas codes.

Agriculture Code
Alcoholic Beverage Code
Business and Commerce Code
Business Organizations Code
Civil Practice and Remedies Code
Education Code
Civil Statutes (Education Auxiliary)
Election Code
Estates Code
Family Code
Finance Code
Government Code
Health and Safety Code
Human Resources Code
Insurance Code
Labor Code
Local Government Code
Natural Resources Code
Occupations Code
Parks and Wildlife Code
Penal Code
Property Code
Special District Local Laws Code
Tax Code
Transportation Code
Utilities Code
Water Code
Civil Statutes (Water Auxiliary)
Civil Statutes (Titles 1 to 32)
Civil Statutes (Titles 33 to 77)
Civil Statutes (Titles 78 to 111)
Civil Statutes (Titles 112 to Final Title)
Texas Probate Code
Constitution of the State of Texas 1876
Code of Criminal Procedure
Effective Dates of Laws
UCC Acknowledgments
Vernon's Texas Rules Annotated

Information about marriage—informal or formal—would probably be located in the Texas Family Code.[2] (And, if you read the previous pages of this book, you were already told that. Close reading pays off.)

If you were to go to the library and locate the physical copy of the Texas Family Code, below is a picture of what you would see.

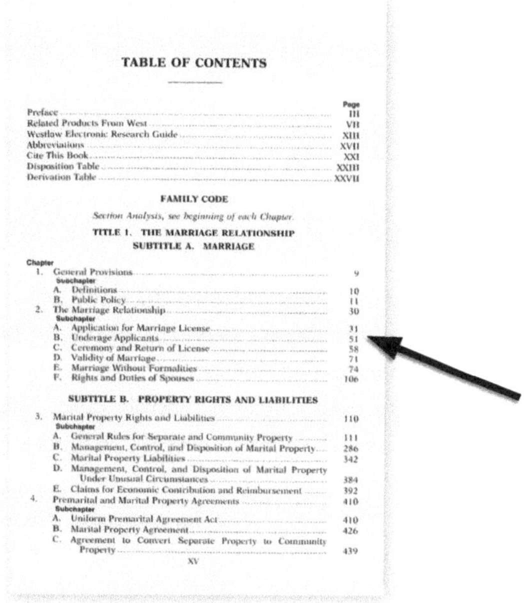

TABLE OF CONTENTS

XV

As you can see, the table of contents in the book version of the statute allows you to see where the section on informal marriage is in relation to the larger code—Title 1, The Marriage Relationship, Subtitle A. Marriages, Chapter 2, Subchapter E. Marriage without Formalities. As a reader, you can then look to the surrounding sections to see if there are other provisions you should peruse because they may affect your reading of the provision that is most relevant to you. For example, in this case, the "Definitions" section located in Chapter 1 of the same title seems relevant because it may define terms in the statute at issue.

Another way to access a state statute is to use an online legal search engine, such as Westlaw or Lexis, as discussed above. Below is what you would find if you looked up the Texas Family Code on informal marriage on Westlaw.

2. You will note that in Texas, as in other jurisdictions, there are both annotated and unannotated statutes. Annotated statutes—like regular statutes—contain the language of the official statute, but, in addition, contain summaries of important judicial decisions related to the included provision(s).

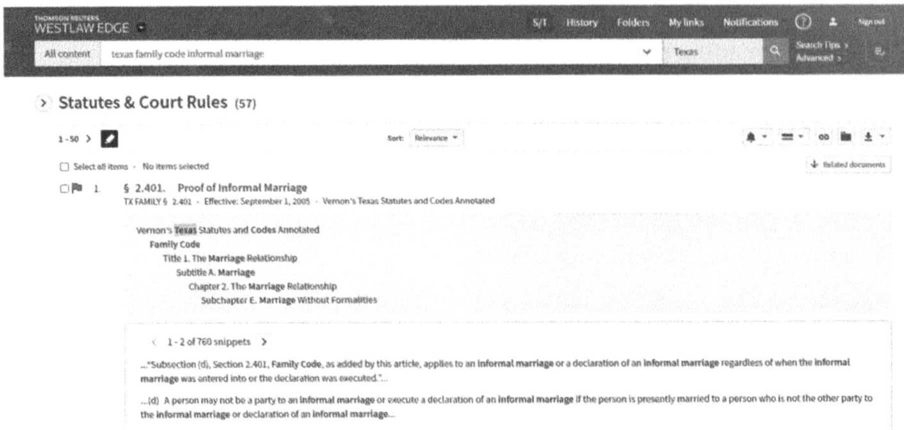

The complete index to the code does not appear automatically online the same way it would if you accessed the statute in hard copy. That said, in just a few easy clicks, you can access a table of contents and peruse the statute online just as you would in hard copy. First, click on "Family Code," and then, if you scroll down, you can click on the various chapters to reveal subchapters and sections.

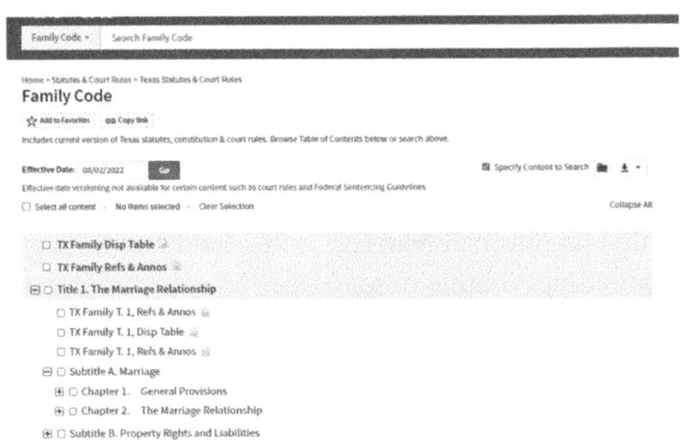

By orienting yourself in the larger Family Code—whether online or in a hard-copy version of the code—you can tell that informal marriage is just one of the ways that a couple can be considered married in Texas.

b. Organization and structure of federal statutes

Like Texas statutes, federal statutes are organized topically; however, instead of subject-matter codes, federal statutes are divided into different, subject-specific numbered titles.[3] There are 50 different titles that contain federal statutes, such as Title 11 (Bankruptcy), Title 26 (the Internal Revenue Code), and Title 49 (Transportation). Each federal title is further broken down into parts, chapters, and sections. Just as with Texas state statutes, you could go to the library and locate a hard copy of a federal statute. If you were to go to the library and locate the physical copy of Title 28 of the federal code, which contains the federal statutes related to the judiciary and judicial procedure, below is a picture of what you would see.

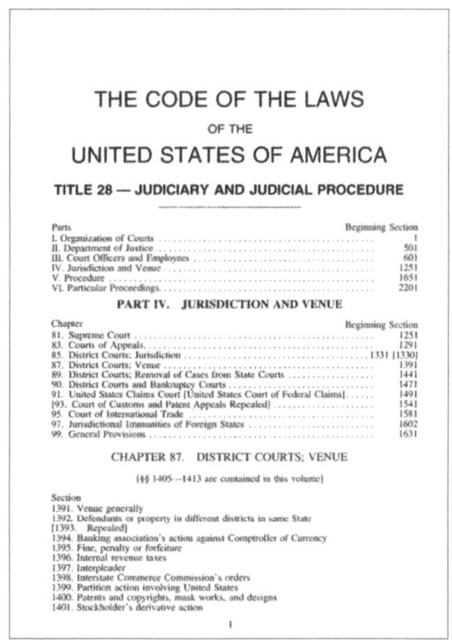

THE CODE OF THE LAWS

OF THE

UNITED STATES OF AMERICA

TITLE 28 — JUDICIARY AND JUDICIAL PROCEDURE

Parts	Beginning Section
I. Organization of Courts	1
II. Department of Justice	501
III. Court Officers and Employees	601
IV. Jurisdiction and Venue	1251
V. Procedure	1651
VI. Particular Proceedings	2201

PART IV. JURISDICTION AND VENUE

Chapter	Beginning Section
81. Supreme Court	1251
83. Courts of Appeals	1291
85. District Courts; Jurisdiction	1331 [1330]
87. District Courts; Venue	1391
89. District Courts; Removal of Cases from State Courts	1441
90. District Courts and Bankruptcy Courts	1471
91. United States Claims Court [United States Court of Federal Claims]	1491
[93. Court of Customs and Patent Appeals Repealed]	1541
95. Court of International Trade	1581
97. Jurisdictional Immunities of Foreign States	1602
99. General Provisions	1631

CHAPTER 87. DISTRICT COURTS; VENUE

[§§ 1405—1413 are contained in this volume]

Section
1391. Venue generally
1392. Defendants or property in different districts in same State
[1393. Repealed]
1394. Banking association's action against Comptroller of Currency
1395. Fine, penalty or forfeiture
1396. Internal revenue taxes
1397. Interpleader
1398. Interstate Commerce Commission's orders
1399. Partition action involving United States
1400. Patents and copyrights, mask works, and designs
1401. Stockholder's derivative action

1

As you can see, the table of contents in the book version of the statute allows you to see where each section falls in relation to the larger code. If you were looking for the federal rule on general venue, you would look in Title 28—Judiciary and Judicial Procedure, Part IV, Jurisdiction and Venue, Chapter 87, Section 1391, Venue generally.

Similar to the different ways you can access Texas statutes, you can access federal statutes using an online legal search engine, such as Westlaw or Lexis, in addition to locating them in hard copy. Below is what you would find if you were to look up section 1391 of Title 28 on Westlaw.

3. There are three versions of the federal codes: the United States Code, the United States Code Service, and the United States Code Annotated. The official version of the code is the United States Code. The other two unofficial versions of the Code contain the official statutory language of the United States Code plus summaries of judicial opinions related to the particular statutes.

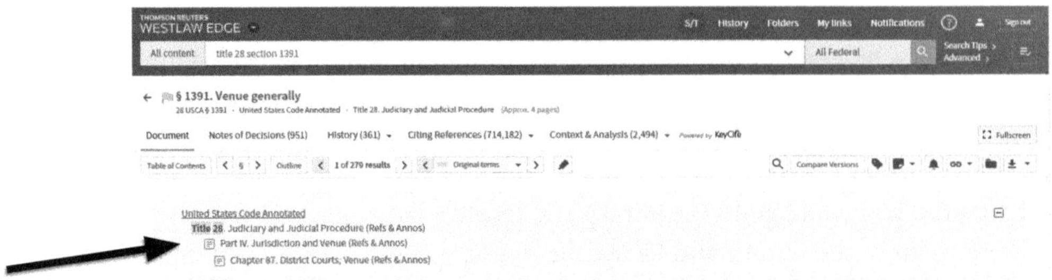

Like the Texas statutes, the table of contents for federal statutes does not automatically appear in its entirety, but by clicking "Title 28. Judiciary and Judicial Procedure," you can open the relevant portions of the table of contents in order to orient yourself in the statute and review other nearby provisions.

c. Applying organizational structure

Now that you understand how statutes are organized, let's turn back to the hypothetical scenario from before. You have successfully located Section 2.401 of the Texas Family Code, which on its face sets forth the standard for establishing an informal marriage in Texas. Now, per step one for reading a statute, you need to "zoom out" of the specific, relevant provision and orient yourself in the Texas Family Code more generally. Doing so will give you general context for what you are reading and will help you determine which, if any, other provisions of the Texas Family Code may be relevant to your client's inquiry.

Using Westlaw, first locate section 2.401 of the Texas Family Code. Review the statute for context.

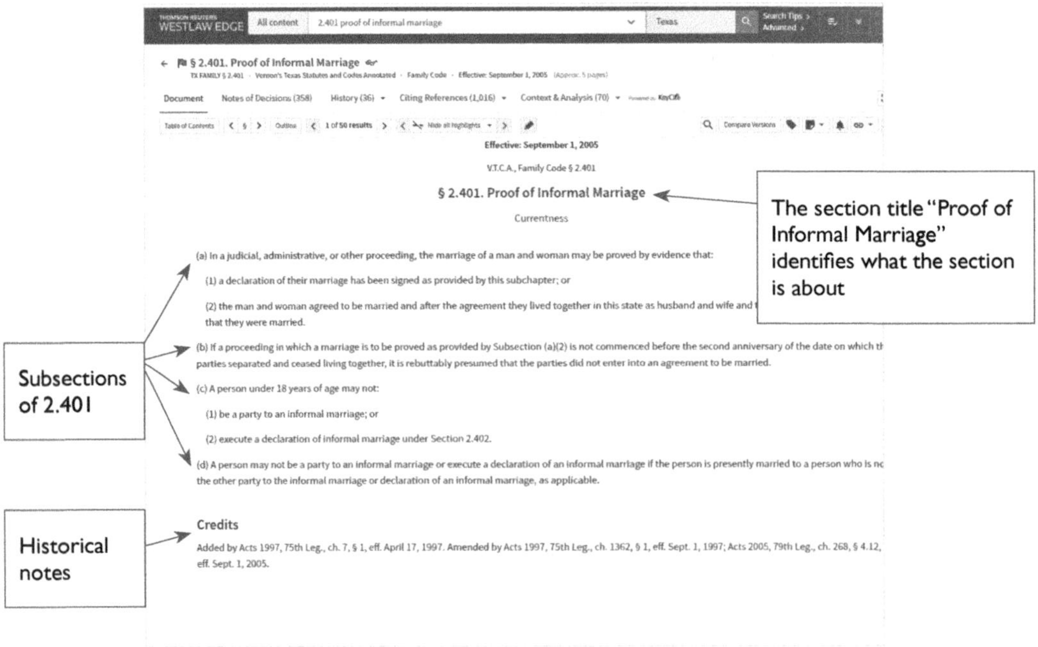

Then back out of the specific section to view the table of contents for the relevant subtitle. You will see the following.

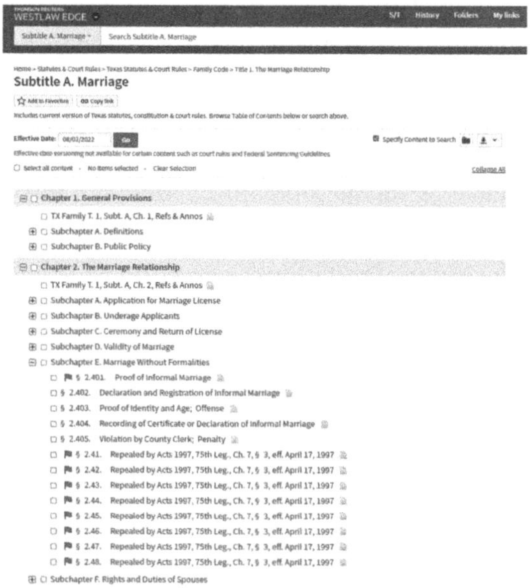

Given this context, you may decide to review the definitions in subchapter A, as well as section 2.403, regarding proof of identity and age related to informal marriages. You will also note that the section you are focused on—section 2.401—contains a red flag. Westlaw's red flag system denotes that this particular provision of the code is no longer good law.[4]

Step two: Skim the statute, paying attention to any headings and any conclusions, to get the statute's context. Make an effort to decipher how the statute operates and to whom or to what it applies. Do not use a highlighter or take notes during this step. Sit on your hands.

The second step required to read a statute is to skim the statute. Like the first step where you determine how the statute you are reading relates to the larger code, during this step, you figure out the statute's general meaning and how its different parts, subparts, sentences, and words relate to one another. You achieve this by discerning the

4. The U.S. Supreme Court held that there was a fundamental right to marry that included same-sex couples. *See generally Obergefell v. Hodges*, 576 U.S. 644 (2015). That decision impacts Texas's ability to allow only a "man and a woman" to get informally married. The statute itself is not overturned, but to the extent that it prohibits same-sex couples from satisfying the requirements of informal marriage, it is unconstitutional and will likely not be enforced.

answers to the following questions while you read: What does the statute allow, prohibit, or require? Does the statute provide any limitations or exceptions? Are there any cross-references mentioned in the statute itself? Are there any terms that need to be defined?

What does the statute allow, prohibit, or require? This inquiry mandates that you—as the reader of the statute—understand both the type of conduct or behavior the statute aims to regulate and how the statute aims to regulate that conduct or behavior (for example, by allowing, prohibiting, or requiring it). A statute allows conduct if it states that conduct is acceptable. A statute prohibits conduct if it forbids or disallows it. A statute requires conduct if it states that certain conduct is compulsory or mandatory.

Does the statute provide any limitations or exceptions? Statutes often provide limitations or exceptions to the rule they set forth. Limitations or exceptions are matters or types of conduct that are not included or covered by the general statutory language. For example, a statute may prohibit parking on the street overnight but provide an exception for local residents who have an overnight parking permit.

Are there any cross-references mentioned in the statute itself? A cross-reference is a reference to another statute or another section of the same statute. Statutes include cross-references to other statutory provisions in order to avoid restating large quantities of material in multiple locations, while signaling to the reader that they are relevant to the provision being read. When a statute contains a cross-reference, that reference effectively incorporates the cross-referenced provision into the statute. As such, it is essential that you, as a good statutory reader, review any and all other statutory provisions cross-referenced in the statute you are reading.

Are there any terms that need to be defined? Oftentimes, statutes will provide definitions of the terms used in the statute. Sometimes these definitions are in the statutory section you are reading, but sometimes they are in a different section or not defined at all within the statute. You should always look up the definitions of any terms used in the statute (either by finding the definition in the statute itself, in caselaw, or in a legal dictionary) to maximize your understanding of the statute.

Skim section 2.401 of the Texas Family Code for answers to these four questions:

SECTION 2.401: PROOF OF INFORMAL MARRIAGE	QUESTION	ANSWER
(a) In a judicial, administrative, or other proceeding, the marriage of a man and woman may be proved by evidence that: (1) a declaration of their marriage has been signed as provided by this subchapter; or	What does the statute allow, prohibit, or require?	The statute allows an informal marriage if there is a declaration or proof of certain requirements/elements.
(2) the man and woman agreed to be married and after the agreement they lived together in this state as husband and wife and there represented to others that they were married. (b) If a proceeding in which a marriage is to be proved as provided by Subsection (a)(2) is not commenced before the second anniversary of the date on which the parties separated and ceased living together, it is rebuttably presumed that the parties did not enter into an agreement to be married.	Does the statute provide any limitations or exceptions?	There are three limitations: 1. If more than two years has passed, it is rebuttably presumed that there was no agreement to be married. 2. If a person is under 18, the person cannot be informally married. 3. If a person is currently married to a third party, the person cannot be informally married.
(c) A person under 18 years of age may not: (1) be a party to an informal marriage; or (2) execute a declaration of informal marriage under Section 2.402. (d) A person may not be a party to an informal marriage or execute a declaration of an informal	Are there any cross-references mentioned in the statute itself?	The statute cross-references section 2.402, which sets forth the requirements for proving an informal marriage by declaration/registration.
marriage if the person is presently married to a person who is not the other party to the informal marriage or declaration of an informal marriage, as applicable.	Are there any terms that need to be defined?	What is an agreement? What is a declaration of marriage?

In short, by skimming the statute, you can discern that it sets forth the requirements for establishing an informal marriage. The statute provides a number of limits on a party's ability to informally marry and includes a cross-reference.

Step three: **Slowly read the statute with painful particularity. Look up terms you do not know, interact with the text, and note what is said, as well as what is not said, in the text. Pay close attention to "watchwords" and grammatical construction. During this step, you may take notes and highlight key parts of the text.**

The third step required to read a statute is that you "zoom in" and review the statute slowly and with particularity. To do this, you need to isolate the "watchwords" in the statute, determine if the statute is setting forth elements or factors, and then break the statute into bite-sized, grammatically sensible pieces to ensure you understand what the statute is—in this case—requiring and who is required to prove what.

Watchwords are deceptively small words in a statute that, if changed, would alter the meaning of the statute entirely. Some legal writing professors refer to these words as red flag words, words of authority, or operative words. The table below highlights the most important words to watch for when reading statutes.

WATCHWORD	MEANING
And	Requires all elements or factors to be met or considered
Either/Or	Requires only one of the elements or factors to be met or considered
If... then	Creates an exception to the standard
Unless	Creates an exception to the standard
Except	Creates an exception to the standard
Should or may	Allows conduct but does not mandate it
Should not or may not	Disallows conduct but does not prohibit it
Will	Provides for a future event
Must or shall	Mandates conduct
Must not or shall not	Prohibits conduct
Provided that	Creates a condition or exception or adds an additional requirement

To determine whether the statute sets forth elements or factors, you must first understand the difference between the two. If a rule is made up of elements, it means that to satisfy the rule you must establish each of (read: all of) the specified elements. If a rule is made up of factors, it means that to satisfy the rule you must weigh a series of factors to determine whether you satisfy the rule, but failure to find one of the factors is not fatal. You may need to try to reorder the structure of the statute into elements or factors by placing the subject of the statute first.

Let's practice the third step by engaging in a slow reading of section 2.401(a). First, highlight the watchwords in the statute.

Section 2.401: Proof of Informal Marriage

(a) In a judicial, administrative, **or** other proceeding, the marriage of a man **and** woman **may** be proved by evidence that:

(1) a declaration of their marriage has been signed as provided by this subchapter; **or**

(2) the man **and** woman agreed to be married **and** after the agreement they lived together in this state as husband and wife **and** there represented to others that they were married.

Next, based on an analysis of the highlighted watchwords, you can quickly see that there are two ways to establish an informal marriage as set forth in subsections (a)(1) and (a)(2) of the statute. Moreover, if one is establishing an informal marriage through the avenue set forth in (a)(2), the use of the watchword "and" between the requirements demonstrates that one will need to establish three **elements** to prove an informal marriage.

Last, try to reorder the requirements of the statute to make it easier to understand how to establish an informal marriage in Texas.

A man and a woman can establish an informal marriage if:

- they sign a declaration of marriage as set forth in this subchapter; or
- they prove three things:
  (1) they agree to be married;
  (2) after agreeing to be married, they live together in Texas as husband and wife; and
  (3) they represent to others that they were married.

Step four: Think about how this particular statute relates to other statutes or other pieces of law (cases possibly) that you have read and/or how it helps you resolve client problems.

The fourth step to reading a statute is to zoom back out again and to assess how the statute you read relates to other laws or helps you resolve your current client's and any future client's issue(s). Here, in the case your client has brought to you, there is no evidence that she or her boyfriend signed a declaration of an informal marriage. Accordingly, it seems that the validity of the boyfriend's divorce filing will turn on whether he can show evidence to support the three elements required for an informal marriage: (1) they agreed to be married; (2) after the agreement they lived together in Texas as husband and wife; and (3) they represented to others that they were married. Moreover, per the statute, your client and her boyfriend must be of different sexes and over 18. Last, if the boyfriend did not file his petition for divorce within two years of ceasing living together with your client, it is presumed they were not informally married, and the boyfriend has a greater hurdle to prove the informal marriage.

As evidenced by this exercise, statutory reading is arduous, perhaps even more arduous than reading those awful Ikea assembly instructions. Reading statutes is often like navigating a new language. To really grasp what the statute is requiring, prohibiting, or limiting, you must refrain from simply power-reading the language of the statute, and, instead, you must read the statute carefully following the four-step process. Although this process is slow going, the depth of understanding it yields will more than make up for the time spent.

We'd like to include a word of caution here. Even after you expend the time and energy necessary to break a statute into its requisite elements or factors, your work understanding the law is likely still incomplete. You will most likely need to invest additional time to understand exactly what one must show to establish at least some of the elements or factors set forth in the statute. For example, although we were able to identify the three elements required to establish an informal marriage in Texas by carefully reading the informal marriage statute, the language of the statute itself does not give us any information about the type of evidence that a plaintiff can use to establish each element. For example, the statute itself does not tell us what it means to "agree to be married." Must the couple exchange rings; sign some sort of written document stating "we agree to be married"; or just orally say they agree to be married? In other words, the arduous work required to read the statute will only get you part way to understanding the legal standard set forth in the statute. You then need to locate and read other legal sources—i.e. regulations, cases, or secondary sources—to help you understand the parameters of the legal standard set forth in the statute.

2. *How to read a case*

Law students are required to read on average 450 pages a week.[5] The vast majority of this reading is comprised of judicial opinions, which lawyers, judges, professors, and law students commonly refer to as cases. Cases are written opinions or decisions authored by judges that specify the resolution of a legal dispute and the reasons for that resolution.

At first, it takes law students hours to read and comprehend cases. In fact, during the first month of law school, new law students tend to be able to read and comprehend only three pages of a case per hour.[6] As students become more familiar with the structure and language of cases, however, their reading becomes more efficient and, thus, quicker. Accordingly, although the care you give to case reading will not vary much from the process set forth in this section, the pace with which you can complete that process will quicken.

Just as with statutory reading, the reading process required for law students and lawyers to "read" a case is much more in-depth than the process required to read a novel or even an undergraduate textbook. The four steps set forth at the beginning of this chapter should serve as your four guideposts for navigating your way through legal opinions as a new law student. In an effort to provide you with a bit more guidance as you navigate the hundreds of cases you will read in your first semester of law school alone, the steps below fine-tune the four steps recommended for legal reading generally to ensure extra care is given to the nuances of case reading.

Step one: Identify the purpose for which you are reading the case. What part of the law are you trying to understand?

Step two: Skim the case to understand the context of the case, such as which court the case comes from and the names and roles of the parties. While you skim, you should identify the different parts of the case, any headings, and any conclusions. Do not use a highlighter or take notes during this step except to indicate where the different key pieces of the case start and stop.

---

5. Sally Kane, *Tips Before Starting Law School*, The Balance Careers (June 25, 2019) https://www.thebalancecareers.com/preparing-for-your-first-year-of-law-school-2164369.

6. Lawnerds.com, *Speed Reading a Case*, http://lawnerds.com/guide/reading.html (last visited April 28, 2024).

Step three: Slowly read the case. Look up terms you do not know, interact with the text, note what is said, as well as what is not said, in the case. Omit sections of the case that are irrelevant to the issue for which you are reading the case. During this step, you may take notes and highlight key passages of the case.

Step four: Think about how this case relates to others you have read and/or how it helps you resolve hypotheticals.

Let's run through a new hypothetical to help you better understand how to read a case.

> Congratulations, you have passed the bar exam and are a newly sworn-in member of the Arkansas Bar! You are a young associate at a small law firm eager to make a good impression on the partner for whom you work. Early in the morning, the partner walks into your office, sits across from your desk, and explains that she has a client meeting later in the afternoon. She explains that she needs you to send her an e-mail memo by noon detailing what is required in order for her client to establish a claim of Title VII religious discrimination in the Fifth Circuit against her employer. The partner hands you a stack of cases and explains she has already done the research but has not read the cases in detail. The case on the top of the pile is *Davis v. Fort Bend County*. You begin your project by reading that case.

Step one: Identify the purpose for which you are reading the case. What part of the law are you trying to understand?

The first step you should complete in order to read a case is a pre-reading step: discern why you are reading the case. At first blush, this question may seem obvious, but usually, it requires you to step back, orient yourself, and think critically about what you need/hope to get out of the case. Your purpose for reading the case will inform the sections of the case on which you focus your time. If you are reading a case for a class—say torts—the purpose for which you are reading will be dictated by the assigned chapter in which the case appears. If you skim through the table of contents of your casebook, you may see that the case you are reading falls within the part on intentional torts, the chapter on battery, and the subsection of that chapter on intent. It follows then that the purpose for which you will be reading that particular case is to understand how you establish the intent element of battery.

Speaking frankly, however, once you complete law school, research does not arrive on your desk in a bound casebook with a table of contents to highlight the importance of each case. Instead, you will need to discern the purpose for which you are reading a case by the work assignment you have been given or the issue your client has asked you to resolve. In the hypothetical above, you have been asked to send an e-mail memo to the partner for whom you work explaining what is required in order for her client to establish a claim of Title VII religious discrimination in the Fifth Circuit against her employer. Accordingly, when you read the first case in the stack of cases the partner hands you, your purpose in reading the case is to understand the requirements for establishing a Title VII religious discrimination claim. With this overarching purpose noted, you can then begin to dig into the case in more detail.

Step two: Skim the case to understand the context of the case, such as which court the case comes from and the names and roles of the parties. While you skim, you should identify the different parts of the case, any headings, and any conclusions. Do not use a highlighter or take notes during this step except to indicate where the different key pieces of the case start and stop.

In order to complete the second step required to read a case, you must first understand the different parts of a case. Not all cases will look the same, and not all cases will contain all the parts described below. In addition, the source from which you get a case—the reporter, Westlaw, Lexis, or another source—also affects the appearance and contents of the case. A case from a reporter only contains the basic case information and the judicial opinion (including concurrences and dissents) itself. On the other hand, cases from online search engines such as Westlaw and Lexis contain research tools and summaries created by editors that precede the judicial opinion itself. These tools and summaries are not part of the case and, thus, are not law. Accordingly, it is critical that you are able to distinguish these research tools and summaries from actual parts of the case so that you do not mistakenly cite to or rely on them as if part of the actual case. Below is the case *Davis v. Fort Bend County* from Westlaw with annotations to help you begin to understand and identify the different parts of a case.

The Citation: shortly after the case caption (or sometimes directly underneath it), you will find the legal citation for the case. The legal citation tells you the court that decided the opinion, when the decision was issued, and the reporter in which it is published.

The Headnotes: a system for identifying the key legal topics and subtopics covered in the case (also called key numbers in Westlaw). Headnotes are not law, and, as such, you should not cite them.

Davis v. Fort Bend County, 765 F.3d 480 (2014)

124 Fair Empl.Prac.Cas. (BNA) 101, 98 Empl. Prac. Dec. P 45,138

The Caption: the title of the case, which, in most instances, sets forth the names of the parties, the court the opinion is from, and the date of the opinion.

765 F.3d 480
United States Court of Appeals, Fifth Circuit.

Lois M. DAVIS, Plaintiff–Appellant
v.
FORT BEND COUNTY, Defendant–Appellee.

No. 13–20610.
|
Aug. 26, 2014.

The Synopsis (called the case summary in Lexis): a summary of the facts and holdings of the case. Case summaries are not law and are drafted by publishers, not the actual judges who heard the case. You should never cite to a case synopsis.

Synopsis

Background: Former county employee brought action against county, alleging retaliation and religious discrimination in violation of Title VII. The United States District Court for the Southern District of Texas, Melinda Harmon, J., 2013 WL 5157191, granted county summary judgment. Employee appealed.

Holdings: The Court of Appeals, Edward C. Prado, Circuit Judge, held that:

[1] genuine issue of material fact existed as to whether employee felt that she was religiously compelled to attend event;

[2] genuine issue of material fact existed as to whether permitting employee to arrange substitute for her shift would impose undue hardship on county;

[3] there was no evidence that county's allegedly retaliatory conduct was materially adverse to employee; and

[4] there was no evidence that county's proffered non-retaliatory reason for terminating employee was pretextual.

Affirmed in part and reversed in part.

Jerry E. Smith, Circuit Judge, filed dissenting opinion.

Procedural Posture(s): On Appeal; Motion for Summary Judgment.

West Headnotes (14)

[1] **Civil Rights**—Accommodations

An employer has the statutory obligation under Title VII to make reasonable accommodations for the religious observances of its employees, but is not required to incur undue hardship. Civil Rights Act of 1964, § 703(a)(1), 42 U.S.C.A. § 2000e–2(a)(1).

5 Cases that cite this headnote

[2] **Civil Rights**—Effect of prima facie case; shifting burden

A Title VII claim for a failure to accommodate religious observances is analyzed under a burden-shifting framework akin to the *McDonnell Douglas* burden-shifting framework; an employee must first establish a prima facie case of religious discrimination and, if she does, the burden shifts to the defendant to demonstrate either that it reasonably accommodated the employee, or that it was unable to reasonably accommodate the employee's needs without undue hardship. Civil Rights Act of 1964, § 703(a)(1), 42 U.S.C.A. § 2000e–2(a)(1).

24 Cases that cite this headnote

[3] **Civil Rights**—Practices prohibited or required in general; elements

To establish a prima facie case of religious discrimination under Title VII, a plaintiff must present evidence that: (1) she held a bona fide religious belief; (2) her belief conflicted with a

Davis v. Fort Bend County, 765 F.3d 480 (2014)
124 Fair Empl.Prac.Cas. (BNA) 101, 98 Empl. Prac. Dec. P 45,138

requirement of her employment; (3) her employer was informed of her belief; and (4) she suffered an adverse employment action for failing to comply with the conflicting employment requirement. Civil Rights Act of 1964, § 703(a)(1), 42 U.S.C.A. § 2000e–2(a)(1).

15 Cases that cite this headnote

[4] **Civil Rights**—Beliefs and activities protected; sincerity

In determining whether a plaintiff has a bona fide religious belief, required for a Title VII religious discrimination claim, a court's inquiry is limited to focusing upon the individual's motivation; specifically, a court's task is to decide whether the individual's beliefs are, in his own scheme of things, religious. Civil Rights Act of 1964, § 703(a)(1), 42 U.S.C.A. § 2000e–2(a)(1).

9 Cases that cite this headnote

[5] **Civil Rights**—Beliefs and activities protected; sincerity

A belief is religious, required for a Title VII religious discrimination claim, if it is a sincere and meaningful belief which occupies in the life of its possessor a place parallel to that filled by God; conversely, whether the belief itself is central to the religion, that is, whether the belief is a true religious tenet, is not open to question. Civil Rights Act of 1964, § 703(a)(1), 42 U.S.C.A. § 2000e–2(a)(1).

5 Cases that cite this headnote

[6] **Civil Rights**—Beliefs and activities protected; sincerity
Civil Rights—Questions of law or fact

The sincerity of a person's religious belief is a question of fact unique to each Title VII religious discrimination case; the specific religious practice must be examined rather than the general scope of applicable religious tenets, and the plaintiff's sincerity in espousing that practice is largely a matter of individual credibility. Civil Rights Act of 1964, § 703(a)(1), 42 U.S.C.A. § 2000e–2(a)(1).

6 Cases that cite this headnote

[7] **Civil Rights**—Beliefs and activities protected; sincerity

Judicial inquiry into the sincerity of a person's religious belief must be handled with a light touch, or judicial shyness in Title VII religious discrimination actions; examining religious convictions any more deeply would stray into the realm of religious inquiry, an area into which courts are forbidden to tread. Civil Rights Act of 1964, § 703(a)(1), 42 U.S.C.A. § 2000e–2(a)(1).

2 Cases that cite this headnote

[8] **Federal Civil Procedure**—Employees and Employment Discrimination, Actions Involving

Genuine issue of material fact existed as to whether county employee felt that she was religiously compelled to attend event breaking ground for a new church and feeding the community, precluding summary judgment on her Title VII religious discrimination claim against county after she was terminated. Civil Rights Act of 1964, § 703(a)(1), 42 U.S.C.A.

§ 2000e–2(a)(1).

4 Cases that cite this headnote

[9] **Federal Courts**—Pleading

District court's ruling on whether affirmative defense has been waived is typically reviewed for abuse of discretion.

5 Cases that cite this headnote

[10] **Federal Civil Procedure**—Employees and Employment Discrimination, Actions Involving

Genuine issue of material fact existed as to whether permitting county employee to arrange a substitute for her shift would impose undue hardship on county, precluding summary judgment on employee's Title VII religious discrimination claim. Civil Rights Act of 1964, § 703(a)(1), 42 U.S.C.A. § 2000e–2(a)(1).

69 Cases that cite this headnote

[11] **Civil Rights**—Practices prohibited or required in general; elements

To set out a prima facie case of Title VII retaliation, a plaintiff must show: (1) that she engaged in activity protected by Title VII; (2) that an adverse employment action occurred; and (3) that a causal link existed between the protected activity and the adverse action. Civil Rights Act of 1964, § 704(a), 42 U.S.C.A. § 2000e–3(a).

42 Cases that cite this headnote

[12] **Civil Rights**—Adverse actions in general

To establish that she suffered adverse employment action, an employee asserting a Title VII retaliation claim must show that a reasonable employee would have found the challenged action materially adverse, which in this context means it well might have dissuaded a reasonable worker from making or supporting a charge of discrimination; this materiality requirement separates significant from trivial harms. Civil Rights Act of 1964, § 704(a), 42 U.S.C.A. § 2000e–3(a).

21 Cases that cite this headnote

[13] **Civil Rights**—Public Employment
Counties—Removal or other adverse action
Public Employment—Exercise of Rights; Retaliation

There was no evidence that county's conduct in subjecting employee to daily 30-minute meeting, removing employee's computer server administrative rights, reducing her staff, and giving direct assignments to her staff was materially adverse to employee, as required to establish an adverse employment action for employee's Title VII claim of retaliation for filing a complaint of sexual harassment. Civil Rights Act of 1964, § 704(a), 42 U.S.C.A. § 2000e–3(a).

8 Cases that cite this headnote

[14] **Civil Rights**—Motive or intent; pretext
Counties—Removal or other adverse action
Public Employment—Motive and intent; pretext

Davis v. Fort Bend County, 765 F.3d 480 (2014)
124 Fair Empl.Prac.Cas. (BNA) 101, 98 Empl. Prac. Dec. P 45,138

There was no evidence that county's terminating employee for failing to report to work was pretext for retaliation after employee complained of sexual harassment, as required for employee's Title VII retaliation claim. Civil Rights Act of 1964, § 704(a), 42 U.S.C.A. § 2000e–3(a).

2 Cases that cite this headnote

Attorneys and Law Firms

***483** Raffi Melkonian, Wright & Close, L.L.P., Darryl E. Scott, Houston, TX, for Plaintiff–Appellant.

Randall Weaver Morse, Assistant County Attorney, Mary Elizabeth Reveles, Richmond, TX, for Defendant–Appellee.

Appeal from the United States District Court for the Southern District of Texas.

Before SMITH, WIENER, and PRADO, Circuit Judges.

The Judge: the judge(s) who heard the case, as well as the judge(s) who authored the opinion, any concurrences, and any dissents.

Opinion

EDWARD C. PRADO, Circuit Judge:

The Opinion: the court's decision and the reasoning behind that decision written by the judge. The opinion is what you can cite to if you cite to the case.

Plaintiff–Appellant Lois M. Davis ("Davis") filed suit against her former employer, Defendant–Appellee Fort Bend County ("Fort Bend"), alleging discrimination and retaliation under Title VII of the Civil Rights Act of 1964, 42 U.S.C. § 2000e–2000e–17 ("Title VII"). The district court granted Fort Bend's motion for summary judgment on both claims. For the reasons stated below, we affirm in part and reverse in part.

I. FACTUAL AND PROCEDURAL BACKGROUND

The Facts: typically the first part of the body of the opinion that sets forth the facts of the case that led to the filing of the lawsuit.

Fort Bend hired Davis in December 2007 as a Desktop Support Supervisor responsible for supervising about fifteen information technology ("IT") technicians. Charles Cook ("Cook") was the IT Director at the time. In November 2009, he hired his personal friend and fellow church member, Kenneth Ford ("Ford"), as Davis's supervisor.

On or about April 1, 2010, Davis filed a complaint with Fort Bend's Human Resources Department, alleging that Cook subjected her to constant sexual harassment and assaults soon after her employment began. Fort Bend placed Davis on Family Medical Leave Act ("FMLA") leave during its investigation of her complaint. The investigation substantiated Davis's allegations against Cook and ultimately led to Cook's resignation on April 22, 2010.

According to Davis, Ford immediately began retaliating against her when she returned to work from FMLA leave. She alleged that Ford "effectively" demoted her by reducing the number of her direct reports from fifteen to four; removed her from projects she had previously managed; superseded her authority by giving orders and assigning different projects and tasks directly to Davis's staff; removed her administrative rights from the computer server; and assigned her tasks that similarly situated employees were not required to perform.

In March 2011, Fort Bend prepared to install personal computers, network components, and audiovisual equipment into its newly built Fort Bend County Justice Center. All technical support employees, including Davis, were involved in the process. As the Desktop Support Supervisor, Davis and her team were to "assist with the testing of the computers [and] make sure all of the computers had been set up properly." The installation was scheduled for the weekend of July 4, 2011, and all employees were required to be present.

On June 28, 2011, Davis informed Ford that she would not be available to work the morning of Sunday July 3, 2011, allegedly "due to a previous religious commitment." Davis testified that "[i]t was a special church service, and that I needed to be off that Sunday[,] ... but I would be more than willing to come in after church services." Davis also testified that she had arranged for a replacement during her ***484** absence, as she had done in the past. Ford did not approve her absence, stating that it "would be grounds for a write-up or termination." After Davis attended her church event

 4

The Procedural History: usually following the recitation of the facts, the opinion will set forth the procedural history of the case—that is, how the case moved through the legal system (e.g., where the case was originally filed and subsequent or related decisions in the case).

The Law of the Case: the legal principles that govern the case. The law may be set forth all at the beginning of the opinion, sprinkled throughout, or a bit of both. Here, the legal lens (standard of review) that the court will use to decide all causes of action in the case is set forth up front. Then, the legal standard for each individual legal issue is set forth in separate sections addressing those issues.

Client's Issue: Religious Discrimination

and did not report to work. Fort Bend terminated Davis's employment.

Davis filed suit against Fort Bend, alleging retaliation and religious discrimination under Title VII, and intentional infliction of emotional distress. The district court granted Fort Bend's motion for summary judgment on all claims and dismissed Davis's action. Davis timely appealed the district court's grant of summary judgment. On appeal, Davis challenges the grant of summary judgment on her Title VII claims, but not on her intentional infliction of emotional distress claim.

II. JURISDICTION AND STANDARD OF REVIEW

The district court had jurisdiction over Davis's Title VII claims pursuant to 42 U.S.C. § 2000e–5(f)(3). Because this is an appeal of a final judgment of a district court, this court has jurisdiction under 28 U.S.C. § 1291.

This court reviews the district court's ruling on summary judgment de novo, applying the same standard as the district court in the first instance. *Turner v. Baylor Richardson Med. Ctr.*, 476 F.3d 337, 343 (5th Cir.2007) (citation omitted). "Summary judgment should be granted when the moving party shows that 'there is no genuine dispute as to any material fact and the movant is entitled to judgment as a matter of law.' " *Willis v. Cleco Corp.*, 749 F.3d 314, 317 (5th Cir.2014) (quoting Fed.R.Civ.P. 56(a)). A genuine dispute of material fact exists when the " 'evidence is such that a reasonable jury could return a verdict for the nonmoving party.' " *Royal v. CCC & R Tres Arboles, L.L.C.*, 736 F.3d 396, 400 (5th Cir.2013) (quoting *Anderson v. Liberty Lobby, Inc.*, 477 U.S. 242, 248, 106 S.Ct. 2505, 91 L.Ed.2d 202 (1986)).

"[A] party seeking summary judgment always bears the initial responsibility of informing the district court of the basis for its motion, and identifying those portions of [the record] which it believes demonstrate the absence of a genuine issue of material fact." *Celotex Corp. v. Catrett*, 477 U.S. 317, 323, 106 S.Ct. 2548, 91 L.Ed.2d 265 (1986). The burden then shifts to "the nonmoving party to go beyond the pleadings and by her own affidavits, or by the 'depositions, answers to interrogatories, and admissions on file,' designate 'specific facts showing that there is a genuine issue for trial.' " *Id.* at 324, 106 S.Ct. 2548. The court must "draw all reasonable inferences in favor of the nonmoving party" and "refrain from making credibility determinations or weighing the evidence." *Turner*, 476 F.3d at 343 (citation and internal quotation marks omitted). A party cannot "defeat summary judgment with conclusory allegations, unsubstantiated assertions, or 'only a scintilla of evidence.' " *Id.* (quoting *Little v. Liquid Air Corp.*, 37 F.3d 1069, 1075 (5th Cir.1994) (en banc) (per curiam)).

III. DISCUSSION

Davis argues that the district court erred when it granted summary judgment for Fort Bend as to her Title VII religious discrimination claim and as to her retaliation claim. We address each argument in turn below.

A. Davis's Title VII Religious Discrimination Claim

[1] As explained below, the district court erred when it granted summary judgment in favor of Fort Bend on Davis's Title VII religious discrimination claim. ***485** Title VII prohibits an employer from discriminating against an employee on the basis of her religion. 42 U.S.C. §§ 2000e–2(a)(1), 2000e(j). "An employer has the statutory obligation to make reasonable accommodations for the religious observances of its employees, but is not required to incur undue hardship." *Weber v. Roadway Express, Inc.*, 199 F.3d 270, 273 (5th Cir.2000).

[2] This court analyzes a Title VII claim for a failure to accommodate religious observances under a burden-shifting framework akin to the *McDonnell Douglas Corp. v. Green*, 411 U.S. 792, 93 S.Ct. 1817, 36 L.Ed.2d 668 (1973), burden-shifting framework. The

employee must first establish a prima facie case of religious discrimination. *Antoine v. First Student, Inc.*, 713 F.3d 824, 831 (5th Cir.2013). If she does, "the burden shifts to the defendant to demonstrate either that it reasonably accommodated the employee, or that it was unable to reasonably accommodate the employee's needs without undue hardship." *Id.* Here, a genuine dispute of material fact exists at both steps.

Analysis Part 1: Prima Facie Case

1. *Davis's Prima Facie Case Survives Summary Judgment*

[3] Davis has presented evidence demonstrating a genuine dispute of material fact on her prima facie case and, thus, survives the first step. As we have previously stated:

> To establish a prima facie case of religious discrimination under Title VII, the plaintiff must present evidence that (1) she held a bona fide religious belief, (2) her belief conflicted with a requirement of her employment, (3) her employer was informed of her belief, and (4) she suffered an adverse employment action for failing to comply with the conflicting employment requirement.

Tagore v. United States, 735 F.3d 324, 329 (5th Cir.2013) (citing *Bruff v. N. Miss. Health Servs., Inc.*, 244 F.3d 495, 499 n. 9 (5th Cir.2001)).

[4] [5] The parties dispute only the first element: whether Davis's observance of her church's July 3rd event was pursuant to her bona fide religious belief. Bona fide religious beliefs include "moral or ethical beliefs as to what is right and wrong which are sincerely held with the strength of traditional religious views." *See, e.g.*, 29 C.F.R. § 1605.1 (citing *United States v. Seeger*, 380 U.S. 163, 85 S.Ct. 850, 13 L.Ed.2d 733 (1965)). A court's inquiry is limited to focusing upon the individual's motivation. Specifically, a court's task is to decide "whether [the individual's beliefs] are, *in his own scheme of things*, religious." *Seeger*, 380 U.S. at 185, 85 S.Ct. 850 (emphasis added). In this regard, a belief is "religious" if it is "[a] sincere and meaningful belief which occupies in the life of its possessor a place parallel to that filled by ... God." *Seeger*, 380 U.S. at 176, 85 S.Ct. 850. Conversely, whether the belief itself is central to the religion, i.e., whether the belief is a true religious tenet, is "not open to question." *Moussazadeh v. Tex. Dep't of Criminal Justice*, 703 F.3d 781, 790 (5th Cir.2012) (quoting *Seeger*, 380 U.S. at 185, 85 S.Ct. 850) (internal quotation marks omitted) (discussing the threshold inquiry into a person's religious belief under the Religious Land Use and Institutionalized Persons Act); *see Tagore*, 735 F.3d at 328–29 (applying *Moussazadeh* to a Title VII religious discrimination claim).

[6] The sincerity of a person's religious belief is a question of fact unique to each case. *Tagore*, 735 F.3d at 328; *Moussazadeh*, 703 F.3d at 791 ("This is doubly true regarding sincerity."). "The specific religious practice must be examined rather than the general scope of applicable religious tenets, and the plaintiff's 'sincerity' ***486** in espousing that practice is largely a matter of individual credibility." *Tagore*, 735 F.3d at 328; *see also Moussazadeh*, 703 F.3d at 791 ("[T]he important inquiry was what the prisoner claimed was important to him." (alteration in original) (citation and internal quotation marks omitted)).

[7] This court has cautioned that judicial inquiry into the sincerity of a person's religious belief "must be handled with a light touch, or judicial shyness." *Tagore*, 735 F.3d at 328 (citation and internal quotation marks omitted). "[E]xamin[ing] religious convictions any more deeply would stray into the realm of religious inquiry, an area into which we are forbidden to tread." *Id.* (alteration in original) (citation and internal quotation marks omitted). Indeed, "the sincerity of a plaintiff's engagement in a particular religious practice is rarely challenged," and "claims of sincere religious belief in a particular practice have been accepted on little more than the plaintiff's credible assertions." *Id.*

[8] We emphasize that this limited inquiry is being decided on summary judgment in this case. Thus, the issue here is whether there exists a genuine dispute of material fact whether Davis sincerely felt that she was religiously

compelled to attend and participate in a special service at church on Sunday, July 3.

In Davis's view, her bona fide belief that she was religiously compelled to attend the event is supported by her testimony that she is a devout member of the Church Without Walls. Specifically, she refers this court to her testimony that she attends at least two services every weekend; she volunteers for the church; the pastor knows her and would vouch for her; and she believed strongly that she "needed" to be at church on Sunday, July 3, 2011, as a religious matter. As the nonmoving party on summary judgment, Davis contends that the court must draw the inference in her favor that her decision to attend church was religious, "at the very least in her own scheme of things."

Fort Bend asserts without analysis or argument that Davis's reason for not working on July 3—breaking ground for a new church and feeding the community—"is not a religious belief or practice." Fort Bend also includes the majority of the district court's reasoning verbatim. The district court noted that "being an avid and active member of church does not elevate every activity associated with that church into a legally protectable religious practice." The district court then found that Davis's "absence from work was due to personal commitment, not religious conviction," because she described her obligation as a "request[ ]" from her Pastor that all members participate in the "community service event."

We disagree with Fort Bend and the district court. Neither addresses whether Davis's religious belief was sincere and, instead, both improperly focus upon the nature of the activity itself. A showing of sincerity, however, does not require proof that the July 3rd church event was in itself a true religious tenet, but only that Davis sincerely believed it to be religious in her own scheme of things. *See Moussazadeh,* 703 F.3d at 791 ("Individuals may practice their religion in any way they see fit, and it is not for the Court to say it is an unreasonable one. A showing of sincerity does not necessarily require strict doctrinal adherence to standards created by organized religious hierarchies." (citation and internal quotation marks omitted)). Thus, even if attendance at the "community service event" was arguably not a religious tenet but a mere request by her Pastor, "[t]hese telling arguments address an issue that is not for federal courts, powerless as we are to evaluate the logic or validity of beliefs found religious and sincerely held." ***487** *See Cooper v. Gen. Dynamics, Convair Aerospace Div., Fort Worth Operation,* 533 F.2d 163, 166 n. 4 (5th Cir.1976) (chastising a district court for having "evaluated the tenet and concluded that it was irrational and specious").

Focusing on the sincerity of Davis's belief, as we must, we hold that her prima facie case survives summary judgment. Davis testified about her devotion to church and that she was "[a]bsolutely not" "just a weekend warrior." Instead, she was actively committed to her church "because [she] believe[d] in something," sometimes attending up to three services every Sunday. Regarding the particular Sunday at issue here, July 3, 2011, she testified that she "needed" to attend "a special church service." She similarly alleged in her complaint that "she would be unavailable for work on Sunday July 3, 2011 due to previous religious commitment." Although her complaint also noted that her "Pastor ***requested*** that all members participate in this highly anticipated ***community service event*** " (emphasis added), we must "refrain from making credibility determinations or weighing the evidence." *Turner,* 476 F.3d at 343; *see, e.g., Seeger,* 380 U.S. at 184, 85 S.Ct. 850 ("Religious experiences which are as real as life to some may be incomprehensible to others." (quoting *United States v. Ballard,* 322 U.S. 78, 86, 64 S.Ct. 882, 88 L.Ed. 1148 (1944))); *Tagore,* 735 F.3d at 328 (holding that plaintiff's sincerity "is largely a matter of individual credibility"). Such restraint is particularly important here, where a court "must refuse to dissect religious tenets just because the believer['s] ... beliefs are not articulated with the clarity and precision that a more sophisticated person might employ." *A.A. v. Needville Indep. Sch. Dist.,* 611 F.3d 248, 261 (5th Cir.2010).

Accordingly, drawing all reasonable inferences in favor of Davis as the nonmoving party, and considering the "light touch" and "judicial shyness" that must be exercised, Davis's testimony about her own sincere belief regarding her religious need to attend a special service at church on Sunday sufficiently evidenced a genuine dispute of material fact whether she held a bona fide religious belief. *See Tagore,* 735 F.3d at 328 ("[C]laims of sincere religious belief in a particular practice have been accepted on little more than the plaintiff's credible assertions.").

Analysis Part 2: Affirmative Defenses

2. *The Burden Shifts to Fort Bend*

At the next step, Fort Bend may assert its affirmative defenses and "demonstrate either that it reasonably accommodated the employee, or that it was unable to reasonably accommodate the employee's needs without undue hardship." *Antoine*, 713 F.3d at 831. On summary judgment, Fort Bend asserted only undue hardship, which "exists when an employer is required to bear more than a de minimis cost." *Id.* at 839 (citation omitted).

[9] Davis argues that, on the merits,[1] Fort Bend did not present evidence that it could not reasonably accommodate her religious observance without an undue hardship. According to Davis, she asked only to be absent the morning of July 3 and promised to report to work directly after the July 3rd event. Not only was this ***488** "short period of absence" minimal under Title VII, but Davis claims she arranged for a substitute for the hours she would be absent. Moreover, Davis contends we should not give credit to Fort Bend's purported undue hardship because Fort Bend permitted another employee to take time off to attend a parade that same weekend.

In response, Fort Bend cites a string of circuit precedent—*see, e.g., Bruff,* 244 F.3d at 501; *Weber,* 199 F.3d at 274; *Eversley v. MBank Dall.,* 843 F.2d 172, 176 (5th Cir.1988); *Brener v. Diagnostic Ctr. Hosp.,* 671 F.2d 141 (5th Cir.1982)—for the proposition that requiring one employee to substitute for another presents an undue hardship. Additionally, Fort Bend asserts that Davis's role as Desktop Support Supervisor was vital to the efficiency of the move. Thus, her absence not only increased the risk that the computers would not be timely installed and functional, but also required other employees to take on additional duties or change their schedules. Finally, Fort Bend disregards the substitute Davis arranged because Davis did not have the authority to make such schedule changes.

The district court found that Davis did not offer any evidence to rebut Fort Bend's undue hardship defense. Davis did provide a fellow supervisor's affidavit, in which the supervisor averred that Ford denied his request to permit his employees to attend church services on July 3rd. But, the district court found that the affidavit instead bolstered Fort Bend's position, reasoning that "all such requests were denied because granting any particular one would have adversely affected other employees." "[R]ather than evidence of religious discrimination," the district court continued, "there is evidence only of a neutral policy denying all requests for time off."

We disagree with Fort Bend and the district court on this issue as well. First, the district court improperly inferred facts against the nonmoving party, Davis, when it concluded that Ford denied the requests "because granting any particular one would have adversely affected other employees." However, because there was nothing in the affidavit hinting at Ford's reason for denying the request, the district court's conclusion was improper. *See Turner,* 476 F.3d at 343 (explaining that a court must draw all reasonable inferences in favor of the nonmoving party on summary judgment). Next, the district court compared Davis to similarly situated employees within the *same* protected class—i.e., those with religious observances. But, the proper comparators are "similarly situated employees *outside* the protected group." *See, e.g., McCoy v. City of Shreveport,* 492 F.3d 551, 556 (5th Cir.2007) (per curiam) (emphasis added). In that regard, Davis testified that Ford permitted another employee time off to attend a Fourth of July parade the weekend of the move.

We also reject Fort Bend's arguments because, even though Fort Bend correctly recites precedent, it misapplies law to facts. Fort Bend correctly asserts that requiring an employee to substitute for Davis's absence may, as a matter of law, impose more than a de minimis cost. *See, e.g., Bruff,* 244 F.3d at 501 ("Requiring one or both counselors to assume a disproportionate workload, or to travel involuntarily with Bruff to sessions to be available in case a problematic subject area came up, is an undue hardship as a matter of law."). Fort Bend is also correct that permitting Davis to be absent may leave it short-handed and, therefore, impose an undue hardship as a matter of law. *See, e.g., Trans World Airlines, Inc. v. Hardison,* 432 U.S. 63, 84, 97 S.Ct. 2264, 53 L.Ed.2d 113 (1977) (holding that to leave the employer ***489** short-handed would involve costs to the employer "in the form of lost efficiency"). But these cases do not apply to the facts here because there was a ready and willing *volunteer* to substitute for Davis.

Substituting a volunteer does not necessarily impose the same hardship on the employer, if any, as requiring an employee to substitute for another's religious observance. In holding that Title VII does not require an employer to substitute employees, the Supreme Court in *Hardison* stated "[t]here were no *volunteers* to relieve Hardison on

Saturdays, and to give Hardison Saturdays off, TWA would have had to deprive another employee of his shift preference at least in part because he did not adhere to a religion that observed the Saturday Sabbath." 432 U.S. at 81, 97 S.Ct. 2264 (emphasis added). In *Eversley,* we relied on this language from *Hardison* to hold that "it is unreasonable and an undue hardship on an employer to require the employer to *force* employees, over their express refusal, to permanently switch from a daytime to a nighttime shift in order to accommodate another employee's different Sabbath observation." 843 F.2d at 176 (emphasis added). Further, in disagreeing with any implication that an "employer may be required to force other employees into a disadvantageous permanent switch of shifts against their wishes," we noted that "the Sixth Circuit seems to have assumed that an employer's attempt to seek out employees who would be *willing* to switch shifts would be a reasonable accommodation for purposes of Title VII." *Id.* (citing *Smith v. Pyro Mining Co.,* 827 F.2d 1081, 1088–89 (6th Cir.1987)).

[10] Here, Davis arranged for a substitute who voluntarily agreed to work Davis's shift that Sunday. That Davis lacked authority to schedule her own substitute does not take away from the fact that there was at least one volunteer to work Davis's shift. With a volunteer substitute available, Fort Bend would not have had incur any cost *requiring* an employee to substitute for Davis, nor would Fort Bend necessarily be left short-handed. *See Antoine,* 713 F.3d at 839–40 (holding that the availability of a voluntary shift swap procedure precluded employer's argument that accommodating plaintiff would have imposed the undue hardship of a "forced, unilateral reassignment by [the employer]"). Because Fort Bend does not argue that permitting Davis's arranged substitute to work in place of Davis would impose an undue hardship, there exists a genuine dispute of material fact whether Fort Bend would have suffered undue hardship in accommodating Davis's religious observance. The district court's grant of summary judgment based upon Fort Bend's undue hardship was error.

Irrelevant Issue: Retaliation

B. Davis's Title VII Retaliation Claim

Separate from a religious discrimination claim, Title VII makes it unlawful for an employer to retaliate against an employee who opposes an employment practice that violates Title VII. 42 U.S.C. § 2000e–3(a).

[11] Because Davis does not present any direct evidence of retaliation, her retaliation claim is evaluated under the *McDonnell Douglas* burden-shifting framework. *See Septimus v. Univ. of Hous.,* 399 F.3d 601, 607–08 (5th Cir.2005) (applying the *McDonnell Douglas* framework in a Title VII retaliation case). The *McDonnell Douglas* framework requires a plaintiff first to demonstrate a prima facie case of retaliation. *LeMaire v. La. Dep't of Transp. & Dev.,* 480 F.3d 383, 388 (5th Cir.2007). To set out a prima facie case of Title VII retaliation, a plaintiff must show "(1) that she engaged in activity protected by Title VII, (2) that an adverse employment action occurred, and (3) that a causal link existed between the protected activity ***490** and the adverse action." *Ikossi–Anastasiou v. Bd. of Supervisors of La. State Univ.,* 579 F.3d 546, 551 (5th Cir.2009) (citations and internal quotation marks omitted). "If the employee establishes a prima facie case, the burden shifts to the employer to state a legitimate, non-retaliatory reason for its decision. After the employer states its reason, the burden shifts back to the employee to demonstrate that the employer's reason is actually a pretext for retaliation." *LeMaire,* 480 F.3d at 388–89 (citation omitted).

Here, Davis meets neither her summary judgment burden at the prima facie stage with respect to Fort Bend's alleged pre-termination actions, nor her burden at the pretext stage with respect to her termination.

[12] As to Davis's prima facie case, the primary dispute is whether adverse employment action occurred. To establish that she suffered adverse employment action, Davis must show that "a reasonable employee would have found the challenged action materially adverse, which in this context means it well might have dissuaded a reasonable worker from making or supporting a charge of discrimination." *Burlington N. & Santa Fe Ry. Co. v. White,* 548 U.S. 53, 68, 126 S.Ct. 2405, 165 L.Ed.2d 345 (2006) (citation and internal quotation marks omitted). This materiality requirement separates "significant from trivial harms." *Id.*

In *White,* the Supreme Court explained that "[t]he antiretaliation provision protects an individual not from all retaliation, but from retaliation that produces an injury or harm." *Id.* at 67, 126 S.Ct. 2405. Thus, "petty slights, minor annoyances, and simple lack of good manners" are not actionable retaliatory conduct; Title VII "does not set forth a general civility code for the American workplace." *Id.* at 68, 126 S.Ct. 2405 (citations and internal quotation marks omitted). Importantly, "the significance any given act of retaliation will often depend upon the particular circumstances. Context matters." *Id.* at 69, 126 S.Ct. 2405. For example,

> A schedule change in an employee's work schedule may make little difference to many workers, but may matter enormously to a young mother with school-age children. A supervisor's refusal to invite an employee to lunch is normally trivial, a nonactionable petty slight. But to retaliate by excluding an employee from a weekly training lunch that contributes significantly to the employee's professional advancement might well deter a reasonable employee from complaining about discrimination.

Id. (citations omitted).

Davis points to several actions as adverse: (1) subjecting her to daily thirty-minute meetings with upper management that were not required of similarly situated employees; (2) superseding her authority by giving orders and assigning different projects and tasks directly to Davis's staff; (3) removing her administrative rights from the computer server; (4) reducing her staff from fifteen to four employees; and (5) terminating her employment. Davis contends that these acts, both individually and in the aggregate, constitute adverse employment action.

[13] Simply listing the employment actions that Davis believes were adverse does not meet her burden on summary judgment because she makes no effort to evidence the circumstances that make those actions "materially adverse." *See* *White,* 548 U.S. at 68, 126 S.Ct. 2405. Again, "[c]ontext matters." *Id.* at 69, 126 S.Ct. 2405. For example, whether removing her administrative rights from the computer server was an actionable "significant" harm or a non-actionable "trivial" ***491** harm may depend upon, at the least, Davis's need for administrative rights. Administrative rights may have been required for Davis to perform her duties, or those rights may have been a convenience. Davis fails to offer any evidence on the matter and, thus, fails to evidence a genuine dispute of material fact.

Ford's thirty-minute meetings, direct assignment of work to Davis's staff and reduction of her staff similarly lack context. *See* *White,* 548 U.S. at 71, 126 S.Ct. 2405 ("Whether a particular reassignment is materially adverse depends upon the circumstances of the particular case...."). Although Davis alleged in her complaint that Ford's "malice and retaliation tactics against [her] caused discord and conflict amongst the IT employees including [her] personal staff," this assertion does not implicate any impact on Davis herself. She does not offer any evidence to show, for example, that these actions were "the result of any fault on [her] part, such as might carry a stigma in the workplace," *Stewart v. Miss. Transp. Comm'n,* 586 F.3d 321, 332 (5th Cir.2009); that "she suffered a diminution in prestige or change in standing among her co-workers" because of these actions, *id.;* that she viewed these actions as a demotion[2] or that such actions embarrassed her, *Aryain v. Wal-Mart Stores Tex. LP,* 534 F.3d 473, 485 (5th Cir.2008); or that these actions made her duties "more arduous," *White,* 548 U.S. at 71, 126 S.Ct. 2405 (internal quotation marks omitted). Without any evidence of the context of these pre-termination actions, there is no genuine dispute whether Davis suffered an "adverse impact" as a result of Ford's pre-termination actions. *See* *Stewart,* 586 F.3d at 332.

[14] Turning to her termination, there is no dispute that it was an adverse action. However, Davis does not present any evidence that Fort Bend's legitimate, non-retaliatory reason for terminating her—that she failed to report to work—was pretext for retaliation. Instead, she argues only that Fort Bend's reason for terminating her was pretext for its *religious discrimination.* This is irrelevant to her *retaliation* claim. *LeMaire,* 480 F.3d at 388–89 ("After the employer states its reason, the burden shifts back to the employee to demonstrate that the employer's reason is actually a pretext *for retaliation.*" (emphasis added) (citation omitted)). Fort Bend has therefore stated a legitimate, non-retaliatory reason that Davis has not

Davis v. Fort Bend County, 765 F.3d 480 (2014)

124 Fair Empl.Prac.Cas. (BNA) 101, 98 Empl. Prac. Dec. P 45,138

rebutted.

In sum, Fort Bend asserted the absence of evidence demonstrating an adverse employment action, and of evidence demonstrating pretext. Davis thus had to bear the burden of producing evidence demonstrating the existence of a genuine dispute of material fact as to these issues, but failed to meet that burden. *See* *Celotex Corp.*, 477 U.S. at 322, 106 S.Ct. 2548. Summary judgment was proper as to Davis's Title VII retaliation claim.

The Disposition: a statement setting forth the resolution of the dispute.

IV. CONCLUSION

The district court's summary judgment on Davis's Title VII religious discrimination claim is REVERSED, and its summary judgment on Davis's Title VII retaliation claim is AFFIRMED. The matter is REMANDED for further proceedings in accordance with this opinion.

The Dissent: the opinion in a case written by one or more judges disagreeing with the court's opinion and explaining the basis for the disagreement.

JERRY E. SMITH, Circuit Judge, dissenting:

In its well-written opinion, the majority errs in holding that our inquiry is limited ***492** to the sincerity of an employee's alleged religious belief; we must also consider whether that belief is "religious" in nature or merely a personal preference or a secular social or economic philosophy. The district court correctly found that Davis's failure to appear for work was motivated by a personal commitment and not a religious belief protected under Title VII. The majority also mistakenly decides that accommodating Davis's belief did not constitute an undue hardship. (I agree with the majority's disposition of the retaliation claim.) Because I would affirm the summary judgment, I respectfully dissent.

I.

A.

The majority strays in opining that courts may not consider the religious nature of an employee's alleged beliefs but instead must focus solely on sincerity. I have no qualm about the majority's discussion regarding the sincerity of Davis's belief, but that is not at issue. The county does not dispute her sincerity, and her opening brief states as much: "*[S]incerity* is not at issue here."

Title VII does not protect beliefs merely because they are sincerely or strongly held.[1] Instead, it protects employees from discrimination based on their "religion," 42 U.S.C. § 2000e–2(a)(1), defined to include "all aspects of *religious* observance and practice, as well as belief," 42 U.S.C. § 2000e(j). As a result, the *prima facie* case for religious accommodation requires the plaintiff to show that he "had a *bona fide* religious belief that conflicted with an employment requirement."[2] The district court found that Davis's belief was not religious: "[Her] absence from work was due to personal commitment, not religious conviction"; the court found that she "did not present a conflict between religious beliefs and employment requirements; [she] presented a conflict of time." *This* is the real issue presented to us on appeal.

Only a couple of sentences of the majority opinion pertain to whether Davis's belief was "religious." In its cursory review, the majority asserts, without analysis, that our "inquiry is limited to focusing upon the individual and whether her belief is sincere, or 'truly held'; whether the belief itself is central to the religion, i.e., whether the belief is a religious tenet, is 'not open to question,' " citing *Moussazadeh v. Texas Department of Criminal Justice*, 703 F.3d 781, 790 (5th Cir.2012) (Smith, J.). Not only is the holding not supported by *Moussazadeh*, but it is contrary to the plain language of Title VII and to the precedents of the Supreme Court, this court, and all of our sister circuits to have addressed this issue.

In *Moussazadeh, id.,* the parties did not dispute that "eating kosher food constitutes a 'religious exercise' " under the RLUIPA. The only issue was whether the prisoner sincerely held that religious belief. Contrary to the majority's selective quotation of six words from its discussion of sincerity, *Moussazadeh* does not hold that courts cannot look into the religious character of a belief. It merely states that "while the 'truth' of a belief is not open to question, there remains the significant question of whether it is 'truly held.' " *Id.* (quoting *United States v. Seeger,* 380 U.S. 163, 185, 85 S.Ct. 850, 13 L.Ed.2d 733 (1965)).

***493** In *Seeger,* the Court provided further guidance on courts' proper role in considering the religiosity of beliefs:

> The validity of what [the plaintiff] believes cannot be questioned. Some theologians, and indeed some examiners, might be tempted to question the existence of the registrant's "Supreme Being" or the truth of his concepts. But these are inquiries foreclosed to Government. As Mr. Justice Douglas stated in *United States v. Ballard,* 322 U.S. 78, 86 [64 S.Ct. 882, 88 L.Ed. 1148] (1944): "Men may believe what they cannot prove. They may not be put to the proof of their religious doctrines or beliefs. Religious experiences which are real as life to some may be incomprehensible to others." Local boards and courts in this sense are not free to reject beliefs because they consider them "incomprehensible." Their task is to decide whether the beliefs professed by a registrant are sincerely held and *whether they are, in his own scheme of things, religious.*
>
> But we hasten to emphasize that while the "truth" of a belief is not open to question, there remains the significant question whether it is "truly held." This is the threshold question of sincerity which must be resolved in every case.

Seeger, 380 U.S. at 184–85, 85 S.Ct. 850. In other words, courts cannot look into whether the religious belief is true—for example, whether the angel Gabriel truly appeared to Muhammad, whether the Middle Way is indeed the path to enlightenment, or whether Jesus is in fact the Christ.[3] Instead, courts are tasked with deciding not only whether the alleged belief is "sincerely held" but also "whether [the beliefs] are ... *religious.*" *Id.* at 185, 85 S.Ct. 850.

The majority holding also conflicts with the decisions of every circuit to have addressed this issue. Consistently with *Seeger,* the First,[4] Fourth,[5] Seventh,[6] Eighth,[7] and Tenth[8] Circuits have held ***494** that courts must consider both whether a belief is religious in nature and whether it is sincerely held. No circuit has held—in a published or unpublished opinion—as the majority does today.

Even this circuit has implied that courts must consider whether the employee's belief is religious in nature.[9] For example, in *Cooper v. General Dynamics, Convair Aerospace Division, Fort Worth Operation,* 533 F.2d 163 (5th Cir.1976), we chided a district court that had evaluated a plaintiff's religious belief, and we "concluded that it was irrational and specious"; we stated that such conclusions are "not for federal courts, powerless as we are to evaluate the logic or validity of beliefs *found religious* and sincerely held." *Id.* at 166 n. 4 (emphasis added) (citing *Seeger,* 380 U.S. at 184–85, 85 S.Ct. 850). Although the majority cites this very language in support of its holding, again it does so having missed the very meaning of the words: We may not, as courts, consider the verity or "validity" or truth of beliefs that are *found religious* and sincerely held. Implicit with this statement, however, is that courts may—and must—find that those beliefs are in fact religious in nature as well as sincerely held.

For thirty years, district courts in this circuit have also considered the religious nature of beliefs when at issue in Title VII cases.[10] Therefore, not only is the majority's opinion in conflict with the direction of the Supreme Court and the holdings of our sister circuits, but it represents a departure from longstanding Fifth Circuit practice. Thus, contrary to the majority's holding, not only may we consider whether an employee's belief is religious in nature under Title VII, but we must do so where, as here, it is disputed.

A belief is "religious" if it is a "sincere and meaningful belief which occupies in the life of its possessor a place parallel to that filled by [ ] God." *Seeger,* 380 U.S. at 176, 85 S.Ct. 850. Such a belief is "not merely a matter of personal preference, but one of deep religious conviction, ... intimately related to daily living." *Wisconsin v. Yoder,* 406 U.S. 205, 216, 92 S.Ct. 1526, 32 L.Ed.2d 15 (1972). These statements "define religious practices to include moral or ethical beliefs as to what is right and wrong which are sincerely held with the strength of traditional views" whenever the religious nature of a belief is at issue. 29 C.F.R. § 1605.1. These include "not only traditional, organized religious such as Christianity, Judaism, Islam, Hinduism, and Buddhism, but also religious beliefs that are new, uncommon, not part of a formal church sect, only subscribed to ***495** by a small number of people, or that seem illogical or unreasonable to others." EEOC Compliance Manual § 12–I(A)(1). But, typically these beliefs concern "ultimate ideas about life, purpose, and death." *Id.*[11] Therefore, to be entitled to constitutional or statutory protection, an observance, practice, or belief must be motivated by this broad definition of "religion" and not mere personal preference or secular philosophy, whether social, political, or economic.[12]

B.

Applying the proper inquiry, we must decide what practice, observance, or belief Davis claims is protected under Title VII. Then we must consider whether she produced evidence that this belief is "religious" in her own scheme of things and whether it conflicted with an employment requirement.

Davis's testimony demonstrates that neither Sabbath-day observance nor her regular attendance at church services conflicted with Fort Bend County's requirement to work on Sunday and therefore are not at issue on appeal.[13] Instead, it was her commitment to participate in her church's special community-service project that she claims was in conflict with her employment requirements.[14] We must therefore decide whether the record supports a finding that religious belief—rather than personal preference or secular philosophy—motivated her commitment.

Davis claims that, for three main reasons, the community-service project constitutes ***496** a religious belief: (1) Davis testifies that she has been a faithful member of her congregation for about four years before the event. In light of her obvious devotion, the only reasonable inference to be drawn from her participation in a church event is that it was motivated by a religious belief. (2) Davis—contrary to the majority's assertion—did not testify that she needed to be off work "as a religious matter." She did, however, refer to the community service as a religious commitment in her complaint, and once in her testimony as a "Sunday religious activity." This alone, her reasoning continues, is sufficient to create a genuine issue of material fact regarding whether she was motivated by a *bona fide* religious belief. (3) Alternatively, Davis claims that her Christian belief in service and "feeding the community" required her participation in the Sunday service event.

First, Davis improperly focuses on the nature of the activity rather than the motivation behind it.[15] Depending on what motivated it, the very same activity can be both protected and unprotected under Title VII. One might be a vegetarian because one adheres to the Jain concept of Ahisma, requiring nonviolence. Or, one might be a vegetarian because one merely believes it to be the healthier food option. The former, motivated by a religious belief, is protected by Title VII; the latter, a personal preference, is not.

Similarly, even an activity ostensibly connected with a church or associated with a religious practice might not be motivated by religious belief and, therefore, would remain unprotected. For example, attending Sunday Mass out of obedience to God's commands is protected religious belief, but attending Mass because one enjoys listening to the choir is not.[16] Likewise, volunteering at a Christmas party in order to worship or celebrate the Christ Child is protected, but doing so out of a sense of social or familial obligation is not.[17] Just because an activity involves an activity or practice that is often associated with religion or religious belief does not end the inquiry: A reasonable jury must be able to find that a *religious* belief conflicted with the employment requirement.

In other words, the fact that Davis—devoted as she may be—participated in an activity associated with her church, at the request of her pastor, does not mean the activity necessarily constitutes a religious practice, observance, or belief.[18] Her participation in *that* activity must be motivated by her own, personal religious belief. Certainly, if she agreed to babysit her pastor's children at the church as a personal ***497** favor to him, Title VII would not apply, no matter her devotion to her faith. By that same token, the court must consider whether Davis produced evidence that her *personal* religious belief—and not necessarily the religious doctrine or tenets of her church or religion as broadly understood—required her participation at the groundbreaking ceremony.

Considering the record as a whole, Davis has failed to provide sufficient evidence to create a genuine issue of material fact. Although she did refer to the community service as a religious commitment in her complaint and once as a "Sunday religious activity" in her testimony, "an employee is not permitted to redefine a purely personal preference or aversion as a religious belief."[19] Mere conclusional language that the belief is "religious," without more, is insufficient.[20] Even if one refers to his personal preference for eating cat food as a "personal religious creed," for example, merely terming the activity or belief as such cannot make "religious" what is not.[21]

Instead, the plaintiff must produce evidence of the motivation behind the practice, observance, or belief that is religious in nature. This is not an onerous or difficult task; testimony by the plaintiff describing this motivation in terms meeting the broad standard for what is "religious" will usually suffice to survive summary judgment. For example, if one were to testify that he believes the goddess Bastet commanded him to eat cat food in worship of her divinity, and he sincerely holds that belief, he has provided sufficient evidence of a *bona fide* religious belief. This is so even if Bastet did not in fact give that command and the record reflects that this is not a generally recognized tenet of Bastet worship.[22] Although this requirement ***498** might often go undisputed or be easily met in most cases,[23] that fact does not absolve the plaintiff from bearing his burden.[24]

Davis did not testify that she "needed" to attend her church's community service project because of "religious" motivation, even under the broad definition of "religious." She states *only* that her "Pastor requested all members participate in this highly anticipated community service event," that she "was in charge of the volunteer program that was responsible for feeding three hundred (300) people," and that her "church depended on her to be there." In other words, Davis "needed" to attend the community service project on Sunday, July 3 not because her personal conception of religion required her attendance but because she had made a personal, social commitment to her pastor and fellow church members who were depending on her being there.

Based on this record, a reasonable jury could not conclude that Davis was motivated by a *bona fide* religious belief. It was her personal preference to prioritize her social commitment to her pastor over her commitment to her employer. Such a personal preference does not constitute a *bona fide* religious belief as a matter of law, and Title VII does not require an employer to accommodate it.

In the alternative, Davis argues for the first time on appeal that her faith requires that she follow Christ's example in "feeding the community." This, she claims, was her motivation in attending the community service project and constitutes a *bona fide* religious belief. This notion too fails. Assuming that the record supported that she was motivated by this religious belief, Davis has failed to provide evidence that her religious belief in "feeding the community" actually conflicted with her employment requirement. Even if her religion required her to feed the community, Davis has failed to show that it required her to do so on Sunday, June 3.[25]

In *Tiano v. Dillard Department Stores, Inc.*, 139 F.3d 679, 682 (9th Cir.1998), the court held that an employer did not have to accommodate an employee's religious belief that she needed to go on a pilgrimage to Medjugorje because the evidence presented evinced no temporal mandate requiring the pilgrimage take place at the time she left. "Otherwise, the employer is forced to accommodate the personal preferences of the employee—the timing of the trip. Title VII does not protect secular preferences." *Tiano*, 139 F.3d at 682. The court held that the mere statement that she "needed" to go was insufficient without corroborating evidence that the timing was motivated by her religious belief and because the record reflected that ***499** there were other opportunities serve as a pilgrim that did not conflict with her work schedule.[26]

Likewise, in *Dachman v. Shalala*, 9 Fed.Appx. 186, 192 (4th Cir.2001), the court held that an employer did not have to accommodate a Jewish employee who claimed she needed leave every Friday to pick up Challah bread for the Sabbath because it was merely her preference to do so on Friday. Although this was inconvenient for her to purchase the bread on Thursday, the employer did not have to accommodate her personal preferences in opting for a Friday pickup.[27]

Similarly, although her personal religious belief might require her to feed the community, Davis has not put forward any evidence that there was a temporal mandate for her to participate in *this* service on *this* particular Sunday. Undoubtedly, she would have had other opportunities to feed the community at times that would not conflict with her work schedule. Also, her testimony suggests that it was her preference to feed the community at that community service event because the church was depending on her after she had volunteered to participate. Therefore, she "[can] not satisfy one crucial element of her *prima facie* case: conflict between her religious belief and employment duties."[28]

Because Davis fails to establish a *prima facie* case, the district court correctly granted summary judgment. Davis has not provided evidence establishing a religious belief that was in conflict with an employment requirement. Instead, the record supports only the conclusion that Davis's personal commitment to her pastor kept her from reporting for work on Sunday, July 3. Because she was not motivated by *religious* belief, or a religious belief that conflicts with employment requirements, Title VII does not require Fort Bend County to accommodate her conflict.

II.

Even assuming Davis created a genuine issue of material fact regarding whether her "religions" belief conflicted with an employment requirement, the majority errs because accommodating Davis's belief constituted an undue hardship. The majority relies heavily on the fact that Davis found a volunteer replacement in holding there to be no undue hardship as a matter of law. The majority maintains that this alone is enough to establish a dispute of material fact to survive summary judgment. In doing so, however, the majority overlooks that the existence of a volunteer alone is insufficient if even the use of the volunteer would have reasonably resulted in "decreased efficiency, economic loss, and increased risk."[29]

***500** More specifically, the majority does not examine the qualifications of the proffered volunteer. Not any volunteer that a plaintiff can convince to substitute will be sufficient to defeat a defendant's establishment of undue hardship.[30] Even the majority would agree that any surgeon demanding accommodation cannot merely substitute the hospital janitor, no matter how willing he is to volunteer. The fact that Davis found a volunteer, although relevant, does not end our inquiry. We must consider whether he is qualified such that the substitution does not constitute only a *de minimis* cost to the employer.

Davis relies solely on the fact that her volunteer had occasionally filled in for her in the past as evidence that she was qualified to fill in for her on Sunday, July 3. That argument is unavailing, however, because (1) Fort Bend County's IT department was engaged in an unusually large and complex undertaking with a strict deadline and little room for error correction that (2) in its reasonable judgment required the attendance and support of all departmental supervisors. Davis does not contend, nor is their evidence to support, a finding that her volunteer was either a qualified supervisor or had filled in for her in the past during a comparably difficult managerial task.

Both sides agree that the move into the new courthouse was an extra-ordinary event within the IT department. It represented a huge undertaking that required months of planning and—as Davis has testified—many long days and nights of preparation by supervisors in the preceding weeks in order to ensure a smooth transition.[31] The IT department had only the extended Fourth of July weekend to complete the transfer and installation of all IT systems within the new courthouse and to ensure that they were functional before the start of business the following week.

Because of the importance and enormity of the task at hand, all supervisors were required to be present to minimize the risk of failure. The director of the IT department, testified via affidavit that he instructed Ford to deny Davis's request to be excused on Sunday because the "absence of a supervisor ... would have required other employees to assume a disproportionate workload." "[Her] role as Desktop Support Supervisor during the holiday weekend move to the Justice Center was vital to the efficiency of the move, her absence increased the risk that the computers would not be installed and functional when the Court system opened for business...." "[B]ecause of the risk and the enormity of the tasks to be completed in such a short amount of time," *all* members of the management team and supervisors were required to work throughout the weekend. And, in fact, all of those managers and supervisors did show up to work throughout the weekend, except for Davis.

Davis does not dispute that her volunteer was not a supervisor but merely a subordinate member of the IT staff. Although the volunteer had occasionally filled in for Davis, the record contains no evidence that she had either filled-in for ***501** Davis during a comparably complex managerial assignment or that she had similar experience or qualifications in tackling such a task. Therefore, Davis did not provide a qualified volunteer to cover her absence.

With this testimony, Fort Bend County met its

responsibility to produce evidence that this action created an undue burden. In response, Davis failed to show a genuine dispute of material fact because she failed to provide evidence of a volunteer with similar job qualifications or that the absence of a supervisor did not increase the risk of economic loss or efficiency.[32] Although reviewing courts must "draw all reasonable inferences in favor of the nonmoving party," courts cannot invent out of whole cloth evidence that *if in the record* would support the nonmoving party's position or draw inferences in favor of the nonmoving party that are unreasonable or unsupported by the evidence *actually in the record*.[33]

Any inference that Davis's volunteer was qualified to replace her in the monumental managerial task is unreasonable based on this record. Replacing a supervisor with an employee who is neither a supervisor nor has similar job qualifications for the task at hand created an increased risk to the county. This is, as a matter of law, a greater than *de minimis* injury.[34] Therefore, accommodation constituted an undue hardship, and the district court properly granted summary judgment on that ground.

Because I would therefore affirm the judgment in its entirety, I respectfully dissent from the conscientious decision of the majority.

All Citations

765 F.3d 480, 124 Fair Empl.Prac.Cas. (BNA) 101, 98 Empl. Prac. Dec. P 45,138

Footnotes

1 Davis also argues that Fort Bend waived the affirmative defense of undue hardship. A district court's ruling on waiver is typically reviewed for abuse of discretion, *Levy Gardens Partners 2007, L.P. v. Commonwealth Land Title Ins. Co.*, 706 F.3d 622, 633 (5th Cir.2013), but the district court has not addressed the issue. Given the "fact-specific" inquiry required, *Woodfield v. Bowman*, 193 F.3d 354, 362 (5th Cir.1999), the district court will be in a better position to decide whether Fort Bend has waived the defense. Accordingly, and because we resolve this issue in Davis's favor regardless, we decline to address waiver.

2 Davis argued in briefing that she was "effectively demoted" when Ford reduced the number of her direct reports, but points us to no evidence in the record that she felt this was a demotion.

1 *Cf.* EEOC Compliance Manual § 12–I(A)(1) (EEOC 2009), *available at* 2008 WL 3862096.

2 *Weber v. Roadway Exp., Inc.*, 199 F.3d 270, 273 (5th Cir.2000); *see also* *EEOC v. Abercrombie & Fitch Stores, Inc.*, 731 F.3d 1106, 1122 (10th Cir.2013).

3 *See* *Ballard*, 322 U.S. at 86–87, 64 S.Ct. 882 ("The religious views espoused by respondents might seem incredible, if not preposterous, to most people. But if those doctrines are subject to trial before a jury charged with finding their truth or falsity, then the same can be done with the religious beliefs of any sect. When triers of fact undertake that task, they enter a forbidden domain.").

4 *See, e.g., EEOC v. Union Independiente de la Autoridad de Acueductos y Alcantarillados de Puerto Rico*, 279 F.3d 49, 56 (1st Cir.2002) ("In order to satisfy this element, the plaintiff must demonstrate both that the belief or practice is religious and it is sincerely held."); *cf. Cloutier v. Costco Wholesale Corp.*, 390 F.3d 126, 130–32 (1st Cir.2004).

5 *See, e.g.,* *Dachman v. Shalala*, 9 Fed.Appx. 186 (4th Cir.2001) ("While an employer has a duty to accommodate

an employee's religious beliefs, the employer does not have a duty to accommodate an employee's preferences.").

6 *See, e.g., Adeyeye v. Heartland Sweeteners, LLC,* 721 F.3d 444, 448 (7th Cir.2013) ("[T]he belief necessitating the accommodation must actually be religious."), *EEOC v. Ilona of Hungary, Inc.,* 108 F.3d 1569, 1575 (7th Cir.1996) ("In order to establish a prima facie case of religious discrimination, a plaintiff must show that the observance or practice conflicting with an employment requirement is religious in nature...."); *Redmond v. GAF Corp.,* 574 F.2d 897, 901 n. 12 (7th Cir.1978) ("We believe the proper test to be applied to the determination of what is "religious" under § 2000e(j) can be derived from the Supreme Court decisions in [*Welsh*], and [*Seeger*], i.e., (1) is the 'belief' for which protection is sought 'religious' in person's own scheme of things, and (2) is it 'sincerely held.' ").

7 *See, e.g., Vetter v. Farmland Indus., Inc.,* 120 F.3d 749 (8th Cir.1997) ("An employer need not accommodate a purely personal preference." (internal quotation marks omitted)); *Brown v. Gen. Motors Corp.,* 601 F.2d 956, 959 (8th Cir.1979) (holding that Title VII "does not require an employer to reasonably accommodate the purely personal preferences of its employees.").

8 *See, e.g., EEOC v. Abercrombie & Fitch Stores, Inc.,* 731 F.3d 1106, 1119 (10th Cir.2013) ("[B]ecause religious beliefs have a distinctive content related to ultimate ideas about life, purpose, and death, logically, even if an applicant or employee claims to be acting for 'religious' reasons, if those reasons actually do not pertain to such ultimate ideas, then that person's conduct would fall outside the protective ambit of Title VII—*viz.,* the conduct would not truly relate to religious matters.").

9 *See, e.g., Anderson v. Browning–Ferris, Inc.,* 29 F.3d 623, *2 & n. 2 (5th Cir.1994) (per curiam) (unpublished); *Eversley v. MBank Dall.,* 843 F.2d 172, 175 n. 2 (5th Cir.1988); *Brown v. Dade Christian Schs., Inc.,* 556 F.2d 310, 324 (5th Cir.1977) (en banc) (Roney, J., dissenting); *Theriault v. Carlson,* 495 F.2d 390, 394–95 (5th Cir.1974).

10 *See, e.g., Brown v. Pena,* 441 F.Supp. 1382, 1385 (S.D.Fla.1977), *aff'd,* 589 F.2d 1113 (5th Cir.1979); *see also Toronka v. Cont'l Airlines, Inc.,* 649 F.Supp.2d 608, 611–12 (S.D.Tex.2009) ("Initially, the Court must determine whether Tornoka's 'moral and ethical belief in the power of dreams based on his religious convictions and traditions of his national origin of African descent' is a religious belief."); *McCrory v. Rapides Reg'l Med. Ctr.,* 635 F.Supp. 975, 979 (W.D.La.1986).

11 *See also Abercrombie,* 731 F.3d at 1119; *Brown,* 556 F.2d at 324 (Roney, J., dissenting) ("[A]s the very cases cited by the plurality demonstrate, the 'religious' nature of a belief depends on (1) whether the belief is based on a theory 'of man's nature or his place in the Universe,' (2) which is not merely a personal preference but has an institutional quality about it, and (3) which is sincere." (citations omitted)).

12 *See Yoder,* 406 U.S. at 216, 92 S.Ct. 1526 ("[I]f the Amish asserted their claims because of their subjective evaluation and rejection of the contemporary secular values accepted by the majority, much as Thoreau rejected the social values of his time and isolated himself at Walden Pond, their claims would not rest on a religious basis. Thoreau's choice was philosophical and personal rather than religious...."); *Anderson,* 29 F.3d at *2 ("The Supreme Court has characterized a 'religious' belief entitled to constitutional or statutory protection as 'not merely a matter of personal preference, but one of deep religious conviction, shared by an organized group, and intimately related to daily living.' " (quoting *Yoder,* 406 U.S. at 216, 92 S.Ct. 1526)); *see also Brown,* 441 F.Supp. at 1385 ("Plaintiff's 'personal religious creed' concerning Kozy Kitten Cat Food [that it contributed to his well-being] can only be described as such a mere personal preference and, therefore, is beyond the parameters of the concept of religion as

protected by the constitution or, by logical extension, by 42 U.S.C. § 2000e et seq."), *aff'd*, 589 F.2d 1113 (5th Cir.1979); *Bellamy v. Mason's Stores, Inc.*, 368 F.Supp. 1025, 1026 (E.D.Va.1973) (holding that the Ku Klux Klan is not a religion under the meaning of Title VII because the "proclaimed racist and anti-semitic ideology" has "a narrow, temporal and political character inconsistent with the meaning of 'religion' as used in § 2000e."), *aff'd*, 508 F.2d 504 (4th Cir.1974).

13 Davis testified that she first learned in March or April that the big move into the new courthouse would take place over the long Independence Day weekend, including Sunday, July 3. When she first learned of the move, she testified that "[she] had no conflict."

14 It was not until a week before the move that she realized that she did not wish to work the following Sunday; her pastor had requested all members participate in the community service event accompanying the ground-breaking for the new chapel on that date, and Davis committed to head the volunteer program tasked with feeding the community throughout the event. She informed the county of this conflict two days before the move.

15 *Cf. Cooper*, 533 F.2d at 168 ("If the employee's conduct is religiously motivated, his employer must tolerate it unless doing so would cause undue hardship to the conduct of his business.").

16 *See, e.g., Anderson*, 29 F.3d at *2 n. 2 (relating how the plaintiff felt obligated to attend his church service not because of Sabbath-day worship but in order to retain his position as usher and trustee of the church).

17 *See, e.g., Wessling v. Kroger Co.*, 554 F.Supp. 548, 552 (E.D.Mich.1982) (finding that a plaintiff's request to volunteer at a Christmas party was "not a religious observance protected by Title VII" because "[i]t was family oriented, a family obligation, not a religious obligation.").

18 *Abercrombie*, 731 F.3d at 1119 ("[A]n applicant or employee may engage in practices that are associated with a particular religion, but do so for cultural or other reasons that are not grounded in religion. If so, an employer's discrimination against that individual for engaging in that practice ... would not contravene Title VII's religion-discrimination provisions. This is true of course because, despite the practice's customary association with religion, the applicant's or employee's motivation for engaging in the practice would not be religious.").

19 *Reed v. Great Lakes Cos.*, 330 F.3d 931, 935 (7th Cir.2003); *see also Seshadri v. Kasraian*, 130 F.3d 798, 800 (7th Cir.1997) ("He claims that this is a religious creed, and he appeals to the provision of Title VII that forbids discrimination on grounds of religion. He refuses, however, to identify the religion. He claims a right not to do so, pointing out that government has no right to require a person to state his religious beliefs or affiliations. True enough; but a person who seeks to obtain a privileged legal status by virtue of his religion cannot preclude inquiry designed to determine whether he has in fact a religion.").

20 *See Turner v. Baylor Richardson Med. Ctr.*, 476 F.3d 337, 343 (5th Cir.2007) ("[A] party cannot defeat summary judgment with conclusory allegations, unsubstantiated assertions, or only a scintilla of evidence." (internal quotation marks omitted)); *Hussein v. The Waldorf–Astoria*, 134 F.Supp.2d 591, 597 (S.D.N.Y.2001) ("[Plaintiff] offers only a conclusory assertion that his religion required him to wear a beard.); *cf. Pedreira v. Ky. Baptist Homes for Children, Inc.*, 579 F.3d 722, 728 (6th Cir.2009) ("Pedreira has not alleged any particulars about her religion that would even allow an inference that she was discriminated against on account of her religion.").

21 *See Brown,* 441 F.Supp. at 1384–85; *see also* *Seshadri,* 130 F.3d at 800; *Hussein,* 134 F.Supp.2d at 597 ("Title VII does not require the accommodation of personal preferences, even if wrapped in religious garb.").

22 *See* *Seshadri,* 130 F.3d at 800 ("It is true that the EEOC, following [*Seeger*], does not think that the plaintiff in a case of religious discrimination must be a member of an authorized church or subscribe to its full menu of orthodox beliefs. We agree. For otherwise Jesus Christ, a heterodox Jew, could not be regarded as having been a victim of religious persecution. Heretics are a principal target of religious persecution."); *EEOC v. Red Robin Gourmet Burgers, Inc.,* No. C04–1201JLR, 2005 WL 2090677, at *3–4 (W.D.Wash.2005) (holding that an employee sufficiently established a *bona fide* religious belief even though the record reflected that the belief lacked scriptural or historical support in the practice of Kemetecism); *see also* *A.A. v. Needville Indep. Sch. Dist.,* 611 F.3d 248, 261 (5th Cir.2010) ("[T]he guarantee of free exercise is not limited to belies which are shared by all of the members of a religious sect." (internal quotation marks and citation omitted)); 29 C.F.R. § 1605.1 ("The fact that no religious group espouses such beliefs or the fact that the religious group to which the individual professes to belong may not accept such belief will not determine whether the belief is a religious belief of the employee or prospective employee.").

23 *See* *EEOC v. Union Independiente de la Autoridad de Acueductos y Alcantarillados de Puerto Rico,* 279 F.3d 49, 56 (1st Cir.2002).

24 *Neely v. PSEG Tex., Ltd. P'ship,* 735 F.3d 242, 246 (5th Cir.2013) ("[T]hough the ADAAA makes it *easier* to prove a disability, it does not *absolve* a party from proving one.").

25 *See, e.g., Anderson,* 29 F.3d at *2–3; *Bush v. Regis Corp.,* 257 Fed.Appx. 219, 221–22 (11th Cir.2007) ("Bush argues that the Sunday shift prevented her from doing field service with her family, which constituted a bona fide religious belief. The record, however, indicates that field service was not required to be performed on Sundays; rather, that was the day Bush and her family *wished* to perform field service.").

26 *Tiano,* 139 F.3d at 682–83 ("She offered no corroborating evidence to support the claim that she had to attend the pilgrimage between October 17 and 26. For example, she did not testify that the visions of the Virgin Mary were expected to be more intense during that period. Nor did she suggest that the Catholic Church advocated her attendance at the particular pilgrimage. In short, her lone unilateral statement that she 'had to be there at that time' was her only evidence.").

27 *Dachman,* 9 Fed.Appx. at 192. ("While an employer has a duty to accommodate an employee's religious beliefs, the employer does not have a duty to accommodate an employee's preferences. In this case, appellant's own testimony confirmed that her decision to pick up the bread on Friday afternoon was simply her preference and not a religious requirement. As such, her employer did not have a duty to accommodate this preference." (citing *Tiano,* 139 F.3d at 682)).

28 *Tiano,* 139 F.3d at 683; *see also* *Dachman,* 9 Fed.Appx. at 192.

29 *Brener v. Diagnostic Ctr. Hosp.,* 671 F.2d 141, 146 (5th Cir.1982) (stating that the proposed solution of having another employee substitute had resulted in decreased efficiency).

30 *See* *Trans World Airlines, Inc. v. Hardison,* 432 U.S. 63, 84, 97 S.Ct. 2264, 53 L.Ed.2d 113 (1977); *see also* *id.* at 85–86, 90 n. 4, 92 n. 6, 97 S.Ct. 2264 (Marshall, J., dissenting) (quoting the EEOC example of undue hardship relied

upon by the majority as "where the employee's needed work cannot be performed by another employee *of substantially similar qualifications* during the period of absence" (emphasis added)).

31 Davis testified that she worked every weekend for about two or three months in preparation for the move.

32 Although the move occurred without any significant issues and employees were released early on Sunday as a result, we cannot allow hindsight bias to cloud our analysis. Instead, we must consider whether accommodation posed an increased risk to the employer *ex ante*, even if that risk did not materialize *ex post*. "Title VII does not require an employer to actually incur accommodation costs before asserting that they are more than *de minimis*." *Bruff v. N. Miss. Health Servs., Inc.*, 244 F.3d 495, 501 (5th Cir.2001); *see also* *Weber v. Roadway Exp., Inc.*, 199 F.3d 270, 274 (5th Cir.2000) (holding that the "mere possibility of an adverse impact ... is sufficient to constitute an undue hardship").

33 *See* *Caban Hernandez v. Philip Morris USA, Inc.*, 486 F.3d 1, 8 (1st Cir.2007) ("In marshaling the facts for this purpose, we must draw all reasonable inferences in the light most favorable to the nonmovant. That does not mean, however that we ought to draw *unreasonable* inferences or credit bald assertions, empty conclusions, rank conjecture, or vitriolic invective." (citation omitted)); *cf.* *Weber v. Roadway Exp., Inc.*, 199 F.3d 270, 274 (dismissing the argument that the district court failed to view all facts and inferences in the light most favorable to the nonmovant by accepting the employer's hypotheticals "regarding the effects of accommodation").

34 *See* *Trans World Airlines*, 432 U.S. at 84, 97 S.Ct. 2264; *Weber*, 199 F.3d at 275 (affirming summary judgment because the only suggested accommodation "would impose more than a *de minimis* cost").

End of Document

Step three: **Slowly read the case. Look up terms you do not know, interact with the text, note what is said, as well as what is not said, in the case. Omit sections of the case that are irrelevant to the issue for which you are reading the case. During this step, you may take notes and highlight key passages of the case.**

The third step you should take when reading a case is to read the case slowly, intentionally, and diligently. This step is where you finally get to dig into the content of the case—that is, where you understand the law and how the law relates to the particular facts. Although a summary of facts is often placed at the beginning of a case—and you should read it at the outset—until you dig into the law, you may not be able to understand which facts are relevant to the specific issues of law. Given this reality, you should read the statement of facts but then go back and reread the facts after you understand the legal issues. Doing so will allow you to ascertain which facts go to each legal issue that you face. That is, which facts are "trigger facts"?

After reading the facts section with a particular focus on the issues relevant to you, begin reading the case paragraph by paragraph and section by section. Typically, a case will contain headings that split its content into sections for you. However, sometimes older cases do not contain headings; in that situation, you should section the case off by creating your own headings, noting where the court begins to grapple with each new legal issue or element of a claim. In addition to sectioning the case, at the close of each paragraph, make sure you understand what the paragraph you just read means. Ask yourself: "What was the purpose of the paragraph in plain English?" Then, note that purpose in the margins. You may need to read paragraphs or even entire sections multiple times to understand the content.

When engaging in close reading, remember to look up any terms or words that you do not understand. In addition, it is smart to circle or highlight watchwords (discussed previously) when a case describes the law.

Below is an example of a section of the sample case—*Davis v. Fort Bend County*—with the types of notes you might make on a case while engaging in deep reading to understand the legal requirements for a Title VII religious discrimination claim.

THE CASE	YOUR MARGIN NOTES
1. Davis's Prima Facie Case Survives Summary Judgment Davis has presented evidence demonstrating a genuine dispute of material fact on her prima facie case and, thus, survives the first step. As we have previously stated: To establish a prima facie case of religious discrimination under Title VII, the plaintiff must present evidence that (1) she held a bona fide religious belief, (2) her belief conflicted with a requirement of her employment, (3) her employer was informed of her belief, and (4) she suffered an adverse employment action for failing to comply with the conflicting employment requirement. *Tagore v. United States*, 735 F.3d 324, 329 (5th Cir.2013) (citing *Bruff v. N. Miss. Health Servs., Inc.*, 244 F.3d 495, 499 n. 9 (5th Cir.2001)).	**Procedural posture:** summary judgment motion on plaintiff's prima facie religious discrimination claim. **Prima Facie:**[7] A prima facie case is a cause of action or defense that is sufficiently established by a party's evidence to justify a verdict in his or her favor, provided such evidence is not rebutted by the other party. Gray highlighting = four elements required to establish a prima facie case of religious discrimination. NOTE: "and" means you need to show all four elements.
The parties dispute only the first element: whether Davis's observance of her church's July 3rd event was pursuant to her bona fide religious belief. Bona fide religious beliefs include "moral or ethical beliefs as to what is right and wrong which are sincerely held with the strength of traditional religious views." *See, e.g.*, 29 C.F.R. § 1605.1. A court's inquiry is limited to focusing upon the individual's motivation. Specifically, a court's task is to decide "whether [the individual's beliefs] are, in his own scheme of things, religious." *Seeger*, 380 U.S. at 185, 85 S.Ct. 850 (emphasis added). In this regard, a belief is "religious" if it is "[a] sincere and meaningful belief which occupies in the life of its possessor a place parallel to that filled by ... God." *Seeger*, 380 U.S. at 176, 85 S.Ct. 850. Conversely, whether the belief itself is central to the religion, i.e., whether the belief is a true religious tenet, is "not open to question." *Moussazadeh v. Tex. Dep't of Criminal Justice*, 703 F.3d 781, 790 (5th Cir.2012).	**Element 1 subrule:**[8] Bona Fide religious belief = moral beliefs as to right and wrong held with strength of traditional religious views **Element 1 subrule:** Whether a belief is a bona fide religious belief turns on whether the individual's belief is religious in his own scheme of things, not whether the asserted belief is objectively a true or established religious tenet.

7. "Prima Facie" may be a term you would look up in a legal dictionary.
8. As will be discussed later, subrules define or explain the general rule, here, the element at issue.

Step four: Think about how this case relates to others you have read and/or how it helps you resolve hypotheticals.

The last step you should complete when reading a case is to think about the case. Really think about what you just read. What are the main takeaways? What rules of law can you glean from the case that might be applicable to your client's case or a future case? Are there limits on the applicability of the case?

3. *How to brief a case*

A case brief is simply a written summary of a case. There are a number of ways to format a case brief and, in all honesty, no one form is perfect. The key takeaway is that you really should brief the cases you read in some format in order to ensure you are reading actively and carefully and to have a record of the highlights of the case to save time in the future. When practicing law, lawyers often continue to brief cases, especially in preparation for an oral argument to help them quickly address any questions a court may have about the implications, law, or facts from any case discussed in the briefing.

Below is a simple form you may use to brief cases. It contains explanations for what each part of the brief is calling for. These explanations will help you as you work to generate your first case briefs for all your classes.

ITEM	DESCRIPTION
Case Citation	This includes the case name located at the top of the case. For example: *Roe v. Wade*. It also includes the reporter volume number, abbreviation, first page of the case, the court writing the opinion, and the date of the opinion.
Parties	These are the key players in the case and how they are related to each other. For example, in an appellate case parties are labeled as Appellant and Appellee or Petitioner and Respondent. However, in your case brief it is helpful to give them their trial court designations (plaintiff or defendant) or label then as their roles (for example, employer and employee).
Procedural History	The procedural history of the case is a summary of how the case got to the court it is in.
Disposition	The disposition is how the court decided the issue procedurally, such as remand, reverse, or affirm.

ITEM	DESCRIPTION
Issue(s) Presented	The issue(s) presented is generally a legal question that the party that filed the case or the appeal wants the court to answer. Sometimes there is more than one issue.
Trigger Facts	Not all facts are relevant; some are relevant for one purpose but not for another. Once you find the issue(s) presented and the holding, you should have a better feel for which facts are truly important. The facts are not the court's holding or reasoning, but rather include the legally significant facts underlying the case and, specifically, the issues before the court.
Rule	The rule is the law the court applied to each issue. It may look like three things: (1) a succinct statement of the governing legal principle that the higher court uses to decide the case (about a sentence in length); (2) a sentence or paragraph in which the higher court answers the issue(s) presented; or (3) a paragraph that describes under what circumstances a person or entity is liable. The rule may be all three. You will sometimes have to edit what the court says—without losing meaning—to shorten the rule.
Holding	The holding(s) are the court's answer(s) to the issue(s) presented. The holdings are not the narrow disposition of the case, for example, "case reversed and remanded," but, instead, are broader substantive holdings that deal with the interpretation of the governing rule. If the issues were stated precisely, the holding can be stated as "yes" or "no" or in short statements taken from the language used by the court. Sometimes it's: "We hold that. . . ."
Reasoning	The reasoning is how the court got to the holding. Put another way how did the court apply the rule (law) to the trigger facts in the case to make its decision. It is generally several paragraphs following the rule in which the court explains *how* and *why* it answered the issue(s) presented as it did. It is a blend of facts and legal language. Pay close attention to this because you will have to show your reasoning when you answer essay questions. Take time to fully wrap your head around how the court explains itself. You will encounter both clear and well-explained reasoning and some fuzzy and hard-to-follow reasoning.

ITEM	DESCRIPTION
Takeaways and Other Notes	For substantive classes, every case is in the textbook for a reason. Before you read and while you read, you should ask yourself over and over, "What is the main takeaway of this case? Why have the authors included this case in the book, and why have they placed the case in this particular section?" Find this and you are golden. But, remember that sometimes your professors will use a case for different or additional reasons beyond what the casebook author intended. Don't get nervous, just try to understand why the professor is assigning the case. In legal writing class, as you brief cases, note here how you will use the case in your written assignment (e.g., what issue you will use it for). You can also note if there is significant dicta (portion of the opinion with legal reasoning that is not essential to the resolution of the issue(s) before the court) or if there are issues discussed that are not relevant to why you are reading the case.

There is a sample case brief in Appendix B for the *Davis* case. You can practice reading *Davis*, brief the case, and then compare it to the sample.

Chapter 3 | Formulaic Legal Writing

In math class, you use formulas. You plug numbers into the formula to get an answer. While the numbers you plug into a formula will change and the answer you get out of the formula will change, the formula itself never changes. Why? Because it works. It gets you from the problem to the answer. In legal writing, we use the CRAC formula to help us get from the problem to the answer. Why? Because it works and, more importantly, it is what your audience—whether that be a partner at a law firm or a judge—expects.

In legal analysis, we use deductive reasoning, meaning we set out our conclusion and then support that conclusion. In the most basic sense, as lawyers, we support our conclusion by applying the law to the facts of our case. In other words, to reach our conclusion we need the law and the facts.

Conclusion = Law + Facts

More specifically, to reach our conclusion we need the law and then we need to apply that law to the facts:

Conclusion = Rule (law) + Analysis (law applied to facts)

Let's do a very easy example. Let's say the Conclusion we want the court to reach is that "Dan was speeding while driving in the school zone." What do we need to show our audience in order for the audience to reach that Conclusion? We need to set forth (1) what the speed limit was in the school zone (law); and (2) how fast Dan was driving (facts).

Let's say we learn that the speed limit in the school zone was 20 miles per hour (law) and that Dan was driving 35 miles per hour (facts). Our CRAC would look like this:

Conclusion:	Dan was speeding in the school zone.
Rule:	The speed limit in a school zone is 20 miles per hour.
Analysis:	Dan was driving 35 miles per hour, which is 15 miles per hour over the speed limit.
Conclusion:	Accordingly, because Dan was driving over the speed limit, Dan was speeding in the school zone.

Of course, as a lawyer, the problems you solve and the legal analysis that you do to find an answer will be much more complicated than the above example. However, the formula will be the same. You will always start with your Conclusion. To show the reader how you reached your Conclusion, you will state the governing law (Rule) and then apply the Rule to the facts of your case (Analysis). You will then repeat your Conclusion. No matter how hard the problem, the formula is the same:

CRAC FORMULA

Conclusion + Rule + Analysis + Conclusion

Formulaic writing makes certain legal writing scholars scoff. They think that formulaic writing stifles creativity, is not the best way to respond to every legal problem, and can lead to boring, dull legal analysis. They are right. If a lawyer spent their entire career sticking to the formulas in this book, that lawyer would never be considered an "excellent" legal writer in the leagues of the late Justice Anthony Scalia or the late Justice Ruth Bader Ginsberg. However, before you learn to run, you have to learn to walk. Before you learn to sing, you have to learn to talk. Formulaic writing teaches you the basics. It teaches you how to think and, thus, how to communicate like lawyers do. It breaks down complex legal analysis into small, simple steps. Formulaic writing, if followed, will cause your legal analysis to be strong and sound. Once your legal analysis is strong and sound, then, in an upper-level writing course, you can work on making it "run" or "sing."

Legal writing is difficult. It is a learned skill, is not something that comes naturally, and is unlike any other type of writing. In law school, we had a friend who was an excellent writer. He had numerous published books, columns, and articles. He had an undergraduate degree in English from a prestigious college. He was talented, smart, and experienced when it came to writing. That is why it came as such a surprise when he got a C in legal writing during his first semester of law school. Although he was a good writer and his grammar was impeccable, his legal analysis was poor.

It is imperative to understand that good writing does not equal good legal writing. Good legal writing is composed of good writing ***plus good legal analysis***. Thus, while formulaic writing can seem "boring," it will teach you how to communicate your legal analysis in a way that is proven to work. Once you have mastered how to "talk" like a lawyer through formulaic writing, you can and should improve upon the formulas and deviate from the formulas to make your writing "run" or "sing." In the next parts of this book, formulaic writing is discussed in detail and in the context of both objective and persuasive writing.

A. Macro formulaic writing: CRAC

As already mentioned, CRAC is an acronym for Conclusion, Rule, Analysis, and Conclusion.[1] CRAC is the structure used to organize legal arguments on a macro level, whether those arguments appear in essay responses on an exam, an objective memorandum to a partner, or a persuasive motion or brief to the court. While different lawyers use different acronyms depending on how they were taught in law school,[2] the result is the same: lawyers first identify the issue by stating the conclusion; lawyers then provide the rule or governing legal authority for the issue; lawyers next apply the rule or governing legal authority to the facts that go to the problem or issue at hand; and lawyers lastly restate their conclusion on the issue.

1. Why use CRAC

A lawyer's effectiveness turns on her ability to explain and to persuade. Many law students are under the wrong impression that a lawyer's success in explaining and persuading hinges on her ability to draft eloquent sentences and complex legal analyses. Truthfully, however, a lawyer's success at its core turns on whether she logically organizes her argument.

2. How to use CRAC

You will use the CRAC structure (Conclusion, Rule, Analysis, and Conclusion) to organize each "issue" in your essay, memo, or brief. That is worth repeating: you use the CRAC structure for each "issue" in your essay, memo, or brief. The reason the word "issue" is in quotation marks is because what constitutes an issue varies depending on the call of the question you are answering and the type of document you are drafting. An issue might be a cause of action, a defense, or an element of a claim. A rookie law student mistake—one that professors see time and time again—is writing one giant

1. When we get to persuasive writing, you will see that we add an extra "C" for "Counter-Analysis" so that your organization is CRACC (Conclusion, Rule, Analysis, Counter-Analysis, Conclusion).

2. There are dozens of variations of CRAC used by various legal writing programs across the nation. For example, some lawyers use IRAC (Issue, Rule, Analysis, Conclusion) or CREAC (Conclusion, Rule, Explanation, Application, Conclusion). The variation turns—for the most part—on the specificity each law school wants to provide via its selected acronym.

CRAC for the entirety of the question even though the question raises more than one "issue."

a. Using CRAC in formal legal writing

For documents such as memoranda, briefs, and motions, the CRACs go in the main body of the document. In memoranda, your CRACs go in the "Discussion" section (the body) under the heading for the corresponding issues. In motions and briefs, your CRACs go in the "Argument and Authorities" section (the body) under the heading for the corresponding issues. Typically, each CRAC is separated by a heading or sub-heading.

If you are writing a memo, to determine how many issues you have (and thus how many CRACs you need), you should look at the assignment instructions. For example, you may be asked: "Please write a memorandum analyzing whether our client, Ms. Piper, has a cause of action for intentional infliction of emotional distress under Texas law." The number of issues you have, which is the same as the number of CRACs you will need, will be tied to the elements of an intentional infliction of emotional distress cause of action under Texas law. You would have four CRACs because, after reading through Texas caselaw, you would find that an intentional infliction of emotional distress cause of action has four elements: "(1) the defendant acted intentionally or recklessly, (2) the conduct was 'extreme and outrageous,' (3) the actions of the defendant caused the plaintiff emotional distress, and (4) the resulting emotional distress was severe."[3]

The assignment instructions may explicitly tell you that there are certain issues that you do not need to analyze and, if that is the case, you will adjust the number of CRACs accordingly. For example, you could be asked, "Please write a memorandum analyzing whether our client, Ms. Piper, has a cause of action for intentional infliction of emotional distress under Texas law. You do not need to discuss whether Defendant's conduct caused Ms. Piper emotional distress or whether the distress Ms. Piper suffered was severe." You would, thus, only have two issues (elements) remaining and, therefore, two CRACs.

b. Using CRAC on essay exams

As discussed in more detail in Part Six, CRAC is the structure you should use when answering bar-style essay exam questions in law school as well as when answering essay-style questions on the bar exam itself.

When faced with an essay question, the first thing you must do is read the entire question and identify the issues because, remember, the number of issues presented in the question itself will dictate the number of CRACs.

Let's look at an example. On a contracts exam, you might be given a set of facts and then asked, "Did the parties form a contract?" To answer this question, you must identify and analyze the issues, which, in the example, are the elements required for con-

3. *Standard Fruit & Vegetable Co., Inc. v. Johnson*, 985 S.W.2d 62, 65 (Tex. 1998).

tract formation. As you have (or will) learn in contracts class, a valid contract has four elements (offer, consideration, acceptance, and mutuality) and, thus, you would have four issues. Because you have four issues, you would have four CRACs. This is because, as always, # of Issues = # of CRACs.

c. Using CRAC on Performance Tasks

As discussed in more detail in Part Six, CRAC is also useful for tackling Performance Tasks ("PT") that you will take on the bar exam, but given the time-pressured nature of exams it is slightly modified and made simpler. Performance Tasks are drafted by the National Conference of Bar Examiners and administered in most states as part of the bar exam. Unlike the essay or short answer questions on the bar exam, which test substantive knowledge of the law, the PTs are unique in that they do not test substantive knowledge of the law. Rather, the PTs are "designed to test an examinee's ability to use fundamental lawyering skills in a realistic situation and complete a task that a beginning lawyer should be able to accomplish."[4] While the task on any given PT can vary, the task always involves written legal analysis. Therefore, the skills you learn in legal writing class will help you succeed on the PTs. What makes the PTs different than the assignments you will do in legal writing class is that the PTs are time-pressured exams where examinees only have 60 to 90 minutes to read the problem, the underlying facts, and the governing law, and then complete the written task—whether that be a memorandum, brief, letter, etc. This extreme time pressure is what makes the PTs difficult.

B. Micro formulaic writing: the building blocks for CRAC

We know that CRAC stands for <u>C</u>onclusion, <u>R</u>ule, <u>A</u>nalysis, and <u>C</u>onclusion. We also know that in both objective and persuasive writing, each issue has a CRAC. But, none of that helps you actually write a <u>C</u>onclusion (first and last "<u>C</u>" of CRAC), a <u>**R**</u>ule ("<u>**R**</u>" of CRAC), or an <u>A</u>nalysis ("<u>A</u>" of CRAC). Faced with this realization, this book's approach to writing does not end with adopting the CRAC formula; it also provides "micro formulas" within CRAC to help you draft the different parts of your CRAC.

C. Where we will use micro formulas

Within the CRAC formula, we will use "micro formulas" to help you learn how to craft <u>**R**</u>ules ("<u>**R**</u>") and how to do Analysis ("<u>**A**</u>"). These micro formulas are covered in excruciating detail in later parts of this book. But to foreshadow what you will learn

---

4. Note that the Multi-State Performance Test "MPT" is a 90-minute exam. The PT, which is part of the NextGen Bar Exam, is 60 minutes. National Conference of Bar Examiners, Multistate Performance Test, http://www.ncbex.org/exams/mpt/, and Performance Tasks, http://www.ncbex.org/exams/nextgen/sample-questions (last visited May 1, 2024).

there, let's look at a few examples. Under the "**R**" of CRAC, the **R**ule has three parts: (i) general rule; (ii) subrules; and, sometimes, but not always, (iii) case illustration(s). Thus, we will use the following micro formulas to help us as we draft our Rules.

Rule = General Rule + Subrules

or

Rule = General Rule + Subrules + Case Illustration

Similarly, we will use micro formulas to help you learn how to draft the most complex part of the Rule—the case illustration. We use the following micro formula to draft a case illustration:

Case Illustration = Topic Sentence + Holding + Trigger Facts + Reasoning

By using formulas beyond just the big CRAC, you will be able to break down the different parts of CRAC, better understand how the parts work individually and together, and make sure that your legal analysis is complete. As an added benefit, with these formulas in hand, you will rarely feel as if you are starting to write with an entirely blank piece of paper.

Chapter 4 | **How to Cite the Law**

A citation is how you attribute what you have written to its source. Proper citing requires that you master both: (1) when a citation is needed; and (2) the proper form of the citation.

A citation serves multiple purposes. First, a citation tells your reader the source/authority of your assertion. For example, let's say you write the following in a motion to the United States District Court for the Northern District of Texas:

> **A plaintiff cannot succeed in a Title VII religious discrimination claim unless it meets the burden to prove that the employee sincerely held a bona fide religious belief.**

If you do not include a citation after that sentence, the authority/source for that assertion is nothing or maybe, at best, you (i.e., new lawyer). That sentence, without a citation, is like telling the reader (here, the district court), "Hey, just trust me that here, a plaintiff cannot win a Title VII claim for religious discrimination if the employee did not hold a bona fide religious belief." The reader will not give much weight to what you have written because you have not told the reader that it is supported by legal authority. That is, you are missing a citation to the source for your assertion that, under Title VII, a plaintiff must prove the employee held a bona fide religious belief. Now, let's say, in your motion to the district court, you write this instead:

> **A plaintiff cannot succeed in a Title VII religious discrimination claim unless it meets the burden to prove that the employee sincerely held a bona fide religious belief. *Davis v. Fort Bend Cnty.*, 765 F.3d 480, 485 (5th Cir. 2014).**

The citation added to the end of the sentence tells the reader that the source/authority for your assertion is the Fifth Circuit Court of Appeals case *Davis*. No longer are you telling the reader, "Hey, just trust me!" Instead, you are telling your reader that, per a Fifth Circuit Court of Appeals case, that is **binding** on a federal district court within the Fifth Circuit, a plaintiff must prove the employee held a bona fide religious belief. As explained previously, a lower court is bound by the precedent of courts above it; accordingly, the district court would find very authoritative your citation to a Fifth Circuit case, which is mandatory (binding), primary authority.

Second, a citation allows the reader to find the source of your assertion. In the above example, the citation was ***Davis v. Fort Bend Cnty.***, 765 F.3d 480, 485 (5th Cir. 2014), and this citation was written in what lawyers commonly refer to as "*Bluebook* form." *The Bluebook* provides "a systematic method by which members of the profession communicate important information about the sources and legal authorities upon which they rely in their work."[1] While a complete summary of *Bluebook* citation form is beyond the scope of this book, suffice it to say that using a citation and putting it in correct *Bluebook* form allows a reader to find and to go to the source you are citing. For case citations, like the one in the example above, the citation consists of four parts, each of which conveys important information to the reader. First is the case name, which consists of the parties' names—***Davis v. Fort Bend County***—followed by a comma.[2] Second is the reporter volume number—**765**, the reporter abbreviation—**F.3d**, and first page of the case—**480**, collectively—**765 F.3d 480.** Third is a comma followed by the specific page(s) of the case where the assertion may be found—**485.** This is called a pincite. Fourth is an open parenthesis followed by the abbreviation for the deciding court and the year of the decision followed by a closed parenthesis and period—**(5th Cir. 2014).**

1	2	3	4
[*Davis v. Fort Bend County*,]	[765 F.3d 480]	[, 485]	[(5th Cir. 2014).]

Specifically, it is the second part of the citation—the reporter volume number, reporter abbreviation, and first page of the case—that is most helpful in allowing the reader to find the case by either (1) going to the book, which is Volume 765 of the Federal Reporter, Third Series on page number 480; or, more likely, (2) entering "765 F.3d 480" in an electronic search database like Westlaw or LexisNexis.

---

1. THE BLUEBOOK: A UNIFORM SYSTEM OF CITATION (Columbia Law Review Ass'n et al. eds., 21st ed. 2021).

2. Full party names should not just be copied in full to create the "case name." Instead, the party names must be abbreviated per the rules for abbreviation set forth in the Bluebook. See Tip #3 below for specific rules on abbreviating case names

Third, a citation helps you avoid plagiarism by attributing what you have written to its source. Black's Law Dictionary defines plagiarism as "the deliberate and knowing presentation of another person's original ideas or creative expressions as one's own work."[3] While the Black's Law definition requires intent on the part of the writer in order to constitute plagiarism, some law schools' honor codes define plagiarism as encompassing conduct that is both deliberate or intentional and conduct that is inadvertent or accidental. The quintessential example of plagiarism is taking the work of another, for example, an essay answer written by a classmate, a former student, a student at another school, etc. and passing it off as your own. Intentional plagiarism can also happen if you, for example, copy and paste from a secondary source that summarizes a rule of law and pass it off as your own summary of the rule of law in a memo or motion by failing to cite to the secondary source or failing to use quotations. Hopefully it goes without saying that you should never do this in law school. Avoiding intentional plagiarism such as this is not something that should need to be taught to law students. You should never pass off the work of another as your own. Doing so will likely cause you not only to fail the given assignment, but also will likely cause you to be referred to the honor council or disciplinary board at your school and, potentially, be reported to the character and fitness section of your state bar.

However, plagiarism happens not only when you intentionally copy the entire work or large parts of the work of another, but it also can happen in more subtle ways. Plagiarism is often caused by failure to properly cite and/or failure to use quotations when taking language from another source. While failing to properly cite or use quotations can be deliberate and done with a bad motive, more often it is the result of not fully understanding the rules of attribution. Thus, learning when to cite and how to cite will help you to avoid plagiarism.

A. Attribution: when to cite and use quotations

As a general matter, you should include a citation after every assertion that is taken from another source. Here is an easy rule to live by: "When in doubt, CITE!"

In the context of first-year legal writing and, specifically, in the context of CRAC, this means that you usually cite to legal authority after almost every sentence in your Rule of CRAC, and you usually cite to legal authority and/or the record (facts of your case) after almost every sentence in your Analysis of CRAC. With respect to the two Conclusions of CRAC, you do not need a citation because your Conclusions will be something you generated as a product of applying the law to the facts such that you did not take it directly from another source.

Below is an excerpt from a CRAC. You will see that every assertion requiring a citation is indicated by the words CITE LAW (if a citation is needed to legal authority) or CITE RECORD (if a citation is needed to the underlying facts of the client's case at issue).

---

3. *Plagiarism*, BLACK'S LAW DICTIONARY (11th ed. 2019).

> Mr. Saint will likely satisfy the fourth element of a prima facie case of religious discrimination. To satisfy the fourth element, the plaintiff must prove that he suffered an "adverse employment action for failing to comply with the conflicting employment requirement." CITE LAW. An adverse employment action includes "ultimate employment decisions" such as those that deal with hiring, firing, or compensation. CITE LAW.
>
> Here, Mr. Saint will likely satisfy the fourth element of his prima facie case because UI did not compensate him after he failed to comply with its policy mandating that employees use a new biometric scanning system to clock in and out. CITE TO RECORD. For ten days after UI's new scanning system's implementation, Mr. Saint continued to work as scheduled but did not use the scanner to sign in and out of work because of his belief that it would administer the "Mark of the Beast." CITE TO RECORD. His August paycheck failed to compensate him for the time he worked on those ten days and, therefore, was an "adverse employment action." CITE TO RECORD; CITE TO LAW. Because Mr. Saint was not compensated for "failing to comply" with UI's required timekeeping system and decisions regarding compensation constitute "adverse employment action," Mr. Saint will likely satisfy the fourth element of a prima facie case of religious discrimination under Title VII. CITE RECORD; CITE LAW.

You should see that almost every sentence in the **R**ule and **A**nalysis of CRAC has a citation after it. The only sentences that do not include a citation in the **R**ule and **A**nalysis sections are topic sentences. This is because topic sentences are kind of like "mini-conclusions" in that they introduce, summarize, and connect for the reader the information in the current paragraph. The topic sentence does not present a new rule or point of law in and of itself, but, instead, summarizes or previews what is in the sentences that follow. Therefore, a citation is usually not needed in a topic sentence unless it quotes from a subrule or part of the case you are illustrating. In summary, you do not need a citation after your topic sentences. "Wait," you say, "I hear what you are saying, but it is confusing me!" To that, we reply, be calm, carry on, and remember the easy rule we live by: "When in doubt, CITE!" Citing after your topic sentence is technically not wrong, rather it is simply stylistically better not to distract from your topic sentence with a citation if your topic sentence is merely previewing your case illustration without quoting from the case. Therefore, if you are confused or "in doubt" about citations and topic sentences, what should you do? CITE.

We know that we need to cite after every assertion that is taken from another source. When we take an assertion from another source word for word, rather than paraphrasing that other source, we need to use quotations to indicate that we are using the exact words from another source. When the material you are quoting from is more than 50 words, you should use a block quote. Otherwise, you indicate you are using the words of another by using quotation marks around the text.

The below text is copied and pasted from the case *Davis v. Fort Bend County*. If you were to quote the entirety of the text word for word, you would put it in block quotation format because it exceeds 50 words. Block quotations do not use quotation marks. Instead, block quotations are indicated by indenting the text on the right and left sides and using single spacing. Note that the citation following a block quote is left-justified, but it is not indented and, thus, not a part of the block quote.

> Focusing on the sincerity of Davis's belief, as we must, we hold that her prima facie case survives summary judgment. Davis testified about her devotion to church and that she was "[a]bsolutely not" "just a weekend warrior." Instead, she was actively committed to her church "because [she] believe[d] in something," sometimes attending up to three services every Sunday. Regarding the particular Sunday at issue here, July 3, 2011, she testified that she "needed" to attend "a special church service." She similarly alleged in her complaint that "she would be unavailable for work on Sunday July 3, 2011 due to previous religious commitment."

Davis v. Fort Bend Cnty., 765 F.3d 480, 487 (5th Cir. 2014).

Block quotes should be used sparingly, if at all, because block quotes are often skipped over by readers. Let's say, instead of using a block quote, you want to form a subrule from the second sentence above. If you want to use the exact words to create that subrule, you need to use quotes and a citation. If you alter the text in any way, you should use brackets inside the quotation to indicate the alteration.

> A court "must" "focus[] on the sincerity of [an employee]'s belief" in deciding whether a "prima facie case survives summary judgment." *Davis v. Fort Bend Cnty.*, 765 F.3d 480, 487 (5th Cir. 2014).

Let's say you do not want to take the language word for word from *Davis*, but, instead, you want to paraphrase the language to create a subrule. Here, you would not need to include quotations, but you would need to include a citation.

> Courts look at whether an employee's belief was sincere in deciding a motion for summary judgment. *Davis v. Fort Bend Cnty.*, 765 F.3d 480, 487 (5th Cir. 2014).

B. How to cite (Bluebook, Indigo Book, state-specific citation forms)

We discussed when you need a citation and why you need a citation, but how do you properly form citations? The short answer is you look to a citation manual like *The Bluebook*, which explains (in painstaking detail) how to cite just about everything under the sun according to the Uniform System of Citation followed in the legal profession. However, *The Bluebook*, while certainly the most prominent legal citation manual, has a few drawbacks. First, if bought new, it costs around $46.00. Second, the publishers keep making new editions, meaning you may be shelling out $46.00 every few years if you want to stay up to date. Third, because the vast majority of *The Bluebook* pages are devoted to constructing citations for the purpose of law review footnotes (something first-year law students will not need to worry about in their first-year legal writing class), it can be a little (a lot) confusing. Enter: *The Indigo Book*.[4] *The Indigo Book* is a (1) free, online resource; (2) that is consistent with *The Bluebook* citation style; and (3) is a whole lot less confusing. To access it, go to https://indigobook.github.io/versions/indigobook-2.0.html or Google "The Indigo Book 2.0."

As law professors, we have found that *The Indigo Book* covers almost everything that you will need to know how to cite in first-year legal writing. And, by using lots of examples and by eliminating law review-specific details, *The Indigo Book* is also much easier for legal writing students to follow. While *The Bluebook* and *The Indigo Book* cover general citations, it is important to be aware that some states have their own state-specific citation manuals that govern citation to state-specific legal authority. For example, Texas, California, and Louisiana—just to name a few—all have their own unique citation systems. If you are writing something to be filed in state court, you should check the see if the state has its own citation form that supersedes *The Bluebook* when it comes to proper citation to state legal authorities.

Whichever legal citation manual or manuals you use, below are our "top four" citation tips. Because in first-year legal writing the most common legal authority you will cite is cases, most of these tips deal with case citations.

Tip #1: Placing long citations, short citations, and *Id.* (Bluebook Rule B10.2; Indigo Book Rule 15).

The first time you cite something, you use the full citation. If you cite the same material again in your paper, you will use either "*Id.*" or a short citation, depending on where the subsequent citation is found. If you are citing to the same single source from the immediately preceding citation, you will use "*Id.*" if the subsequent citation is at the same page number (pincite), or you will use "*Id.* at ___." if you are citing to the same

4. The Indigo Book: A Manual of Legal Citation (Christopher Sprigman & Jennifer Romig et al. eds., Public.Resource.Org. 2d ed. 2021), https://indigobook.github.io/versions/indigobook-2.0.html (last visited May 1, 2024).

single source but to a different page number/pincite. If you are citing to something you have previously cited, but it is not from the immediately preceding citation, you will use the short form citation (*see* tip #2 for how to form a short citation). Look at the example below. Note that the citation in the first and second sentences are full citations because, in the example, it is the first time the writer is citing *Davis* and *Tagore*. The third and fourth sentences use the citation "*Id.*" because they are also citing to *Tagore*, the immediately preceding citation and the same page. The fifth sentence cites the *Davis* case again and uses a short citation because *Davis* has already been cited, but here, "*Id.*" is inappropriate because the citation immediately preceding the last sentence is not *Davis*.

> An employee satisfies the first element of a Title VII claim for religious discrimination whenever he establishes that he holds a bona fide religious belief. *Davis v. Fort Bend Cnty.*, 765 F.3d 480, 487 (5th Cir. 2014). In analyzing this element, the "specific religious practice must be examined rather than the general scope of applicable religious tenets, and the plaintiff's 'sincerity' in espousing that practice is largely a matter of individual credibility." *Tagore v. United States*, 735 F.3d 324, 328 (5th Cir.2013). Indeed, courts hold the first element is met "on little more than the plaintiff's credible assertions." *Id.* The sincerity of a plaintiff's engagement in a particular religious practice is "rarely challenged" and, when it is, the court must analyze the issue "with a light touch, or 'judicial shyness.'" *Id.* Furthermore, in deciding whether a belief is bona fide, the court "is limited to focusing upon the individual's motivation" and a court's task is to decide whether the individual's beliefs are, "in his own scheme of things, religious.'" *Davis*, 765 F.3d at 485 (citing *United States v. Seeger*, 380 U.S. 163, 185 (1965)).

It is inappropriate to use "*Id.*" if the preceding citation cites more than one source. In the example below, because the first sentence cites two sources, it is inappropriate to use "*Id.*" after the second sentence because it would be unclear which authority (*Davis* or *Tagore*) you are referring to for the source of the second sentence. Instead, you would use a short citation after the second sentence to indicate the source.

> A plaintiff cannot succeed in a Title VII religious discrimination claim unless it meets the burden to prove that the employee sincerely held a bona fide religious belief. *Davis v. Fort Bend Cnty.*, 765 F.3d 480, 487 (5th Cir. 2014); *Tagore v. United States*, 735 F.3d 324, 328 (5th Cir. 2013). Bona fide religious beliefs include "moral or ethical beliefs as to what is right and wrong which are sincerely held with the strength of traditional religious views." *Davis*, 765 F.3d at 485.

Tip #2: Example case citations—going from long to short.

How do you transform a full citation into a short citation? We are glad you asked. Citation manuals tell you all the different parts of a citation, what the parts mean, and how to piece them together. That is all well and good, but, if you are like a lot of law students, what you really want is an example. Below are some example case citations in long-form and short-form (and how to get from long to short). As you draft your citations, you can look back to these examples and others and "check" yourself. Do you have all your commas? Is your spacing right? Do you have a pincite?

REPORTED CASE EXAMPLE (*Bluebook* Rule B10.1, B10.2; *Indigo Book* Rule 11, 15)

Long: *Bruff v. N. Miss. Health Servs., Inc.*, 244 F.3d 495, 497 (5th Cir. 2001).

Bruff ~~*v. N. Miss. Health Servs., Inc.*~~, 244 F.3d ~~495,~~ **at** 497 ~~(5th Cir. 2001)~~.

Short: *Bruff*, 244 F.3d at 497.

Id. or *Id.* at __.

UNREPORTED CASE EXAMPLE (*Bluebook* Rule B10.1.4, B10.2; *Indigo Book* Rule 12.4): Note that some cases are not assigned to reporters. For these cases, you include the case name, docket number, citation to either Westlaw or Lexis, the word at star pagination, and, inside the parentheses, the court and the complete date (as opposed to just the year).

Long: *Pok Seong Kwong v. Am. Flood Research, Inc.*, No. 302CV2189-R, 2004 WL 906173, at *2 (N.D. Tex. Apr. 16, 2004).

Pok Seong Kwong ~~*v. Am. Flood Research, Inc.*, No. 302CV2189-R~~, 2004 WL 906173, at *2 ~~(N.D. Tex. Apr. 16, 2004)~~.

Short: *Pok Seong Kwong*, 2004 WL 906173, at *2.

Id. or *Id.* at *__.

Note: When using "*Id.*" for these unreported citations, if citing to a different page, you will use the star pagination. For example: *Id.* at *3.

Tip #3: Tables—some of them—are your friends.

The Bluebook has 16 tables in its white pages and two tables in its blue pages. While you will rarely, if ever, look at most of them, there are a few that you will regularly use.

Most Used Tables for Citations

ABBREVIATIONS FOR:	WHERE TO FIND:	SUMMARY/ EXAMPLE:
Court documents	*Bluebook* Bluepages Table 1	Use this table to help formulate citations to court documents in your case. For example, if you were citing to a Defendant's Motion for Summary Judgment filed in your case, you would abbreviate it "Def.'s Mot. Summ. J."
Case names	*Bluebook* Table 6 (Indigo Table 11)	Use this table to find which words in case names are abbreviated when citing cases. For example, if your case was American Association of Restaurants v. Smith National Laboratory, when referring to the case name in a citation, the following words would need to be abbreviated: *Am. Ass'n of Rests. v. Smith Nat'l Lab.*
Court names	*Bluebook* Table 7 (Indigo Table 9)	Use this table when citing cases to determine how to abbreviate the type of court that decided the case in the citation. Note that the court is coupled with the geographical location. For example, for a citation to an administrative court case, you would use the abbreviation "Admin. Ct." to refer to the court. In a citation to a federal district court case, you would use the abbreviation "D." to refer to the court.
U.S. geographical locations	*Bluebook* Table 10.1 (Indigo Table 12.1)	Use this table for geographical terms (U.S. states, cities, and territories) in case citations. For example, Alabama is "Ala."; Missouri is "Mo."; and Wyoming is "Wyo."
Months	*Bluebook* Table 12 (Indigo Table 17)	Use this table when a month is used in a citation. Every month except May, June, and July are abbreviated.
Periodicals	*Bluebook* Table 13 (Indigo Table 18)	Use this table to abbreviate periodical names in citations. For example, Harvard Law Review is abbreviated "Harv. L. Rev."

Tip #4: When to use signals (Bluebook Rule 1.2; Indigo Book Rule 4).

Signals can precede a citation to inform the reader about the relationship between the assertion and the authority cited for that assertion. *The Bluebook* and *Indigo Book* divide signals into four categories: (1) signals that indicate support (*E.g., Accord, See, See also, Cf.*); (2) signals for comparison (*Compare ... with ...*); (3) signals for contrast

(*Contra*, *But see*, *But cf.*); and (4) signals for background or general information (*See generally*). Note that if no signal is used, it means that the authority cited directly states the assertion.

For a complete discussion of what each signal means, you should refer to *The Bluebook* Rule 1.2 (or *Indigo Book* Rule 4). However, you should know that signals are very important in legal writing. The use or misuse of a signal can completely change the meaning of what you are saying to the reader.

To illustrate this, let's look at an example. The following is an excerpt from *Brener v. Diagnostic Ctr. Hosp.*, 671 F.2d 141, 146–47 (5th Cir. 1982), where the court upheld a finding that the employer provided a reasonable accommodation and discussed that courts recognize a duty of employees to cooperate:

> A reasonable accommodation need not be on the employee's terms only. Here, Brener did not fully explore the possibilities for accommodation within the pharmacy's flexible scheduling system before he sought additional action from the hospital. In such circumstances, he cannot reject the hospital's efforts as inadequate.

Brener v. Diagnostic Ctr. Hosp., 671 F.2d 141, 146–47 (5th Cir. 1982).

Let's say you wanted to write the following:

> The employee must completely explore the possibilities within the employer's proposed accommodation before asking for a different accommodation. *Brener v. Diagnostic Ctr. Hosp.*, 671 F.2d 141, 146–47 (5th Cir. 1982).

If you do not include a signal, the lack of the signal signifies to the reader that *Brener* directly states your assertion. However, is it accurate that *Brener* directly states that assertion? Go back and reread the excerpt. What do you think? Not exactly. Rather, it would be more accurate to say that *Brener* "supports" that assertion or that the assertion "follows from it."[5] Accordingly, you should use a "*See*" signal before the citation.

> The employee must completely explore the possibilities within the employer's proposed accommodation before asking for a different accommodation. *See* *Brener v. Diagnostic Ctr. Hosp.*, 671 F.2d 141, 146–47 (5th Cir. 1982).

---

5. The Bluebook, *supra* note 1, R. 1.2.

Chapter 5 | Grammar and Style

Grammar is the way in which language is structured. The part of grammar that is most relevant to your work as a lawyer is known as syntax and construction. Syntax and construction provide the basic rules that allow us to understand each other, both in terms of the spoken and the written word. These rules dictate, for example, the parts of speech, the use of punctuation, the use of capitalization, and pronoun and antecedent agreement. Style, on the other hand, is the gray area among the rules of grammar. Style is a set of preferences and often imposes arbitrary rules affecting voice and tone. Style has nothing to do with syntax. Both grammar and style are central to becoming a successful legal writer. Rules of grammar are 100 percent learnable. Style, however, as you can imagine, is a bit more squirrelly, especially given that style preferences may vary depending on your audience. Below we have captured the top eight—widely accepted—rules of grammar and style for legal writers. Be mindful that while grammar rules are black and white, proper style may vary from situation to situation.

A. Why grammar and style are important

Grammar matters. It is that simple. First, the use of improper grammar affects a law student's grades in legal writing. Second, the use of improper grammar impacts a lawyer's credibility to her clients, peer lawyers, and judges. Furthermore (and probably more importantly), the use of improper grammar affects both law students' and lawyers' abilities to communicate effectively and precisely.

The last thing you want as a law student or as a new lawyer is for someone to focus on your poor grammar rather than on the arguments you are making on your client's behalf. If you think we are creating an issue that does not exist, think again. For example, a federal judge in the Eastern District of Kentucky commented on the lawyer's grammar: "Once again [] counsel is reminded that he should at least make a pretense of having proofread his documents before filing them in federal court. The Court was hesitant to even cite to [counsel's] brief here, given the poor quality of counsel's writing."[1]

Improper or unintended grammatical issues can also affect the substance of what law students and lawyers are trying to communicate. For example, an inadvertently omitted or a misplaced comma can completely change the meaning of a sentence in a brief, a clause in a contract, or a provision in a municipal code. A judicial opinion out of Ohio illustrates the ramifications of improper grammar. A local ordinance in West Jefferson, Ohio, was drafted to read as follows: "it is illegal to park on a village street '**any motor vehicle camper**, trailer, farm implement and/or non-motorized vehicle for a continued period of twenty-four hours.'" A local woman woke up at 5:30 p.m. (she works nights) and discovered that her green pickup truck had been towed and the local police issued her a citation for violation of the ordinance. In assessing whether it was improper to tow the resident's motor vehicle, the Ohio court noted:

> By utilizing rules of grammar and employing the common meaning of terms, 'motor vehicle camper' has a clear definition that does not produce an absurd result. If the village desires a different reading, it should amend the ordinance and insert a comma between the phrase 'motor vehicle' and the word 'camper.' As written, however, legislative intent is clear from looking at the language used in the ordinance itself.[2]

This lack of a comma worked to the local woman's advantage. Her green pick up truck was a motor vehicle but not a motor vehicle camper so the plain language of the ordinance did not apply to it. However, is that what the drafters meant? Probably not. They probably forgot the comma between "motor vehicle" and "camper."

B. Quick review: the top nine most important grammar and style rules for legal writing

There are numerous grammar rules crucial to a law student's or a young lawyer's ability to draft articulate, clear, and accurate sentences. Unfortunately, given curricular shifts in undergraduate and high school education, there is an ever-increasing number of college graduates who are unfamiliar with the rules of grammar and style that form the basis for how we speak and write. The purpose of this section is not to teach or re-

1. *Colyer v. Speedway, LLC*, 981 F. Supp. 2d 634, 641 n.5 (E.D. Ky. 2013).
2. *W. Jefferson v. Cammelleri*, 12th Dist. No. CA2014-04-012, 2015-Ohio-2463, 2015 WL 3824456, ¶ 18.

teach you English grammar in its entirety. Instead, this section aims to highlight the top nine rules of grammar and style most critical to a lawyer's work. As such, if as you navigate writing courses in law school, you realize that you are deficient in your understanding of the rules of English grammar, we encourage you to seek additional help to shore up your grammar abilities.[3]

1. Rule one: plain language

Using bigger words does not make you seem smarter. How about we repeat that for emphasis: using multisyllabic, thesaurus-found words does not make you (or make you appear) smarter. Instead, the smartest lawyers are those who can take the law—which is necessarily complex on its own—and make it easy to understand. One of the primary ways law students and young lawyers begin to do this is by constantly reminding themselves to use plain, simple English in their writing.

How do you do this? Follow these few failsafe tips.

Tip #1: When possible, leave Latin where it originated—in ancient times—and prefer simple words over complex ones.

To use arcane phraseology to expound on the state of jurisprudence is, well, absurd. For whatever reason, many entering law students are under the impression that to be a lawyer they have to "sound" like one and that to sound like a lawyer they need to use complex and multisyllabic words. Truthfully speaking, however, what clients pay lawyers to do is to take the law and to make it understandable. So, the reality is that using plain English is the best way to communicate orally and in writing because, simply put, it is the best way to ensure that others are understanding what you are saying or writing.

What does this mean for lawyers in particular? At times as a lawyer, you will need to use terms of art; after all, there are some terms that cannot be simplified without introducing inaccuracies (for example, "battery" cannot be replaced with "hit" and "family violence" cannot be replaced with "abuse"). However, aside from terms of art, lawyers should avoid using legalese and Latin phrases in their writing. Brian Garner has written a number of books dedicated to helping lawyers simplify their language; below is a sampling of legal and "stuffy" terms he suggests you avoid using and some suggested alternative phrasing for each.[4]

---

3. There are a number of resources available to law students to help them shore up their understanding of English grammar. A few of our favorite resources are listed here: WILLIAM STRUNK & E.B. WHITE, THE ELEMENTS OF STYLE (Pearson, 4th ed. 2014); BRYAN GARNER, THE REDBOOK (West, 5th ed. 2023); ANNE ENQUIST ET AL., JUST WRITING: GRAMMAR, PUNCTUATION, AND STYLE FOR THE LEGAL WRITER (Wolters Kluwer, 6th ed., 2022).

4. GARNER, *supra* note 3, at 219.

GARNER SAYS INSTEAD OF THIS	TRY THIS
Ab initio	From the start
Forthwith	Now
Herein	Here
Sui generis	Unique
To wit	Namely
Inter alia	Among other things

Tip #2: Use (parallel) lists.

Legal readers think in terms of factors and elements. As a result, legal readers appreciate and easily comprehend information when it is presented in numerated or bulleted lists. Given this reality, when the content you are explaining lends itself to it, create a numerated or bullet-pointed list to help your reader navigate the elements, factors, or conditions you are explaining. In addition, when using lists in your legal writing, be mindful to make your lists parallel in terms of construction. What does that mean? Make sure that each item in the list follows the same grammatical structure. For instance, if the first item in the list begins with a past participle,[5] all listed items should begin with a past participle. This parallel structure will make it easier for your reader to see how the different listed items relate to one another.

NON-PARALLEL LIST

There are three elements required to establish an informal marriage in Texas:

1. the couple must agree to be married;
2. cohabitation as husband and wife after the agreement; and
3. representation to others that they were married.

PARALLEL LIST

To establish an informal marriage in Texas, a couple must show that they:

1. agreed to be married;
2. cohabitated as husband and wife after the agreement; and
3. represented to others that they were married.

Tip #3: Keep your sentences concise and easy to follow.

Generally speaking, your sentences should average around 18 words in length. You should have some sentences that are far fewer than 18 words, and you may have some others woven in that are a bit longer. The variation in sentence length helps keep your reader engaged and focused (too many similarly constructed sentences risks lulling your reader to sleep). Sentence length is important not only for ease of reading, but also because it affects your reader's comprehension. As a good rule to follow, we recom-

5. A past participle is a form of a verb usually ending in -ed and expressing a completed action.

mend that you discipline yourself to highlight any sentence that is more than 25 words in your legal writing. Once you have flagged a long sentence, ask yourself whether the long sentence can be improved by splitting it into two sentences or removing unnecessary words or phrases.

In addition to length, draft your sentences in a way that makes it easy for your reader to identify the subject, verb, and object of the sentence. This aim is typically accomplished by locating the subject and verb near the front of your sentences and avoiding writing in the passive voice (see Grammar Rule Two, *infra*, for more on passive voice).

Tip #4: Make sure your writing passes the readability test.

The best way to test the readability of your document is to read it aloud and make sure you—as both the reader and the writer—can follow the content you drafted. Obviously, this readability test is somewhat inaccurate because you drafted the text and are at an advantage in trying to understand it as you read it aloud. Given this reality, there are two other ways to ascertain the readability of your legal writing. The first is to listen to it as Google Docs or another document reader reads it aloud. This approach will highlight long, complex sentences so that you can go back and fix them after the read-through. The second option is to run readability statistics in Microsoft Word. The generally accepted rule is that all writings—including legal writings—should have a readability score around a 40 or 50 and be within a middle or high school range. You can review the readability statistics of any document you draft in Microsoft Word by selecting "show readability" as an option (on a PC computer go to File menu > Options > Proofing tab)[6] and then running a grammar and spell check of your document. Below you will see the readability results from the Objective Memorandum in the Appendix.

Readability Statistics

Counts	
Words	5,271
Characters	27,482
Paragraphs	53
Sentences	224
Averages	
Sentences per Paragraph	5
Words per Sentence	23.3
Characters per Word	5
Readability	
Flesch Reading Ease	37.7
Flesch-Kincaid Grade Level	12.3
Passive Sentences	6.6%

OK

6. On a Mac computer, go to Word > Preferences > Spelling and Grammar > Show readability statistics.

Tip #5: Omit any extra words.

Mark Twain nailed it when he said, "If I had more time, I would have written a shorter letter." Deadlines, which are constant for lawyers, often leave little time for editing. Moreover, working against the clock often results in less time to edit and, thus, longer writings.

Truth be told, it is not **hard** to get rid of extraneous words and tighten your writing, but it does take time and diligence. Given that a lawyer's success is tied directly to her ability to communicate ideas in writing, clarity of communication is crucial. This reality means that it will always behoove you to carve out the time Twain did not have to shorten your writings and tighten the language you use to express your ideas. To get the most bang for your buck when working to omit extra words, focus on the following areas.

- **Replace common but compound phrases with single words meaning the same thing**. Some examples are below.

COMPOUND	SIMPLE
With reference to	About
With regard to	Regarding
By virtue/means/reason of	By
In connection with	With
In order to	To
With respect to	About
With the exception of	Except for
Until such time as	Until
As a consequence of	Because of
As a matter of	In fact
Despite the fact that	Although
In spite of the fact that	Although
Due to the fact that	Because

- **Replace weak verbal phrases that contain adverbs + verbs with a better, stronger verb.** For example, instead of writing "the general counsel walked slowly home after his full workday," you could write "the general counsel plodded home after his full workday." Similarly, instead of writing, "Defendant quickly ate the bag of gummy bears before anyone could see," you would write, "Defendant devoured the bag of gummy bears before anyone could see."

- **Avoid redundant phrases**, such as "null and void," "whether or whether not," "peace and quiet," "free and clear," or "true and correct."
- **Remove extra intensifiers and qualifiers.** New legal writers often fall into the trap of adding in intensifiers or qualifiers because they are insecure about their ability to communicate the law effectively. Locate such words in your writing, and simply put, remove them. Some examples of words to search for and remove include: clearly, extremely, somewhat, very, essentially, generally, perhaps, really, and highly.

2. *Rule two: passive voice*

In grammar-speak, the "voice" of a verb refers to the relationship of the subject to the action expressed by the verb. When a sentence is written in the active voice, the subject of the sentence is doing the action of the verb. When a sentence is written in passive voice, the subject of the sentence is the one on whom the action is being done. In other words, in a sentence written in passive voice the subject is passive. Let's look at a sentence drafted in passive voice and then redrafted in active voice to help you understand the difference between active and passive voice. In both sentences the subject of the verb is underlined and the verb is bolded and italicized.

> **Passive voice:** Alabama law ***was studied*** by first-year <u>students</u> from Faulkner Law.
>
> **Active voice:** First-year <u>students</u> from Faulkner Law ***studied*** Alabama law.

Why does it matter whether a sentence is active or passive? The voice of a sentence matters because legal writing should be primarily written in active voice. There are a number of reasons why legal writers should use active voice instead of passive voice when they write. First, active voice is more concise and impactful than passive voice. In a profession that values clarity, precision, and efficiency, the clearer and more concise, the better. Second, text written in active voice is easier for the reader to understand because it clearly identifies the subject of the sentence and the doer of the action. Third, because legal writing often focuses on evaluating an actor's conduct, legal writers should employ active voice because it emphasizes the actor. Despite the general preference for writing in active voice, legal writers may write in passive voice when the actor of the verb is unknown or when the writer wants to hide or de-emphasize the actor. For example, if a lawyer represents someone in a criminal case, he may not want to say "Defendant brandished a knife." Instead, in such an instance, the lawyer may prefer to write "A knife was brandished." Reframing the sentence in this way—by using the passive voice—allows the lawyer to de-emphasize the proximity of his client (Defendant) to the knife and tries to prevent a reader from associating his client with a weapon.

Given the preference for writing in active voice, a significant challenge for law students and young lawyers is identifying the "voice" employed in their writing and, then, converting any sentences written in passive voice into active voice. So how do you identify passive voice?

> **Option one:** Look for sentences that contain a "to be" verb plus the word "by." A "to be" verb includes is, was, were, be, or has been.
>
> The law ***was*** overturned ***by*** the U.S. Supreme Court. = Passive Voice
>
> **Option two:** Look for sentences that contain a "to be" verb plus an implicit version of the word "by" that can be identified using the "by zombies" trick. If you can insert "by zombies" after the verb in a sentence and the sentence still makes sense, then the sentence is probably passive voice.
>
> The law ***was*** overturned [***by zombies***]. = Passive Voice
>
> The law ***was*** devastating to the farmers. = Active Voice (adding "by zombies" would not make sense)

Once you have identified sentences that are drafted in passive voice, your next job is to convert those sentences to active voice. You can do this in three easy steps:

Step one: Identify the subject, verb, and object of the sentence. The verb is the action word in the sentence that describes what the subject is doing. The subject is what or who the sentence is about. The object is the person or thing that receives the action of the verb.

Step two: Make the subject do the action of the verb.

Step three: Make sure the verb matches the subject in terms of singularity/plurality.

Let's practice these three steps with the following sentence, currently drafted in passive voice: **The battery was committed by the boy when he hurled his phone at his teacher.**

Step one: Identify the subject, verb, and object of the sentence.

The battery **was committed** by **the boy** when he hurled his phone at the teacher.

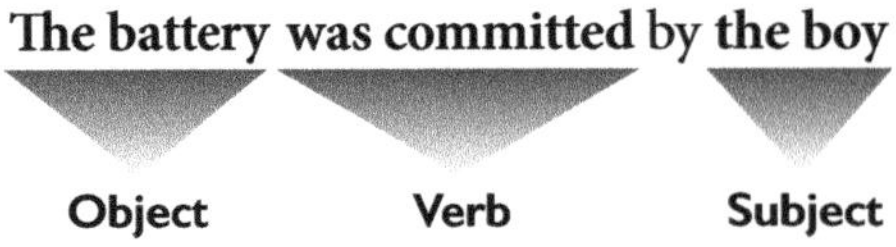

Step two: Make the subject do the action of the verb.

The boy committed the battery when he hurled his phone at his teacher.

Subject **Verb** **Object**

Step three: Make sure the verb matches the subject in terms of singularity/plurality.

Here, the boy and the battery were both singular, so shifting the organization of the sentence does not require a change to the singularity or plurality of the verb.

3. *Rule three: commas*

Commas are punctuation marks used to separate various parts of a sentence. Use of commas can provide clarity to writing and can help communicate the content of a sentence more effectively. Unfortunately, commas are frequently misused. This misuse may stem from failure to learn the rules related to commas or it may stem from learning inaccurate rules—for example, the rule often espoused by grade school teachers telling you to place a comma wherever you would pause if you read your sentence aloud. As a result of this dearth of knowledge and application of incorrect rules, we have a mix of overuse of commas and then—possibly in overreaction to the previously mentioned erroneous rule—an equal amount of missed comma usage.

There is, however, hope. Although there are more uses for and rules related to commas than there is space in this book, there are a handful of key comma rules that can improve your usage exponentially. To help, below you will find the top ten most commonly missed and misapplied comma rules, each with an example or two.

Comma rule #1: Use a comma to separate each item in a series (the Oxford comma).

There have been hot debates over the necessity of the Oxford comma—the comma that precedes the final item in a multi-item list. Some believe that the Oxford commas is superfluous. Others believe that the Oxford comma should be placed as a matter of course. Through debate, what has become clear is that the absence of the Oxford comma does not always affect the meaning of a sentence. However, at times, failing to include the Oxford comma will change the meaning of what is written.

Legal writers and legal readers prefer consistency and predictability. Because of this tendency for consistency, we recommend that, as a matter of course, you include the Oxford comma even where it is not absolutely necessary. Including it where unnecessary does not change the meaning of the sentence, but omitting it in some circumstances can upend what is written. Err on the side of inclusion.

Oxford comma: I invited the grandmothers, Alice, and Amy.

No Oxford comma: I invited the grandmothers, Alice and Amy.

With the Oxford comma, I have invited grandmothers (plural) plus a person named Alice and a person named Amy. Without the comma, I have invited a grandmother named Alice and a grandmother named Amy.

Comma rule #2: Use commas to set off quotations.

The comma serves as a signal to the reader that you are starting or ending a quote. Accordingly, you should use commas in the following instances: (1) when you have a statement before your quote, use the comma to signal a quote is coming; (2) when you start with a quote, use the comma to signal the quote has ended; and (3) when a statement interrupts your quote, do both—use a comma to let your reader know the first part of the quote has ended and a comma to let your reader know the rest of the quote is coming. Below you will find an example of each type of quote-based comma.

When introducing a quote: Ygritte said, "You know nothing, John Snow."

When following a quote: "I am the one who knocks," Walter White said.

When interrupting a quote: "Clear eyes, full hearts," Coach Taylor yelled, "can't lose."

Comma rule #3: Use commas after introductory words or phrases.

An introductory word (here, first, finally, etc.), a phrase (a phrase does not have its own subject and verb), and a clause (a clause has its own subject and verb), all set the stage for the main part of the sentence. Use a comma after the introductory word, phrase, or clause to let your reader know the introduction is over and you are moving on to the main part of the sentence.

Introductory word: Loudly, she explained her position to the judge.

Introductory phrase: Typing quickly, Meredith finished the brief before the deadline.

Introductory clause: After they finished the final, Brian's study group went out for dinner.

Comma rule #4: Use commas to join independent clauses joined by a coordinating conjunction.

When a sentence is made up of two separate, independent clauses (called a compound sentence), you should use a comma together with a coordinating conjunction to separate each independent clause. An independent clause is a clause that could stand alone as a sentence. Students often remember coordinating conjunctions through the mnemonic FANBOYS (for, and, nor, but, or, yet, so). Compare the following two sentences:

> **Compound sentence:** Jeff won the moot court competition, **and** he submitted the best brief.
>
> **Simple sentence:** Jeff won the moot court competition and submitted the best brief.

Comma rule #5: Use commas to set off nonessential information in a sentence.

When a sentence contains a nonrestrictive phrase or clause—meaning a phrase or clause that adds nonessential information to the sentence—the nonrestrictive clause should be set off by commas. A phrase or clause is nonrestrictive if, when the clause is removed from the sentence, the sentence retains its meaning. An example of a nonrestrictive clause is the bolded part of the example sentence below.

> Several law students, judges, and attorneys attended the speech, **which began at 1 p.m.**, regarding how to reduce pollution.

Some students deeply struggle to figure out whether a clause is restrictive or nonrestrictive. Generally speaking, a clause that is framed by "that" is typically restrictive and a clause that is framed by "which" is generally nonrestrictive.

> **Correct restrictive sentence:** Cars that are manual are difficult to drive.
>
> **Incorrect nonrestrictive sentence:** Cars, which are manual, are difficult to drive.

The fact that the cars are manual is essential to the meaning of the sentence. Therefore, it should be a restrictive clause using "that." If it is put in a non-restrictive clause ("which"), removing the clause changes the meaning of the sentence. The writer is not saying that all cars are difficult to drive. Rather, the writer is saying that cars with a manual transmission are difficult to drive.

The problem with using that general rule to determine the type of clause you are dealing with is that many students and lawyers use "which" and "that" incorrectly. Truthfully, the category a clause falls into will depend on the context and meaning of each sentence. The illustration below is a way to visualize the example sentence to determine whether it is restrictive or non-restrictive.

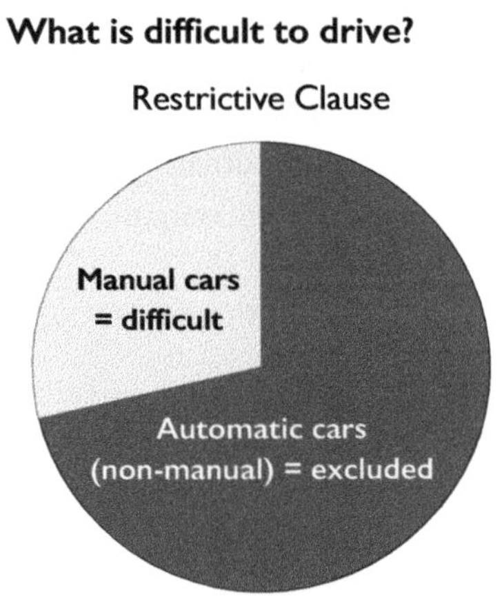

Comma rule #6: Do not use a comma to offset a restrictive phrase.

If a sentence contains a phrase or clause that is restrictive—that is essential to the sentence for its meaning to be clear—you should NOT set the restrictive clause off with commas.

> Lawyers who work hard will receive a raise.

If you remove the phrase "who work hard" you still have a complete sentence, but you have lost the meaning—that only lawyers who work hard get raises. We are not trying to say every lawyer will get a raise. Because it is essential to the meaning of the sentence, you **do not** need a comma.

> The podcast that covered Adnan Syed's case became very popular.

Similarly, if you remove the phrase "that covered Adnan Syed's case" you would have a complete sentence, but it would not be clear which podcast you were describing.

Comma rule #7: Use commas between adjectives that describe the same noun.

When multiple adjectives describe the same noun, you should separate those adjectives with a comma. Hint: If you can put *and* or *but* between the adjectives, a comma will probably belong there.

> The judge is a tall, distinguished man.

Because you could write "tall and distinguished," you need a comma.

> When I was in law school, I lived in a bright red house near campus.

Because you would not say that you lived in a "bright and red house," you do not need a comma between the adjectives.

Comma rule #8: Use a comma to separate a direct address from the rest of the sentence.

Use a comma when you are directly addressing someone or something. If the direct address comes at the beginning or end of a sentence, use one comma to set it off. If the direct address comes in the middle of the sentence, use a pair of commas to set it off.

> Elle Woods, your LSAT score is impressive!
>
> Get the confession, Perry Mason, or you could lose the case!

Comma rule #9: Use a comma with numbers, dates, addresses, and titles.

For dates, set off the year from the rest of the sentence with a pair of commas.

> On June 13, 1966, the U.S. Supreme Court issued its opinion in *Miranda v. Arizona*.

For addresses, separate out the elements of an address with a comma. The exception is the zip code.

> Judge Learned Hand was born in Albany, New York, in 1872.
>
> Please send a copy of the brief to the Dallas County Clerk at 1201 Elm Street, Dallas, Texas 75270.

For titles, where a title follows a name, separate out the name with a pair of commas.

> Johnnie Cochran, J.D., helped defend O.J. Simpson.

For numbers, if writing a number more than three digits, use commas to separate the numbers into groups of three (e.g., 200,000).

Comma rule #10: Do not put a comma where a period should go.

Do not run two independent clauses together by using a comma instead of a period. This use of a comma creates what is called a comma splice or a run-on sentence. There are a few options for fixing this. You could split the sentence at issue into two separate sentences; you could create an introductory phrase and use a comma; or you could add a coordinating conjunction and a comma.

> **Incorrect:** He forgot to study, he failed the test.
>
> **Correct:** He forgot to study. He failed the test.
>
> **Correct:** After he forgot to study, he failed the test.
>
> **Correct:** He forgot to study, and he failed the test.

4. *Rule four: semicolons vs. colons*

The default rule you should follow is that you should use semicolons and colons sparingly. Why? Because more often than not, writers misuse and/or overuse semicolons and colons. If you decide to employ a colon or a semicolon, the rules below will help you ensure your usage is proper.

a. Semicolons

Semicolons have two common uses. First, you should use a semicolon (instead of a comma) to separate listed items or items in a series when there are internal commas in the list or series.

Compare the following:

> **Series separated with commas:** The judge ruled on three motions in court today: a motion to dismiss, a motion in limine, and a *Daubert* motion.
>
> vs.
>
> **Series separated with semicolons:** The judge heard three cases today: *In re Adams*, an undue influence case; *Tom v. Phill*, a battery case; and *United States v. Erie*.

Second, you can (but need not) use a semicolon instead of a period to separate two independent clauses. Often writers will use a semicolon in lieu of a period when the reader wants to highlight the connection between the two independent clauses by tying them together. Another alternative to using a semicolon to separate two independent clauses is to add a coordinating conjunction (a FANBOY as explained in comma rule #4) and then use a comma to separate the independent clauses.

Compare the following:

> **Two independent clauses separated with a period:** The attorney argued passionately. He was disappointed when the judge denied his motion for summary judgment.

vs.

Two independent clauses separated with a semicolon: The attorney argued passionately; he was disappointed when the judge denied his motion for summary judgment.

vs.

Two independent clauses separated by a comma and a coordinating conjunction (FANBOY): The attorney argued passionately, and he was disappointed when the judge denied his motion for summary judgment.

b. Colons

Colons, like semicolons, have multiple uses. In most instances, the use of a colon is a stylistic choice because there are other, grammatically correct punctual marks that you could use in place of the colon. There are a few central ways to use the colon.

First, you can use colons to introduce an item or a series of items. When using a colon in this way, you do not capitalize the first item after the colon (unless for some other reason it should be capitalized).

> In law school you are required to read many things: statutes, cases, textbooks, and even regulations.

Second, you can use colons between two sentences if the second sentence emphasizes or illustrates the first.

> Reflecting back, the first year of law school was incredibly hard: we had to read hundreds of cases, attend long lectures, take regular quizzes, and sit for long exams.

Third, you can use colons to introduced bulleted or numbered lists.

> Undue influence requires proof of three elements:
>
> 1. the existence and exertion of an influence;
> 2. the influence overpowered the mind of the testator; and
> 3. the execution of the will only occurred because of the influence.

5. *Rule five: punctuation in quotations*

Quotation marks designate words, phrases, or sentences that are quoted. We already discussed the importance of quotations, how and when to use them, and the different ways to express quoted material in your writing (inline quotations or block quotations). Once students figure out where to use quotations, they often struggle with the placement of punctuation in and around quoted material. The rules that dictate where punctuation goes in relation to quotations are not hard, but many students are not introduced to the proper rules before law school.

> **Periods:** Final periods go ***inside*** quotation marks. It does not matter whether the period is part of the original quotation or whether you are adding it as the final period.
>
> **Commas:** Commas go ***inside*** quotation marks. It does not matter whether the comma is part of the original quotation or whether you are adding it as a final comma before the quote ends.
>
> **Semicolons and colons:** Semicolons and colons go ***outside*** the quotation marks, even if there was a semicolon or colon included as part of the quotation at the end of the material quoted.
>
> **Question marks and exclamation marks:** Question marks and exclamation marks ***sometimes go inside and sometimes go outside***. They go inside the quotation marks if they are included as part of the original quotation, but they go outside the quotation marks if they were not part of the original quotation.

Another quotation-related grammar rule that often throws law students off is the use of single versus double quotation marks. In legal writing, you only use single quotation marks for nested quotations (that is, for quoted material within quoted material). When you refer to terms of art, unless those terms are part of a nested quotation, you should use traditional double—not single—quotation marks. Similarly, if you are indicating that a phrase is odd, informal, or ironic, you should also use traditional double quotation marks around that phrase.

6. Rule six: subject-verb agreement

The subject of a sentence must agree with the verb. This means that if the subject of a sentence is singular, the verb of the sentence must also be singular. On the other hand, if the subject of the sentence is plural, the verb must also be plural.[7]

---

7. An oddity of English grammar is that to make a verb singular you have to add an "s," and to make a verb plural, typically you omit the "s." On the other hand, to make a noun (or subject) singular you omit the "s," while to make a noun or subject plural you have to add an "s."

Singular verb

The law student studies hard.

Singular subject because one student

Plural verb

UNT Dallas College of Law students study hard.

Plural subject because refers to more than one student

Although the rule itself is simple, there are a handful of pronouns (called indefinite pronouns) that, when used as subjects, make it hard to discern whether to use a singular or plural verb. For indefinite pronouns, you will need to memorize whether they take a singular or plural verb.

INDEFINITE PRONOUNS THAT ALWAYS TAKE A SINGULAR VERB	INDEFINITE PRONOUNS THAT ALWAYS TAKE A PLURAL VERB	INDEFINITE PRONOUNS THAT CAN TAKE EITHER A SINGULAR OR PLURAL VERB (DEPENDING ON USAGE)
Anyone	Both	All
Everyone	Few	Any
Someone	Many	More
Anybody	Others	Most
Somebody	Several	Some
Nobody		
Each		
One		
Either		
Neither		

For the third category, to determine whether the particular pronoun requires a singular or plural verb, you need to identify whether the subject is singular or plural. When the pronoun is acting as a singular subject, use a singular verb; otherwise, use a plural verb.

7. *Rule seven: hyphens, en dashes, and em dashes*

Hyphen -

En dash –

Em dash —

Although similar in appearance, the hyphen, the en dash, and the em dash are punctuation marks distinct from one another in terms of appearance and purpose.

The **hyphen** is the most commonly used type of dash, and it is also the shortest in terms of its length. Unfortunately, because many people do not know there are different types of dashes, the hyphen (also the most easily accessible dash on a keyboard) is often misused where an en dash or em dash would be appropriate. A hyphen should not be used as punctuation but, instead, should be used to combine different types of compound words and adjectival phrases. One of a hyphen's main purposes is to combine modifiers with nouns they modify. In particular, one should hyphenate certain compound modifiers that come before nouns, such as "well-established rule" or "little-known fact." Second, one should also hyphenate the modifiers "all," "ex," and "self" when they come before nouns, such as "all-time," "ex-spouse," or "self-doubt." Third, one should use a hyphen before elect, such as a "president-elect." Fourth, one should hyphenate compound numbers that modify a noun, such as "twenty-two cases" or "twenty-two-year-old judge." Fifth, one should hyphenate two parties who are combined to modify a noun, such as "attorney-client privilege." Sixth, one should use a hyphen between "e" and any other word when "e" is meant to abbreviate electronic, such as "e-mail," "e-memo," or "e-commerce." The hyphen is easily inserted into text by using the hyphen key on the keyboard.

An **en dash** is the least frequently used dash. An en dash means "to" or "through" and is used to connect numbers and occasionally words. For example, an en dash should be employed in the following sentence:

> The salary for first-year public defense attorneys, $50,000–$60,000, is enough for a young lawyer to live on.

You also use en dashes between page ranges, including page ranges in citation sentences. To insert an en dash in Microsoft Word, under the "Insert" tab, one must click "Symbol," click "More Symbols," then under "Special Characters" click "En Dash." Most prgrams also have shortcuts set up for the en dash.

An **em dash** is the longest of the dashes. Like a comma, colon, or parenthetical, the em dash is a punctual mark of separation that tells the reader that what follows bears some relation to what it preceded. Em dashes should be used (1) to signal the beginning and end of the list; (2) to set off an introductory list containing commas; (3) to show abrupt shifts; (4) to cue the reader to shocking or surprising information; or (5) as punctuation in place of parentheses or to set off a non-restrictive clause. For example: **My house—1920s Tudor with only 2,000 square feet—was appraised at $800,000!**

To insert an em dash in Microsoft Word, follow the instructions above for "en dash" but select "Em Dash" from the "Special Characters" menu.

8. Rule eight: capitalization

Most law students understand basic capitalization rules by the time they begin high school. That said, there are a few capitalization rules that are either tricky or specific to legal writing. These capitalization rules are worth a quick review.

CATEGORY	RULE	EXAMPLE
Titles/job/ roles	Capitalize official titles or roles if they come before and are attached to the name. But do not capitalize the title if it comes after the name.	Judge Emily Miskel Emily Miskel, judge
Geography	Capitalize specific geographical regions but not points of the compass or directions.	North America Let's travel north.
Acronyms	Use capital letters for every letter of almost all acronyms.	SCOTUS (acronym for Supreme Court of the United States)
Court	The word court is ***only*** capitalized in the following instances: (1) when referring to the Supreme Court of the United States; (2) when the name of the court is spelled out, e.g., the United States District Court for the Northern District of Texas; (3) when referencing the specific court that you are practicing before or the one that will rule on your case.	The Court overturned its own decision rendered in *Roe v. Wade.* We ask this Court to grant summary judgment. vs. The court in *Rothermel* reviewed the elements of undue influence.
Defendant/ Plaintiff	The plaintiff and defendant are capitalized only when referring to the parties in your particular case.	Defendant moved for summary judgment, and, in response, Plaintiff appealed. vs. The defendant in *Rothermel* had two children.
Order/ Motion	Titles of documents (such as motions or orders) are capitalized when they are referring to a document that has been filed in the same matter in which you are filing your document.	Defendant requests that the Court grant her Motion for Summary Judgment. vs. Drafting a motion for summary judgment is a hard skill to learn.

9. Rule nine: correct personal pronoun usage

Using the correct personal pronouns is important and, in a professional environment like the practice of law, expected. As such, if you **know** which pronouns a person uses, you **must** use those pronouns. You should endeavor to be consistent in employing a person's pronouns both to show respect for the person's pronoun preferences and to avoid confusion. As such, if Adam uses he/him pronouns, use those pronouns whenever referring to Adam. In other words, don't switch between he/him and they/them pronouns when referencing Adam, because he does not use they/them pronouns.

Sometimes it isn't clear which pronouns a person uses. If you don't know, what should you do? Below are some helpful hints designed to help you navigate situations where a person's pronouns are unknown.

Ask. If you're in a position to ask a person which pronouns they use, do so. This approach is often the best one and can save you from any potential embarrassment caused by guessing or from awkward prose caused by other work arounds. Looking forward to your future legal practice, you would be smart to have a question about which pronouns a client uses on your client intake forms.

Avoid using pronouns. Pronouns can sometimes be avoided altogether. One workaround is to use a party's or person's name—that is, employ a proper noun instead of a pronoun. For example, let's say we're not sure what pronouns Sam uses. We can get around having to make any assumptions by using Sam's name. Instead of "She/He/They entered the convenience store" you can simply say, "Sam entered the convenience store" without creating any ambiguity or confusion. Another work around is to use a party's role in lieu of using a pronoun. "The defendant entered the convenience store."

Refer to a person as the court does. If a judge or judicial opinion has previously used pronouns to describe a person, use those pronouns.

Consider employing singular they when a sentence calls for a gender-neutral pronoun. The previously accepted use of the masculine pronoun—he—as gender-neutral is a construct of the past. Instead, employment of a person's specified pronouns—whether he, she, or singular they—is now required when it is known. When a sentence requires a gender-neutral pronoun, use of the singular they is emerging as a preferred approach. Although the legal field is slow to change, norms in this area are evolving, and students should attempt stay up to date as our modern sense of equity and representation continue to progress.

Part 2 | **Objective Legal Writing**

Before reading this part of the book, you should skim through the objective memorandum in the Appendix.

Students often suffer from so-called "Law and Order" syndrome. Misled by the often-watched (and idolized) television lawyers, students mistakenly believe that a lawyer's job turns on his, her, or their ability to engage in oral advocacy and argument. As alluded to in Part I of this book, however, a lawyer's primary job is not oral advocacy but writing. Lawyers write, and they write a lot. To make this more difficult, the type of writing that lawyers do varies. There are two primary types of writing that lawyers do: objective legal writing and persuasive legal writing. This part of the book focuses on objective writing.

Chapter 6 | What Is Objective Writing?

Objective writing is often referred to as predictive writing. No matter what you call it—objective or predictive—the purpose of this type of legal writing is to present a balanced analysis of the law, given the facts presented. In other words, objective legal writing does not take a position and then design an argument to further or support that position. Instead, objective writing answers a question and then sets forth and applies legal authority to explain that answer to the reader. There is a small twist here that can be confusing to students. Objective writing, while neutral and balanced in its approach and analysis of the law, is not devoid of persuasion. After all, once you have neutrally analyzed the law, the purpose of your memorandum is—in many ways—to show your reader how you reached your result and, implicitly, to have them agree with your ultimate prediction. This nuanced persuasion is decidedly different than the persuasion at the core of persuasive writing; however, it is disingenuous to suggest objective writing does not have any desire to persuade its reader, given that you want to show the reader your prediction is correct.

A. Types of objective writing

Objective writing itself can take a few different forms. The most common type of objective writing, especially in the first year of law school, is a formal objective legal memorandum ("objective memo") drafted for internal office purposes or for clients. An objective memo—regardless of its audience—involves the presentation of a question, a brief answer, and then an often lengthy, detailed analysis explaining how the lawyer-author arrived at his, her, or their answer based on the law and facts at hand.

Law students are often introduced to objective memos during the first semester of their first year of law school. The reason for this early introduction is that an objective memo is a great mechanism for assessing and then fine-tuning a developing lawyer's ability to write and engage in deep legal analysis. In addition, objective memos are often assigned to summer legal interns and junior lawyers. Accordingly, it is important to have exposure to the form and content of such documents before a potential employer uses that written product to assess your potential as a future employee.

Truth be told, objective memos are becoming less common in practice, at least in their formal and lengthy form. Instead, clients and lawyers alike are relying more on abbreviated versions of objective memos to cut client costs and to account for the quicker pace of the practice of law. After all, to draft a lengthy analysis necessarily requires a significant amount of a lawyer's time and, thus, a significant monetary investment by a client. As a result, students and young lawyers will often be asked to draft abbreviated e-mail memos (also called e-memos), in lieu of formal objective memos.

In addition to objective memos and e-mail memos, there are other forms of objective writing that students and young lawyers will likely encounter during practice. For example, when serving as a clerk or intern for a court, a student may be asked to draft a bench memorandum. A bench memo is a form of objective writing drafted by a judicial intern or clerk to advise a judge on how to decide a case (or an issue in a case) by offering an objective review of both sides of the case (or the issue). Unlike the briefs that the parties submit to the court in a case—where each party presents its side of the argument (with brief discussion of counterarguments)—a bench memo summarizes and develops both sides' arguments, recognizes the strengths and weaknesses of those arguments, and recommends a course of action. Another common form of objective writing is a client letter. Client letters vary in terms of form based on the content they aim to cover. Some client letters will be longer and contain deeper analysis, while others may be shorter and more conclusory.

Although you will likely encounter all of these types of objective writing in practice, this part of the book will focus on introducing you to the two primary forms of objective writing that most students and summer interns encounter: the objective memo and the e-mail memo.

B. Understanding and identifying the purpose, audience, length, and tone for objective writing

Each form of objective writing and, in fact, each assignment itself, regardless of form, will vary in terms of length, audience, tone, and purpose. Some objective memos, for example, are simply requests for legal research, while others require legal research plus an analysis of how that research is likely to apply to a specific scenario or a specific set of facts. In other words, although two assignments may both call for an objective memo, the ultimate product for each assignment may look and sound different depending on what the particular issue or assignment demands.

So how do you determine the form, audience, length, and purpose of whatever objective writing you have been asked to draft? Well—wait for it—**it depends**. You need to take time to understand what you are being asked to do and what product you are being asked to produce. You need to assess who the reader or readers of what you are drafting will be. After all, who your reader is will affect both the content and the tone of your objective writing. Last, you need to assess the expected length of the writing. The length of any piece of objective writing will depend, in part, on who your reader is, but it may also be informed by time and cost constraints.

Although each assignment will vary depending on its specific assigned task, below is a chart that should help you think through issues of purpose, audience, length, and tone for the various types of objective writing.

	FORMAL OBJECTIVE MEMO	E-MAIL MEMO	CLIENT LETTER	BENCH MEMO
PURPOSE	Formal memoranda objectively inform a reader about what the law is and then suggest what the outcome will likely be when the law is applied to a particular set of facts.	E-mail memoranda communicate the crux of legal research or basic legal analysis in a streamlined e-format, which is easily read on a phone, computer screen, or tablet.	Client letters summarize legal analysis, often originally captured in a formal objective memo, in a way that the client can understand and that focuses on the bottom line more than on the process of getting to the bottom line.	Bench memoranda objectively inform the reader what the law is, summarize what the parties' arguments are, and then convey what the outcome should be when the law is applied to the facts of the case.
AUDIENCE	A supervising lawyer or a client	A supervising lawyer or a client	A client	A judge or judicial clerk

LENGTH	Length depends on issues covered but is typically more than ten pages.	Length is typically one screen, but if longer, the e-mail should be easily readable and digestible in e-format (on a phone, computer screen, or tablet).	Length is limited to a few pages, often single-spaced.	Length depends on issues covered but is typically more than ten pages.
TONE	Tone is professional and formal and presents a deep but balanced view of the law and facts.	Tone is professional, but often the content and language are streamlined.	Tone is professional but is adjusted if the client is a non-lawyer to explain the law in layperson terms and to clearly communicate the bottom-line recommendation.	Tone is decisive in its assessment of the strengths and weaknesses of each party's case.

Chapter 7 | What Is an Objective Memo?

Objective memos remain—for better or worse—a type of document that all lawyers are expected to be able to draft. As alluded to previously, objective memos can vary in terms of content and exact format, depending on the specific assignment given and the audience for whom the memo is drafted. Despite these potential differences, however, at their core, all objective memos are expected to answer a specific question and are designed to explain the basis for that answer—in terms of law and fact—in a clear and organized fashion. This chapter of the book will introduce you to the basic format and content of an objective memo. Once you enter practice, you may need to tweak the form, content, and/or style of your objective memo to comply with the particular nuances of your office, your supervisor, and your practice area. This introduction, however, will ensure you have the basic constructs to succeed when tasked with drafting an objective memo in law school or in practice.

A. Overview of the organization of an objective memo

Objective memos are rigid in terms of their macro structure and the order in which that macro structure appears in the memo itself. While the particular formatting may vary somewhat from law firm to law firm, practice area to practice area, and classroom to classroom, readers expect to find the basic six sections of an objective memo in, generally speaking, the same predictable order: (1) the heading; (2) the question(s) presented; (3) the brief answer(s); (4) the statement of facts; (5) the discussion; and (6) the overall conclusion. The discussion section of an objective memo is the core of the legal analysis of the memo. Each of the six parts of the objective memo, however, is important and plays a distinct role. The following sections will provide you with guidance regarding how to format and draft each of the six sections of an objective memo. The picture below captures the framework of the six sections of your objective memo.

MEMORANDUM

TO:

FROM:

DATE:

SUBJECT:

QUESTION PRESENTED

BRIEF ANSWER

STATEMENT OF FACTS

DISCUSSION

CONCLUSION

B. The heading

The heading provides basic information regarding the subject, the audience, and the author of the objective memo. It allows the author to give the memo's reader macro context regarding what she is about to read. The heading also provides future readers (maybe colleagues in the law firm who are grappling with a similar case) with client and subject matter context for the objective memo. Importantly, the heading also identifies the date on which a memo was drafted. The date is important because it tells the reader—both current and future—that it sets forth the law as of the date of the objective memo's drafting and thus may not capture subsequent changes to the law. Below is an example of what a heading should look like.

MEMORANDUM

TO:	Dominique Baker
FROM:	Neu Loiya
DATE:	September 16, 2024
SUBJECT:	United Information, Inc. (30408.123): Title VII Liability Analysis

As illustrated by the example, your heading should identify the product as a memo and then contain "To," "From," the "Date" of the memo, and the "Subject" of the memo. The label "Memorandum" should be emphasized using boldface, all-caps, and underlining and should be centered on the page. In addition, the heading should be easy to read, and the tabbing should be evenly spaced.

C. The question(s) presented

Nearly every objective memo has the primary purpose of answering a legal question or multiple legal questions for the reader (and then explaining that answer). The question grappled with in an objective memo is written out immediately following the objective memo's heading and is called the "Question Presented." Obviously, if there is only one question at issue, there will be only one question presented, whereas if there are multiple questions at issue in the objective memo, there will be multiple questions presented, and, in that case, the heading will be "Questions Presented."

1. The purpose of question(s) presented

The question presented tells the reader the exact legal problem that will be answered and explained in the objective memo. Moreover, because the question presented appears at the opening of an objective memo, the statement of the question provides a framework for the reader to navigate the rest of the objective memo.

2. The number of question(s) presented needed

This may seem self-evident, but you need the same number of questions presented as the number of macro issues addressed in the objective memo. Typically, this means that you will have one question presented for each cause of action or affirmative defense at issue. Note that you should not draft a question presented for each element of a claim for a couple of reasons. First, if you draft multiple, separate questions presented asking whether each element is satisfied, you never ask (or answer) the real question at issue—whether a party is likely to be successful in establishing the larger cause of action. Second, if—trying to avoid the problem just mentioned—you pose multiple element-based questions each in the context of the larger cause of action, the answer to each question posed will necessarily be no! For example, you necessarily cannot establish a prima facie case of religious discrimination under Title VII by satisfying just element one (because a Title VII prima facie case requires that an employee prove all four elements).

3. Formulas for drafting question(s) presented

There are lengthy articles and entire book chapters dedicated to different formats one can use to draft a question presented. Despite the many options, there are two universally accepted formats for drafting a question presented, and these are the two formats you should learn and (at least in your legal writing course) use. The first—and the most traditional—is the under/can-does-is/when approach. The second—and more modern—is the multi-sentence approach. Below you will find a formula for and an example of each format. Regardless of which format you ultimately decide to use, a good question presented will identify the governing law and set forth the legally relevant ("trigger") facts on which the issue will turn.

UNDER/CAN-DOES-IS/WHEN FORMULA

Under	+	Controlling jurisdiction and law governing the question presented	+	**Can/ Does/ Is**	+	Legal question being asked	+	**When**	+	Trigger facts (or the facts that will determine the outcome of your client's case)?

UNDER/CAN-DOES-IS/WHEN EXAMPLE

Under Title VII of the Civil Rights Act of 1964, as interpreted by the Fifth Circuit, can UI avoid liability for a religious discrimination claim by showing that reasonably accommodating Mr. Saint's religious belief would cause UI undue hardship when UI's implementation of the new biometric-scanner timekeeping system increased a UI supervisor's efficiency and saved UI an estimated $4,000 annually?

MULTI-SENTENCE FORMULA

Sentence stating the general law.	+	Sentence (or two or three sentences) stating the trigger facts.	+	Question-based sentence asking about the legal issue?

MULTI-SENTENCE EXAMPLE

Sentence stating the general law.

Sentence(s) stating the trigger facts.

Sentence asking about the legal issue.

Title VII of the Civil Rights Act of 1964, as interpreted by the Fifth Circuit, provides that an employer can avoid liability under Title VII if it can show it is "unable to reasonably accommodate [the] employee's … religious observance or practice without undue hardship on the conduct of the employer's business." 42 U.S.C. § 2000e(j). UI replaced its manual timekeeping system with a new biometric scanning timekeeping system that Mr. Saint's religious belief prohibited him from using. UI's implementation of this new biometric scanning timekeeping system (in lieu of a manual system that Mr. Saint requested to continue using) increased a UI supervisor's efficiency and saved UI an estimated $4,000 annually. Can UI prove that accomodating Mr. Saint with the manual system would rise to the level of undue hardship and, thus, allow UI to avoid liability under Title VII?

4. *Top tips for drafting question(s) presented*

As you draft your question presented, keep the following tips in mind:

Tip #1: Try to keep your question presented as brief as possible so it is easy for your reader to comprehend.

Tip #2: Phrase your question presented in a way that has a definitive yes or no (or likely yes or likely no) answer.

Tip #3: Phrase your question presented to be neutral rather than conclusory; in other words, the question presented should be a real question rather than a rhetorical one (or one that by design mandates a certain answer).

D. The brief answer(s)

The brief answer provides the bottom-line answer to the question presented and a few critical reasons for that conclusion. The brief answer appears near the beginning of the objective memo, and it immediately follows the question presented.

1. *The purpose of brief answer(s)*

The purpose of the brief answer is to provide the reader with a succinct answer to the question presented without the reader being forced to wade through the entire objective memo. In addition to simply providing an answer up front, the brief answer serves to provide the reader with a framework as she navigates the entirety of the memo.

2. *The number of brief answer(s) needed*

You need a brief answer for each question presented in your objective memo. In other words, # of questions presented = # of brief answers.

3. *Formula for drafting a brief answer*

The formula for drafting your brief answer is designed to give your reader the quick answer to the question presented followed by an explanation for that answer. Therefore, you will begin your brief answer with the direct answer to the question asked above in your question presented. The answer should begin with a simple "Yes" or "No" that usually includes a degree of certainty ("Likely, yes" or "Likely, no"). It is usually wise to couple your answer with a degree of certainty if the answer is not 100 percent certain (which is often the case). Because in an objective memo you are applying law to a set of facts, which may not be fully developed or clear, the answer you will predict is not an absolute certainty most of the time. Also note that "maybe" is not a proper answer because it is not an answer at all. You are tasked with predicting an outcome, and, therefore, you must make a prediction one way or the other. That is, your job as a lawyer is to answer the question asked and "maybe" is not helpful.

After you give your direct answer ("Likely, yes."), you will expand that answer to a complete sentence linked to the question asked with key reasoning ("UI will likely establish that providing Mr. Saint with a reasonable accommodation would cause the company undue hardship because it would impose more than a de minimis cost on its finances, efficiency, and other employees. Accordingly, because it can likely establish the affirmative defense of undue hardship, a court will not find UI liable for Title VII religious discrimination.").

BRIEF ANSWER FORMULA

Pick one of the following answers that indicate the appropriate degree of certainty of your conclusion: 1. Yes. 2. Likely, yes. 3. Likely, no. 4. No.	+	State the answer linked to the question presented.	+	Discuss the presence or absence of any elements/components in the same order they are addressed in the discussion section of the memo.

BRIEF ANSWER EXAMPLE

Likely, yes. UI will likely establish that providing Mr. Saint with a reasonable accommodation would cause the company undue hardship because it would impose more than de minimis cost on its finances, efficiency, and other employees. Accordingly, because it can likely establish the affirmative defense of undue hardship, a court will not find UI liable for Title VII religious discrimination.

Notice that in the brief answer you do not need citations. You do not need citations because your brief answer is your summary of what follows in the discussion section of your objective memo. Notice also that the brief answer is—wait for it—brief. You should keep your brief answer to no more than a paragraph in length because the reader will ultimately get the complete explanation in the body of the discussion section of your objective memo.

Keep in mind that what your brief answer looks like is necssarily connected to which question presented format you used. If you used Under/Does/When format for your question(s) presented, your brief answer explanation will likely be longer (and may include a citation to the governing rule as you explain). Take a look at the below example.

[UNDER/DOES/WHEN] QUESTION PRESENTED

Under Texas's Recreational Use Statute, is the City of Austin immune from liability when Ms. Zadie was a spectator at a gymnastics event at City of Austin's Gymnastics Center and was injured after exiting the event?

BRIEF ANSWER

No. Under Texas's Recreational Use Statute, a city is immune from liability in a premises defect action if (1) the plaintiff is injured while engaging in recreational activities; and (2) the city's conduct was not grossly negligent. Tex. Civ. Prac. & Rem. Code Ann. § 75.002(f). The Recreational Use Statute does not apply to spectators at sporting events because spectating at a sporting event does not fall under the statutory definition of recreation. Because Ms. Zadie was not engaged in recreation at the time of her injury, the Recreational Use Statute does not apply to limit the City's liability.

If you used the multi-sentence format for your question(s) presented, your brief answer explanation will likely be shorter and may not include a citation to legal authority (especially if that legal authority is already cited in your question(s) presented). Take a look at the below example. Notice how it differs from the one above.

[MULTI-SENTENCE] QUESTION PRESENTED

Under Texas's Recreational Use Statute, a city is immune from liability in a premises defect action if (1) the plaintiff is injured while engaging in recreational activities; and (2) the city's conduct was not grossly negligent. Tex. Civ. Prac. & Rem. Code Ann. § 75.002(f). Ms. Zadie was a spectator at a gymnastics event at City of Austin's Gymnastics Center and was injured after exiting the event. Is the City of Austin immune from liability under the Recreational Use Statute?

BRIEF ANSWER

No. The Recreational Use statute does not apply to spectators at sporting events because spectating at a sporting event does not fall under the statutory definition of recreation. Because Ms. Zadie was not engaged in recreation at the time of her injury, the Recreational Use Statute does not apply to limit the City's liability.

E. Statement of facts

The statement of facts is the section of your memo where you explain the factual foundation for your client's legal question. In other words, this is where you tell the story. A statement of facts should not include legal conclusions or legal argument; instead, it should include only the facts. Therefore, you should not say in your statement of facts "Defendant was recklessly driving" because that is a legal conclusion. Instead, you would show by the facts that Defendant was reckless. For example, "Defendant was driving 25 miles above the speed limit in a school zone." That is, your statement of facts should show, not tell. The facts in your statement of facts will be used again in your Analysis. In an Analysis of the above example, you would apply the law to the fact provided and conclude that Defendant was recklessly driving.

1. What facts you should include in your statement of facts

The statement of facts should include the facts of the case on which the resolution of the question(s) presented turns. Generally speaking, you should include the following three categories of facts in your statement of facts:

> **Legally Significant Facts (or Trigger Facts):** These facts are determinative, key, and critical, these are facts in your client's case that will affect a court's analysis.
>
> **Background or Procedural Facts:** These are facts that provide **context** for understanding your client's situation, the roles of the people involved in the legal issue, and the current status of the pending question(s).
>
> **Emotional Facts:** These are facts that are not necessary to resolve the legal issues but that help the reader understand what motivated the parties to act or react in a particular way.

You may find it hard at the beginning to determine which facts are legally significant. You cannot understand this until you have a firm grasp of the legal standard for the issue your memo is addressing. Typically, the best way to determine legal significance is to review the facts in relation to the elements or defenses at the center of the cause of action at issue. For example, if you were to draft a statement of facts for the objective memo assessing whether Mr. Saint is likely to succeed in holding UI liable for religious discrimination, you would review the facts that you know and try to discern which known facts are relevant to each element of and each defense to a Title VII claim. You might begin by creating a chart to help you link the facts to the law and, thus, to help you figure out which facts are legally significant.

Below is an example table that sets forth the elements and defenses relevant to Mr. Saint's claim and begins to capture a few of the key facts related to the first element of Mr. Saint's prima facie case—bona fide religious belief. Notice that because the second, third, and fourth elements of Mr. Saint's prima facie case are not at issue for purposes of the objective memo, we have omitted them from the table to avoid distraction. You can practice identifying legally significant facts by filling in additional facts from the record relevant to each element and defense listed in the table.

ELEMENT OF OR DEFENSE TO TITLE VII CLAIM	RELEVANT FACT(S)
The employee had a bona fide religious belief	Mr. Saint was an Evangelical Christian. Mr. Saint participated in organized religion from early in his childhood until 2016, when he deactivated his membership with St. Jaguar Community Church. By 2018, Mr. Saint no longer participated in organized religion. As part of his religion, Mr. Saint believes in the Mark of the Beast and Antichrist. Mr. Saint informed UI that using a biometric scanning system—like the retinal scanner mandated by UI—conflicted with his religion because using such a system would give him the Mark of the Beast as cautioned against by the Bible. Mr. Saint steadfastly refused to use the biometric scanner in any capacity.
The employer offered the employee a reasonable accommodation	
The employer could not reasonably accommodate the employee without undue hardship	

When you have completed the chart, you will then draft the statement of facts (usually in chronological order, not by element) being mindful to include each of the facts identified in your chart.

In addition to the legally significant facts, your objective memo's statement of facts should also include background facts and, possibly, a select number of emotional facts. You should be judicious when including background and emotional facts; in other words, be careful not to include too many emotional or background facts. Including too many will make it harder for your reader to identify those facts that affect the outcome of the case—the legally significant or trigger facts. Emotional facts, in particular, are a powerful tool when you are engaging in persuasive writing (covered later in this book). But, emotional facts also have an important role in objective writing because the power of certain emotional facts may affect the weight a particular trigger fact is given or how the trigger fact may be viewed later by a judge, jury, client, or opposing party.

After you have drafted your entire objective memo, you should go back and review your statement of facts. Compare the facts that you used in the discussion section (specifically in the Analysis) and make sure that each of those facts is also included in your statement of facts. In addition, make sure to note the facts that you include in your statement of facts that you do not use in your discussion. Do you need them to provide background or to show your reader potential emotional facts that may come up if the case goes forward? If so, you can leave them. However, if not, you should you omit them from your statement of facts so as not to distract your reader.

2. How to tell a story objectively in your statement of facts

Remember the purpose of the objective memo: to predict the likely outcome of the law's application to the facts of your client's case. You, as the drafter of an objective memo, need to maintain a neutral perspective and to objectively set forth the law and the facts. Maintaining this neutral perspective is often one of the hardest parts of drafting an objective memo, especially for new legal writers. The already mentioned ("Law and Order" syndrome) is typically to blame; after all, students have grown up watching lawyers creatively "spin" and frame facts in order to win cases. But, you must resist the temptation. You must present the facts on both sides and present them in a neutral way. When you write persuasively (as we discuss later in this book) you will get to select facts to highlight and facts to diminish in order to advocate and to persuasively frame your case. But all parts of your objective writing should remain, well, objective or neutral.

In order to ensure your statement of facts is objective in nature, ask yourself the following questions:

> **Question one:** Do you include facts from both sides' perspectives? That is, do you include the facts that are in favor of finding a particular element, cause of action, or defense, as well as those that might cut against finding a particular element, cause of action, or defense?
>
> **Question two:** Do you characterize facts or state them in neutral terms? Often a signal that you are characterizing facts is the use of adverbs or adjectives in your statement of facts. Highlight adjectives and adverbs in your statement of facts and then ask yourself whether they are part of the facts or, instead, constitute your characterization of the facts. Omit them if they are your characterization (or opinion).

3. How to organize your statement of facts

There are a number of ways you can organize your statement of facts. As you grow as a legal writer and as you grapple with more complex problems, you will have flexibility in how you present the story—by the order in which the events took place (in chronological order), by each element of a claim, by each claim, or by each event or actor. How you organize your facts will be dictated by how best to explain what happened in the context of the legal question at issue. That said, for now (and always as a default), you should organize your statement of facts chronologically.

To order your statement of facts chronologically, you will often have to create a timeline on which you record the events and facts collected from various documents, interviews, and e-mails. After all, facts—even in an interview—are often not given to you in perfect chorological order. As a lawyer, one of your main jobs will be to become an expert in the facts of your case. Learning how to organize facts from various sources into a timeline or chronology will help you with this task. There are a number of tools available that will help you create a chronology, including Microsoft Office's Timeline, Chronology Marker, or Timeline-Diary and Notes. Below is an example of the beginning of a factual chronology for the events giving rise to Mr. Saint's Title VII religious discrimination claim and UI's related affirmative defenses.

2016	Mr. Saint deactivated his membership in St. Jaguar Community Church. This same year, Mr. Saint began working for UI, which employed a manual timekeeping system that required employees to clock in and out of work with their supervisors using their IDs.
2018	Mr. Saint stopped attending church services.
JULY 2023	UI announced it was moving from its manual timekeeping system to a retina-based biometric-scanning timekeeping system. After this announcement, Mr. Saint sent a letter, e-mails, and a Religious Accommodation Request form to UI through Mr. Saint's supervisor, Ms. Kathy Edwards, and UI's Human Resources Manager, Mr. Sean Farmor, asserting his religious belief that use of biometric scanners could "mark" him and citing a Bible verse regarding the "Mark of the Beast."
AUGUST 1, 2023	UI implemented the retina-based biometric-scanning timekeeping system but allowed Mr. Saint to continue using the manual timekeeping system.
AUGUST 11, 2023	UI's manual timekeeping system was no longer available to Mr. Saint.
AUGUST 21, 2023	Mr. Saint received his paycheck from UI and that paycheck did not include compensation for the hours Mr. Saint worked but did not clock in between August 11, 2023, and August 21, 2023.
AUGUST 22, 2023	Mr. Saint resigned from UI.

4. *Use of headings in your statement of facts*

It is often helpful to use headings in your statement of facts to help guide your reader through the events. In persuasive writing, factual headings are an additional opportunity to frame the facts in your client's favor. In objective writing, headings can improve readability and comprehension of your statement of facts, making it easier for your reader to follow the events that are at the center of the question(s) presented. For example, think about the facts related to Mr. Saint's religious discrimination claim. After you order the facts chronologically, can you insert headings to help your reader follow the events? Below are sample headings that you might employ to help break up the statement of facts in Mr. Saint's case and guide your reader from event to event. Note the sample headings are topical in nature but chronologically ordered.

> **Heading one:** Mr. Saint claims to be an Evangelical Christian and previously participated in organized religion.
>
> **Heading two:** Mr. Saint's employer, UI, moved from using a manual system to a retina-based biometric-scanning system for employees to clock in and out of work.
>
> **Heading three:** Mr. Saint asserted his religious belief against using the biometric scanner.
>
> **Heading four:** UI offered Mr. Saint the option of scanning his right hand instead of his retina, but Mr. Saint refused the accommodation.
>
> **Heading five:** Mr. Saint resigned after UI did not compensate him for the time he worked after the manual timekeeping system was deactivated.

5. *Tips for drafting your statement of facts*

When drafting your statement of facts keep the following tips in mind:

Tip #1: Tell your reader the story of the case. A story is easier to follow than a series of facts not woven together for the reader.

Tip #2: Use the past tense. The events you are detailing in your statement of facts already happened. As a result, you should use the past tense.

Tip #3: Use role designations, in addition to names. A role designation identifies the role of the person in the cause of action (not his role in the case procedurally but factually). For example, in the objective memo you are drafting related to Mr. Saint, you should refer to the key actors in terms of their names and their factual roles in the case—Mr. Saint, the employee, and UI, the employer. Using such role designations will allow your reader to better relate the key players in your case to the players involved in the legal precedent you will rely on in the discussion section of your objective memo.

Tip #4: **Provide context.** Begin your statement of facts by providing the context of your client's story and end your statement of facts reminding your objective reader what your memo will address.

Tip #5: **Vary your sentence and paragraph length.** Employ both short and long sentences to keep your reader interested. Related to this, make sure to divide your statement of facts into digestible paragraphs—not too long or too short—that are organized topically.

Tip #6: **Organize your thoughts intentionally and use chronological order.** It is much easier for a reader to follow a story if it is presented in chronological order because this is the way the readers are used to hearing stories—from beginning to end.

Tip #7: **Describe the legally significant facts (trigger facts) with precision and detail.** Trigger facts are the facts on which your case will turn. It is critical that your reader is able to identify and understand these critical facts.

Tip #8: **CITE after every sentence.** In the "real" world, sometimes you will not need to include citations to the record (factual documents) in your objective memo's statement of facts (especially where the facts on which you are relying come primarily from interviews of your own client). That said, it is important to get in the habit of citing, and it is critical to learn correct and consistent citation form, including the correct citation form for factual documents.

F. The discussion

The discussion section of your objective memo is the heart of your memo in terms of substance and length. The discussion section is where you set forth the law in detail, explain the law, and then apply the law to your client's facts to show your reader how you reached your conclusion or predicted outcome.

The discussion section itself can (and usually should) be broken into multiple parts. For example, in the objective memo drafted for UI, the discussion section begins with an introduction in the form of an introductory roadmap, and then, the remainder of the discussion is divided into two sections, one for the cause of action and one for the affirmative defenses. Under the section for affirmative defenses (because there are two) there are two subheadings. You see the CRACs for each issue (there are three) go under heading I. (bona fide religious belief), heading II.A (reasonable accomodation), and heading II.B (undue hardship). The outline below (extracted from the objective memo drafted for UI) shows you how to set up the macro-organization of a discussion section of an objective memo.

> **DISCUSSION**
>
> [Introductory Roadmap Goes Here]
>
> I. **PRIMA FACIE CASE HEADING GOES HERE.**
> [CRAC for Element 1 Goes Here]
>
> II. **AFFIRMATIVE DEFENSE HEADING GOES HERE.**
> [Mini Roadmap Setting Out the Two Ways to Establish an Affirmative Defense Goes Here]
> A. Affirmative Defense 1 Heading Goes Here.
> [CRAC Affirmative Defense 1 Goes Here]
> B. Affirmative Defense 2 Heading Goes Here.
> [CRAC Affirmative Defense 2 Goes Here]

Let's say that instead you were asked to write an objective memo on the cause of action of undue influence, which has three elements. Assuming you were asked to discuss all three elements, your memo would look like the below example and not need subheadings (or a mini roadmap). The macro-organization of the objective memo's discussion section is simply three headings (one for each element).

> **DISCUSSION**
>
> [Introductory Roadmap Goes Here]
>
> I. **ELEMENT 1 HEADING GOES HERE.**
> [CRAC for Element 1 Goes Here]
>
> II. **ELEMENT 2 HEADING GOES HERE.**
> [CRAC for Element 2 Goes Here]
>
> II. **ELEMENT 3 HEADING GOES HERE.**
> [CRAC for Element 3 Goes Here]

1. Introductory roadmap

A discussion section of an objective memo rarely, if ever, covers only a single issue. Instead, although there may be a single question presented, that single question typically requires an analysis of multiple elements, factors, or possible defenses to determine the answer. In light of this underlying complexity, your objective memo will typically begin with an introductory roadmap.

An introductory roadmap is exactly what it sounds like: it provides a map outlining the organization of your discussion section. It reminds your reader of the question presented and the answer reached, but more importantly, it provides a very broad overview of the analytical steps required to get from the question presented to the answer. In addition, your introductory roadmap should mention any otherwise relevant elements or defenses that your discussion may not cover so that, in addition to what is forthcoming, your reader also knows what not to expect in the discussion ahead.[1] Of course, to the extent an introductory roadmap includes statements of the law, it must also include citations.

a. Purpose of an introductory roadmap

To understand the purpose of an introductory or overall roadmap, remove yourself from the law for a minute. Think about the following two ways in which your mom can give you the same instructions to meet her at Buc-ee's[2] in Terrell, Texas.

> **Alternative 1:** Your mom tells you to leave the law school and meet her at Buc-ee's in Terrell, Texas.
>
> **Alternative 2:** Your mom tells you to leave the law school and meet her at Buc-ee's in Terrell, Texas, by taking the following steps: (1) take I-30 East; (2) stay right onto US-80 E; (3) keep straight on TX-557 E Spur; (4) take the ramp to the right and follow the signs for FM-148; (5) turn right onto FM-148; and (6) arrive at Buc-ee's on the right (if you reach Medical Drive you have gone too far).

Which alternative will better help you understand how to get from the law school to Buc-ee's to meet your mom? Obviously, the second alternative is much easier to follow because it tells you how to get there.

An introductory roadmap in an objective memo should do essentially what alternative two in the Buc-ee's scenario above does: it reminds the reader of the issue and the conclusion, and then outlines the exact path that the objective memo will take to get there. After all, readers absorb what they are reading better when they first understand

1. At times, an element, claim, or defense may be omitted from a lawyer's analysis by instruction (stated in the assignment itself) or because the parties have stipulated to it.

2. Do not know what Buc-ee's is? It is only THE greatest gas station Texas has to offer.

the purpose and organization of what they are about to read. Compare two alternative introductory roadmaps for the discussion section of the objective memo for UI.

Alternative 1 (poorly drafted roadmap):

> **DISCUSSION**
>
> Mr. Saint is unlikely to hold UI liable for Title VII religious discrimination. Although Mr. Saint will very likely be able to establish a prima facie case of religious discrimination, UI will likely be able to avoid liability by establishing that it could not reasonably accommodate Mr. Saint without undue hardship, and, thus, Mr. Saint's Title VII claim will likely fail.

Alternative 2 (roadmap that shows analytical process):

> **DISCUSSION**
>
> Mr. Saint is unlikely to succeed in his attempt to hold UI liable for Title VII religious discrimination. Title VII prohibits an employer from discriminating against an employee based on the employee's religion. 42 U.S.C. § 2000e–2(a)(1). Religion "includes all aspects of religious observance and practice, as well as belief." 42 U.S.C. § 2000e(j). The Fifth Circuit employs a burden-shifting framework to analyze Title VII religious discrimination claims. *Davis v. Fort Bend Cnty.*, 765 F.3d 480, 485 (5th Cir. 2014). Under this framework, the plaintiff must first establish a prima facie case of religious discrimination. *Id.* If the plaintiff establishes a prima facie case, the burden shifts to the defendant to demonstrate that it reasonably accommodated the employee or could not reasonably accommodate the employee without undue hardship. *Id.* First, Mr. Saint is very likely to establish a prima facie case of religious discrimination against UI. To establish a prima facie case of religious discrimination under Title VII, a plaintiff must prove that (1) he had a bona fide religious belief; (2) his belief conflicted with an employment requirement; (3) his employer was informed of his belief; and (4) he suffered an adverse employment action for failing to comply with the conflicting employment requirement. *Tagore v. United States*, 735 F.3d 324, 329 (5th Cir. 2013). Because, at this point, UI does not contest elements two, three, and four, only the first element of Mr. Saint's prima facie Title VII

> case remains at issue. Second, UI is very unlikely to avoid liability by establishing that it offered Mr. Saint a reasonable accommodation. Third, however, UI will likely be able to avoid liability by establishing that it could not reasonably accommodate Mr. Saint without undue hardship. Therefore, Mr. Saint's Title VII claim will likely fail.

The first alterative introductory roadmap is not terrible, but it does not help the reader forecast the four elements required for a prima facie religious discrimination claim or the two alternate affirmative defenses available to UI that the memo will set forth and analyze. In contrast, the second alternative, provides the reader with a better understanding for how the objective memo will analytically get from the question to its answer by setting forth the both the prima facie elements and the affirmative defenses in the order they will be discussed, explaining which elements are not contested (and therefore not discussed in the memo), and then explaining which remaining elements and affirmative defenses are and are not satisfied.

b. Formula

Unfortunately, there is no single, precise formula for drafting an introductory roadmap. The reason for this is because the structure of each roadmap will depend, in large part, on the complexity of the issues covered in the objective memo. How many claims does it address? How many elements or factors are required for each claim? Are there any affirmative defenses?

Generally speaking, however, a roadmap usually follows the following formula.

ROADMAP FORMULA

Conclusion on objective memo's cause of action.	+	List of elements, factors, and affirmative defenses and any overarching subrules that apply to all elements or affirmative defenses.	+	Conclusion on objective memo's cause of action with a brief explanation tying the conclusion to the elements or factors and affirmative defenses.

c. Mini-roadmaps under subheadings

Now that you understand the purpose of an introductory roadmap—to forecast the basic steps of analysis necessary to get from the memo's question presented to its brief answer—do you think there are other places that you might want to use roadmaps in your discussion? Of course! Generally speaking, any time you have a large section of your memo that is subdivided into multiple smaller sections you will insert a mini-roadmap between the larger section heading and the first subdivision heading. This is called a mini-roadmap, and its purpose is to forecast the steps involved in the analysis of that subdivision.

For example, an employer can avoid liability for a Title VII religious discrimination claim by establishing one of two statutorily allowed affirmative defenses: (1) the employer offered the employee a reasonable accommodation or (2) offering a reasonable accommodation would cause the employer undue hardship. Thus, when you begin drafting that section of your objective memo, you may decide to do a large section heading about the employer's ability to avoid liability through an affirmative defense followed by two subheadings—one for each available defense. If you decide to use such a structure, include a mini-roadmap forecasting why the text below is divided into multiple subsections and telling your reader the result of the analysis of the totality of those separate subsections. Below is an example of a mini-roadmap for the affirmative defenses and then the subheadings (text omitted) that would follow.

> **II. UI will likely avoid liability for Title VII religious discrimination based on an affirmative defense.**
>
> UI will likely be able to avoid liability for religious discrimination because it can establish an affirmative defense to the Title VII religious discrimination claim. An employer can avoid liability for Title VII religious discrimination by establishing one of two affirmative defenses: the employer can either show that it offered the employee a "reasonable" accommodation for his religious conflict or that it was "unable to reasonably accommodate [the] employee's . . . religious observance" because doing so would have imposed "undue hardship on the conduct of the employer's business." 42 USC § 2000e(j); *see also Davis*, 765 F.3d at 487. Although UI will not likely be able to prove that it offered Mr. Saint a reasonable accommodation, UI likely can show it could not reasonably accommodate Mr. Saint's religious belief without undue hardship, and, thus, UI will likely avoid Title VII liability.
>
> A. UI is unlikely to prove the affirmative defense of reasonable accommodation.
>
> B. UI is likely to prove the affirmative defense of undue hardship.

If you are still struggling to grasp when or where you include a mini-roadmap in your discussion, understand that they are not always necessary. That said, if your discussion section includes a heading on top of a subheading with no text in between the two (like Heading Two on the next page), it is a good indication that you may need to insert a mini-roadmap between the two headings.

DISCUSSION

[Introductory Roadmap Goes Here]

A. HEADING ONE

B. HEADING TWO

[Mini-Roadmap Goes Here]

1. SUBHEADING ONE

2. SUBHEADING TWO

2. *CRAC: objective writing*

After your introductory roadmap, what comes next in your discussion is the substantively hard work of an objective memo: your legal analysis drafted in the form of issue-based CRACs. Remember, your legal analysis should, generally speaking, always take the form of CRAC because this is the organizational structure that lawyers use to frame their arguments. While the CRAC structure is more malleable once you master the basic skills of legal reasoning, during your first year of law school you should employ it religiously. Before you begin drafting the CRACs in your discussion section, you have to figure out how many issues you have to address in your discussion and, thus, how many CRACs you need to draft.

When you are writing your objective memo, you will need the same number of CRACs as the number of issues you have been asked to address. That is, # of issues = # of CRACs. In other words, the number of CRACs will be dictated by the assignment itself and by how many issues the assignment asks you to address. However—and here is the important part—you may need additional CRACs because, as we discussed earleir in the book, macro issues often contain elements or factors. If an issue requires the analysis of three separate elements, you then need a CRAC not for the macro issue, but, instead, for each element you must address in order to assess the macro issue.

For example, in the Appendix e-mail assigning you the work on Mr. Saint's case, Dominique Baker writes, "I am hoping you have some time to help me on this matter by drafting a formal memorandum that I can forward to UI in which you assess the likelihood UI will be held liable for violating Title VII." Based on the assignment, you might think that you need a single CRAC, assessing liability under Title VII. However, Ms. Baker has helped you out by forecasting that liability under Title VII requires that you complete a two-part analysis looking at (1) whether Mr. Saint will likely establish a prima facie case of Title VII religious discrimination and (2) whether, if Mr. Saint is successful establishing a prima facie case, UI can avoid liability by proving one of two affirmative defenses available under Title VII. Ms. Baker then explains that, although a prima facie religious discrimination claim typically requires an employee to prove four elements, the only element at issue in Mr. Saint's prima facie case is the first element—whether he held a bona fide religious belief. Because only one element of the prima facie case is at issue as well as two possible affirmative defenses, you now know you really have three separate "issues"[3] and you will, thus, need three separate CRACs in the discussion section of your objective memo. Using this information, you now know the basic structure of the discussion section of your memo (that is, the outline of your legal analysis and each issue you need to tackle using the CRAC analytical structure).

> **DISCUSSION**
>
> [Introductory Roadmap Goes Here]
>
> I. **MR. SAINT WILL LIKELY ESTABLISH A PRIMA FACIE CASE OF RELIGIOUS DISCRIMINATION UNDER TITLE VII.**
>
> [CRAC for Element 1 Goes Here]
>
> II. **UI WILL LIKELY AVOID LIABILITY FOR TITLE VII RELIGIOUS DISCRIMINATION BASED ON AN AFFIRMATIVE DEFENSE.**
>
> [Mini-roadmap Goes Here]
>
> A. UI is unlikely to prove the affirmative defense of reasonable accommodation.
>
> [CRAC for Affirmative Defense 1 Goes Here]
>
> B. UI is likely to prove the affirmative defense of undue hardship.
>
> [CRAC for Affirmative Defense 2 Goes Here]

In some instances, the number of elements of a claim may precisely reflect the number of CRACs in your discussion. For example, Ms. Baker could ask, "Please draft a formal memorandum analyzing whether Mr. Saint is likely to succeed in establishing his prima facie case," without any qualifications or exclusions. You would, thus, have four issues (four elements) and, therefore, four CRACs.

Once you determine the number of CRACs and what issues are at the core of each CRAC, you then need to begin the hard work: analyzing each issue following the CRAC formula. The sections that follow will walk you through precisely how to do this, starting with "C" (Conclusion), then "R" (Rule), then "A" (Analysis), and then the final "C" (Conclusion).

3. A word of caution: because your discussion section contains three issues and, thus, has three CRACS, it does not always mean that you should have three separate questions presented. This seeming disconnect can be confusing for new law students. You need to make sure you draft your question(s) presented in a way that allows for your objective memo to answer the ultimate question posed—in this case, the likelihood that UI will be held liable.

3. CRAC: creating objective opening and closing Conclusion sentences

Every issue in your objective memo will begin **and** end with a Conclusion—a statement of the conclusion or result of your legal analysis of that issue. Unlike John Grisham novels that build for hundreds of pages to a surprise ending, good legal analysis gives away the ending up front. The reason that all legal analyses begin with the conclusion is that readers absorb more if they understand—in advance—the significance of what they are about to read. Thus, by leading with the conclusion of your analysis, you are helping your reader better comprehend your argument. In addition, by beginning your legal analysis with your Conclusion, you will keep your analysis better organized and focused. Given these benefits, you should begin each separate legal analysis by stating the conclusion for the issue you are addressing and then closing out that issue's legal analysis by restating that same, substantive conclusion.[4]

a. How to write objective Conclusions

Conclusion sentences in your objective memo tell your reader the resolution of the legal issue being addressed. While there are only two Conclusions (two "C"s) in each CRAC, you will have three forms of conclusions for each issue you are addressing because, in addition to your opening and closing conclusion sentences, you will also include a conclusory heading before your CRAC on each issue. Conclusory headings orient the reader (by clearly dividing the larger discussion section into smaller issue-based sections) and, just like opening and closing conclusion sentences, give away the result of the legal analysis to come on that particular issue. Typically, at least one of the three conclusions (often the closing conclusion) will include a key reason or key fact to explain the basis for the conclusion.

In objective writing, conclusion sentences can be qualified. In other words, your Conclusion need not be 100 percent certain but, instead, can include some finessing language such as "likely" or "unlikely." For example, in the memo for UI, there are conclusion sentences for each element at issue and each affirmative defense, and each conclusion is qualified as opposed to certain. Below is the opening Conclusion for element one.

---

4. It is important to note that conclusory-based headings do not serve as the "C" or Conclusion required at the beginning of each CRAC. Instead, you will have a conclusion-based heading, and then, following that heading, the first sentence of your text will restate the conclusion of your analysis. For many law students, the repeated conclusions (the conclusory-based heading, the opening Conclusion and the closing Conclusion) seem overly repetitive. However, headings and the text of an argument itself serve entirely different roles. In fact, a reader may only read the headings or, alternatively, may skip the headings altogether and just dig into the text of the argument. Given the different roles of the headings and the text, it is helpful for readers to have the conclusion provided in both places. That said, for stylistic purposes, as discussed *infra*, you should vary the length and content of the conclusion-based headings and your opening and closing conclusion sentences so they are not identical in form.

> Given Mr. Saint's consistent representations to UI and actions surrounding his religious belief against using UI's new biometric-scanning system, Mr. Saint will likely establish the first element required for religious discrimination.

Notice how this Conclusion forecasts to the reader the result of the lawyer's analysis on the first element. Moreover, rather than the lawyer guaranteeing the result, the lawyer qualifies her conclusion by noting that the result is "likely" rather than certain. Lawyers qualify their answers in objective memos because, at the early stages of a case (typically when objective memos are drafted), a lawyer likely does not have all the facts of the case, and additional facts discovered later may affect the lawyer's conclusion. In other words, using qualified conclusion language gives a lawyer some "wiggle room" to adjust her analysis later if/when she learns new or different information that affects the outcome of a particular issue or the case more generally.

b. How to vary your different objective Conclusions

In addition to the general struggle law students have adjusting to the substantive redundancy of legal writing (and legal analysis), many law students have difficulty figuring out how to elegantly vary their conclusion sentences to communicate the same substantive conclusion in all the places an experienced reader expects it, while avoiding linguistic redundancy. Generally speaking, there are a few techniques you can use to vary your conclusion sentences.

> **Technique one:** Conclude in a broad, non-specific way (in relation to the named element or issue, omitting the detail).
>
> **Technique two:** Conclude by setting forth the details of the issue or element on which you conclude.
>
> **Technique three:** Conclude in a way that also explains the primary reason or reasons for the conclusion.

The examples below, based on the objective memo drafted for UI, illustrate how to vary conclusion sentences using these techniques to avoid redundancy.

CONCLUSORY HEADING FOR AFFIRMATIVE DEFENSE TWO (TECHNIQUE ONE)

> UI is likely to prove the affirmative defense of undue hardship.

OPENING CONCLUSION FOR AFFIRMATIVE DEFENSE TWO (TECHNIQUE TWO)

> UI can likely establish that offering Mr. Saint a "reasonable" accommodation would have imposed undue hardship on its business.

CLOSING CONCLUSION FOR AFFIRMATIVE DEFENSE TWO (TECHNIQUE THREE))

> Because UI can provide evidence of the "mere possibility" that it could have experienced undue hardship—precisely what was missing in *Ford*—if forced to offer Mr. Saint an accommodation not requiring use of the scanner, it will likely establish the second affirmative defense under Title VII.

You will notice that, as illustrated by the three examples above, by making even small variations in the drafting of your conclusion sentences, you are able to minimize the redundancy that your reader might otherwise experience, especially when the issue or element being addressed is a fairly simple or brief one.

4. CRAC: creating objective Rules

Your Rule is the second part of your CRAC, and as such, it directly follows the opening Conclusion. Rule statements are the scaffolding of all legal analysis. Without clearly articulated rules, there would be nothing to apply facts to and no standard to use predict a resolution of the legal problem presented. In other words, pay attention because this section of the book is especially important.

Objective rule statements are generally comprised of three parts: the general rule, subrules, and one or more case illustrations. Given the importance of rule statements to the success of your legal analysis, it is critical that you learn to identify and draft all parts of a legal rule. Moreover, it is important while you are still mastering legal analysis that you always include all three parts of a Rule (with one exception discussed in the section on case illustrations later in this part of the book) and that you do so in the required order—from the general rule to the subrules to the case illustration(s).

Each of the three parts of a Rule plays a unique role. First, the general rule is the part of the rule where you state the law governing the element or claim at issue. Second, subrules are specific rules that explain the general rule. Subrules often define terms from the general rule, identify how courts determine whether the general rule is satisfied (e.g., factors), or identify evidence that is needed to satisfy the general rule. Third, case illustrations demonstrate how the general rule (and its subrules) have been applied in prior cases. In other words, case illustrations provide examples of the general rule in action.

These three parts of a Rule—the general rule, subrules, and case illustrations—work together to explain the law at issue to the reader. Moreover, these three parts of a Rule help define the parameters of the legal standard at issue from its broadest application (the general rule) to its narrowest (the case illustration). A well-drafted and complete Rule is central to your reader's understanding of the legal standard at issue and, thus, her ability to follow how you apply the law to the facts to arrive at your predicted outcome.

Let's look at an example of a rule statement that contains all three parts of a Rule to better understand what these three parts look like. Below is the rule statement for the first element from the objective memo for UI. The three parts of the Rule are labeled for you.

With practice, all law students and lawyers alike should be able to master drafting excellent legal rules by following the guidelines provided in this book. The next few sections will walk you through how to draft each of the three parts of an objective Rule.

General Rule

Subrules: From Broad to Narrow

To satisfy the first element of a religious discrimination claim, a plaintiff must prove that he had a "bona fide religious belief." *Id.* In other words, the first element requires a plaintiff to prove two things: first, that his belief is religious and, second, that his belief is bona fide. A bona fide religious belief includes "moral or ethical beliefs as to what is right and wrong [that] are sincerely held." *Davis*, 765 F.3d at 485. In determining whether a plaintiff's belief is a religious belief, a court must ask "whether [the individual's beliefs] are, in his own scheme of things, religious." *Id.* (citing *United States v. Seeger*, 380 U.S. 163, 185 (1965)). A plaintiff's belief may constitute a "religious belief" despite its incomprehensibility or imprecision. *Id.* at 487 (first quoting *Seeger*, 380 U.S. at 184; and then quoting *A.A. ex rel. Betenbaugh v. Needville Indep. Sch. Dist.*, 611 F.3d 248, 261 (5th Cir. 2010)). Put another way, "a belief is 'religious' if it is '[a] sincere and meaningful belief which occupies in the life of its possessor a place parallel to that filled by . . . God.'" *Id.* at 485 (citing *Seeger*, 380 U.S. at 176). Because the belief's trueness or centrality as a religious tenet is "not open to question," whether a belief is religious is ultimately a question of sincerity. *See id.* Courts hesitate to challenge a plaintiff's sincerity, inquiring with "a light touch" and "judicial shyness" and performing a limited assessment of a plaintiff's credibility based on his representations and actions relating to his asserted belief. *Tagore*, 735 F.3d at 328 (citing *Moussazadeh v. Tex. Dep't of Crim. Just.*, 703 F.3d 781, 792 (5th Cir. 2012)). To be sincere, an employee's reliance on a religious belief must stem from conviction and not convenience. *Hansard v. Johns-Manville Prods. Corp.*, No. 1902, 1973 WL 129, at *2 (E.D. Tex. Feb. 16, 1973).

An employee's consistent representation that she holds a particular religious belief coupled with action consistent with that belief supports a finding of sincerity. In *Davis*, the Fifth Circuit held that the employee's representation and action evidenced sincerity such that she, at minimum, raised a genuine issue of material fact as to the sincerity of her belief. 765 F.3d at 485–86. In that case, the employee notified her employer that she could not work on a particular Sunday because she had a special church service to attend that involved breaking new ground and feeding the community. *Id.* at 486–87. The employee attended the church event, was fired for being absent from work without approval, and then sued her employer for religious discrimination under Title VII. *Id.* at 484. At trial, the employee testified about her devotion to the church, stating that she "believed strongly" that she "needed" to attend a "special church service." *Id.* at 486. The employee further testified about her active commitment to her church, referencing her frequent church attendance and participation. *Id.* at 487. The Fifth Circuit reasoned that the district court erred when it granted summary judgment because it improperly inquired into the nature of the activity and its status as "a true religious tenet," whereas it should have looked to the employee's credibility and asked whether the employee sincerely believed that the activity was religious "in her own scheme of things." *Id.* The Fifth Circuit further reasoned that the employee's representation and action surrounding her belief that she was religiously required to attend a special church service, through her testimony, sufficiently evidenced a genuine issue of material fact as to whether she sincerely believed the event to be religious. *Id.* at 487. Accordingly, the employee's prima facie case survived summary judgment for a trier of fact to later determine whether the employee held a bona fide religious belief. *Id.*

Case illustration

a. CRAC: general rule, the first part of an objective Rule

The general rule is the first part of your Rule, that is your three-part rule statement in objective writing. A general rule is a succinct statement of the law that governs the legal element at issue in the subsection you are drafting. General rules are not hard to identify because they are usually explicitly set forth in a case or a statute.

In addition, general rules are also not terribly hard to draft because, most often, they are the specifically stated elements of a claim or the affirmative defense. In objective writing, which is neutral in perspective, you should usually draft your general rules using the same language used in the source for the rule. In fact, if you do not mirror the general rule language provided by the source but, instead, paraphrase that general rule language, you risk introducing unintended inaccuracy or persuasive spin into your supposedly neutral statement of the law. You should draft all general rules in the present tense (because the general rule is currently the law) and follow your general rule statement by a citation to the case or statute from which it came.

Let's practice finding and drafting general rules by turning to Mr. Saint's case. In the memo for UI, we know that the core issue is whether Mr. Saint is likely to succeed in holding UI liable for religious discrimination under Title VII. If we look at one of the seminal cases on religious discrimination in the Fifth Circuit,[5] *Tagore v. United States*, what are the general rule(s) for establishing a prima facie religious discrimination claim? See if you can find them in the excerpt below that was copied and pasted directly from *Tagore*.

> Title VII prohibits an employer from discriminating against an employee on the basis of her religion, unless the employer is unable to reasonably accommodate the employee's religious exercise without undue hardship to its business. 42 U.S.C. §§ 2000e–2(a)(1), 2000e(j). To establish a prima facie case of religious discrimination under Title VII, the plaintiff must present evidence that (1) she held a bona fide religious belief, (2) her belief conflicted with a requirement of her employment, (3) her employer was informed of her belief, and (4) she suffered an adverse employment action for failing to comply with the conflicting employment requirement.

We know that general rules are the statement of the law that governs the issue and that general rules often take the form of an element or elements of a claim. Here, *Tagore* identifies four elements required to establish a prime facie case of religious discrimination.

> ...the plaintiff must present evidence that (1) she held a bona fide religious belief, (2) her belief conflicted with a requirement of her employment, (3) her employer was informed of her belief, and (4) she suffered an adverse employment action for failing to comply with the conflicting employment requirement.

Because there are four elements, there are four separate general rules (each of the four elements). As previously discussed, because there are four elements of the claim, you would normally have four separate CRACs (one for each of the four elements). The

5. 735 F.3d 324, 328 (5th Cir. 2013).

general rule for the Rule of each CRAC is actually the element you are addressing. You will note, however, that in the memo for UI, the second, third, and fourth elements are uncontested and, therefore, are not included as part of the objective memo's analysis.

If you look to the first element, what is the general rule for element one? The general rule for element one is the element itself. Easy enough, right? See the sample general rule for the first element of religious discrimination from the memo for UI.

> To satisfy the first element of a religious discrimination claim, a plaintiff must prove that he had a bona fide religious belief. *Tagore*, 735 F.3d 324, 329 (5th Cir. 2013).

This general rule, as discussed above, objectively restates the element set forth *Tagore* without paraphrasing terms of art such as "bona fide" and "religious belief." Instead, the language from the general rule's source—*Tagore*—is used. In addition, as discussed above, this sample general rule is written in present tense and is followed by a citation to the case from which the general rule was taken—*Tagore*.

If you step back for a minute and take a look at the macro-organization of the discussion section of UI's memo, you will notice that the issues are presented using parallel structure or, in other words, with the same introductory language and using the same basic grammatical structure. By using parallel structure across the elements (or across the affirmative defenses), you can help your reader see the similarities between them and, thus, help your reader follow and relate the different general rules to one another. For your convenience and to further help you discern how to employ parallelism, below are the general rules for the two affirmative defenses written in parallel structure taken from the objective memo.

AFFIRMATIVE DEFENSE	GENERAL RULE
Affirmative Defense One	An employer can avoid liability under Title VII if it can show it offered the employee any reasonable accommodation.
Affirmative Defense Two	An employer can avoid liability under Title VII if it can show it could not accomodate the employee's religious practice without undue hardship on the employer's business.

b. CRAC: subrules, the second part of an objective Rule

Subrules are the second part of your three-part rule statement in objective writing. Subrules are short excerpts from cases that explain the parameters and meaning of the general rule. Subrules ensure that your reader understands the general rule at issue and how that general rule is (or is not) satisfied. You should draft subrules, like the general rule, in present tense. In addition, just like for general rules, each subrule should be followed by a citation to the legal authority where the subrule was found.

As discussed above, identifying and drafting general rules is not a difficult task. You review the seminal case or a statute and locate the general rule; then, you insert it into your CRAC after your opening Conclusion. But, for your reader, simply reading a general rule does not really help her understand the legal standard at issue. For example, if you step back and read the general rule for the first element of a prima facie case of religious discrimination—"To satisfy the first element of a religious discrimination claim, a plaintiff must prove that he had a bona fide religious belief"—do you understand what it means? Do you understand how to figure out whether a particular belief is "bona fide"? Not really.

This is where subrules come into play. The main purpose of subrules is to explain the general rule. Subrules define terms in the general rule, set forth tests that courts use to determine whether the general rule is satisfied (for example, the factors a court weighs in considering a general rule), and identify what evidence does or does not satisfy the general rule. Subrules are typically woven together using a technique called bridging. Bridging occurs when you pull language from the general rule into your subrules and, also, when you build on your subrules by pulling language from one subrule and repeating it in the next subrule. Using this bridging technique improves the flow of your subrules, while simultaneously reducing the need for artificial transition words, such as "next," "then," "moreover," or "in addition," which can distract your reader. Subrules are also drafted in a particular order—from the most general to the narrowest.

Let's look at the memo for UI again to better understand how to draft subrules. Below we have excerpted the general rule and the subrules for element one from the objective memo for UI.

> To satisfy the first element of a religious discrimination claim, a plaintiff must prove that he had a "bona fide religious belief." *Id.* In other words, the first element requires a plaintiff to prove two things: first, that his belief is religious and, second, that his belief is bona fide. A bona fide religious belief includes "moral or ethical beliefs as to what is right and wrong [that] are sincerely held." *Davis*, 765 F.3d at 485. In determining whether a plaintiff's belief is a religious belief, a court must ask "whether [the individual's beliefs] are, in his own scheme of things, religious." *Id.* (citing *United States v. Seeger*, 380 U.S. 163, 185 (1965)). A plaintiff's belief may constitute a "religious belief" despite its incomprehensibility or imprecision. *Id.* at 487 (first quoting *Seeger*, 380 U.S. at 184; and then quoting *A.A. ex rel. Betenbaugh v. Needville Indep. Sch. Dist.*, 611 F.3d 248, 261 (5th Cir. 2010)). Put another way, "a belief is 'religious' if it is '[a] sincere and meaningful belief which occupies in the life of its possessor a place parallel to that filled by . . . God.'" *Id.* at 485 (citing *Seeger*, 380 U.S. at 176). Because the belief's trueness or centrality as a religious tenet is "not open to question," whether a belief is religious is ultimately a question of sincerity. *See id.* Courts hesitate to challenge a plaintiff's sincerity, inquiring with "a light touch" and "judicial shyness" and performing a limited assessment of a plaintiff's credibility based on his representations and actions relating to his asserted belief. *Tagore*, 735 F.3d at 328 (citing *Moussazadeh v. Tex. Dep't of Crim. Just.*, 703 F.3d 781, 792 (5th Cir. 2012)). To be sincere, an employee's reliance on a religious belief must stem from conviction and not convenience. *Hansard v. Johns-Manville Prods. Corp.*, No. 1902, 1973 WL 129, at *2 (E.D. Tex. Feb. 16, 1973).

This example does a nice job demonstrating the use of bridging. The highlighted terms use repetitive language to bridge or transition from one subrule to the next. Similarly, the highlighted terms are repeated from the general rule into the subrules to help create cohesion in the larger rule statement. This example also illustrates the proper way to order subrules—from broad to narrow. The image on the following page is a pictorial illustration of that order.

GENERAL RULE

- **To satisfy the first element of a religious discrimination claim, a plaintiff must prove that he had a bona fide religious belief.**

SUBRULES

- **In other words, the first element requires a plaintiff to prove two things: first, that his belief is religious and, second, that his belief is bona fide. *Id.***
  - **A bona fide religious belief includes "moral or ethical beliefs as to what is right and wrong [that] are sincerely held."**
    - **In determining whether a plaintiff's belief is religious, a court must ask "whether [the individual's beliefs] are, in his own scheme of things, religious."**

- **A plaintiff's belief may constitute a "religious belief" despite its incomprehensibility or imprecision.**
  - **Put another way, "a belief is 'religious' if it is '[a] sincere and meaningful belief which occupies in the life of its possessor a place parallel to that filled by . . . God.'"**
    - **Because the belief's trueness or centrality as a religious tenet is "not open to question," whether a belief is religious is ultimately a question of sincerity.**
      - **Courts hesitate to challenge a plaintiff's sincerity, inquiring with "a light touch" and "judicial shyness" and performing a limited assessment of a plaintiff's credibility based on his representations and actions relating to his asserted belief.**
        - **To be sincere, an employee's reliance on a religious belief must stem from conviction and not convenience.**

As you can see from the example, the general rule is the broadest of the rules in the rule statement. Then, following that broad general rule, is the first subrule, which broadly identifies the standard that courts use to assess the first element. Thereafter, the subrules get narrower—first defining the terms (e.g., religious and "bona fide") and then identifying the type of evidence that satisfies or does not satisfy the terms.

i. How to find objective subrules

For practicing lawyers, mining cases for subrules is a relatively quick, easy, and—some lawyers would even say—fun task. Finding subrules, however, is often difficult for law students. It is difficult because law students—beginning ones especially—do not know where to look or what to look for when trying to find subrules.

Let's talk through those two difficulties, so you don't get stumped when looking for subrules. In terms of what to look for, subrules are, at their core, snippets of law that define or explain the larger rule at issue. In terms of where to look, subrules usually come from statutes or caselaw. In caselaw, subrules typically follow the statement of the general rule. Some cases will have all the general rules and subrules grouped together, while other cases will break each general rule out and follow each general rule with subrules that explain that particular general rule. While some cases are subrule gold mines (meaning they contain subrule after subrule), others may have no relevant subrules. In addition to the easy-to-grab subrules included in the text of cases, each case addressing a particular legal issue also presents the opportunity to synthesize a subrule based on what that case adds to pre-existing expectations at the time. This type of subrule is called a synthesized or implicit subrule because you as a reader have to discern them from your understanding of the case rather than just grabbing them from the text of the case itself.

Let's continue working with the first element of religious discrimination to practice finding subrules. You should begin your search for subrules by reviewing caselaw that discusses the first element required for religious discrimination (there may, in fact, be some cases that do not grapple with the first element at all—you can set those cases aside for purposes of finding element one subrules). Based on your prior, careful reading of the general rule for element one, you can probably spot a few terms of art that need defining. "Bona fide," for example, is at the core of the element and is a phrase that jumps out because you probably do not know what it means. Using this term as an example, you will look in the relevant caselaw to find out how courts have interpreted "bona fide," or, in other words, you will look for subrules to help explain this part of the general rule. As you search, keep in mind that typically an entire case will not address a single element of a claim. So, if you are looking for subrules related to a particular element (here, element one), usually the best place to start looking is in the part of a case that specifically addresses the element or factor at issue.

Below is an excerpt from *Davis v. Fort Bend County*.[6] This excerpt is from the part of *Davis* that deals with the first element of a prima facie religious discrimination claim. Because this case includes headings in its opinion, it is very easy to determine which part of the opinion addresses which element.

> Bona fide religious beliefs include "moral or ethical beliefs as to what is right and wrong which are sincerely held with the strength of traditional religious views." *See*, e.g., 29 C.F.R. § 1605.1 (citing *United States v. Seeger*, 380 U.S. 163, 85 S.Ct. 850, 13 L.Ed.2d 733 (1965)). A court's inquiry is limited to focusing upon the individual's motivation. Specifically, a court's task is to decide "whether [the individual's beliefs] are, in his own scheme of things, religious." *Seeger*, 380 U.S. at 185, 85 S.Ct. 850 (emphasis added). In this regard, a belief is "religious" if it is "[a] sincere and meaningful belief which occupies in the life of its possessor a place parallel to that filled by ... God." *Seeger*, 380 U.S. at 176, 85 S.Ct. 850. Conversely, whether the belief itself is central to the religion, i.e., whether the belief is a true religious tenet, is "not open to question." *Moussazadeh v. Tex. Dep't of Criminal Justice*, 703 F.3d 781, 790 (5th Cir. 2012) (quoting *Seeger*, 380 U.S. at 185, 85 S.Ct. 850) (internal quotation marks omitted) (discussing the threshold inquiry into a person's religious belief under the Religious Land Use and Institutionalized Persons Act); *see Tagore*, 735 F.3d at 328–29 (applying *Moussazadeh* to a Title VII religious discrimination claim).

What, if any, parts of the excerpt from *Davis* help the reader better understand the meaning of the "bona fide" term we identified above? What parts help the reader better understand any other aspect of the first element required for religious discrimination? This excerpt has many potential subrules—it is a goldmine of sorts.

As you read and find potential subrules in cases like this one, you should keep track of those subrules in an organized way (and usually by element). When you have finished reviewing all the relevant caselaw, you may have a handful of subrules that appeared in multiple cases. This repetition is a sign that a particular subrule is likely important to understanding the general rule. In other words, if there are certain repeated subrules, you will likely want to include those as subrules in your Rule. In addition, by keeping track of all subrules, including recording similar subrules that appear across cases, it will position you to select the best (in objective writing the best subrule means the one that is the clearest) version of the subrule to use in your Rule.

---

6. 765 F.3d 480, 485 (5th Cir. 2014).

The table below is an example of one method you can use to record subrules while you read caselaw. Note that because the citations are not in final form, the subrules captured in the table are in pre-writing format and are not final work product.

Subrules for Element I

DAVIS V. MONROE COUNTY	*HANSARD V. JOHN MANVILLE PRODS. CORP.*	*TAGORE V. UNITED STATES*
Bona fide beliefs include "moral or ethical beliefs as to what is right and wrong which are sincerely held with the strength of traditional religious views." *Davis*, 485.		
The religiosity of an employee's belief turns on "whether [the individual's beliefs] are, in his own scheme of things, religious" and if the belief is "[a] sincere and meaningful belief which occupies in the life of its possessor a place parallel to that filled by ... God." *Davis*, 485.		
In assessing whether a belief is a religious belief determining whether the belief is a true religious tenet, is "not open to question." *Davis*, 485.		

A few of the key subrules related to element one are filled in from *Davis*. For practice, you should review *Hansard*[7] and *Tagore*.[8] Based on your review, you should then identify and record any additional subrules from those cases that help explain further the first element of religious discrimination.

ii. Structural subrules

A primary purpose of objective writing is to explain the law in a way that your reader can grasp. Fulfilling this purpose presents a challenge for two reasons. First, courts are, unfortunately, not always clear or precise when they explain the law and, as

7. *See Hansard v. Johns-Manville Prods. Corp.*, No. 1902, 1973 WL 129 (E.D. Tex. Feb. 16, 1973).
8. *See Tagore v. United States*, 735 F.3d 324 (5th Cir. 2013).

a result, the relationship between the general rule and subrules or between the subrules themselves can become hazy. Second, as a first-year law student, you are a new legal reader and, therefore, understandably a bit insecure in your ability to comprehend and ultimately explain the law.

One tool you can use to help you better explain the law are structural subrules. Structural subrules do not add substance to the legal standard; instead, they isolate and then call out the structures or subdivisions in a general rule to make it easier for you to explain and, thus, easier for your reader to understand. Let's look at the first element in the objective memo for UI again as an example.

General Rule

Structural subrule

> To satisfy the first element of a religious discrimination claim, a plaintiff must prove that he had a "bona fide religious belief." *Tagore*, 735 F.3d at 329. In other words, the first element requires a plaintiff to prove two things: first, that his belief is religious and, second, that his belief is bona fide. *Id.*

In the example above, the element itself—bona fide religious belief—is not only a mouthful, but is a tangle of two different requirements—religiosity and the bona fides of that religiosity. To tackle the element as one single requirement risks that a reader (and writer for that matter) might get confused moving between the different requirements of the element. Moreover, although even without adding a structural subrule, a good writer would still opt to organize the various subrules into the two-required parts of the element, by identifying and including a structural subrule, the writer is able to overtly explain the ordering and organization of the subrules that follow to the reader. By so doing, the writer enables the lazy reader to put her feet up, lean back in her chair, take a sip of tea, and follow along without having to work to understand the organizational construct of the rule.

iii. How many subrules do you need to find?

Law students always ask how many subrules they need for each element. Unfortunately, there is no universal number. Instead, the number of subrules needed will depend on the complexity of the general rule that the subrules aim to explain and on how much legal precedent there is interpreting that particular general rule. Generally speaking, if you have fewer than three subrules, you should critically reflect on whether the subrules you rely on are truly sufficient to explain the general rule to your reader. On the other hand, if you have, say, ten subrules, you should reflect on whether each subrule adds to your reader's understanding of the general rule or whether some of the subrules are redundant or should be modified and converted to case illustrations. The key to determining the number of subrules is assessing whether each subrule adds meaningful content.

c. CRAC: case illustrations, the third part of an objective Rule

Case illustrations are the third and final part of your three-part rule statement in objective writing. Case illustrations provide examples of the general rule and subrules "in action." People learn by example, and that is what case illustrations do—they provide specific examples of the application of the rule at issue to a set of past facts and the result that followed.

For purposes of understanding case illustrations, let's look back at the objective memo for UI, but, this time, let's look at the second affirmative defense, instead of Mr. Saint's prima facie case. Under Title VII, even if Mr. Saint successfully proves a prima facie case of religious discrimination, UI can avoid liability by showing that offering Mr. Saint a reasonable accommodation would cause the company undue hardship. The general rule and an abbreviated version of the subrules for this affirmative defense are below.

> An employer can avoid liability under Title VII if it can show it is "unable to reasonably accommodate [the] employee's ... religious observance or practice without undue hardship on the conduct of the employer's business." 42 U.S.C. § 2000e(j). Undue hardship exists when an employer must "bear more than a de minimis cost" to reasonably accommodate its employee's religious belief. *Weber v. Roadway Exp., Inc.*, 199 F.3d 270, 273 (5th Cir. 2000). An employer need not wait to feel the accommodation's impact or attempt to accommodate the employee to establish an undue hardship; instead, an employer can establish undue hardship by showing evidence that the "mere possibility of an [accommodation's] adverse impact" could impose more-than de minimis costs on the employer. *Id.* at 274–75. In the Fifth Circuit, courts have recognized the requisite undue hardship in a variety of circumstances:
>
> - An employer can establish more than de minimis costs by showing that a religious accommodation is inflexible to the employer's business demands. *Id.* at 275.
> - An employer can establish more than de minimis costs by showing that an accommodation could adversely impact its finances, employees, or efficiency. *Favero*, 939 F. Supp. at 1288; *Weber*, 199 F.3d at 273.
> - An employer can establish more than de minimis financial costs through economic loss or an increase in wage expenditure. *Brener v. Diagnostic Ctr. Hosp.*, 671 F.2d 141, 146 (5th Cir. 1982); *Favero*, 939 F. Supp. at 1288.
> - An employer can demonstrate more than de minimis costs without quantifying the hardship in economic terms but by showing that providing a "reasonable" accommodation could "require coworkers to unfairly perform extra work" or decrease company efficiency. *Tagore v. United States*, 735 F.3d 324, 330 (5th Cir. 2013); *Brener*, 671 F.2d at 146.

You may think after reading this rule and subrule, "That's all well and good, but give me an example. Give me an example of a case where the court held conduct met that standard or an example of a case where the court held conduct did not meet that standard."

In response to this need for more precision in your explanation of the rule, you may decide to illustrate a case to establish what sort of evidence or conduct in precedent (past) cases has been held to be sufficient to establish the "undue hardship" required to avoid Title VII liability. After all, this is the role of case illustrations—they provide the reader with examples of the rule being applied to a factual scenario and the result of that application.

In some instances, however, one case illustration alone may still not be "enough" for your reader to understand the **R**ule. This happens most often when the rule requires the assessment of the parameters of behavior. In such a scenario, you may decide to use two case illustrations to show the reader an example of the type of evidence that has been held to satisfy and not satisfy the rule (that is, to establish "parameters of behavior"). For example, for "undue hardship" you may decide to illustrate two cases: one on each end of the spectrum, i.e., one where the court held that the consequences a company would experience by offering an employee a reasonable accommodation would rise to the level of undue hardship (establishing the second affirmative defense) and one where the court held that the consequences a company would experience by offering an employee a reasonable accommodation did not rise to the level of undue hardship (not establishing the second affirmative defense).

By having a case illustration from each end of the spectrum (standard met vs. standard not met), later in your **A**nalysis (CR**A**C), you will be able to compare and contrast your client's facts to the facts of the illustrated cases to objectively predict where your client's facts fall on the spectrum, that is where your client's case falls in relation to the two illustrated cases. Using two case illustrations—where such caselaw is available—is especially important in objective writing. As an added benefit, by using two case illustrations, your Analysis will more naturally address and dispose of counter arguments.

As a matter of qualification, now that you understand how helpful case illustrations can be, it is important to note that case illustrations are not always needed. Sometimes, the rule and subrules are so straightforward that no one would ask, "Can you give me an example of that?" In these situations, a case illustration is not necessary.

For example, let's say the issue is who can recover damages under the bystander doctrine. Below is the general rule (first sentence) and subrule (second sentence) you would find for the third element of the bystander doctrine.

> Under the third element of the bystander doctrine, the bystander must show that they are "closely related" to the victim of the accident in order to recover damages. *Freeman v. City of Pasadena*, 744 S.W.2d 923, 924 (Tex. 1988). A bystander is "closely related" if the bystander is one of the "parents, siblings, children, [or] grandparents of the victim." *Garcia v. San Antonio Housing Auth.*, 859 S.W.2d 78, 81 (Tex. App.—San Antonio 1993, no writ).

Do you need a case illustration to help you determine if the bystander-mother is "closely related" to the victim such that she can recover damages? No, it is straightforward! You do not need an example to explain the rule. When this is the situation, <u>R</u>ule = general rule + subrules. In other words, when this is the situation, your <u>R</u>ule will only have two, instead of three, parts.

Having provided this qualification, it is worth repeating that, generally, in objective writing your <u>R</u>ule will include a case illustration. In fact, generally, in objective writing you should use two case illustrations per issue or element—one that holds the element is satisfied and one that holds the opposite.

i. Parts of a case illustration

Each case illustration has four parts: (1) a topic sentence; (2) the holding of the case on the element or issue for which you are illustrating the case; (3) the trigger facts related to the element or issue for which you are illustrating the case; and (4) the court's reasoning or how the court applied the facts to the law to reach its holding. That is, case illustration = topic sentence + holding + trigger facts + reasoning. Case illustrations should be drafted in past tense,[9] and every sentence of your case illustration (except for potentially your topic sentence) should be followed by a citation to the illustrated case.

Let's work through *Tagore v. United States* to draft each of the four parts of a case illustration related to the second affirmative defense to Title VII liability.

Part one: Topic sentence stating the reason you are illustrating the case.

The first sentence of your case illustration is the topic sentence of the paragraph. This topic sentence highlights the importance of the illustrated case for the reader; that is, it states precisely what the illustrated case adds to the legal standard set forth in the general rule and subrules. Note that because a topic sentence endeavors to identify what the case adds to the legal standard, the topic sentence is never simply a reworded statement of either the general rule or a subrule.

---

9. Case illustrations are drafted in past tense because the cases you are illustrating were decided in the past (in other words, they are past examples of the law being applied to a past set of facts).

Many students find it easier to draft topic sentences after they back up and ask themselves the following questions: "Why am I illustrating this case" and "What principle do I want my reader to take away from this case illustration?" Many find it easier to leave a place holder for the topic sentence and to fill in the topic sentence after drafting the entire case illustration. Waiting to write your topic sentence is often easier because the topic sentence summarizes the key reason you included the case in your Rule and, often, you might not understand what that key reason is until you have pieced together the whole case illustration. Below is an example topic sentence from the objective memo.

> An accommodation that requires other employees to take on additional time-consuming, work or to do their assigned work in a way that lessens their effectively constitutes an undue burden

As you can see from the topic sentence this case is going to give the reader an example of how undue hardship can be met if the accomodation adversely affects co-employees.

Part two: The holding of the illustrated case on the issue for which you are illustrating it.

In the second sentence of your case illustration, you will state the court's holding with respect to the specific element at issue (as opposed to the holding of the court with respect to the entire cause of action).

Remember the holding sentence needs to communicate the court's decision on the elements or issue you are illustrating the case to show. The holding is not a rule. The holding is not a disposition.

> In *Tagore*, the Fifth Circuit held that the employer's failure to offer an employee her proposed accommodation did not violate Title VII, as a matter of law, because accommodating the employee could have imposed more-than de minimis costs on its employees and efficiency. *Tagore*, 735 F.3d at 330.

Part three: The trigger facts related to the issue for which you are illustrating the case.

After stating the specific holding of the case, next you will set forth the facts underlying the court's holding. These facts are called the trigger facts—they are the facts that were essential to the court's holding with respect to the element at issue.

Students sometimes struggle to decide which facts to include because they do not know which facts are "trigger facts." How do you determine which facts are "trigger facts?" The easiest way to identify trigger facts is by reviewing the general rule and sub-rules for the issue or element you are using the case to illustrate. Trigger facts are those facts that are relevant to—or triggered by—the rule you've set forth. In addition, you want to make sure you include "trigger facts" that are particularly similar to or distinct from the facts of your case.

> In that case, the employee's religious belief required her to wear a kirpan—an article resembling a knife—but a federal law prohibited possession of "dangerous weapon[s]" in the public office where she worked. *Id.* at 326–27. The employer denied the employee entry to her workplace when she wore the kirpan, refusing to offer the employee her proposed accommodation—wearing a dulled kirpan blade. *Id.* at 326.

Part four: The court's reasoning or how it got from the trigger facts to its holding on the issue for which you are illustrating the case.

Finally, after you state the trigger facts, you will set forth the court's reasoning. The court's reasoning consists of how/why the court reached its holding based on the trigger facts and legal standard before it. What was the court's reasoning in holding that the defendant's conduct you just described met the standard? The reasoning is what connects the trigger facts to the holding—it shows why the court reached the result it did.

> The Fifth Circuit, affirming the district court's grant of summary judgement, reasoned that the proposed accommodation would impose more-than de minimis employee cost because it would require the employer's security guards to ascertain whether the kirpan blade was sharp or dull—a dangerous weapon or not—each time the employee entered the building, which constituted extra "time-consuming" work. *Id.* at 330. The Fifth Circuit also recognized that such an inquiry would impose more-than de minimis efficiency costs on the employer because requiring security guards to determine whether the kirpan was a dangerous weapon every time the employee entered the building would be "impractical, and detrimental to the broad vigilance required at the entrance to public offices." *Id.* Accordingly, the employer avoided liability under Title VII, as a matter of law, by establishing that it was unable to reasonably accommodate the employee without undue hardship. *Id.*

As you advance in your legal writing career, you will see that there are other effective ways to illustrate cases. However, a strong case illustration will always in some order include a topic sentence, the holding, the trigger facts, and the court's reasoning. Therefore, as a legal writing beginner, employing the case illustration formula (set forth below) is a failsafe way to make sure your case illustrations are strong and complete.

ii. Formula for case illustrations

CASE ILLUSTRATION FORMULA

Topic Sentence	**+**	**In** [insert case name], **the court held** [insert conclusion for element or issue you are illustrating the case for]	**+**	**In that case,** [insert trigger facts from case related to element or issue you are illustrating the case for]	**+**	**The court reasoned that** [insert court's reasoning for issue or element you are illustrating the case for]

iii. Pulling it together

Turning back to Mr. Saint's case, the objective memo's **Rule** for the second affirmative defense to Title VII liability contains two case illustrations. These two illustrations not only provide the reader with examples of how courts have applied the legal standard in the past, but as discussed above, their polarity defines the parameters of the legal standard—in one illustration the court held that offering the employee a reasonable accommodation would cause the employer undue hardship, and, in the other, the court held there was insufficient evidence that offering the employee a reasonable accommodation would cause the employer undue hardship.

Undue Hardship

An accommodation that requires other employees to take on additional time-consuming, work or to do their assigned work in a way that lessens their efficiency constitutes an undue burden. In *Tagore*, the Fifth Circuit held that the employer's failure to offer an employee her proposed accommodation did not violate Title VII, as a matter of law, because accommodating the employee could have imposed more-than de minimis costs on its employees and efficiency. *Tagore*, 735 F.3d at 330. In that case, the employee's religious belief required her to wear a kirpan—an article resembling a knife—but a federal law prohibited possession of "dangerous weapon[s]" in the public office where she worked. *Id.* at 326–27. The employer denied the employee entry to her workplace when she wore the kirpan, refusing to offer the employee her proposed accommodation—wearing a dulled kirpan blade. *Id.* at 326. The Fifth Circuit, affirming the district court's grant of summary judgment, reasoned that the proposed accommodation would impose more-than de minimis employee cost because it would require the employer's security guards to ascertain whether the kirpan blade was sharp or dull—a dangerous weapon or not—each time the employee entered the building, which constituted extra "time-consuming" work. *Id.* at 330. The Fifth Circuit also recognized that such an inquiry would impose more-than de minimis efficiency costs on the employer because requiring security guards to determine whether the kirpan was a dangerous weapon every time the employee entered the building would be "impractical, and detrimental to the broad vigilance required at the entrance to public offices." *Id.* Accordingly, the employer avoided liability under Title VII, as a matter of law, by establishing that it was unable to reasonably accommodate the employee without undue hardship. *Id.*

No Undue Hardship

On the other hand, unsubstantiated assertions that any reasonable accommodation would impact other employees or impact the employer financially are insufficient to establish undue hardship. In *Ford v. City of Dallas, Texas*, the court held that an employer failed to meet its burden of proving that offering any reasonable accommodation would be unduly burdensome. No. 3:05-C-1676-D, 2007 WL 2051016, at *1 (N.D. Tex. July 12, 2007). In that case, the employee sued her employer for religious discrimination under Title VII for failing to accommodate her religious belief against working on the Sabbath. *Id.* The employer claimed that accommodating the employee would require it to create an entirely new position for the employee and hire additional employees—which it claimed were more-than de minimis costs—but failed to offer supporting evidence. *Id.* at *5. The court reasoned that the employer's unsubstantiated assertion failed to establish that all conceivable accommodations would have imposed more-than de minimis costs. *Id.* at *4–5. Accordingly, the employer did not avoid liability under Title VII, as a matter of law, because it failed to support its claimed inability to reasonably accommodate the employee without undue hardship. *Id.*

By having this complete picture of the law "in action" (an understanding of when a court has held the second affirmative defense is satisfied and when the court has held the second affirmative defense is not satisfied), the reader is best positioned to understand the parameters of the rule at issue. In addition, with this lay of the land, the reader is ready to understand the Analysis (CRAC) that will follow the Rule.

5. CRAC: drafting objective Analysis

The "A" of CRAC or the Analysis is arguably the most important part of CRAC because it is where the law meets your client's facts. After you have set forth the basic rule (the general rule) and explained that rule (subrules and case illustrations), you will apply the law to the facts of your case in the Analysis. That is, you take the Rule and apply it to the facts of your client's case to support your predicted outcome—the Conclusion—on the issue.

Remember in math class when your teacher told you that you must "show your work"? Your middle school math teacher made clear that it was not sufficient to simply say 712 ÷ 8 = 89. Instead, you had to show your teacher how you got from the problem to the answer. You did this by showing your teacher your long division in a step-by-step manner, rather than by just showing your teacher the answer.

```
       89
   ________
8 |   712
      -64
        7↓
       64
      -72
        0
```

Think of the Analysis section of your CRAC as the place in your legal analysis where you "show your work." In your Analysis, you are showing your reader your work for the following equation: Rule for the issue + client's facts for the issue = your Conclusion on the issue.

In the Analysis section, you should not add any new legal authority for the issue. Instead, all legal authority for the issue should be in your Rule. In the Analysis section, you should also not add any new facts. Instead, all facts for the issue should be in your statement of facts. When you think about it, as you write your Analysis, it is really just a mixing and matching of what is already in your Rule (legal authority for the issue) with what is already in your statement of facts (facts for the issue). If you have a well-written, complete Rule and a well-written, complete statement of facts, then the Analysis should be the easiest part of your memo to write. In a way, the Analysis writes itself!

In practice, however, students struggle with the Analysis. The main reason for this struggle ties back to a fear of redundancy. Law students mistakenly think that because they have already drafted the rule in the Rule section (and the reader has read it) and set forth the facts in the statement of facts (and the reader has read it) they can just tie them together with a conclusion or conclusory analysis—facts + Rule = Conclusion (voila!). This is wrong. You **must** show your reader how to take the facts and apply them to the law. The reader is not in your head. Thus, to show your reader how you got to your Conclusion, you must show them, step by step. Failing to do so leaves the reader to do the work and risks that the reader does not apply the right (or the most significant) facts to the Rule and, thus, does not, in the end, understand or agree with your predicted conclusion.

In order to show your work in your Analysis, make sure your Analysis section has two parts:

Part one: You will start your Analysis section of CRAC with a sentence predicting what happens when the Rule is applied to the facts.

Part two: Then, you will prove the prediction (part one) through either pure rule-based reasoning (if it is a straightforward application) or a combination of analogical reasoning and rule-language bridging (if it is not a straightforward application).

a. Part one of an objective Analysis

As described below, in your Analysis, you will use either rule-based reasoning or analogical reasoning with rule-language bridging. Regardless of which you use, you will start your Analysis in the same way. The first sentence of your Analysis will predict what happens when you compare the facts of your case to the Rule. This first part can be described as a topic sentence or mini-conclusion. Indeed, because it serves as a topic sentence/mini-conclusion, it is the only sentence in your Analysis that will likely not need a citation.[10]

(ex. 1) Here, a court will likely hold that Mr. Saint held a bona fide religious belief.

(ex. 2) Mr. Saint will likely satisfy the first element of his religious discrimination claim because, like the employee in *Davis*, and distinct from the employee in *Hansard*, Mr. Saint was consistent in his representations and actions surrounding his religious belief, which weighs in favor of a court finding Mr. Saint's belief to be sincere

Next, in part two, you will prove your prediction in part one.

10. Note that if you, for example, quote from a subrule in your part one sentence, you would then need a citation to that law. However, if your part one sentence is a topic sentence that merely summarizes part two below it, no citation is needed.

b. Part two of an objective Analysis

After you state your prediction as to what happens when you compare your facts to the Rule (part one), you will prove why that result occurs by using either (1) pure rule-based reasoning or (2) analogical reasoning and rule-language bridging.

A note about citations: in part two of your Analysis, you will be discussing both the law and the facts of your client's case. Therefore, after each sentence in part two of your Analysis, you will need a citation. Depending on the subject of the sentence, that citation may be to the law, the record, or both.

i. Pure rule-based reasoning analysis

Rule-based reasoning is used when the application of the rule to your facts is straightforward. You use rule-based reasoning in your Analysis when your Rule is so straightforward that you did not need an example (case illustration). That is, if you did not include a case illustration in your Rule, you will use pure rule-based reasoning in your Analysis because there will be no example case with which you can compare and/or contrast.

You conduct rule-based reasoning by tying language from the rule to your facts to predict an outcome. Let's use the bystander doctrine example from earlier to see how rule-based reasoning analysis works. First, let's review the Rule!

RULE

General Rule → Under the third element of the bystander doctrine, the bystander must show that they are "closely related" to the victim of the accident in order to recover damages. *Freeman v. City of Pasadena*, 744 S.W.2d 923, 924 (Tex. 1988). **Subrule** → A bystander is "closely related" if the bystander is one of the "parents, siblings, children, [or] grandparents of the victim." *Garcia v. San Antonio Housing Auth.*, 859 S.W.2d 78, 81 (Tex. App.—San Antonio 1993, no writ).

Let's say that the facts of your case were that the victim of an accident was Martha and the bystander who witnessed the accident was Paula, Martha's daughter. Your Analysis using rule-based reasoning might look like the example below.

ANALYSIS

Analysis Part 1 → Paula will satisfy the third element of the bystander doctrine. **Analysis Part 2** → Because Paula is Martha's daughter, she is "closely related" to the victim Martha and, as such, can recover damages. *Freeman*, 744 S.W.2d at 924; *Garcia*, 859 S.W.2d at 81; Mem. from A. Partner to File (Jan. 30, 2024).

You see that the Analysis using rule-based reasoning is straightforward. Here, the facts of our client's case are that Paula, the bystander, is the victim's, Martha's, daughter. Applying the law in the Rule (a bystander is closely related if they are a child of the victim) to the facts of this case (Paula, the bystander, is a child of the victim, Martha), is a straightforward application.

Here is another example using a statute. In many states, an establishment, like a bar or restaurant, that sells alcohol can be liable under the state's Dram Shop Act if the establishment's employees over-serve a patron and that patron's intoxication causes a plaintiff's injury. An affirmative defense to an establishment's liability is called the "safe harbor" provision. In Texas, for example, the Dram Shop Act provides that an employee's actions that violate the Dram Shop Act are not attributable to the employer-establishment if (1) the employer-establishment required its employees to attend a Texas Alcohol and Beverage Commission ("TABC") approved "seller training program"; (2) the employee actually attended the program; and (3) the employer did not directly or indirectly encourage the employee to violate the Dram Shop Act.[11]

The first two elements of the affirmative defense are straightforward. The employer-establishment either did or did not require employees to attend TABC-approved training, and the employees either did or did not attend. Thus, the Rule for each of these elements will be straightforward. There is nothing really to explain and, thus, a case illustration is not needed. Therefore, the application of the Rule to the facts in the Analysis will also be straightforward and will use rule-based reasoning.

Let's say that the evidence showed that the establishment, Chip-Home Bar & Grill, as a condition of employment, required its employees to attend TABC-training, and the evidence showed current training certifications for all employees. Below is what the Rule and Analysis (rule-based reasoning analysis) might look like for the first two elements.

The first element of the safe harbor provision is satisfied when the employer-establishment "requires its employees to attend a commission-approved training program." Tex. Alco. Bev. Code Ann. § 106.14(a)(1).	Rule
Here, Chip-Home satisfies the first element.	Analysis Part 1
Chip-Home's training manual contains a section that requires all employees to attend TABC-training as a condition of employment. Mem. from A. Partner to File (Nov. 30, 2023). Because Chip-Home "requires" TABC training attendance for all its employees, it can establish the first element of the safe harbor provision. *Id.*	Analysis Part 2
The second element of the safe harbor provision is satisfied when it is shown that "the employee has actually attended such a training program." Tex. Alco. Bev. Code Ann. § 106.14(a)(2).	Rule
Here, Chip-Home satisfies the second element.	Analysis Part 1
Chip-Home has evidence of training certificates that show all employees had attended TABC-training and had a current TABC certification. Mem. from A. Partner to File (Nov. 30,	Analysis Part 2

11. Tex. Alco. Bev. Code Ann. § 106.14(a).

2023). Because Chip-Home's employees "actually attended" the required TABC training, it could establish the second element of the safe harbor provision. *Id.*

You see that rule-based reasoning is a simple, straightforward application of the Rule to the facts of the client's case.

ii. Analogical reasoning + rule-language bridging

Most often, however, the rules and the application of your client's facts to them are not so straightforward. Therefore, pure rule-based reasoning is insufficient. Instead, you will need to use a combination of analogical reasoning and, what we will call, rule-language bridging.

When the Rule is not straightforward, in order to fully explain the law in the Rule, you must include case illustrations to provide the reader with examples of when the Rule was satisfied and was not satisfied. If you included case illustrations in your Rule, you will need to conduct analogical reasoning in your Analysis. Analogical reasoning means reasoning by analogy. You will use analogical reasoning to compare the facts of your case to the precedent cases that you have illustrated. You will show that your case is either like the precedent case such that your case requires the same result or that your case is unlike the precedent case such that your case requires a different result. When employing analogical reasoning, you should compare discrete facts from the case you illustrated to the corresponding discrete facts in your case. When you use analogical reasoning in your Analysis, you are conducting fact-to-fact comparisons to show your reader that the facts of your case are either like or unlike the facts of the precedent case.

Just because you included case illustrations in your Rule and are doing analogical reasoning in your Analysis to compare and contrast your facts to those cases, it does not mean that you get to simply ignore the general rules and subrules from your Rule in your Analysis. You will still apply the general rule and subrules to your facts; however, that application is less straightforward than pure rule-based reasoning. Instead, you will "bridge" the language from the rules and subrules to your facts in your Analysis. This rule-language bridging is used in combination with analogical reasoning to comprise your Analysis.

Let's first start with a non-legal example to understand how analogical reasoning works.

JAKE'S EXPERIENCE

Jake is a college student. He is taking English Literature 101 with Professor Plum. In Professor Plum's syllabus, he includes a provision that provides: "Late assignments will not be accepted unless there are extraordinary circumstances. Extraordinary circumstances include circumstances that were unforeseeable and that could not with proper planning have been avoided."

> Jake had a paper due on May 15 by 8 a.m. He was supposed to submit a hard copy of the paper to Professor Plum's office by that time. He left his apartment at 7 a.m. on May 15 to drive to the college, which was only 20 minutes away. On his way, Jake got a flat tire after hitting a nail. He stopped to change the tire as fast as he could and immediately went to the college. He did not arrive to the college until 8:30 a.m., and as a result, the paper he submitted was late.
>
> Jake is wondering whether his late paper will be accepted. He hires you to do some research and predict an outcome for him.

The first thing you do is look at the syllabus and find the written rule in the syllabus governing late submissions of assignments in Professor Plum's class. The "rule" states as follows: "Late assignments will not be accepted unless there are extraordinary circumstances. Extraordinary circumstances include circumstances that were unforeseeable and that could not with proper planning have been avoided."

From the rule language alone, can you predict whether Jake's late paper will be accepted? Not really. The rule is not very straightforward. What would be helpful, you think, are examples of when Professor Plum applied the rule either to accept or to reject submissions of other students. It would also be helpful, you think, to figure out for these past examples what the circumstances were that caused the student's paper to be late, what decision Professor Plum made with respect to the late paper, and what reasoning he applied to make his decision. That is, to further explain the rule, you need past examples of when the rule was met and was not met. You need case illustrations!

You walk around campus and find two students who had similar experiences regarding late assignments and Professor Plum.

SARA'S EXPERIENCE

> Sara tells you that she had a paper due for Professor Plum and submitted it 23 hours late. Sara tells you that she left her house at 7:30 a.m. to submit the paper by 8 a.m. because the college is only 15 minutes away from her house. While she was driving to the college to submit the paper, her car was hit by a student on a bicycle. While Sara was uninjured, the student on the bicycle was severely injured. Sara had to wait with him until the ambulance arrived and then rode in the ambulance with him to the hospital. When she got to the hospital, the (very scared) student asked Sara to stay with him until his parents arrived because he had no friends. His parents did not arrive until 10 p.m. When Sara left the hospital, the building housing Professor Plum's office was locked. She turned in the paper the next morning at 7 a.m. as soon as the building was open. Professor Plum accepted the paper because he said that (1) being hit in a car by a bicycle is not something that happens normally or could have been easily avoided and (2) Sara was not at fault.

> Professor Plum said it was important to his decision that Sara acted as a Good Samaritan by staying at the hospital with the injured student and that Sara was diligent in submitting the paper as soon as the building opened the next day.

> **MOLLY'S EXPERIENCE**

> Molly tells you that she had paper due for Professor Plum and left her house to submit it an hour before it was due (even though the college was only five minutes away). A police officer stopped Molly on her way to submit the paper. Molly said she had never in her life received a ticket and was only going four miles over the speed limit. The police officer eventually let Molly go with a warning. But the stop caused Molly to not arrive at the college to submit her paper until 8:05 a.m.—five minutes after it was due. Professor Plum did not accept the paper because he said that (1) it is foreseeable that one will get a ticket if driving too fast and (2) Molly was at fault and proper planning (in the form of not speeding) could have avoided the situation and resulting late paper.

These "case illustrations" give you more insight into the meaning of the rule and into when Professor Plum (the authority) has held the rule to have been satisfied and not satisfied. Now that you have a full explanation of the rule, you need to apply it to Jake's facts to predict an outcome.

To do so, you should use analogical reasoning to predict whether Jake's case is more like Sara's, where the late paper was accepted, or more like Molly's, where the late paper was rejected. That is, where does Jake fall on the Molly/Sara spectrum?

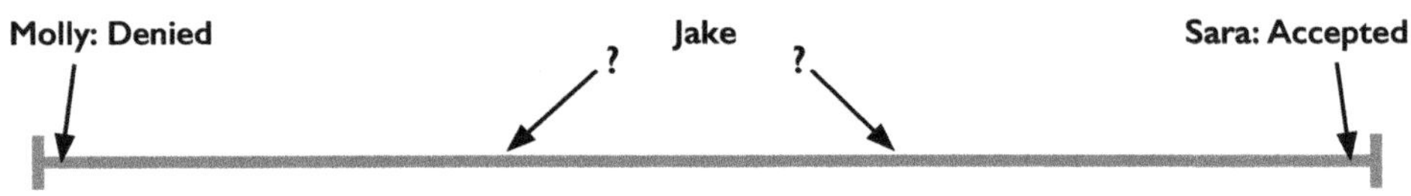

Analogical reasoning is an unnecessarily fancy word for comparing and contrasting. We must compare the facts of Jake's case to the facts of Molly's case and to the facts of Sara's case to predict whether Professor Plum will find that Jake's late submission was caused by extraordinary circumstances, like Sara's, or not, like Molly's. We must take similar facts from Jake's experience and put them side by side with similar facts from Sara's experience and Molly's experience to reach our prediction.

So, what's your prediction? Will Professor Plum likely accept Jake's late paper like he did Sara's late paper? Or, will Professor Plum likely reject Jake's late paper like he did Molly's late paper? Where did you put the facts of Jake's case on the Molly–Sara spectrum?

Let's say you predict that Professor Plum will accept the late assignment. While Jake's facts are not as strong as Sara's, you conclude Jake's facts are more like Sara's facts than Molly's facts.

Part one of your Analysis—the topic sentence—would be: "While Jake's case is not as strong as Sara's case, it is likely that Professor Plum will accept Jake's late assignment." Then, you would need to show your work in part two through analogical reasoning and rule-language bridging. Specifically, you need to tie Jake's facts to the "rule" in the syllabus and compare and contrast Jake's facts with Sara's and Molly's. You must show how you reached your prediction, why you reached your prediction, and what your thought process was.

Not showing your work. Similar to Sara's case, Jake's flat tire was unforeseeable. Unlike Molly's case and like Sara's case, Jake was not at fault for his flat tire. Like Sara, he could not have prevented his flat tire.

Showing your work. Like Sara, who was in a car accident that was not caused by her own fault, Jake had a flat tire, which Professor Plum will likely find is not caused by his own fault. Similar to being hit by a bike, running over a nail is not something that can be avoided. However, unlike being hit by a bicycle, it is far more common to get a flat tire. While getting a flat tire is likely more foreseeable than being hit by a bike, it is likely that Professor Plum will still find that getting a flat tire is unforeseeable because there is nothing Jake could have done to avoid it. Unlike Molly, whom Professor Plum found could have avoided getting pulled over by not speeding, Jake could not have avoided getting a flat tire. What makes Jake's case weaker than Sara's is that, unlike Sara, whom Professor Plum found acted like a Good Samaritan, Jake did not do anything to help another person. However, like Sara who submitted her late paper as soon as feasible, Jake submitted his late paper as soon as he could. Jake's paper, which was submitted 30 minutes late, was closer to being submitted on time than Sara's paper, which was submitted 23 hours late.

You see how the two examples differ. In the first example, you do not show your thought process. You do not show the reader step by step how you got to your prediction. It is much like not showing your work in math class. In the second example, you show the reader how and why you got to your prediction. You are comparing and contrasting fact to fact with the examples (precedents) and you are connecting your facts with the "rule" language through rule-language bridging (foreseeable, unforeseeable, could have avoided, etc.).

1. Analogical reasoning formula

ANALOGICAL REASONING BASED ANALYSIS FORMULA

Topic Sentence + Evidence Sentences + So what Sentence + Conclusion

Repeat as needed

If you are using analogical reasoning in your Analysis, you will have had one or more case illustrations in the Rule of your CRAC. You must compare and contrast the facts of your case to the precedent cases you illustrated. If you have cases on both ends of the spectrum—one where the element or issue is met and one where the element or issue is not met—you must show the reader where your case falls on the spectrum between the two precedent cases.

For example, in the objective memo, the writer illustrates two cases for the first element of Mr. Saint's prima facie religious discrimination claim in the Rule: *Davis*, where the court held the first element was satisfied, and *Hansard*, where the court held the first element was not satisfied. In the Analysis, you start with part one, which is your prediction as to whether a court will find the facts of your client's case more like *Davis* or more like *Hansard*.

Then you must prove part one through the analogical reasoning set forth in part two. To do analogical reasoning, you must do two things. First, you must take a trigger fact from your case and put it next to a similar trigger fact from a precedent case and compare or contrast the two facts. You should repeat this for each trigger fact or set of trigger facts. That is, you must do a fact-to-fact comparison and/or contrast with both your illustrated cases. Second, and as explained in more detail below, as you do your fact-to-fact comparison and/or contrast, you must tell the reader why that comparison or contrast matters. That is, you must bring it full circle for the reader. Why should the reader care that your facts are similar to or different from a precedent case? What does that mean? Why and how is that significant?

To help you engage in fact-to-fact comparisons and contrasts, you can use and repeat the following "formula" sentences.

> **To compare:** Like [precedent case], where [trigger fact from precedent case], here, [similar trigger fact from your case].
>
> **To contrast:** Unlike [precedent case], where [trigger fact from precedent case], here, [different trigger fact from your case].

By using this formula, it will force you to show your work and to use a parallel structure. Take a look at the example below from the objective memo for UI.

> Like *Davis*, where the employee once informed her employer that she could not work on a particular Sunday because she strongly believed she needed to be at church for an event, Mr. Saint repeatedly told UI that he could not use the biometric scanner because of his Evangelical Christian belief that Revelation 13:16–18 indicates that the "Mark of the Beast" is a "symbolic mark" and that "technology will be used to carry out its implementation." 765 F.3d at 483; Ex. 2; Ex. 5 at 2; Ex. 8; Ex. 13.

You will see that the sentence takes a discrete trigger fact from the illustrated case *Davis* in the Rule (employee previously asserted she could not work on Sunday because of her beliefs) and compares it to a similar discrete trigger fact from your client's case (Mr. Saint repeatedly told UI he could not scan because of his beliefs).

To do fact-to-fact comparisons and contrasts, you need not strictly adhere to the formula. It is okay to deviate from the exact words of the formula as long as you are comparing and contrasting between your case and the precedent case on a fact-to-fact level. In the example below from the objective memo for UI, while the rigid formula is not used, the writer is contrasting the facts of the client's case to those of one of the illustrated cases. The differences are explained side by side and are obvious to the reader.

After you do comparisons or contrasts, you must tell the reader why this matters. You see that the last sentence is where the reader is told why the contrast between the facts of your client's case and the case *Hansard* matters. That is, the last sentence brings full circle the purpose of the fact-to-fact analysis.

> Unlike *Hansard*, where the employee asserted on select occasions that he could not work Sundays due to his religious belief against working for profit on Sundays, Mr. Saint was steadfast in his communications to his employer that he could not use the biometric scanner because of his religious belief in the "Mark of the Beast." 1973 WL 129, at *1; Ex. 5 at 2; Ex. 8. Although the employee in *Hansard* claimed that his religious belief against working on Sundays was "lifelong," he admitted to not always following his represented belief. 1973 WL 129, at *2. Despite the employee's attempt to justify his inconsistency by explaining that his belief reemerged following a "miraculous" event, he admitted to still working some Sundays even after his belief's renewal. *Id.* Unlike these inconsistent actions that the *Hansard* employee displayed surrounding his represented belief, Mr. Saint's actions reflect consistency because he never once used the scanner, he requested continuous exemptions from UI's new scanning policy, and he ultimately resigned rather than succumbing to use of the scanner. Ex. 2; Ex. 4; Ex. 5 at 2; Ex. 8; Ex. 12 at 5:14–15; Ex. 13. Thus, unlike *Hansard*, Mr. Saint's belief could hardly be argued to be based on "convenience rather than conviction" because Mr. Saint's made clear his religious belief forbade him from using the scanning technology, which he consistently refused to use, even though it inconveniently cost him his job. *See Hansard*, 1973 WL 129, at *2.

2. Using rule-language bridging with analogical reasoning

In your Analysis, even though you are using analogical reasoning to compare your facts to the illustrated cases, it does not mean that you get to ignore rule-based reasoning. Rather, you should still be connecting your facts with the language of the general rule and subrules for the issue. However, because the application of the rule-language to your facts is not straightforward or sufficient in and of itself, the term we like to use for incorporating the rule language in this instance is rule-language bridging.

In part two of your Analysis, in addition to doing analogical reasoning, you should take "soundbites" or terms from the general rule and subrules and tie those soundbites to your facts and analysis of the issue. That is, you pull language from your general rule and subrules into your Analysis and incorporate such language throughout. In this way, you are making sure that your Analysis is using everything in your Rule—not just the case illustrations. Below is an example from the objective memo's Analysis for the second affirmative defense. Notice how both analogical reasoning (comparing facts to *Ford*) and rule-language bridging (taking language from a subrule from *Weber*) are used together.

> In addition, unlike in *Ford*, where the employer failed to prove that it had explored more than one accommodation, UI explored alternative accommodations when it e-mailed PalmVein asking for help resolving Mr. Saint's conflict and offered Mr. Saint the options to scan his right hand or left thumbprint instead of his retinas. Ex. 5; 2007 WL 2051015, at *5. Thus, unlike in *Ford*, UI did not establish that all conceivable accomodations would impose more than de minimus costs. *See Ford*, 2007 WL 2051015, at *5.
>
> Distinct Because UI can provide evidence of the "mere possibility" that it could have experienced undue hardship—precisely what was missing in *Ford*—if forced to offer Mr. Saint an accommodation not requiring use of the scanner, it will likely establish the second affirmative defense under Title VII. *See Weber*, 199 F.3d at 274.

G. The overall conclusion

The overall conclusion to your objective memo is where you tie together the conclusions reached in each of the parts of your discussion to state a more global conclusion. The overall conclusion of your memo restates the conclusion articulated in the brief answer(s) and then sets forth the central reason(s) for that core conclusion. The overall conclusion does not summarize your entire memo. On the other hand, the conclusion also does not simply set forth a single conclusion sentence for the claim or cause of action at issue. Instead, typically a paragraph in length, the overall conclusion reminds the reader of the brief answer(s) and briefly restates the reasons for that conclusion. Below is a sample conclusion from the objective memo drafted for UI.

> Mr. Saint can very likely establish a prima facie case of religious discrimination under Title VII because, he can probably show that he had a bona fide Evangelical Christian belief against using biometric scanners and the remaining elements of his prima facie claim are uncontested. However, because any permanent accommodation not involving the use of the scanner would impose undue hardship on UI, UI can likely avoid liability under Title VII by asserting that it could not "reasonably" accommodate Mr. Saint without undue hardship. Accordingly, Mr. Saint is unlikely to establish a Title VII religious discrimination claim against UI.

You will note that this conclusion restates the answer to the ultimate question—will Mr. Saint be successful holding UI liable for religious discrimination under Title VII—and then explains its answer in terms of the element and affirmative defenses analyzed in the discussion.

Chapter 8 | E-mail Memos

With the increasing pressure from clients to reduce legal costs and the increasing demand for instantaneous or real-time communication, lawyers often find themselves drafting abbreviated legal analysis in e-mail memos (often referred to as e-memos) rather than drafting more lengthy and formal memos. Typically, the exact format and depth of an e-mail memo will depend on the exact question or request to which the e-mail memo is responding. Generally, e-mail memos are substantively similar to formal objective memos; however, the formalities are often fewer, and the length is often abbreviated. Accordingly, in addition to understanding the intricacies of drafting formal objective memos, it is crucial to understand the art of drafting e-mail memos in the legal profession.

A. The realities of e-mail[1]

E-mail is the most common method of communication that lawyers use today.[2] Despite the frequency of its use, however, the reality is that e-mails are dangerous. Yes, that is right, using e-mail to communicate is as fraught with risk when used as part of your lawyering job as it is when it is used as part of your personal life. Why? In all honesty, there are

1. You should also apply the realities related to e-mail communication and the risks and dangers associated therewith to text-based communications with other lawyers, clients, or opposing counsel. In fact, communication by text is arguably riskier because there is little litigation related to the application of the attorney-client privilege and text messages.

2. *See* Kristen Konrad Robbins-Tiscione, *From Snail Mail to E-Mail: The Traditional Legal Memo in the Twenty-First Century*, 58 J. Legal Educ. 32, 32 (2008).

countless reasons that e-mailing is dangerous, but there are four reasons specifically worth mentioning here.

First, e-mail is effectively unerasable. Even though you may delete an e-mail from your computer, it still exists on the sender's device, and more poignantly, it likely remains in a technology "cloud" just waiting to be uncovered. Second, e-mail is discoverable. This means—setting aside issues of privilege—one side to a lawsuit can force the other side to hand over old, even seemingly erased, e-mails as part of litigation. Third, e-mail often lacks the context to properly determine the tone in which it should be read. This reality means that e-mails are subject to multiple interpretations and, thus, are subject to massive misinterpretation. Fourth, e-mail is forwardable to anyone and publicly postable with just a single click on any social media platform, including Instagram, SnapChat, and X. This means that e-mails are not private.

These realities do not mean we should not use e-mail to communicate. But these realities do mean that we should be mindful of the content, style, and tone we use when e-mailing. As lawyers, e-mails should not be off-the-cuff communications. Instead, lawyers, in particular, need to be diligent and careful about what they say when communicating by e-mail.

B. The parts of an e-mail memo

Given the realities of e-mail, you should err on the side of formality whenever communicating electronically. Part and parcel to this, you should be mindful to include the typical parts of an e-mail.

Subject line: Select a subject line that tells the reader what to expect in the e-mail and that is specific enough to differentiate it from the millions of other e-mails in the recipient's inbox.

Salutation: The salutation is the opening greeting of your e-mail. When selecting an appropriate salutation, pick a salutation that reflects the formality of the relationship you as the sender have with the recipient. Always err on the side of being too formal and always use a person's highest title when addressing the person. For example, if Samantha Smith is a judge and a professor, you should address her as Judge Smith because being a judge is a higher honor than being a professor. Generally, the following are acceptable salutations (which should be followed by a colon or comma at the outset of an e-mail): Dear Mr. Smith, Dear Ms. Smith, Dear Robert (used only if a close relationship), Dear Professor Smith, or Dear Director Smith.

As a general practice, try to determine the recipient's gender by doing outside research before you send him, her, or them an e-mail. If, even after research, you remain uncertain of a person's gender, you may use "Mx." as a gender-neutral way to address him, her, or them.

Similarly, you should avoid using Mrs. or Miss when addressing women. In many states and countries, it is offensive to use Miss or Mrs. because doing so defines a woman in terms of her marital status; in fact, the European Union has banned the use of both terms as sexist.

Last, despite the fact that you may associate the terms with respect, you should avoid using the terms Ma'am and Sir to address an e-mail recipient. Many people find these terms facially offensive. Others find the fact that the writer did not do the requisite research to determine his, her, or their actual name before sending an e-mail offensive.

First sentence: The first sentence of your e-mail should restate the question asked or the issue that you are addressing in your e-mail.

Body: The body of your e-mail should be brief but should answer the question asked in detail. The content of the body of an e-mail will vary depending on the type of question being addressed in the e-mail. For multi-paragraph e-mails, you should not forget to employ normal paragraphs with the first line indented just as you would in a formal letter. The body of an e-mail may present a good opportunity to use bullet points. Although bullet points are sometimes considered too informal for a letter, bullets or lists often allow an e-mail author to more clearly and succinctly cover multiple issues without the need for extensive transitions.

Closing sentence: The closing sentence of an e-mail, especially an e-mail from a junior lawyer to his supervisor, often takes the form of a sentence offering to answer any further questions and to do additional follow-up work.

Signature block: A signature block includes a closing that is appropriately formal followed by one's full name and contact information. Often students and other professionals include favorite quotations or shout-outs to their favorite sports' teams. Such add-ons to one's signature block should be omitted because they may be offensive, or they may create an unintended tone to the e-mail. A few universally accepted closings include "Best Regards," "Sincerely," or "Respectfully."

Privileged notation: Use the same confidentiality and privilege warnings on an e-mail that you would use on a paper document.

C. Practitioners' expectations of e-mail memos

As lawyers increasingly rely on e-mail memos to communicate research findings and legal analysis, it is important to understand what lawyers typically expect when they ask a junior lawyer to share the results of her work by e-mail. Lawyers agree that e-mail memos are best when they do the following:[3]

- Include an upfront answer to the question asked that includes the core reason for the answer.

3. Brad Desnoyer, *E-Memos 2.0: An Empirical Study of How Attorneys Write*, 25 J. Leg. Writing Inst. 213, 249–61 (2021).

- Include, where appropriate, applications of the law to the facts and a clear recommendation.
- Include explanatory parentheticals as part of the citations in lieu of lengthy case illustrations.
- Follow proper *Bluebook* citation form.
- Rely on citation signals when appropriate.
- Attach applicable authority.
- Are completed within 24–48 hours from when the request for work is received.

D. E-mail etiquette

Aside from being careful to draft your e-mail with the requisite parts as described above and being mindful of lawyer-specific e-mail memo expectations, there are a few general rules of e-mail etiquette that you should keep in mind whenever you draft (and ultimately send) an e-mail.

- Take the same care when you draft an e-mail that you would when drafting a written letter. What does this mean? It means use good grammar, be mindful of the tone of your e-mail, and print out your e-mail and proofread it before you hit send.
- Draft the e-mail "to" yourself rather than drafting it to the person to whom you are actually writing the e-mail. This method provides protection in case you accidently hit send before the e-mail is complete. In such an instance, it will simply send to you rather than sending an unfinished e-mail to a client, supervising lawyer, opposing counsel, or judge.
- Think before you write. Is the subject you are writing about appropriate for an e-mail communication, or would it be better to draft a formal letter, handle it by phone, or maybe even address it in person?
- Use the subject line. Make the subject line of the e-mail specific enough so that your audience knows what the e-mail addresses and so that you can find it later if you need to search for it in your e-mail outbox.
- Use the attachment function. Consider attaching documents that support your analysis in your e-mail, such as cases, statutes, or affidavits. In addition, name any attachments so that the reader knows what they are.
- Be mindful of length. Although the old "one screen" rule for an e-mail does not strictly apply anymore (especially now that most of us are accustomed to reading on screens of varying sizes), be aware that an e-mail is intended to be

succinct. If the communication you need to send is longer than a standard size computer screen, think about converting it to a word document and attaching it as a more formal communication to a summary e-mail.

- Use a professional "System" or "web-safe" font (that is, a font assumed to be on most user's devices), such as Times New Roman, Georgia, Ariel, Veranda or Tahoma. While you are at it, use a traditional font color, such as black or navy blue.

E. Sample e-mail memo

So, what do all of these parts of an e-mail look like when properly put together? In advance of asking you to write a formal objective memo, a partner from the law firm, Dominique Baker, calls you and requests a quick e-mail memo identifying the requirements for a Title VII religious discrimination claim. Ms. Baker explains that she needs the e-mail in advance of a meeting with the client, United Information, Inc., in two hours. Faced with this task, you do some preliminary research and turn up the *Davis v. Fort Bend County* case (located in the section of this book discussing how to read a case). After reading the case, you draft the following professional e-mail with all the necessary parts.

From: Loiya, Neu <NeuLoiya@lawfirm.com>
Sent: Thursday, July 25, 2024, 8:15:32 AM
To: Baker, Dominique <dbaker@lawfirm.com>
Subject: United Information, Inc. (Client 30408.123): Title VII Religious Discrimination

Dear Ms. Baker

The purpose of this e-mail is to identify the legal requirements for Mr. Saint to establish a Title VII religious discrimination claim in the Fifth Circuit against United Information, Inc. (UI).

The Fifth Circuit employs a burden-shifting framework to analyze Title VII religious discrimination claims. *Davis v. Fort Bend Cnty.*, 765 F.3d 480, 485 (5th Cir. 2014). Under this framework, an employee has the initial burden to establish a prima facie case of religious discrimination. A prima facie case of religious discrimination requires the employee to prove the following four elements:

1. he had a bona fide religious belief;
2. his belief conflicted with an employment requirement;

3. his employer was informed of his belief; and
4. he suffered an adverse employment action for failing to comply with the conflicting employment requirement. *Id.*

Once the employee has satisfied his burden, the burden shifts to the employer to demonstrate that it reasonably accommodated the employee or could not reasonably accommodate the employee without undue hardship. *Id.*

For your convenience, I have attached the *Davis* case to this e-mail and have highlighted the relevant language.

Please let me know if I can provide you with any additional help on this case or any future cases.

Best Regards,

Neu

Neu Loiya
Baker & Jones, LLP
106 S. Harwood, Suite 400
Dallas, Texas 75201
(214) 555–1234 (telephone)
(214) 555–6709 (facsimile)

PRIVILEGED AND CONFIDENTIAL: Communication Subject to the Attorney-Client Privilege and the Attorney-Work-Product Doctrine

Part 3 | **Persuasive Legal Writing**

Before reading this part of the book, you should skim through the Motion for Summary Judgment and Memorandum in Support Thereof and the Response in Opposition to the Motion for Summary Judgment in the Appendix.

When you were younger, you may have had a relative say something to the effect of, "You are so good at arguing! You should be a lawyer!" Generally, when people hear the term lawyer, their minds go to the lawyers in a courtroom in a television drama. These lawyers are glamorous. They stand before a judge and jury in an old-fashioned-looking courtroom that is necessarily filled with mahogany. These lawyers give lengthy speeches, arguing their client's position with furor and passion. They wave their arms. They pound their fists. And, with a carefully scored musical background, they persuade you—the audience—to feel something.

When you came to law school, you might have thought that right out of the gate you would be passionately arguing like the lawyers on television. We call this the "Law and Order" syndrome. Instead, in your doctrinal courses, you found yourself reading case after case after case. There was no arguing, but, instead, there was learning the law and learning about the way judges make decisions. In your legal writing course, you did not get to argue either at first. Instead, you started with objective writing, where you were told to not take a position but, instead, to provide a balanced analysis of the law.

This part of the book focuses on transitioning from objective writing to persuasive writing. "Hooray," you say. "I finally get to argue?" Yes and no. Lawyers do not simply argue: they persuade. In this part of the book, we will tackle persuasive writing, and you will learn how to make persuasive legal arguments. Moreover, by using the same problem as the one used in the objective writing part of this book, you will be able to see the difference between objective and persuasive writing.

When reading this part of the book, you will often need to turn back to the objective writing part of this book to refresh your memory on the foundational skills introduced when you learned how to write objective legal documents. This part of the book builds on the foundational skills introduced in the context of objective writing to transform your writing from objective to persuasive.

Chapter 9 | What Is Persuasive Writing?

The reason most legal writing programs start with objective writing and then move to persuasive writing is that you must understand the law before you can apply it persuasively. In other words, persuasive writing must start with an objective analysis of the law and an objective analysis of your client's case. You need to look at the law and facts objectively so that you can discern the strengths of your case, the obstacles you must overcome, and, therefore, your best plan of attack to "win."

While the tools you learned in objective writing will help you as you turn to persuasive writing, there are key differences between the two.

	OBJECTIVE WRITING	PERSUASIVE WRITING
GOAL	To provide a predictive/ informative analysis of how the law will be applied to a set of facts	To advocate for your client's position by persuasively arguing for a desired outcome
AUDIENCE	Supervising attorney or clients	Court (judge, judicial staff, judicial clerks)
DOCUMENT	Objective memo or e-mail	Motion or brief
FORMULA	CRAC (Conclusion, Rule, Analysis, Conclusion)	CRACC (Conclusion, Rule, Analysis, Counter-analysis, Conclusion)

These differences impact both the form and the tone of the writing a lawyer must do when engaging in persuasion. To better understand what is involved in persuasion, you need to understand the goal, audience, form, and formula underlying persuasive writing.

A. Goal of persuasive writing

In objective writing, your goal is to predict an outcome. You do not have a side. You do not have a position. You do not have a bias. Instead, you are charged with conducting an even-handed and balanced analysis of the law as applied to the facts. In objective writing, you do not advocate for a certain outcome but, instead, predict which outcome is most likely based on the legal authority. You must inform your audience.

In persuasive writing, your goal is very different. Your goal is to persuade your audience. You have a side. You have a position. You have a bias. You are charged with advocating for your client's position. You do this by framing the law in a way that best suits your client, framing your client's facts in the light most favorable to her, and persuasively applying the law to your client's facts to argue for a specific outcome. You must persuade your audience to agree with your position.

B. Audience in persuasive writing

In order to write persuasively, you must know your audience and, specifically, the needs of that audience. In persuasive writing, your audience is the court, which is comprised of the judge (or judges), the judicial staff, and the judicial clerks. What do courts need? A trial court's biggest "need" is sufficient information to make a decision that is in line with legal precedent because a trial court does not want to be overturned on appeal. Therefore, in order to meet this need, you must persuade the trial court judge that a decision in your client's favor is in line with legal precedent. Trial courts do not make law, but they apply the law. Moreover, in persuading a trial court, your focus needs to be on precedent. Argument of what the law "should be" or policy arguments will not be as persuasive to a trial court as arguments focused on what the law is.

On the other hand, if your audience is the highest court in your state (e.g., the Texas Supreme Court) or the Supreme Court of the United States, the needs of your audience are different. Because these are courts of discretionary review, oftentimes there is no legal precedent that governs the issue, and, instead, the court must effectively make the law. Thus, the highest courts need you, as an advocate for your client, to tell them what the law should be and why that law is in line with public policy. The needs of an intermediate appellate court fall in between the needs of a trial court and the needs of the highest court. Intermediate appellate courts must make decisions in line with the binding precedent of the state supreme court or the U.S. Supreme Court. However, intermediate appellate courts will also be persuaded by what the law should be and by policy arguments, unlike trial courts.

Importantly, regardless of which court you are before, it is crucial to remember that your audience is a judge—not a jury. Persuading a judge is very different than persuading a jury. While a jury might be persuaded by appeals to emotion, a judge expects a sound and logical legal argument. That is not to say judges are devoid of human emotion or that emotion has no place in persuading a judge, but any appeal to a judge's emotion should be subtle (normally through how you frame your client's facts) and secondary to an appeal to the judge's logic.

C. Types of persuasive writing

Persuasive writing can take many different forms. The form your persuasive writing will take depends on the procedural posture of your case, the tribunal you are before, and the issue(s) being addressed.

1. District court motions

In the district or trial level court, documents that contain legal arguments and ask the court to take action are called "motions." The party filing the motion (the party asking the court to take action) is called the movant. When the movant files a motion, the other side (the non-movant) will usually file a "response" or "opposition" to that motion, asking the court to deny the action or relief requested by the movant. Oftentimes, the moving party, after having been served with the non-movant's opposition, will get an opportunity to file a written response to the non-movant's opposition, which is called a "reply."

There are a variety of different motions that come up in a trial court, and the format of these motions depends on the trial court you are before and the type of motion you are filing. For example, some trial courts require you to file a "motion," which is usually one or two pages asking for the relief you want, and an accompanying "memorandum of law," which is where you make your legal arguments in detail. Other trial courts simply require you to file only a single document that is a "motion," which includes the requested relief and the legal arguments in support. Thus, before writing a motion, it is important to check the local rules of procedure.

Pre-trial motions are motions that are filed after the case is filed and before the start of the trial. Pre-trial motions range from generally non-controversial (e.g., a motion for an extension of time to file something) to controversial but not dispositive (e.g., a motion to transfer the case to a different venue or a motion to compel discovery) to dispositive (e.g., a motion to dismiss or a motion for summary judgment). Dispositive motions are arguably the most important pre-trial motions because they can result in the final resolution of a specific issue in the case (e.g., a single cause of action is dismissed) or the final resolution of the case in its entirety (e.g., all causes of action are dismissed).

In addition to pre-trial motions, there are motions that arise both during trial (trial motions) and after trial (post-trial motions). For example, during trial, after the plaintiff has presented its case in chief, a defendant may file a motion for directed verdict (or a motion for judgment as a matter of law) asking the court to enter judgment in favor of the defendant without allowing the case to go to the jury. Some common post-trial motions include motions for judgment notwithstanding verdict (asking the court to disregard the jury's verdict and enter a contrary one because no reasonable jury could have reached the verdict issued) or a motion for new trial (asking the court for a new trial because of significant error or insufficient evidence to support the jury's verdict).

2. *Appellate briefing*

If a party wants to challenge a decision of a trial court, it can file an appeal to an appellate court. The party filing the appeal is called the appellant, and the party on the other side responding to the appeal is called the appellee or respondent. In the typical intermediate court of appeals case, the appellant first files an opening brief setting out the issues to be resolved on appeal and the legal arguments in support. The appellee/respondent then files a brief responding to the appellant's opening brief. Then, the appellant has the opportunity to file a reply brief.

After the intermediate court of appeals decides the case on appeal, the losing party may choose to file a petition for review to the highest appellate court (either a state supreme court or SCOTUS) asking the highest appellate court to review the decision of the intermediate appellate court. Because the highest appellate courts are courts of discretionary review, the highest appellate court may or may not decide to review the intermediate appellate court's decision. If the highest appellate court decides to review the case, it will grant the petition for review. If review is granted, the petitioner (party asking for relief) will file an opening brief on the merits; the respondent (other party) will file a responding brief on the merits; and the petitioner will be given an opportunity to file a reply brief. As you can see, this process is much like the process of an intermediate appellate court.

D. Formula for persuasive writing

The good news is that the formula you will use for persuasive writing is almost identical to the CRAC formula that you used for objective writing. In persuasive writing, you will use the formula CRACC. The new "C" following the Analysis stands for Counter-analysis, which is discussed below. The other parts of CRAC (Conclusion, Rule, Analysis, Conclusion) remain, but you will learn how to make these parts persuasive rather than objective.

Chapter 10 | Motion Writing

This book focuses on trial court motions, as opposed to appellate briefs, to teach you persuasive writing. This is because, throughout your career as a lawyer, you are far more likely to write or respond to trial court motions than to write or respond to appellate briefs. While most lawyers will regularly write and respond to motions in trial courts, normally only a small percentage of lawyers who specialize in appellate law will regularly write appellate briefs. As an example, while federal courts handle more than 50,000 cases each year, only 10 percent of those decisions are appealed to the Supreme Court, yielding only 100 arguments a year before our highest federal court.[1]

A. What is a motion for summary judgment?

In this book, we use a motion for summary judgment as our vehicle to learn persuasive writing. Before we dive into motion writing, it is important that you understand the vehicle we are using as an example and how it comes into play in the life cycle of a civil case. We try to explain the concept of summary judgment as simply as possible given that this is not a book on civil procedure. However, it is important that you understand how summary judgment works so that you will be able to give context to and not be confused by the persuasive writing example we use in this book.

1. United States Courts, *Appellate Courts and Cases—Journalist's Guide*, https://www.uscourts.gov./statistics-reports/appellate-courts-and-cases-journalists-guide (last visited May 1, 2024).

A motion for summary judgment is a pre-trial motion that is filed in the vast majority of civil cases. To understand a motion for summary judgment, let's look at *Loesch-Simmons v. Wal-Mart Stores Texas, LLC.*[2]

The facts of the case are straightforward. While at Wal-Mart, Alicia Loesch-Simmons slipped and fell on water on the floor, which caused her serious injuries. Ms. Loesch-Simmons did not know the source of the water, and she could not determine if any Wal-Mart employee knew about the water before she fell.

What does Ms. Loesch-Simmons do next? She files a civil lawsuit. Ms. Loesch-Simmons (Plaintiff) sued Wal-Mart (Defendant) for negligence, gross negligence, and malice in federal district court in Houston, Texas. Below is a basic chart showing where summary judgment usually fits into a civil lawsuit.

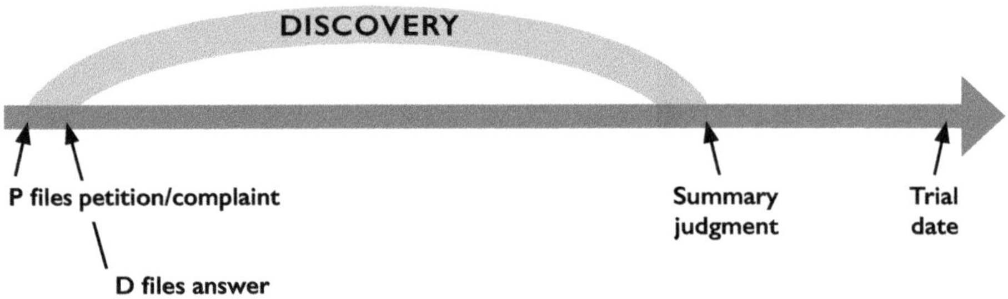

After a plaintiff files a lawsuit by filing a complaint with the causes of action, the defendant will file an answer denying the plaintiff's allegations. The parties will then conduct discovery. Discovery, simply put, is where the parties gather evidence and information related to the case. Motions for summary judgment are usually brought after discovery is well underway or even complete (although, technically, motions for summary judgment do not have to be brought after discovery) and before trial.

Summary judgment is a procedural device whereby a court can dismiss and eliminate unmeritorious claims or defenses. In federal cases, Federal Rule of Civil Procedure 56(a) provides the summary judgment standard: "The court shall grant summary judgment if the movant shows that there is no genuine dispute as to any material fact and the movant is entitled to judgment as a matter of law."

What does that standard mean? It means that the moving party, usually the defendant,[3] must show that the admissible evidence establishes that there is no genuine dispute of material fact as to the plaintiff's causes of action such that the defendant is en-

2. *Loesch-Simmons v. Wal-Mart Stores Tex., LLC*, No. CV H-17-777, 2018 WL 3105027, (S.D. Tex. June 25, 2018).

3. As you will learn in civil procedure, either the plaintiff or the defendant can move for summary judgment on either their own cause of action or defense on the other side's cause of action or defense. However, it is most common for a defendant to move for summary judgment on a plaintiff's cause of action. Therefore, we use that as an example here.

titled to judgment (the defendant wins) as a matter of law. Put another way, if the defendant conclusively disproves one or more elements of the plaintiff's causes of action, then summary judgment must be granted.

You can think of summary judgment as a screening device or filtering mechanism. If a plaintiff has brought a cause of action, and there is no genuine dispute of material fact with respect to that cause of action such that the defendant is entitled to judgment as a matter of law, then the plaintiff's cause of action does not deserve to go to trial. In fact, a trial would be a waste of time and resources because there are no fact issues, and, as such, there is nothing for a jury to decide. Granting summary judgment, however, is a big deal because it takes away a plaintiff's case (or a part of a plaintiff's case) and a plaintiff's right to have that case (or that part of her case) decided by a jury. Therefore, when deciding a motion for summary judgment, the court will exercise caution by putting the thumb on the scale in favor of the non-movant (plaintiff), in whose favor all doubts, evidence, and inferences will be made.

Back to Ms. Loesch-Simmons case. One of the claims Ms. Loesch-Simmons brought against Wal-Mart was for gross negligence. Wal-Mart moved for summary judgment on Ms. Loesch-Simmons' gross negligence claim. The elements required to prove gross negligence are: "(1) viewed objectively from the actor's standpoint, the act or omission ... involve[d] an extreme degree of risk, considering the probability and magnitude of the potential harm to others, and (2) the actor [had] actual, subjective awareness of the risk involved, but nevertheless proceed[ed] in conscious indifference to the rights, safety, or welfare of others."[4]

Let's get a few things straight as we work through this summary judgment example.

- **At trial, who has the burden to prove the elements of gross negligence?** The plaintiff, Ms. Loesch-Simmons, because it is her cause of action.
- **At trial, how many elements of the gross negligence claim must Ms. Loesch-Simmons prove to succeed?** All of them. If she cannot prove one, she will lose.
- **In Wal-Mart's motion for summary judgment, how many elements of Ms. Loesch-Simmons' gross negligence claim must Wal-Mart conclusively disprove to get its motion granted?** Just one. If Wal-Mart can show there is no genuine dispute of material fact with respect to at least one element of Ms. Loesch-Simmons' gross negligence claim, then summary judgment will be granted. This is because if Ms. Loesch-Simmons cannot prove one element, she cannot prove her cause of action, which has two elements.

4. *Loesh-Simmons*, 2018 WL 3105027, at *2 (quoting *Mobil Oil Corp. v. Ellender*, 968 S.W.2d 917, 921 (Tex. 1998)).

When Defendant Wal-Mart moved for summary judgment with respect to Ms. Loesch-Simmons' gross negligence claim, Wal-Mart argued that there was no genuine dispute of material fact with respect to the first element of "extreme risk" or the second element of knowledge. Remember, although Wal-Mart moved on both elements, it only needs to prove there is no genuine dispute of material fact with respect to one to win.

How do you think the court ruled? How would you rule? Looking at the evidence (even in the light most favorable to Ms. Loesch-Simmons), is there a fact issue with respect to whether water standing on the floor involves an "extreme risk" or that Defendant Wal-Mart knew of the risk? The court said "no" to both.

First, the court looked at a precedent case involving a 77-year-old customer who was injured at a store after tripping on a ridge at the base of a concrete ramp. The evidence in that case showed that three months prior to the accident the store, which averaged 50,000 patrons per month, only received a single report of someone tripping over the same ridge. The court reasoned that, although management knew about the ridge before the customer tripped, there was still no evidence that showed an extreme degree of risk.[5] Applying that precedent case to Ms. Loesch-Simmons, the court held that if a "known permanent hazard" like the concrete ridge did not qualify as an extreme risk, then water standing on the floor certainly did not.[6]

Second, the court held that there was no evidence of knowledge because Ms. Loesch-Simmons admitted she did not see anything before she fell, and she provided no evidence that any Wal-Mart employee saw anything.[7]

Therefore, Ms. Loesch-Simmons' claim was unmeritorious and did not deserve to go to trial because there would have been nothing for the jury to decide. Therefore, Wal-Mart sustained its burden to prove it was entitled to summary judgment.

As you can see, summary judgment is an important procedural device. It would have been a waste of resources to allow Ms. Loesch-Simmons' claim to proceed to trial. By granting summary judgment, the court dismissed Ms. Loesch-Simmons' gross negligence claim.

In the summary judgment context, a party moving for summary judgment (the movant) is always arguing that there is no dispute of material fact such that the movant is entitled to judgment as a matter of law. The party opposing the motion for summary judgment (the non-movant) is always arguing the opposite: there is, at a minimum, a genuine dispute of material fact such that the case deserves to move forward.

Refer to the sample motion for summary judgment and sample opposition in the Appendix of this book. Can you find the standard for summary judgment in both documents? How do they differ?

---

5. *Id.* (citing *Wal-Mart Stores, Inc. v. Alexander*, 868 S.W.2d 322, 326 (Tex. 1994)).

6. *Id.*

7. *Id.* at *3.

B. Overview of the formal parts of a motion

When filing a motion or opposition (for simplicity's sake, we use the term "motion" to refer to both), what is required will vary from jurisdiction to jurisdiction. However, as a general matter, a motion will include a notice of motion, memorandum of law, supporting evidence, and a proposed order. The heart of the motion is the memorandum of law because this is where the party includes its statement of facts as well as legal argument and supporting authorities. In the party's memorandum of law, will be the following sections:

- **Caption and Title:** The caption and title include general information about the case (court, document number, party names, and title of the document being filed) and are located at the top of the first page of the document.
- **Introduction:** The introduction is the first thing the court will read and is a summary of the arguments made in the document.
- **Statement of Facts:** The statement of facts provides the relevant facts that the court must know to decide the issue before it.
- **Legal Standard:** The governing legal standard provides an overview of the standard that governs the court's decision when deciding the motion. Depending on the type of motion, the standard will vary.
- **Argument and Authorities:** The argument and authorities section contains the meat of the argument (the CRACCs).
- **Conclusion:** The conclusion consists of one to two sentences restating the relief requested in the motion.
- **Signature Block:** The signature block contains the signature and contact information for the author of the motion or opposition.

These sections will be discussed in more detail below. While these sections can generally be found in any trial court motion, regardless of the specific type of motion, some jurisdictions require additional or different sections. Therefore, it is always wise to check the local rules of your jurisdiction to see if any additional or different sections are needed.

C. Caption and title

The caption appears on the top part of the first page of a motion. It identifies the court where the case is pending, the docket number, and the parties. The caption is the same on any trial court filing for a particular case, regardless of which party files it or what type of case document is filed. Under the caption is the title of the document in ALL CAPS, centered, and bolded. While the caption stays the same regardless of what type of document is being filed, the title changes depending on whom the document belongs to and what the document is addressing or seeking. Below is an example of a case caption and a title for filing that is a memorandum of law in support of a motion for summary judgment.

UNITED STATES DISTRICT COURT
NORTHERN DISTRICT OF TEXAS
DALLAS DIVISION

<table>
<tr><td>U.S. Equal Employment
Opportunity Commission,
Plaintiff

vs.

United Information, Inc.,
Defendant</td><td>§
§
§
§
§
§
§
§</td><td>

CIVIL ACTION NO. 4:2024-CV-00970</td></tr>
</table>

<u>DEFENDANT UNITED INFORMATION, INC.'S MEMORANDUM OF LAW IN SUPPORT OF ITS MOTION FOR SUMMARY JUDGMENT</u>

Defendant United Information, Inc. (UI) moves for summary judgment pursuant to Federal Rule of Civil Procedure 56 as to Plaintiff's Title VII claim for religious discrimination.

D. Introduction

Following the caption and title is the introduction. The introduction is the first part of your motion that the court will read. Given this, the introduction is your first opportunity to persuade the court. Because your introduction is your first impression to the court on the issue, it is incredibly important.

An introduction should give the court a preview or summary of your argument. After reading the introduction, the judge should know the main points of your argument and the relief you are requesting. You should think of the introduction like this: if a judge were to have only two minutes to read your motion, you would have her read the introduction because it would contain the overall relief you request and the key reasons for granting or denying that relief. Put another way, the introduction is the "CliffsNotes" version of your motion or opposition.

1. Why you should write the introduction last

Your introduction is a preview or summary of the content of your argument (which is contained in the argument and authorities section of your motion or opposition). Even though the introduction is the first thing the court reads, we recommend that you write it last for a couple of reasons. First, it is much easier to write a summary of your argument after you have written the full content of your argument. Indeed, if you wait to write your introduction until after the content of your argument is finalized, you will often save time by cutting and pasting portions of your argument into your introduction. Second, if you write your introduction before finalizing the content of your argument, and the content of your argument changes, you will then have to go back and edit your introduction. Save time and write your introduction last.

2. *How to organize your introduction*

There is not one way to organize an introduction, and approaches to introductions vary greatly among lawyers. However, a theme of this book is simplicity. Rather than showing you dozens of sample introductions done every which way, we will provide you with an organizational structure that works and can be applied to write an introduction for any motion or opposition. As you progress through law school and into practice, you may adjust this approach to fit your particular style.

FORMULA FOR AN INTRODUCTION

First, persuasively state the overall conclusion you want the court to reach.

Second, persuasively state the overarching rule for the issue.

[If the non-movant, dispose of any issues the movant does not address in its motion].

Third, incorporating the legal standard, preview your arguments regarding the issue in the order that they will be discussed. This "preview" should include an application of the law to the facts.

[Repeat steps two and three for additional issues].

Fourth, persuasively restate the overall conclusion you want the court to reach.

EXAMPLE INTRODUCTION

This Court should grant summary judgment as to Plaintiff U.S. Equal Employment Opportunity Commission's Title VII claim for religious discrimination. ← **Part 1** Title VII prohibits an employer from discriminating against an employee on the basis of his religion. 42 U.S.C. §§ 2000e(j), 2000e–2(a)(1). ← **Part 2** To establish a prima facie case of religious discrimination, Plaintiff has the burden to prove four elements: (1) employee Abraham Saint "held a bona fide religious belief"; (2) the "belief conflicted with a requirement of [his] employment"; (3) the "employer was informed" of the belief; and (4) Mr. Saint "suffered an adverse employment action for failing to comply with the conflicting employment requirement." *Davis v. Fort Bend Cnty.*, 765 F.3d 480, 485 (5th Cir. 2014). ← **Part 3** First, UI proves Plaintiff cannot establish a prima facie case because there is no genuine issue of material fact as to the first essential element. The summary judgment evidence proves that Mr. Saint's professed evangelical Christian belief in the "Mark of the Beast" arose more than five years after departing his church and after an open and public disavowal of religion on Facebook. This Court should grant summary judgment because Mr. Saint's belief was grounded in convenience rather than conviction such that Plaintiff cannot prove the essential element of a "bona fide religious belief."

Repeat Part 2 and 3 →

Second, even if this Court were to hold that summary judgment is not warranted because Plaintiff can establish a genuine issue of material fact regarding its prima facie case of Title VII religious discrimination, this Court should still grant summary judgment because UI can prove one of the following: (1) it "reasonably accommodated the employee"; or (2) "it was unable to reasonably accommodate the employee's needs without undue hardship." *Antoine v. First Student, Inc.*, 713 F.3d 824, 831 (5th Cir. 2013). First, UI proves that it reasonably accommodated Mr. Saint. Within hours of receiving notice of Mr. Saint's alleged religious conflict, UI began seeking a solution. Ten days after learning of Mr. Saint's religious belief, UI offered Mr. Saint the reasonable accommodation of scanning his left thumb instead of his retina—thereby avoiding the forehead and right hand referenced in Revelation 13:16–18. After UI offered Mr. Saint this reasonable accommodation, Mr. Saint did not object in any way that UI's offered accommodation would violate his religious beliefs. Despite UI's attempts to find a reasonable solution with Mr. Saint, he failed to communicate or cooperate and, instead, resigned without notice. UI's accommodation was reasonable, and, therefore, this Court should grant summary judgment.

Last, in the alternative, UI shows that Mr. Saint's specific accommodation request—continuing to clock in and out directly with his supervisor—would cause UI undue hardship. It is undisputed that Mr. Saint's accommodation request would put at risk the more than $4,000 in savings UI associated with the implementation of the scanning system and require UI to reallocate other employees and resources to accommodate Mr. Saint. Accordingly, this Court should also grant summary judgment because Mr. Saint's requested accommodation would cause undue hardship.

Part 4 → (points to the final line above)

As you see in the motion's example introduction, first Defendant UI begins the introduction by persuasively stating the overall conclusion it wants the court to reach (to deny the motion for summary judgment). Second, UI persuasively states the overarching rule for the issue (the four elements of a prima facie case for religious discrimination). Third, incorporating the legal standard (the summary judgment standard), UI previews its argument on the first issue (that Mr. Saint's belief was not bona fide) by bringing in both key facts and law on the issue. Because there is more than one issue, UI repeats steps two and three for the issues of reasonable accommodation and undue hardship. Finally, UI ends the introduction by persuasively restating the overall conclusion it wants the court to reach (to deny the motion for summary judgment).

If you look at the example introduction to the opposition to the motion for summary judgment in the Appendix, the non-movant's introduction looks similar to the movant's introduction. The main difference is that after the non-movant states the overarching rule for the issue, the non-movant disposes of any issues the movant did not address in its motion. In the book's problem, UI does move for summary judgment on elements two, three, or four of the prima facie case of religious discrimination. Therefore, Plaintiff EEOC points this out in the introduction: "Defendant does not dispute and, therefore, concedes fact issues as to the second, third, and fourth elements of the EEOC's prima facie case." Why would the non-movant do this? The non-movant wants to narrow the issues for the court and highlight the fact that the movant is not disputing three of the four elements of the prima facie case at the summary judgment stage of the case.

As your legal writing skills progress, the introduction section of a motion is often a great place to set out a memorable theme for the motion or case, weave in policy arguments, incorporate some storytelling, and experiment with more persuasive writing techniques. In other words, the introduction—which is often the court's entry spot into your client's argument—is a great place to add a reasonable amount of flair to your legal writing. A word to the wise: note that you want to add a **reasonable** amount of flair in your introduction, not convert your introduction into a passage from a suspense novel or an opening statement issued by a T.V. lawyer in a jury trial.

There are many examples of introductions that provide the reader with the content they need to understand the legal arguments to come while also drawing in the audience. Take a look at the following excerpt from the introduction section of the Petition for Writ of Certiorari in *California v. Texas* (the Affordable Care Act case) (citations omitted for brevity and ease of reading).[8]

---

8. Pet. for Writ of Cert., *California v. Texas*, No. 19-840, 2020 WL 58603 (U.S. Jan. 3, 2020).

EXAMPLE INTRODUCTION

> The Patient Protection and Affordable Care Act (ACA) affects the health and well-being of every American and has transformed our Nation's healthcare system. One of its hundreds of provisions is 26 U.S.C. §5000A. As originally enacted, that provision required most Americans either to maintain a minimum level of healthcare coverage or to pay a specified amount to the Internal Revenue Service. This Court upheld that provision as an exercise of Congress's taxing power, affording individuals a "lawful choice" between buying insurance or paying the tax. In 2017, Congress amended Section 5000A to set at zero the amount of the tax imposed on those who choose not to maintain healthcare coverage—thus rendering the minimum coverage provision effectively unenforceable. At the same time, Congress left every other provision of the ACA in place....
>
> The decision below is both ripe for review and incorrect on every point. As the dissent explains, after the 2017 amendment to the ACA, Section 5000A "does nothing more than require individuals to pay zero dollars to the IRS if they do not purchase health insurance, which is to say it does nothing at all." The individual plaintiffs lack "standing to challenge a law that does nothing" and the state plaintiffs have failed to substantiate their alleged fiscal injuries. In any event, there is no constitutional problem. As amended, Section 5000A is merely a precatory provision that (at most) encourages Americans to buy health insurance but does not compel anyone to do anything. Finally, any question of severability in this case requires no extended analysis. Severability turns on the intent of Congress, and here "Congress removed the coverage requirement's only enforcement mechanism but left the rest of the Affordable Care Act in place." It "is difficult to imagine a plainer indication that Congress considered the coverage requirement entirely dispensable and, hence, severable." There is no need for any "searching inquiry" into hundreds of distinct provisions, and no reason for this Court to defer review given the enormous practical significance of this case.

This introduction nicely illustrates a few effective techniques you might want to consider employing in your introduction. First, the introduction includes a few short and simple sentences that stand out in contrast to the longer ones and draw the reader's attention in: for example, "[t]he decision below is both ripe for review and incorrect on every point." Second, the introduction is short relative to the Petition itself and avoids restating every argument covered by the pages that follow. Last, the introduction is undeniably clear. Even though issues that end up before the Supreme Court are necessarily complex, this introduction distills the arguments down in a way that any reader—even one not familiar with the issue at hand—can navigate.

E. Statement of facts

After your introduction, you will include a statement of facts. Much like your statement of facts in objective writing, your persuasive statement of facts should also include the legally relevant facts that go to the issue or issues before the court. However, in persuasive writing, you are not just telling a story—you are telling a story from a point of view. Do not underestimate the power and importance of a statement of facts in persuasive writing. As Justice Louis Brandeis said: "Let me write the statement of facts, and I care not who writes the law."[9]

1. How a persuasive statement of facts differs from an objective one

In objective writing, your statement of facts objectively sets forth both sides of whatever story you are telling. You do not have a point of view; instead, your goal is to tell a neutral, complete story. You include trigger facts (along with some background facts and potentially a few emotional facts), but as an objective writer, you are not trying to frame the facts in a way that makes the reader feel one way or another.

It is well known that there are two sides to every story. In persuasive writing, you want the court to agree with your client's side of the story. Therefore, the way you frame your statement of facts will be in the way that is most favorable to your client. You will not mislead the court, omit facts, or make up facts to tell your client's story, but, instead, you will frame the facts in a way that emphasizes the facts that are "good" for your client and de-emphasizes the facts that are "bad."

Let's say that the facts are as follows: Plaintiff, Mary Miller, 83, was walking home from church when an unleashed Rottweiler rescued and owned by Defendant, Michael John, ran up to Ms. Miller and bit her leg. This bite caused Ms. Miller's leg to bleed. Ms. Miller immediately went to an urgent care center, where she was given 25 stitches in her leg. At the time of the bite, Ms. Miller was on a small stretch of grass on Mr. John's property that sits between the sidewalk and the street.

Ms. Miller plans to bring a cause of action under California Civil Code Section 3342, which provides, "The owner of any dog is liable for the damages suffered by any person who is bitten by the dog while in a public place or lawfully in a private place, including the property of the owner of the dog, regardless of the former viciousness of the dog or the owner's knowledge of such viciousness."

The statute can be broken down into three elements: (1) the owner's dog bit the plaintiff; (2) the plaintiff was injured; and (3) the bite occurred while in a public place

9. Michael R. Fontham & Michael Vitiello, Persuasive Written and Oral Advocacy in the Trial and Appellate Courts 37 (Wolters Kluwer Law & Business 2012).

or lawfully in a private place. Therefore, the trigger or legally significant facts are the facts that go to each element.

Compare how the facts may be stated objectively, as opposed to persuasively for each side.

OBJECTIVELY

While Plaintiff was walking home, Defendant's dog bit and injured Plaintiff. The injury occurred on a small stretch of grass on Defendant's property that sits between the sidewalk and the street.

PERSUASIVELY FOR PLAINTIFF

Ms. Miller, who is 83, was walking home from church on the public sidewalk. While resting on a patch of grass between the public sidewalk and the public street in front of Defendant's home, Defendant's Rottweiler—who was not on a leash—attacked her. The Rottweiler's teeth sank into Ms. Miller's leg, causing a three-inch gash. To stop the bleeding, Ms. Miller had to have 25 stitches sewn into her leg.

PERSUASIVELY FOR DEFENDANT

Plaintiff was bitten by Mr. John's rescue dog. At the time of the injury, Plaintiff was sitting on Mr. John's private property without permission.

Note how the same story is told differently for the plaintiff and for the defendant. The trigger facts are only those included in the objective version: (1) Defendant's dog bit Plaintiff; (2) Plaintiff was injured; and (3) the location of the injury. In the persuasive versions, each story includes these same trigger facts, but the story is different for each side. For starters, each side is personalizing himself/herself and de-personalizing the other side. Plaintiff refers to herself as Ms. Miller and refers to Defendant as generic "Defendant." Whereas, Defendant does the opposite. Notice how, if you are telling the story from Plaintiff's side, you are including background facts and emotional facts that paint a picture favorable to your client. Does it legally matter that Plaintiff was walking home from church or that she was 83 years old? No. Does it legally matter for the strict liability statute that the dog was a Rottweiler or that it was unleashed? No. However, these facts are favorable to Plaintiff and help tell her side of the story. If you represent Defendant, you would not include these facts, and omitting them would not be "dishonest" because they are not legally significant. Rather, the trigger fact is that a dog bit Plaintiff. No more. And, you will notice that Defendant points out that the dog was a rescue animal, which is an emotional fact favorable to Defendant.

Also, look at how, with respect to the bite, Plaintiff's side of the story is told actively and with strong verbs like "attacked" and "sank." On the other hand, Defendant's side of the story is told passively and generally. With respect to the injury, Defendant simply states that there was an injury, while Plaintiff goes into detail about the injury. Finally, with respect to the location, Plaintiff emphasizes that the place of injury was between two public places to set up Plaintiff's argument: that the location of the injury was public. In contrast, Defendant emphasizes that the location was on his private property.

In persuasive writing, it is your job to tell a truthful, complete story but to tell it in a way that is framed favorably for your client.

2. *Telling your client's "side of the story" through emphasis and de-emphasis*

In persuasive writing, your statement of facts must, like objective writing, include all legally significant or trigger facts. You must tell a complete story. Also, like objective writing, in persuasive writing, your statement of facts should not contain legal argument or legal conclusions. So, how do you make your statement of facts persuasive? First, let's talk about what not to do. Do not omit "bad" facts or fabricate "good" facts. This will not make your statement of facts persuasive. Instead, omitting bad facts (or making up good facts) is both counterproductive and destructive because the other side will include the omitted facts, which will bring to the court's attention your lack of candor and cause you to lose credibility with the court.

Rather, to make your statement of facts persuasive, you should present the same facts as the other side (the legally significant facts) but do so in a way that is most favorable to your client by emphasizing good facts and de-emphasizing bad facts.

Use the following seven tips to emphasize and de-emphasize:

Tip #1: Space. Spend more space/words on facts that you want to emphasize than on facts that you want to de-emphasize.

Consider the following example from the briefs in the case *Morse v. Frederick*,[10] which involved whether a school district had violated a student's First Amendment rights when the school district punished the student for displaying a banner reading "Bong Hits 4 Jesus" at an Olympic Torch Relay, which students attended as part of a school-sanctioned event.

EXCERPT FROM SCHOOL DISTRICT'S STATEMENT OF FACTS

Joseph Frederick, a Juneau-Douglas High School student, and several of his schoolmates positioned themselves on the sidewalk opposite the campus to await the torch relay. Pet. App. 25a. Before the torch arrived, Principal Deborah Morse approached this group to investigate the throwing of snowballs and beverage bottles that originated from their vicinity. J.A. 24, 41, 43. As the torchbearers and television camera crews approached, Frederick and his friends unfurled a large banner emblazoned with the phrase "BONG HiTS 4 JESUS." Pet. App. 25a. Frederick's banner—which measured (by his estimation) 14 feet long—was clearly visible to the large

10. *Morse v. Frederick*, 551 U.S. 393 (2007).

number of students assembled on campus. J.A. 24; Pet. App. 70a; Opp'n to Pet. at 1 n.1.[11]

EXCERPT FROM STUDENT'S STATEMENT OF FACTS

Frederick, an eighteen-year-old resident of Juneau, Alaska, stood among a crowd of students and adults on a public sidewalk in front of private homes and awaited the arrival of the Olympic Torch Relay. J.A. 9–10, 15–16. When the Olympic torch neared, he and several others held up a banner that read "Bong Hits 4 Jesus" in the hopes of attracting the attention of television crews covering the event. J.A. 27–28, 67.[12]

Notice how the school district is giving more space to the details about the displaying of the banner (a good fact for the school district), whereas the student is giving it less space.

Tip #2: Location. You can de-emphasize bad facts by "hiding" them in an introductory clause.

For example, "Although Ms. Jones had a D.W.I. last year, since that time she has stopped drinking alcohol; attended Alcoholics Anonymous meetings twice a week; and started volunteering for Mothers Against Drunk Driving." The bad fact (D.W.I.) is de-emphasized by its location in the introductory clause, and the reader's focus is on the good facts (sobriety, meetings, and volunteering).

Tip #3: Passive Voice. While, generally speaking, you want your writing, including your statement of facts, to be written in active voice, passive voice can and should be used when it has the purpose of de-emphasizing the actor.

For example, if you represent the defendant in a criminal case for murder, which sounds better for your client?

Passive voice: The victim was shot.
Active voice: Defendant shot the victim.

Passive voice allows you to state the legally significant fact without emphasizing the actor.

11. Br. of Pet'r at 4, *Morse v. Frederick*, 551 U.S. 393 (2007) (No. 06-278), 2007 WL 118979, at *4.
12. Resp't Br. at 1, *Morse v. Frederick*, 551 U.S. 393 (2007) (No. 06-278), 2007 WL 579230, at *1.

Tip #4: Noun and Verb Choice. You can persuade in your statement of facts through your choice of words, specifically your choice of nouns and verbs.

In the earlier dog-bite example, notice how the Defendant dog owner used the generic noun "dog," while the Plaintiff used the specific noun "Rottweiler," and how the Defendant used the weak verb "was bitten," while Plaintiff used the strong, vivid verb "attacked." These word choices were made deliberately to tell the story in the light most favorable for each side.

Tip #5: Show. Don't Tell. Your statement of facts should be free from your "opinions" or your legal conclusions.

You should be telling a story that allows the reader to reach his or her own opinions and conclusions—one that is favorable for your client. Consider the following in a statement of facts: "Mary's academic performance was poor." That sentence is really the writer's opinion. That is, the writer is essentially telling the reader to "trust me" that Mary's academic performance was "poor" (whatever that adjective "poor" means in the mind of the writer). Now consider the following in a statement of facts: "Mary's grade point average was a 1.5 out of 4.0." This is a fact, and from this fact, the reader will draw her own conclusion that Mary's academic performance was poor. The second example is showing the reader. The first example is only telling the reader. Do you see how the second example is more powerful? If you see an adjective or an adverb in your statement of facts, it should be a red flag causing you to pause and ask yourself whether you need to revise the sentence to show, not to tell.

Just as you should not include opinions in your statement of facts, you should also not include legal conclusions or argument. In your statement of facts, it would be improper to say, "The doctor committed malpractice by leaving a sponge in Plaintiff's stomach during the operation." The first part of the sentence is a legal conclusion and argument. While this sentence would be fine in your argument and authorities section, it is improper in your statement of facts. Instead, in your statement of facts, you would simply say, "The doctor left a sponge in Plaintiff's stomach during the operation." From this, the reader would draw her own conclusion that the doctor committed malpractice.

Tip #6: "Good" Absent Facts Should Be Included. Depending on the facts of your case, it might be that the absence of a fact or facts is, in and of itself, a good fact for your client.

You should include absent facts in your statement of facts. For example, let's say you represent the plaintiff in a defamation cause of action, and you are trying to prove that the defendant acted with negligence in publishing a false, defamatory story. To show this negligence, you might include absent facts or facts showing what the defendant did

not do. For example, "Defendant did not reach out to Plaintiff for comment. Defendant did not run a fact check on the story. Defendant did not check the background of his one anonymous source." Things the defendant failed to do—absent facts—can be "good" facts for your client and should be included in your statement of facts.

Tip #7: Soundbites Can Be Powerful. In persuasive writing, your factual record may include party or witness depositions, letters, sworn discovery responses, or other "quotable" documents. You can and should selectively quote from these documents if it will help you to persuasively tell your client's side of the story.

For example, Defendant's MSJ in the Appendix of this book selectively quotes the depositions to describe Mr. Saint's relationship with religion:

> While Mr. Saint grew up in St. Jaguar Community Church, his attendance at church "rapidly decreased" beginning in 2016. Ex. 6; Ex. 14, Saint Dep. 3:4–8. In 2017, Mr. Saint posted to his Facebook page that he was "[t]ired of praying to someone that doesn't change anything #overit." Ex. 7. In 2018, he posted to his Facebook page: "When you run into people from your old church and they ask why you have [sic] been in a while. Awkward." *Id.* He clarified in response to a comment on his 2018 post that he was not a "church guy" anymore. *Id.* While Mr. Saint claims to still be an evangelical Christian and a member of St. Jaguar Community Church, he "stopped attending church completely in 2018." Ex. 14, Saint Dep. 3:2–8.

You should see how these quotes help Defendant to persuasively present its side of the story: that Mr. Saint did not have a genuinely held religious belief. Note that it is okay to use adjectives in the statement of facts when they are part of a quote from the factual record because, in this context, the adjectives are not the writer's opinion but, instead, part of the facts of the case.

3. *How to organize your statement of facts*

Just like in objective writing, your statement of facts should, in the vast majority of cases, be organized chronologically. Chronological order is the easiest for the reader to follow; therefore, unless you have a reason to stray from chronological order, it should be your default organizational structure for your statement of facts. To organize your statement of facts chronologically, you should start by creating a timeline and then, using this timeline, pull in your legally significant facts (trigger facts).

Why might you stray from chronological order? Let's say that your facts deal with two different sets of parties. For example, let's say you have a case against a product manufacturer and a retailer of the product for an injury caused by the product. You might choose to group your facts as follows: (1) facts related to the injury, (2) facts related to the manufacturer, and (3) facts related to the retailer. Using strict chronological order might be confusing as there are really three different "timelines."

To keep your statement of facts organized, you should always use descriptive subheadings to keep your reader on track and to break up your facts. See how the statement of facts subheadings in Defendant's MSJ versus those in Plaintiff's MSJ Opposition tell two sides of the same story:

DEFENDANT'S MSJ

IV. STATEMENT OF FACTS

A. Mr. Saint ceased attending church or publicly associating with religion before he started working at UI.

B. UI implemented a new, uniform system for employees to clock in and out of work electronically .

C. Mr. Saint objected to new system based on his alleged religious be-lief that it would impose the "Mark of the Beast."

D. UI quickly offered Mr. Saint an accommodation.

E. Mr. Saint never responded to UI's offered accommodation.

PLAINTIFF'S MSJ OPPOSITION

> **IV. STATEMENT OF FACTS**
>
> A. Mr. Saint is a lifelong Evangelical Christian who believes technology will assign the "Mark of the Beast."
>
> B. Defendant implemented a new policy requiring employees to clock in and out of work using a biometric scanner.
>
> C. Mr. Saint promptly objected to using the biometric scanner based on his sincerely held religious belief that the scanner would impose the "Mark of the Beast."
>
> D. Mr. Saint proposed a reasonable accommodation of continuing to sign in and out with his supervisor—as he had done his entire tenure working for Defendant.
>
> E. Defendant ignored Mr. Saint's request to be exempt from using the scanner and instead claimed it would only accommodate him by forcing him to use the objectionable scanner on another body part.
>
> F. The accommodation Mr. Saint proposed had already been implemented for another employee—however, Defendant refused to offer it to Mr. Saint.

4. Citing to the record

Your statement of facts should include citations to the factual "record," i.e., the evidence of the case. In trial court motions, the factual record is usually attached to the motion or opposition as a number of exhibits. Just as when you cite to legal authority, your citations to the factual record in your statement of facts should be in Bluebook form and should include use of *id.* where proper. Refer to Bluebook Bluepages B17.1.1 and B17.2, and Bluepages Table 1 for how to formulate citations to the factual record.

Example deposition cite: Ex. 14, Saint Dep. 3:9–10.

F. Legal standard

After the statement of facts and before you get into the meat of your argument, you will include a section on the legal standard according to which the court will decide the specific type of motion before it. A legal standard is different than a rule. A legal standard is the lens through which a court reviews the issue based on the procedural posture of the case. It is not cause of action specific; rather, it is specific to the procedural posture of the case and the type of motion before the court. For example, whenever a trial court is deciding a motion for summary judgment, regardless of whether it is a motion for summary judgment regarding a negligence cause of action, defamation cause of action, premises liability cause of action, breach of contract cause of action, or so forth, it will use the same legal standard to decide the motion. That uniform legal standard for motions for summary judgment is as follows: a motion for summary judgment will be granted only when there is no genuine dispute of material fact, and the movant is entitled to judgment as a matter of law.

1. Where to find the legal standard

Legal standards for trial court motions are set forth in both the rules of procedure and caselaw. For example, the standard for summary judgment in federal court is set forth in Federal Rule of Civil Procedure 56: "The court shall grant summary judgment if the movant shows that there is no genuine dispute as to any material fact and the movant is entitled to judgment as a matter of law."[13] The standard is elaborated on by caselaw, which provides that "[o]n summary judgment the inferences to be drawn from the underlying facts ... must be viewed in the light most favorable to the party opposing the motion."[14] Whenever a federal trial court decides a motion for summary judgment, this legal standard or summary judgment "lens" is used. In contrast to a motion for summary judgment, when a motion to dismiss is filed, which is at a different procedural posture in the case, the court uses a different lens. The standard for a motion to dismiss filed in federal court is set forth in Federal Rule of Civil Procedure 12(b): a court shall grant a motion to dismiss if a plaintiff's complaint "fail[s] to state a claim upon which relief can be granted."[15] This standard is also elaborated on in caselaw, which provides a motion to dismiss for failure to state a claim will be granted only if "it appears beyond doubt that the plaintiff can prove no set of facts in support of his claim which would entitle him to relief."[16] Regardless of what type of claim the defendant moves to dismiss (negligence, breach of contract, etc.), the lens the court will use to decide the motion to dismiss is the same.

2. How to state the legal standard of review persuasively for your client

You should state the standard of review that governs your motion in a way that is favorable to your client. Both the motion and the opposition will include the same standard, but each will frame it differently. One side (the movant) wants the standard to be met, while the other side (the non-movant) does not. The standard itself will not

13. Fed. R. Civ. P. 56.
14. *United States v. Diebold, Inc.*, 369 U.S. 654, 655 (1962).
15. Fed. R. Civ. P. 12(b)(6).
16. *Gibson v. United States*, 781 F.2d 1334, 1337 (9th Cir. 1986), *cert. denied*, 479 U.S. 1054 (1987).

change, but how it is framed and explained will. After all, each side needs to state the standard in the way that is persuasive for her client.

SUMMARY JUDGMENT STANDARD FROM MSJ

> Summary judgment is proper when the evidence presented does not establish a genuine dispute of material fact, and the moving party is entitled to judgment as a matter of law. Fed. R. Civ. P. 56(c). To succeed on a motion for summary judgment, the moving party need not negate the elements of the nonmoving party's case; rather, summary judgment should "be granted so long as whatever is before the district court demonstrates that the standard for the entry of summary judgment, as set forth in Rule 56(c), is satisfied." *Lujan v. Nat'l Wildlife Fed'n*, 497 U.S. 871, 885 (1990) (citations omitted). To meet its initial burden, the moving party need only establish that there is no genuine dispute of material fact. *Duffy v. Leading Edge Prods., Inc.*, 44 F.3d 308, 312 (5th Cir. 1995) (citation omitted). The moving party "may do so by pointing out 'the absence of evidence supporting the nonmoving party's case.'" *Id.* Once the moving party meets its initial burden, the nonmoving party must come forward with admissible evidence establishing the existence of a genuine dispute of material fact. *Id.* A material fact is limited to those facts whose "resolution could affect the outcome of the action." *DIRECTV Inc. v. Robson*, 420 F.3d 532, 536 (5th Cir. 2005) (citations omitted). There is no genuine dispute of material fact "unless there is sufficient evidence favoring the nonmoving party for a jury to return a verdict for that party." *Anderson v. Liberty Lobby, Inc.*, 477 U.S. 242, 249 (1986). Evidence that is "merely colorable" or "not significantly probative" is insufficient to defeat summary judgment. *Id.*
>
> For a Title VII religious discrimination claim, there are two ways in which this Court could grant summary judgment. First, this Court should grant summary judgment because UI proves there is no genuine issue of material fact as to at least one of the four elements of Plaintiff's prima facie case. *See Tagore v. United States*, 735 F.3d 324, 329 (5th Cir. 2013). Second, even if UI fails to prove there is no genuine issue of material fact as to a least one of the four elements of Plaintiff's prima facie case, summary judgment is still warranted if UI can prove there is no genuine issue of material fact that either it "reasonably accommodated the employee, or that it was unable to reasonably accommodate the employee's needs without undue hardship." *Davis*, 765 F.3d at 487.

SUMMARY JUDGMENT STANDARD MSJ OPPOSITION

Under Federal Rule of Civil Procedure 56(a), summary judgment is not appropriate unless the movant meets its burden to prove that there is no genuine dispute as to any material fact and that it is entitled to judgment as a matter of law. Fed. R. Civ. P. 56(a); *Matsushita Elec. Indus. Co. v. Zenith Radio Corp.*, 475 U.S. 574, 587 (1986). Under the "stringent criteria for summary judgment," the movant has the burden of proof, and "a court can only enter a summary judgment if everything in the record pleadings, depositions, interrogatories, affidavits, etc. demonstrates that no genuine issue of material fact exists." *Keiser v. Coliseum Props., Inc.*, 614 F.2d 406, 411 (5th Cir. 1980). The movant must prove "beyond peradventure all of the essential elements of the claim or defense." *Bank One, Tex., N.A. v. Prudential Ins. Co. of Am.*, 878 F. Supp. 943, 962 (N.D. Tex. 1995) (citing *Fontenot v. Upjohn Co.*, 780 F.2d 1190, 1194 (5th Cir. 1986)). In reviewing the motion, "the court must view the facts in the light most favorable to the non-moving party" and "any doubt as to the existence of a genuine issue of material fact must be resolved against the moving party." *Coury v. Moss*, 529 F.3d 579, 584 (5th Cir. 2008); *Keiser*, 614 F.2d at 411. While the court must review all the evidence in deciding a motion for summary judgment, it is not permitted to make credibility determinations or weigh evidence because those tasks, "along with the drawing of legitimate inferences from the facts, are for the jury, not the court." *Reeves v. Sanderson Plumbing Prods., Inc.*, 530 U.S. 133, 135 (2000). Summary judgment is "a lethal weapon, and courts must be mindful of its aims and targets and beware of overkill in its use." *Brunswick Corp. v. Vineberg*, 370 F.2d 605, 612 (5th Cir. 1967).

This Court should deny summary judgment because Defendant fails to negate the EEOC's prima facie case for recovery under Title VII, and the EEOC proves there is, at a minimum, a fact issue as to the sole element Defendant challenges—whether Mr. Saint held a bona fide religious belief. Because Defendant cannot conclusively disprove EEOC's prima facie case, the burden shifts to Defendant to prove as a matter of law either a reasonable accommodation or that it was unable to reasonably accommodate Plaintiff without undue hardship. *Antoine*, 713 F.3d at 831. Defendant fails to meet its burden to prove either beyond peradventure and as a matter of law. Accordingly, this Court should deny summary judgment.

Both sides present and cite the same standard, but the movant states the standard positively and broadly because the movant wants the standard to be met (summary judgment *must be granted* when), whereas the non-movant states it negatively and narrowly because the non-movant does not want the standard to be met (a court *must deny* summary judgment unless). After stating the standard, each side explains it in a way that is favorable to her client. The explanations of the standard are both correct, but the movant explains the standard in a way that emphasizes the parts more favorable to the standard being met (framing the standard as less difficult to meet), whereas the non-movant explains the standard emphasizing parts favorable to the standard not being met (framing the standard as difficult to meet).

G. Argument and authorities

The meat of your legal argument will go in a section titled "Argument and Authorities" or "Argument," depending on the style in your jurisdiction. The argument and authorities section of a motion is like the discussion section of an objective memo, except it is persuasive. That is, it is an argument, not a neutral discussion. In persuasive writing, you should give some thought as to how you organize the issues in your argument and authorities section in order to maximize your persuasion. If you have multiple causes of action or defenses that you need to address, you should start with your strongest argument first. For example, let's say as the defendant you are moving for summary judgment on the plaintiff's cause of action and on your own affirmative defense. You "win" whether summary judgment is granted as to either. Therefore, you should start with whichever—the cause of action or the affirmative defense—you believe gives you the strongest chance of winning the motion.

Similarly, within a single cause of action or defense, in persuasive writing, you may choose to start with your "best" element, even if that element is typically set forth as the last element of the cause of action. For example, if a defendant is moving on a plaintiff's cause of action, the defendant will win if it meets its burden to show no genuine dispute of material fact with respect to only one of the elements of plaintiff's cause of action. While the defendant may choose to argue there is no genuine issue of material fact on all of the elements, it only needs to disprove one in order to win. Therefore, the defendant may choose to start with the element on which the court is mostly likely to find there is no genuine dispute of material fact and address the remaining elements in the order of their strength. However, if all of the elements are equally "strong," it probably makes sense to address them in the order in which they typically appear so the motion is the most logical.

When responding to a motion, you need not adopt the other side's organization. Rather, you can organize your arguments in the order of their strength. The exception to this rule is that it may make sense to simply follow the other side's organization as the non-movant where you must "win" on all issues and are not raising any new issues not covered by the movant's motion. For example, in a motion for summary judgment where the defendant has moved on all three elements of a plaintiff's three-element claim, to "win" the plaintiff must "win" on all three elements. That is, the plaintiff must show the court all three elements are equally strong such that the order of them does not matter and reordering the elements will simply make the opposition harder for the court to follow.

1. Overall roadmap

Just as in the discussion section of an objective memo, in the argument and authorities section of your motion you begin with an overall, introductory roadmap. Because, in your motion, you already have an introduction section that summarizes and previews the arguments in the body of your motion, the overall roadmap at the beginning of the argument and authorities section is a little more "bare bones" than the one in the discussion section of an objective memo.

The overall roadmap should state the overall conclusion you want the court to reach and then list the arguments you will make in the order that they will be discussed. If there is anything that will not be discussed, you should dispose of that issue in the roadmap. Additionally, if there are any favorable "subrules" that apply generally to all of the issues or elements addressed in your motion, you can include those in the overall roadmap as well.

DEFENDANT'S MSJ OVERALL ROADMAP

Notice how Defendant begins with the overall conclusion it wants the court to reach in the first sentence. Then, Defendant lists the arguments in the order they will be discussed.

> VII. ARGUMENT AND AUTHORITIES
>
> The Court should grant summary judgment on Plaintiff's religious discrimination claim. First, the undisputed evidence proves that Mr. Saint did not hold a "bona fide religious belief," one of the essential elements of its prima facie case. Second, even if Plaintiff can create a fact question on its prima facie case, the undisputed evidence proves that (1) UI offered a reasonable accommodation and/or (2) the accommodation Mr. Saint requested would have caused undue hardship.

PLAINTIFF'S MSJ OPPOSITION ROADMAP:

Notice how Plaintiff's roadmap looks similar to Defendant's roadmap. Because Plaintiff must "win" on all three issues, Plaintiff organizes its argument in the same order Defendant does.

> **VII. ARGUMENT AND AUTHORITIES**
>
> This Court should deny summary judgment as to the EEOC's Title VII claim for religious discrimination. First, there is, at a minimum, a genuine issue of material fact that Mr. Saint sincerely held a bona fide religious belief. Second, Defendant has failed to conclusively prove that it offered Mr. Saint a reasonable accommodation. Third, Defendant has failed to conclusively prove that accommodating Mr. Saint's religious belief would impose an undue hardship on Defendant.

2. *Mini-roadmaps under subheadings*

Just as in objective writing, any time you have a large section of your argument and authorities section that is subdivided into multiple small sections, you will insert a mini-roadmap between the larger section heading and the first subdivision heading. The mini-roadmap will simply list your arguments for that subdivided section. In the below argument and authorities example (text omitted), large sections A and B are subdivided into small sections so there is a mini-roadmap immediately under those headings. Section C is not subdivided and, therefore, does not need a mini-roadmap.

> **V. ARGUMENT AND AUTHORITIES**
>
> [*Overall Roadmap*]
>
> A. [Cause of action A]
>
> [*Mini-Roadmap*]
>
> 1. Element 1
> 2. Element 2
>
> B. [Cause of action B]
>
> [*Mini-Roadmap*]
>
> 1. Element 1
> 2. Element 2
> 3. Element 3
>
> C. [Cause of action C]

3. CRACC: persuasive writing

For persuasive writing, you will use the formula CRACC to present your legal arguments for each issue. CRACC stands for Conclusion, Rule, Analysis, Counter-analysis (new "C"), and Conclusion. Other than Counter-analysis, which is new, the other parts of CRAC are, in terms of other titles, the same in persuasive writing as in objective writing. However, in this section of the book, you will learn how to make those parts persuasive. In order to transform the parts of CRACC into a persuasive argument, you must have first mastered stating the parts of CRAC objectively. Therefore, it may be helpful to review the corresponding objective CRAC sections in Part Two of this book as you read through this part.

4. CRACC: creating persuasive opening and closing Conclusion sentences

Just as in objective writing, in persuasive writing, every issue in your motion or opposition will begin and end with a conclusion sentence (first and last "C" of CRACC)—a statement of the conclusion or desired result of your legal analysis of that issue. The purpose for these conclusions is slightly different in persuasive writing than in objective writing. Although persuasive conclusions—like objective conclusions—help the reader to better understand the significance of what she is about to read, persuasive conclusions also serve the purpose of advocating for a client's desired outcome. In other words, instead of concluding by telling the reader what you **think** the outcome may be, in persuasive writing you conclude to tell the reader (the court) what you **want** the outcome to be.

Conclusion sentences in your motion tell the court your desired outcome of the legal issue being addressed. Although there are two "C"s or Conclusions in CRACC (the opening conclusion sentence and closing conclusion sentence), you will actually have three forms of Conclusions for each issue you are addressing—the third being the conclusory subheading that goes above each CRACC.

Unlike in objective writing where the conclusion states the predicted outcome based on a neutral assessment of the law and facts, in persuasive writing the conclusion requests that the court make a determination in favor of your client on the issue. Thus, you can see the conclusion sentences in Defendant's MSJ are polar-opposite to those in Plaintiff's MSJ Opposition. This is because each party wants opposite outcomes: the defendant wants summary judgment to be granted, and the plaintiff wants summary judgment to be denied. The defendant wants the court to hold there is no genuine dispute of material fact on the elements, and the plaintiff wants the court to hold the opposite. The chart below shows these opposing conclusions for the first element of religious discrimination addressed in the motion and opposition.

	DEFENDANT (MSJ)	PLAINTIFF (OPPOSITION)
Conclusory heading for element 1	This Court should grant summary judgment because no fact issue exists as to whether Mr. Saint's religious belief was sincerely held when Mr. Saint was okay with some marks of the beast but not others.	Defendant's Motion for Summary Judgment should be denied because there remains genuine disputes of material fact as to whether Mr. Saint's religious belief was bona fide.
Opening Conclusion for element 1	First, this Court should grant summary judgment because the undisputed evidence proves that Mr. Saint did not hold a bona fide religious belief.	First, this Court should deny summary judgment because the evidence shows that a genuine issue of material fact exists as to whether Mr. Saint sincerely held a bona fide religious belief.
Closing Conclusion for element 1	Accordingly, because the undisputed evidence establishes that Mr. Saint does not have a sincere bona fide religious belief—an essential element of Plaintiff's prima facie case—the Court should grant summary judgment.	Accordingly, this Court should deny summary judgment because there is at a minimum, a genuine issue of material fact as to whether Mr. Saint's belief in the "Mark of the Beast" is so sincerely held as to establish a bona fide religious belief.

5. CRACC: creating persuasive Rule statements

Just as in objective writing, after your opening conclusion sentence ("C") is your Rule ("R" of CRAC). Rules are the scaffolding for all legal analysis—regardless of whether that legal analysis is objective or persuasive. In fact, in persuasive writing, courts (and their judges and clerks) do not decide cases based on what you as a lawyer think but, rather, on what the law is (that is, the legal rules applicable to your case). Just like in objective writing, in persuasive writing, Rules have three parts: the general rule, subrules, and the case illustration(s).

These three parts of the Rule—from a macro standpoint—look the same in persuasive writing and in objective writing. First, the general rule is where you state the law governing the element or claim at issue. Second, the subrules explain the general rule by defining key terms from the general rule and identifying how courts determine whether the general rule is satisfied. Third, case illustrations explain (or illustrate) how that general rule (and its subrules) have been applied in prior cases involving similar facts. In other words, just like in objective writing, in persuasive writing, the three parts of the Rule—the general rule, subrules, and case illustrations—work together to explain the law to the court and to define the parameters of the legal standard from its broadest application (the general rule) to its narrowest (the case illustration).

However, unique to persuasive writing, the Rule serves as a persuasive tool in a lawyer's toolbelt. Sometimes this is confusing to students. "I do not understand," they say. "How can the law be persuasive? The law is the same for both sides, right?" Yes, the governing law for the issue will be the same for both sides. That is, for example, element one of a religious discrimination claim is the same for both sides: element one requires that the plaintiff held a bona fide religious belief. You do not make the law persuasive by changing it or misstating it. Rather, how you make the law persuasive is through how you frame it. Unlike in objective writing, in persuasive writing you must be intentional in how you frame the general rule, how you select and frame subrules, and how you select case illustrations. So, although the content and the structure of the persuasive Rule is, generally speaking, similar to that of the objective Rule, in the end (as you will learn in detail below) the persuasive Rule's substance and style are unique.

a. CRACC: general rule, the first part of a persuasive Rule

Just as in objective writing, in persuasive writing the general rule is the first of the three parts of your Rule and is drafted in the present tense. Moreover, just as in objective writing, in persuasive writing the purpose of the general rule is to provide a succinct statement of the law for the issue. This is important because courts are not persuaded by what **you** think. Rather, courts want to follow the law and the legal precedent that governs the issue. Therefore, while you want to state your general rule in the way that is most persuasive for your client, you cannot, in an attempt to make the general rule persuasive, "change" the law to make it better for your client than it really is. Instead, to make the general rule persuasive, you must state the rule from the point of view or angle that is most favorable to your client in relation to the issue.

Let's work through an example together. The seminal case *Davis v. Fort Bend County* sets forth the general rule for element one of religious discrimination as follows: "To establish a prima facie case of religious discrimination under Title VII, the plaintiff must present evidence that (1) she held a bona fide religious belief. . . ."[17]

In objective writing, it would be okay to simply copy *Davis*'s statement of the first element as your general rule for the first element without putting much more thought into it. In objective writing, you want the general rule to be accurate and complete, but how you frame it is not particularly important.

In persuasive writing, like in objective writing, what is quoted above from *Davis* is the general rule for element one. The general rule does not change. However, in persuasive writing, you would not want to simply state the general rule exactly as it is

---

17. *Davis v. Fort Bend Cnty.*, 765 F.3d 480, 485 (5th Cir. 2014).

written in *Davis* in your motion or opposition. Rather, you need to frame the general rule in a way that is favorable to your client. To figure out how to frame the general rule persuasively, follow these four steps:

Step one: Figure out what your client wants in relation to the general rule.

To frame the general rule persuasively, you must first ask yourself: what does my client want in relation to this issue (here, element one)? If you represent Plaintiff, it wants this element to be satisfied. If you represent Defendant, it does not want this element to be satisfied. Both sides want the opposite outcome. Therefore, while the general rule for both sides will be the same law, the way the parties frame the general rule will be opposite.

Step two: Present the general rule in a way that supports what your client wants.

Now that you know what your client wants in relation to the general rule, you will emphasize the rule in way that supports your client's desired outcome. When you are learning to emphasize and de-emphasize parts of a general rule, consider the following two questions: (1) does my client benefit if I state the rule positively or negatively; and (2) does my client benefit if I state the rule broadly or narrowly? Beginning a rule statement by stating the outcome you want for your client will lead the reader toward that position (these are called Jedi mind tricks).

The party that wants the element to be satisfied (here, Plaintiff) will frame the general rule positively and broadly. Positively because the party wants the element to be satisfied—that is, the party wants the court to hold the element has been met. Broadly because the party wants to frame the element in a way that makes it seem easier to meet, as if a broader array of facts will satisfy the element. On the other hand, the party that wants the element to not be satisfied (here, Defendant) will frame the general rule negatively and narrowly. Negatively because the party wants the element to not be satisfied. Narrowly because the party wants the element to seem more difficult to satisfy such that it narrows its perceived application.

The chart below provides examples of positive, broad language and negative, narrow language that can be used to frame general rules.

Positive and broad	"The element is satisfied whenever ..." "A party meets the element anytime ..." "A party only need to show ... to satisfy element ..."
Negative and narrow	"The element is not satisfied unless ..." "A court will not hold the element is satisfied except when ..."

Step three: Emphasize or de-emphasize the burden of proof in the general rule.

Whichever side does not have the burden of proof on the element will, when framing the general rule, emphasize the burden of the other side. The party that does have the burden of proof will de-emphasize the heaviness of the burden. Looking again at the example here, because religious discrimination is Plaintiff's cause of action, Plaintiff has the burden of proof at trial and, as such, Plaintiff will de-emphasize its burden, while Defendant will emphasize it.

Step four: Make sure your general rule is accurate and complete.

Your general rule, while persuasive, must remain accurate. The final step is to make sure your general rule remains true to the actual legal standard. That is, while you have ***re-framed*** the general rule you need to make sure you have not ***changed*** the general rule.

In summary, unlike in objective writing where the general rule is often—in essence—cut and pasted into the memo from its source, in persuasive writing you should not just cut and paste the general rule into your motion or opposition. Instead, you need to think about framing the general rule in a way that is most persuasive for your client. Below is an example of a general rule written three ways: objectively, persuasively in favor of the defendant, and persuasively in favor of the plaintiff.

OBJECTIVE MEMO

This sample general rule for element one from the objective memo is, in essence, the statement of the rule as it appears in the caselaw with little adjustment and no spin.

> To satisfy the first element of a religious discrimination claim, a plaintiff must prove that he had a "bona fide religious belief." *Davis*, 765 F.3d at 485.

PLAINTIFF'S MSJ OPPOSITION

This sample general rule for the first element from Plaintiff's MSJ Opposition is written positively ("element is satisfied") and broadly ("whenever"), thus, maximizing the chances that a reader will find the element satisfied. Additionally, the burden of proof is de-emphasized.

> An employee satisfies the first element of a Title VII claim for religious discrimination whenever he establishes that he holds a bona fide religious belief. *Davis*, 765 F.3d at 485.

DEFENDANT'S MSJ

This sample general rule for the first element from Defendant's MSJ is written negatively ("will not meet her burden to show") and narrowly ("unless") and, thus, lessens the chances that the reader will find the element satisfied. Defendant's framing of the general rule also emphasizes that the Plaintiff has the burden to satisfy this element.

> A plaintiff cannot succeed in a Title VII religious discrimination claim unless he meets the burden to prove that the employee sincerely held a bona fide religious belief. *Davis*, 765 F.3d at 485.

b. CRACC: subrules, the second part of a persuasive Rule

Subrules perform the same role in persuasive writing as they do in objective writing: they explain the general rule. Also, just like in objective writing, persuasive subrules are drafted in the present tense. Unique to persuasive writing, subrules are another persuasive tool in a lawyer's toolbelt that support the client's legal position and persuade the reader that the requested outcome is the right one.

Generally speaking, the art of generating a persuasive rule statement turns on your selection of subrules that support your argument and emphasize or frame the law in a way that supports the result your client wants. There are a few things to keep in mind when making subrules persuasive. First, as was noted in the discussion of general rules, you cannot misrepresent the law. You must accurately state the law and cannot change the law by changing subrules or omitting crucial subrules. Second, the key to making subrules persuasive is through your framing of subrules with your client's desired outcome in mind. Unlike in objective writing, where you want to provide the court with a complete, neutral picture of the law, in persuasive writing you want to present the court with an accurate picture of the law that is framed in favor of your client's position. Therefore, when it comes to subrules, you need not include all subrules that define the general rule. Rather, you must include, what we will call, "crucial subrules"—subrules that define key terms in the general rule. With respect to other subrules, you should only include ones that are favorable for your client.

For the first element, an example of a crucial subrule is that in determining whether an employee's belief is bona fide, the courts look at the sincerity. Notice how this subrule is included in the objective memo, Defendant's MSJ, and Plaintiff's MSJ Opposition. However, examine how it is framed differently by each side. Similar to general rules, you see that Plaintiff, who wants the standard satisfied, frames the subrule positively, whereas Defendant does the opposite. The framing of your subrules (in addition to the perspective from which they are written) deeply affects their persuasion.

OBJECTIVE CRUCIAL SUBRULE FOR ELEMENT ONE

> A bona fide religious belief includes "moral or ethical beliefs as to what is right and wrong [that] are sincerely held." *Davis*, 765 F.3d at 485.

PLAINTIFF'S MSJ OPPOSITION'S PERSUASIVE CRUCIAL SUBRULE FOR ELEMENT ONE

> A court will hold an employee's belief is bona fide as long the belief is sincerely held, and the plaintiff's sincerity in his belief is largely a matter of "individual credibility." *Tagore v. United States*, 735 F.3d 324, 328 (5th Cir. 2013).

DEFENDANT'S MSJ'S PERSUASIVE CRUCIAL SUBRULE FOR ELEMENT ONE

> A belief is not bona fide unless it is "sincerely held with the strength of traditional religious views." *Davis*, 765 F.3d at 485.

With respect to the other subrules, you will see that the ones Plaintiff includes and the ones Defendant includes are not the same. Rather, the parties pick and choose the subrules that are favorable in order to frame the law persuasively for their sides.

PLAINTIFF'S MSJ OPPOSITION'S EXAMPLE PERSUASIVE SUBRULES FOR ELEMENT ONE

> Indeed, courts hold the first element is met "on little more than the plaintiff's credible assertions." *Tagore v. United States*, 735 F.3d 324, 328 (5th Cir. 2013). The sincerity of a plaintiff's engagement in a particular religious practice is "rarely challenged" and, when it is, the court must analyze the issue "with a light touch, or 'judicial shyness.'" *Id.* (citing *Moussazadeh v. Tex. Dep't. of Criminal Just.*, 703 F.3d 781, 791–92 (5th Cir. 2012)). Furthermore, in deciding whether a belief is bona fide, the court "is limited to focusing upon the individual's motivation," and a court's task is merely to decide whether the individual's beliefs are, "in his own scheme of things, religious.'" *Davis*, 765 F.3d at 485 (citing *United States v. Seeger*, 380 U.S. 163, 185 (1965)).

DEFENDANT'S MSJ'S EXAMPLE PERSUASIVE SUBRULES FOR ELEMENT ONE

> While the correctness of an employee's religious belief cannot be questioned, the sincerity of the employee's belief may (and must) be scrutinized. *Hansard v. Johns-Manville Prods. Corp.*, No. 1902, 1973 WL 129, at *2 (E.D. Tex. Feb. 16, 1973). Even where a foundation is laid for an employee's religious belief, "the court must determine the individual plaintiff's sincerity in relying on those religious beliefs." *Id.* Further, an employee's reliance on a religious belief must stem from conviction and not convenience. *Id.*

In comparing the subrules in Plaintiff's MSJ Opposition and Defendant's MSJ, notice how they differ. Both sides are accurately stating the law (all of these subrules are real and really explain the general rule of bona fide religious belief). However, Plaintiff includes subrules favorable to its position, such as how the sincerity of a person's religious belief is subjective, "rarely challenged," and approached with "judicial shyness." On the other hand, Defendant includes different subrules favorable to its side (and does its best to frame the law for bona fide religious belief in a way that makes it seem like this element is more difficult for a plaintiff to establish). Defendant emphasizes in its subrules that the court "must" scrutinize an employee's belief and that the belief "must" stem from conviction. However, Defendant has to work harder in its framing than Plaintiff does. Defendant doesn't have the luxury of including the nice soundbite quotes Plaintiff includes because the law is actually pretty unfavorable to defendants and pretty favorable to plaintiffs on this element.

c. CRACC: case illustrations, the third part of a persuasive Rule

Persuasive case illustrations are designed to, like case illustrations in objective writing, provide an example of how another court has applied the rule at issue in a different case. Persuasive case illustrations—just like with persuasive general rules and persuasive subrules—also serve as another tool in the persuasive lawyer's toolbelt because they help persuade the reader to give the lawyer the outcome she seeks.

Persuasive case illustrations contain the same four parts as objective case illustrations: (1) a topic sentence; (2) the holding of the case on the element or issue for which you are illustrating it; (3) the trigger facts related to the element or issue for which you are illustrating it; and (4) the court's reasoning or how it applied the facts to the law to reach its holding. Moreover, just like in objective writing, persuasive case illustrations should be drafted in the past tense.

Unlike in objective writing, where you select cases to illustrate in order to provide your reader with an accurate and full picture of the law, in persuasive writing, you select cases to illustrate that will help you persuade the court to reach the outcome your client wants. To do this, you should select cases to illustrate that are "good law" (meaning they have not been overturned), have facts similar to the facts of your case, and reach the outcome that your client wants on the issue for which you are illustrating the case. That is, unlike in objective writing where you illustrate factually similar cases on both ends of the spectrum (one where the element was satisfied and one where it was not), in persuasive writing you generally illustrate only factually similar cases that reach the same outcome that you want. For example, if you represent the plaintiff and you are looking for cases to illustrate for element one of your cause of action, you would be looking for cases that are factually similar to your case **and** that held element one was satisfied. (You would not want to illustrate a case that was factually similar to your case but held that element one was not satisfied because that is not the outcome you want.) Then, in your Analysis ("A"), you would argue to the court that your case is so like the favorable illustrated case(s) that the court should reach the same outcome as the court(s) reached in the illustrated case(s) on that element.

Thus, the difference between case illustrations in objective and persuasive writing is less about changing the illustration on a sentence level and more about which cases you pick to illustrate. In persuasive writing, case illustrations look the same in that you are still including a topic sentence (although the topic sentence should be stated persuasively for your client), the court's holding, the trigger facts, and the court's reasoning. However, in persuasive writing, you are only illustrating cases that reach the same outcome that you want the court to reach on the element or issue for which you are illustrating the case. That is, the biggest difference between objective case illustrations and persuasive case illustrations is the cases that you pick.

Below are three case illustrations related to the first element of religious discrimination that demonstrate how the selection of a case or cases to illustrate affects the potential outcome and the persuasive effect of the case illustration.

OBJECTIVE EXAMPLE

The first example contains two case illustrations that are drafted objectively to provide a complete and neutral picture of the parameters of the element at issue (here, element one).

An employee's consistent representation that she holds a particular religious belief coupled with action consistent with that belief supports a finding of sincerity. In *Davis*, the Fifth Circuit held that the employee's representation and action evidenced sincerity such that she, at minimum, raised a genuine issue of material fact as to the sincerity of her belief. 765 F.3d at 485–86. In that case, the employee notified her employer that she could not work on a particular Sunday because she had a special church service to attend that involved breaking new ground and feeding the community. *Id.* at 486–87. The employee attended the church event, was fired for being absent from work without approval, and then sued her employer for religious discrimination under Title VII. *Id.* at 484. At trial, the employee testified about her devotion to the church, stating that she "believed strongly" that she "needed" to attend a "special church service." *Id.* at 486. The employee further testified about her active commitment to her church, referencing her frequent church attendance and participation. *Id.* at 487. The Fifth Circuit reasoned that the district court erred when it granted summary judgment because it improperly inquired into the nature of the activity and its status as "a true religious tenet," whereas it should have looked to the employee's credibility and asked whether the employee sincerely believed that the activity was religious "in her own scheme of things." *Id.* The Fifth Circuit further reasoned that the employee's representation and action surrounding her belief that she was religiously required to attend a special church service, through her testimony, sufficiently evidenced a genuine issue of material fact as to whether she sincerely believed the event to be religious. *Id.* at 487. Accordingly, the employee's prima facie case survived summary judgment for a trier of fact to later determine whether the employee held a bona fide religious belief. *Id.*

In contrast, an employee's consistent representation that he holds a particular religious belief coupled with action inconsistent with that belief negates a finding of sincerity. In *Hansard*, the court held that the employee failed to establish the requisite sincerity because his actions were inconsistent with his asserted religious belief. 1973 WL 129, at *2. In that case, the employee, a New Testament Christian, told his employer that he could not work on a particular Sunday because it conflicted with his religious belief against working for profit on Sundays. *Id.* at *1–2. The employee was fired after refusing to work that Sunday, and he then sued his employer for religious discrimination under Title VII. *Id.* at *1. The employee was raised in the Church of Christ but dropped his membership and claimed to be a New Testament Christian years later. *Id.* at *2. The employee had occasionally refused to work Sundays but admitted to not always following his "lifelong" belief against working for profit on Sundays. *Id.* at *1–2. The court reasoned that the employee's attempt to frame his action as consistent failed because although he attested to his belief's reemergence following a "miraculous" event, his testimony about when the alleged event occurred and his admission to working several Sundays following the event remained inconsistent. *Id.* at *2. The court explained that the employee's inconsistent action surrounding his religious belief against working Sundays suggested that his belief was grounded more in convenience than conviction, thus, negating a finding of sincerity. *Id.* Accordingly, the employee failed to prove that he held a bona fide religious belief. *Id.*

PERSUASIVE DEFENDANT EXAMPLE (FROM DEFENDANT'S MSJ)

Defendant illustrates Hansard—a case where the court held the first element of religious discrimination was not satisfied—because Defendant wants the court in its case to reach the same outcome as the court in Hansard with respect to element one (holding it is not satisfied).

A religious belief based in convenience will not satisfy the first element of a religious discrimination claim. In *Hansard*, the court held that the employee's "religious conviction against working for profit on Sundays" was not sincerely held. *Id.* at *3. In that case, the employee refused to work on Sundays because of his Christian religion. *Id.* at *1. The employee, while claiming his belief was "lifelong," admitted he did not always follow it. *Id.* The employee dropped out of the Church of Christ he attended because of "the hypocrisy within the organized church," which caused him to become a "New Testament Christian." *Id.* In addition, although the employee claimed to have experienced a "revival" of his religious conviction after his infant son purportedly "miraculously" recovered after a difficult birth, the employee "worked several Sundays after the alleged miraculous recovery." *Id.* The court, while not questioning the correctness of the employee's belief, reasoned that the employee's reliance on the belief "appears to be grounded more in convenience than conviction" because he worked some Sundays but not others. *Id.* at *2.

PERSUASIVE FOR PLAINTIFF EXAMPLE (FROM PLAINTIFF'S MSJ OPPOSITION)

Plaintiff illustrates Davis—a case where the court held the first element of religious discrimination was satisfied—because Plaintiff wants the court in his case to reach the same outcome as the court in Davis with respect to the element one (holding it is satisfied).

An employee's testimony as to his sincere religious belief is sufficient to defeat summary judgment. In *Davis*, the Fifth Circuit, overturning the district court's grant of summary judgment, held that the employee's testimony that she sincerely felt she was religiously compelled to attend a church event created a genuine dispute of material fact whether she held a bona fide religious belief. 765 F.3d at 485–86. In that case, the employee told her employer she could not work on a certain Sunday because she had a special church service to attend that involved breaking new ground and feeding the community. *Id.* at 486–87. The employee testified that she was a devout member of her church and "strongly believed" she "needed" to be there for the event. *Id.* at 486. The Fifth Circuit reasoned that the district court erred by improperly focusing on the nature of the activity itself. *Id.* at 486–87. [In finding that the employee's belief was sincere, and, therefore, bona fide,] the Court of Appeals explained that the focus was properly not on whether a "church event was in itself a true religious tenet," but only whether the employee "sincerely believed it to be religious in her own scheme of things." *Id.* The Fifth Circuit further reasoned that "drawing all reasonable inferences in favor of [the employee] as the nonmoving party, and considering the 'light touch' and 'judicial shyness' that must be exercised," the employee's "testimony about her own sincere belief regarding her religious need to attend a special service at church on Sunday sufficiently evidenced a genuine dispute of material fact whether she held a bona fide religious belief." *Id.* at 487.

If you compare each example, you can see that, unlike in objective writing, parties in persuasive writing are usually only illustrating cases that reach the result they want on the issue or element. Additionally, in persuasive writing, a party will be more mindful to illustrate the case in a way that frames the case in the best light for its position. For example, the party will take favorable sound-bites out of the court's reasoning and highlight favorable trigger facts to draw special attention to them. Notice how in the case illustration immediately above, Plaintiff soundbites the standard of review (which is favorable to Plaintiff) in the court's reasoning:

The Fifth Circuit further reasoned that "**drawing all reasonable inferences in favor of [the employee] as the nonmoving party, and considering the 'light touch' and 'judicial shyness' that must be exercised,**" the employee's "testimony about her own sincere belief regarding her religious need to attend a special service at church on Sunday sufficiently evidenced a genuine dispute of material fact whether she held a bona fide religious belief." *Id.* at 487.

In the next section—the Analysis ("A")—the parties will argue that their case is like the illustrated (favorable) cases such that the same outcome is warranted in their case.

6. CRACC: creating persuasive Analysis

Just as in objective writing, after your Rule is your Analysis ("A" of CRACC). In your Analysis, you will apply the law for the issue, which you have just stated persuasively in the Rule for the issue, to your facts for the issue, which you have stated persuasively in the statement of facts, to argue for the outcome you want the court to reach on the issue.

We tell students that if you have a persuasive Rule for the issue and you have all the facts stated persuasively for the issue or element in your statement of facts, then writing an Analysis is a little like copying, pasting, and matching. Your Analysis is really just a combination of your Rule and facts on that issue or element, both of which you have already stated persuasively elsewhere in your motion before you get to the Analysis of the issue or element.

We recommend not writing the Analysis for any issue until you have finalized the statement of facts and all three parts of the Rule for the issue or element. Obviously, you may need to go back and edit or tweak those sections after you have written your Analysis, but, because the Analysis is the product of these two parts, it makes sense to write your Analysis after those parts are completed.

In persuasive writing, the organization of your Analysis is similar to that in objective writing, except you are arguing—not predicting.

a. Part 1 of Analysis made persuasive

In part one of your Analysis, you will argue what happens when you apply the Rule for the issue to the facts for the issue or, put another way, you will argue what result the court should reach when applying the Rule for a particular issue to the facts for that same issue. Compare part one of the Analysis stated objectively, stated persuasively for the plaintiff, and stated persuasively for the defendant on the same issue.

> **Part 1 stated objectively**: Mr. Saint will likely satisfy the first element of his religious discrimination claim because, like the employee in *Davis*, and distinct from the employee in *Hansard*, Mr. Saint was consistent in his representations and actions surrounding his religious belief, which weighs in favor of a court finding Mr. Saint's belief to be sincere.

> **Part 1 stated persuasively for the defendant**: Here, this Court should reach the same conclusion as *Hansard* and hold Plaintiff fails to prove the first element of its claim because the undisputed evidence demonstrates that Mr. Saint's purported religious belief, which prevented him from scanning his retina, was not sincere.

> **Part 1 stated persuasively for the plaintiff**: Here, like *Davis*, Mr. Saint establishes a genuine issue of material fact exists as to the sincerity of his bona fide religious belief in the "Mark of the Beast."

b. Part 2 of Analysis made persuasive

In part two, you will support or prove your argument in part one. If the application of the Rule to the facts for the issue is straightforward, you will use pure rule-based reasoning. Otherwise you will use a combination of analogical reasoning and rule-language bridging. Let's look at each type of proof separately.

i. Pure rule-based reasoning made persuasive

Pure rule-based reasoning is simple and covered in detail when we introduced objective writing in Part Two. Because pure rule-based reasoning is only used when the application of the rule to the facts is straightforward, there is really nothing to "argue." In a sense, "it is what it is." Thus, the difference between pure rule-based reasoning in objective writing and persuasive writing is really only a change in tone. You simply change your tone from predictive to persuasive. Review the bystander example. Below is a comparison of the Analysis using pure rule-based reasoning both objectively and persuasively. You will see the difference is subtle because the Analysis is so straightforward that "it is what it is."

OBJECTIVE EXAMPLE

Part 1 ⟶ Paula will satisfy the third element of the bystander doctrine. Because Pau-
Part 2 ⟶ la is Martha's daughter, she is "closely related" to the victim Martha and, as such, can recover damages. *Freeman*, 744 S.W.2d at 924; *Garcia*, 859 S.W.2d at 81; Mem. from A. Partner to File (Jan. 30, 2024).

PERSUASIVE EXAMPLE

Part 1 ⟶ It is undisputed that Paula satisfies the third element of the bystander doc-
Part 2 ⟶ trine. Because Paula is Martha's daughter, this Court should find that she is "closely related" to the victim Martha and, as such, can recover damages. *Freeman*, 744 S.W.2d at 924; *Garcia*, 859 S.W.2d at 81; Mem. from A. Partner to File (Jan. 30, 2024).

ii. Analogical reasoning and rule-language bridging made persuasive

Just like in objective writing, it is essential that you "show your work" in persuasive writing. Imagine this conversation:

You: "Judge, you should reach the result we want because our case is like the precedent case that reached the result we want."

Judge: "Okay, why?"

You: "Because our case is exactly like the precedent case."

Judge: "Okay, but how?"

You: "Because it is just like the precedent case and is on all fours with the facts of that case."

Judge: "Okay ... why?"

Total nightmare! You are arguing, but there is no meat. You are not showing the court why your argument is correct. You must show your work. Here is what lawyers sometimes do when writing before a court. They write beautiful Rule statements for a particular issue, and, then, in the Analysis, they simply write something like, "Accordingly, because the facts in this case meet the standard, this Court should deny summary judgment." As said by one court, there "is the duty to cite evidence and authority **and explain why [the] same mandates the result desired by the [party] .... One does not**

satisfy this burden by merely uttering conclusions."[18] You cannot merely utter the conclusion that you want the court to reach, you must show the court that the conclusion you want the court to reach is the correct one.

In persuasive writing, you will normally use a combination of analogical reasoning and rule-language bridging in your Analysis.

1. Analogical reasoning: arguing your case is like precedent case such that same result is warranted

Because, in your Rule, you will have only illustrated cases that reach the same result you want the court to reach (favorable cases), in your Analysis when you do analogical reasoning you are arguing that your case is similar to, or better than, the favorable illustrated cases such that the court should reach the same result as the illustrated cases. Unlike in objective writing, in persuasive writing you are not comparing and contrasting but arguing that your case is so like the illustrated case that the same result is warranted. Therefore, the "formula" you will use to do your fact-to-fact analysis (analogical reasoning) is one of comparison, not contrast: **"Like [favorable precedent case], where [trigger fact from precedent case], here [similar trigger fact from our case]."** Similarly, if your case is "better" or "stronger" than the illustrated case on the issue, you will argue that. Here is an example from Plaintiff's MSJ Opposition related to reasonable accommodation:

> More than *Universal*, where the employer at least attempted to accommodate one of the employee's religious needs, here, Defendant did not attempt to eliminate the conflict between Mr. Saint's religious need to avoid using the biometric scanning technology *at all* and Defendant's employment requirements.

For element one, Defendant's MSJ Opposition illustrated *Hansard*—a case where the court held the first element was not satisfied, which is what Defendant wants the court to hold in the present case. Using analogical reasoning, Defendant compares the facts of his case to the illustrated case to show that the two are similar such that the same result is warranted in the present case as was reached by the court in *Hansard*. Additionally, Defendant not only compares, but argues why this comparison matters throughout. The example below uses the two-part analysis formula **and** explicitly tells the court why the comparison matters (**see** bold sentences below).

18. *Foster v. Westinghouse Elevator Co.*, No. 07-96-0322-CV, 1997 WL 360948, at * 2 (Tex. App.—Amarillo June 27, 1997, writ denied) (emphasis added).

Part 1 → Part 2 →

Here, this Court should reach the same conclusion as *Hansard* and hold Plaintiff fails to prove the first element of its claim because the undisputed evidence demonstrates that Mr. Saint's purported religious belief, which prevented him from scanning his retina, was not sincere. Like the employee in *Hansard*, who claimed to have a "lifelong" belief but dropped out of church, Mr. Saint claims to be an evangelical Christian, but has not attended church regularly since 2016—two years before he started working at UI. *Hansard*, 1973 WL 129, at *2; Ex. 14, Saint Dep. 3:2–8; Ex. 6. Mr. Saint's pastor said Mr. Saint "stopped attending church completely in 2018." Ex. 6. Additionally, like the employee in Hansard, who criticized the hypocrisy in the church, Mr. Saint posted to his Facebook page that he was "[t]ired of praying to someone that doesn't change anything #overit." *Hansard*, 1973 WL 129, at *2; Ex. 7. In 2018, he posted the following on his Facebook page: "When you run into people from your old church and they ask why you have [sic] been in a while. Awkward." *Id.* He clarified in response to a comment on his 2018 post that he was not a "church guy" anymore. Id. Furthermore, Jonathan Anderson, who started working at UI at the same time and classified Mr. Saint as "like a big brother," was not aware Mr. Saint was religious. Ex. 11, Anderson Dep. 3:2–6. Mr. Anderson said Mr. Saint "never said anything about [religion]" and that Mr. Saint never mentioned going to church. *Id.* at 3:7–10. **Accordingly, given Mr. Saint's public separation from religion, Mr. Saint's beliefs were not "sincerely held with the strength of traditional religious views."** *See Davis*, 765 F.3d at 485.

Moreover, like the employee in *Hansard*, who worked some Sundays but not others such that his alleged beliefs were inconsistent, **Mr. Saint's beliefs are likewise inconsistent in that he is okay with some "marks of the beast" but not others.** *Hansard*, 1973 WL 129, at *2. The biblical passage on which Mr. Saint relies for his religious belief—Revelation 13:16–18—defines the number of the beast to be 666. Ex. 13. Mr. Saint's address and cell phone number both include the number of the beast: 666 Heaven St. and 972-666-0123. Ex. 8; Ex. 14, Saint Dep. 2:14–17. Mr. Saint refused to clock in using the retina scanner, fearing the "Mark of the Beast," yet he admitted that he is "over religion" and lives in a house and used a cell phone both bearing the number of the beast. Ex. 8; Ex. 14, Saint Dep. 2:14–17. **This evidence proves that, like the employee in *Hansard*, Mr. Saint's belief was one of "convenience rather than conviction" and was not "sincerely held with the strength of traditional religious views."** *See Hansard*, 1973 WL 129, at *2; *Davis*, 765 F.3d at 485.

2. Rule-language bridging made persuasive

Just as in objective writing, in persuasive writing you will connect the persuasive language in your Rule for the issue to the facts in your Analysis. By connecting the language of the general rule and subrules to the facts, you are showing the court how the facts satisfy (or fail to satisfy) the Rule. That is, you are showing your work.

Look at the example from Plaintiff's MSJ Opposition. The bold text is rule-language bridging (i.e. language that Plaintiff has carried down from the Rule for the issue into the Analysis):

> Here, like *Davis*, Mr. Saint establishes a genuine issue of material fact exists as to the sincerity of his bona fide religious belief in the "Mark of the Beast." Like *Davis*, where the employee provided evidence that she was a devout member of her church and that she "strongly believed" she "needed" to be there for a church event, here, Mr. Saint testified that as an Evangelical Christian, he strongly believed that Revelation 13:16–18 indicates that the "Mark of the Beast" is a "symbolic mark" and that "technology will be used to carry out its implementation." *Davis*, 765 F.3d at 486; Ex. 2; Ex. 3; Ex.8; Ex. 14, Saint Dep. 4:2–10. Like *Davis*, where the court held it was improper to focus on whether the activity was a **"true religious tenant,"** here, it was improper for Defendant to interject its own interpretation of the Bible to determine whether Mr. Saint's religious belief about the scanner was somehow wrong. *Davis*, 765 F.3d at 486; Ex. 5 at 1–2. Similar to *Davis*, where the employee informed her employer that she would not be able to attend one of the required days for installation due to her prior religious commitment, here, Mr. Saint immediately informed his supervisor and the Human Resources manager that he could not use the new biometric scanning technology because of his belief in the "Mark of the Beast" being assigned through that exact type of technology. *Davis*, 765 F.3d at 484; Ex. 1; Ex. 2; Ex. 3; Ex 14, Saint Dep. 3:13–15. Following *Davis*, which is binding on this Court, Mr. Saint's testimony about *his* own sincere belief regarding what was **"religious in [his] own scheme of things"** is sufficient to create a genuine issue of material fact on summary judgment without more. *Davis*, 765 F.3d at 487. Accordingly, it is proper for this Court to assess Mr. Saint's religious belief with **"judicial shyness"** and hold that the bona fide religious belief element is met, for the purpose of establishing a genuine issue of fact, **"on little more than the plaintiff's credible assertions."** *Id.* at 484, 487.

Notice also that, in addition to using soundbites from the law, Plaintiff has incorporated soundbites from its statement of facts into the Analysis. Recall that when we discussed making your statement of facts persuasive, we discussed that it was smart to use soundbites to tell your client's side of the story. Because the facts in the Analysis should match the facts for the issue in your statement of facts, you will often have soundbites in your Analysis from the facts of your case.

c. Example of objective versus persuasive Analysis on same element

Now that you know how to make an Analysis persuasive, closely examine the complete Analysis sections for element two taken from the Appendices. As you compare the three different Analysis sections, label the two parts of each Analysis section, underline where analogical reasoning is used, circle where rule-language bridging is used, and highlight the parts of the Analysis where the writer tells the reader why the comparison (and contrast for the objective Analysis) matters.

OBJECTIVE ANALYSIS EXAMPLE

UI will likely establish the second affirmative defense because, like the employer *Tagore*, and distinct from the employer in *Ford*, UI will likely establish that letting Mr. Saint sign in and out without using the scanner would impose more than de minimis financial and efficiency-based costs on UI. In *Tagore*, the accommodation at issue—requiring security guards to ascertain the dullness of a kirpan blade when the employee entered the building—was time-consuming, impractical, and detrimental to the employer's broad safety efforts. *Tagore*, 735 F.3d at 330. Similarly, here, the accommodation at issue—manual time and attendance supervision—would impose a time burden on Ms. Edwards and would upend UI's broad fraud prevention efforts. Ex. 5 at 3; Ex. 12 at 4:16–5:2. Although requiring Ms. Edwards to manually timekeep for Mr. Saint may seem to require less effort than the *Tagore* requirement that security guards ascertain the kirpan blade's dullness each time the employee enters the building, both impose more than de minimis costs because they both require employees to "unfairly perform extra work." *Tagore*, 735 F.3d at 330. The court's willingness in *Tagore* to find the requirement of determining whether an article is a "dangerous weapon" unduly burdensome—a duty seemingly inherent to the role of a security guard—suggests that a court would be even more inclined to find the requirement that Ms. Edwards manually check Mr. Saint in and out—a duty that goes beyond her existing role—unduly burdensome. Ex. 5 at 3; Ex. 9. Therefore, following *Tagore*, a court here would likely also find that requiring Ms. Edwards to perform this extra work is time-consuming and impractical, as it would decrease her efficiency at spearheading recruitment and training efforts—duties that more aptly support UI's broader goals and purpose for adopting the new software policy in the first place. Ex. 9; Ex. 5 at 3; Ex. 12; Ex. 1; Ex. 4. As such, it would "require coworkers to unfairly perform extra work" and impose more than a de minimus cost. *See Tagore*, 735 F.3d at 330; *Favero*, 939 F. Supp. at 1288.

The broad fraud concern in Mr. Saint's case at first blush may seem less significant than the security concern in *Tagore* because the *Tagore* accommodation implicates safety risks and illegal conduct, arguably more serious matters than fraudulent timekeeping. *Tagore*, 735 F.3d at 326–27. However, the cases remain alike because the court's analysis in *Tagore* did not hinge on the nature of the impact—safety, legal, or fraud—but on the accommodation's adverse effect on the employer's goal of viligance. *Id.* at 330. Like how the court considered the employer's vigilance concerns in *Tagore*, here, a court would weigh other timekeeping systems' susceptibility to fraud—an issue tied to UI's financial and efficiency costs—against the overall effectiveness of its company-wide scanner requirement at alleviating its fraud concerns. *Id.*; Ex. 12 at 4:16–5:2; Ex. 5 at 3. Consequently, a court will likely hold that UI can avoid liability under Title VII by establishing that it could not reasonably accommodate Mr. Saint without undue hardship. *Id.*

Unlike in *Ford*, where the employer's unsubstantiated assertion—that making a particular accommodation would impose more-than *de minimis* costs through the creation of a new position and hiring of additional employees—failed to support a court in finding undue hardship, UI's assertion—that it would be unduly burdensome to offer Mr. Saint an accommodation not requiring the use of the scanner—goes beyond a conclusory claim. 2007 WL 2051015, at *5. In contrast to the employer in *Ford* who offered only broad assertions of cost without any substantiation, UI can provide testimony and documentation that any accommodation not requiring the use of the scanner could impose more than de minimis costs to its finances, employees, and efficiency. Ex. 1; Ex. 4; Ex. 5; Ex. 9; Ex. 12 at 4:16–5:2. In addition, unlike in *Ford*, where the employer failed to prove that it had explored more than one accommodation, UI explored alternative accommodations when it e-mailed PalmVein asking for help resolving Mr. Saint's conflict and offered Mr. Saint the options to scan his right hand or left thumbprint instead of his retinas. Ex. 5; 2007 WL 2051015, at *5. Thus, unlike in *Ford*, UI did not establish that all conceivable accomodations would impose more than de minimus costs. *See Ford*, 2007 WL 2051015, at *5.

PERSUASIVE FOR PLAINTIFF ANALYSIS EXAMPLE

Here, like in *Ford* and *Alderman*, Defendant cannot demonstrate a genuine issue of material fact as to undue hardship. As in *Ford*, where the employer offered only one unsubstantiated assertion as the basis for its claim that providing a reasonable accommodation would constitute an undue hardship, here the only support Defendant offers as to its claim of undue hardship is the unsubstantiated statement of one employee, Mr. Saint's supervisor, who testified she refused to perform "extra work" to manually keep Mr. Saint's time. 2007 WL 2051016, at *2; Ex. 5, at 3. Moreover, while Defendant claims the biometric scanning system was implemented to avoid losses associated with suspected fraudulent time-keeping and employees forgetting their codes, Defendant fails to provide evidence indicating that Mr. Saint ever falsified his time records or forgot his code. Ex. 12, Edwards Dep. 4:17– 23, 5:1–2. Accordingly, like *Ford*, Defendant has failed to "to adduce any evidence" that allowing Mr. Saint to manually clock in and out "would have involved more than a de minimis cost." 2007 WL 2051016, at *2.

Furthermore, even if the Court were to accept that conclusory testimony alone is sufficient to show that allowing Mr. Saint to check in and out with his supervisor would have constituted an undue hardship, Defendant failed to prove that Mr. Saint's religious belief could not have been accommodated in some other manner without undue hardship or that such accommodation would constitute "unequal treatment." *See Hardison*, 432 U.S. at 81. While Mr. Saint's *preferred* accommodation was clocking in and out with his supervisor, he informed Defendant he was willing to sign in and out of work "using an alternative method." Ex. 2. Like *Ford*, Defendant has provided no evidence as to whether other methods of accommodation were explored such that Defendant fails to meet its burden to show "that all conceivable accommodations" would have imposed an undue hardship. 2007 WL 2051016, at *2. Defendant cannot "claim that it is unable to offer *any* reasonable accommodation without such hardship" because it did not explore any other accommodations whatsoever—rather, it simply denied Mr. Saint's proposed accommodation and forced him to use the objectionable scanner. *See Philbrook*, 479 U.S. at 68–69; Ex. 5 at 1–2. Moreover, Defendant cannot demonstrate that manually keeping Mr. Saint's time would result in "unequal treatment;" indeed, the opposite is true. *See Hardison*, 432 U.S. at 81. Defendant implemented manual time-keeping for another employee on non-religious grounds and its own policy requires a manual component for employee time-keeping. Ex. 12, Edwards Dep. 5:7–11; 6:2–3; Ex. 9.

Similarly, this Court should follow *Alderman* because it is not an undue hardship per se to allow an employee to continue to use a historically utilized business practice. *Alderman*, 332 F. Supp. 2d at 935. Like in *Alderman*, where the employee had a 14-month history of refraining from working on Sundays, here, Mr. Saint clocked in and out of work using the previously used manual time-keeping system for years before the new system was implemented. 332 F. Supp. 2d at 935; Ex. 12, Edwards Dep. 2:21–22. Further, as in *Alderman*, where the employer alleged that allowing the employee to continue being off on Sundays—as he always had been—would constitute an undue hardship, here, Defendant alleges that allowing Mr. Saint to continue clocking in with the manual system—the one used by all of Defendant's employees for years—would be an undue hardship. 332 F. Supp. 2d at 935; Ex. 5, at 3. However, like the employer in *Alderman*, Defendant has offered no evidence that Mr. Saint's practice of using the manual clock-in system placed an undue hardship on Defendant in the years prior to implementation of the biometric scanning system, nor that it would constitute a future undue hardship. Rather, another employee, Marvin Svelt, was permitted—after the implementation of the scanner—to "clock in by simply checking with Ms. Edwards." Ex. 14, Saint Dep. 4:16–18. Defendant—in allowing Mr. Svelt to "continue manual time-keeping" because he lost an eye and had broken arms—noted that it "understood that Svelt's unique situation makes it impossible for him to comply with the scanning requirements right now." Ex. 5 at 3; Ex. 12, Edwards Dep. 5:9–12. While Defendant admitted that it was aware of Mr. Saint's "strong religious beliefs" that made it impossible for him to use the scanner, Ms. Edwards said allowing Mr. Saint to do the same would be "extra work." Ex. 5 at 3; Ex. 12, Edwards Dep. 5:16–6:3. If allowing an employee to clock in and out manually did, in fact, impose an undue hardship, Defendant would have not allowed Mr. Svelt to do it. Maintaining a manual component to its time-keeping process is also inconsistent with Defendant's bald claim of undue hardship due to manual time-keeping. At the very least, as in *Alderman*, there is an "obvious dominance of material fact issues" and a lack of evidence that any accommodation of Mr. Saint's religious beliefs would cause Defendant undue hardship. 332 F. Supp. 2d at 937.

PERSUASIVE FOR DEFENDANT ANALYSIS EXAMPLE

Here, the Court should follow *Tagore* and find that Mr. Saint's requested accommodation to check in with his supervisor would pose an undue hardship on UI. Like the employee in *Tagore*, who insisted on wearing a kirpan at least three inches long in violation of the employer's policy and causing additional work on the security officers, Mr. Saint deemed only one accommodation acceptable—checking in and out his supervisor. 735 F.3d at 330; Ex.8. Just like the accomodation in *Tagore*, here, the proposed accomodation would require Mr. Saint's supervisor "unfairly to perform extra work to accommodate" Mr. Saint such that it would cause an undue hardship. 735 F.3d at 330; Ex. 5 at 3; Ex. 8. Specifically, allowing Mr. Saint to continue to sign in and out with Ms. Edwards would cause her to do extra work that would take away from her ability to do innovative projects and trainings. Ex. 5 at 3. Thus, like *Tagore*, where the court reasoned that the requested accommodation would pose an undue hardship because asking the employer's security officers, on a daily basis, to ascertain the dullness of the blade would be "time-consuming" and "impractical," here, too, requiring Ms. Edwards to keep track of Mr. Saint's time every day by hand would be "time-consuming" and "impractical." 735 F.3d at 331; Ex. 5 at 3; Ex. 8.

This Court should also find *Weber* persuasive because of the burden Mr. Saint's request would have put on a co-worker. Like *Weber*, where the court reasoned that the employee's "only suggested accommodation, that of skipping over assignments involving women . . . would impose more than a de minimis cost," here, Mr. Saint's only proposed accommodation of clocking in and out with his supervisor would impose significant costs. 199 F.3d at 275; Ex. 12, Edwards Dep. 4:17–5:2. The very reason that UI implemented the scanning system was to capture savings of more than $4,000 previously stemming from the inefficiency of checking employees in and out manually (e.g., Mr. Saint's requested accommodation) and to eliminate "costly positions" for addressing timekeeping fraud. Ex. 12, Edwards Dep. 4:17–5:2. Therefore, allowing Mr. Saint to clock in and out manually with his supervisor, would involve far "more than a de minimis cost" on UI and, therefore, impose an undue hardship such that UI is excused from providing the accommodation. *See Hardison*, 432 U.S. at 84. Additionally, like in *Weber*, where the court reasoned an undue hardship is present if "the proposed accommodation would force changes in the schedules of other employees and alter the employer's otherwise neutral procedure," forcing Ms. Edwards to unwillingly assume additional duties to accommodate Mr. Saint would force a change in her schedule and alter the "neutral" procedure of using the scanner for all employees. 199 F.3d at 275; Ex. 12, Edwards Dep. 5:4–6.While Mr. Saint suggests that his request was reasonable because his supervisor already kept time for another employee, that arrangement was temporary and expired after that employee recovered from his arm injuries. Ex. 12, Edwards Dep. 5:7–14. Here, like the employees in both *Tagore* and *Weber*, Mr. Saint requested a "permanent" accommodation. *Weber*, 199 F.3d at 275; *Tagore*, 735 F.3d at 330; Ex. 8. To accommodate Mr. Saint in his preferred manner would force UI to create permanent, additional duties for Mr. Saint's supervisor, reducing her efficiency—the opposite of what the costly scanner system was designed to do. Ex. 12, Edwards Dep. 4:16–23.

7. CRACC: creating persuasive Counter-analysis

As mentioned above, the organization of persuasive writing shifts from CRAC to CRACC. Although the added letter "C" (which stands for Counter-analysis) is new, the concept of counter-analysis is not. Rather, while it was not called counter-analysis, in objective writing you did a form of counter-analysis in your objective Analysis ("A" of CRAC) when you contrasted the facts of an illustrated case from the facts of your case.

For example, review the objective memorandum in the Appendix. For the CRAC on element one, the writer predicted that the element would be satisfied as her "C" or

Conclusion. The writer then illustrated two cases as part of the Rule ("R"): *Davis* and *Hansard*. In the Analysis ("A"), the writer supported her Conclusion (that element one would be satisfied) by comparing the facts of the client's case to the facts of *Davis* (where the court held element one was satisfied) and by contrasting the facts of the client's case to the facts of *Hansard* (where the court held element one was not satisfied). This contrasting is a form of counter-analysis. To support her prediction that element one would be satisfied, the objective writer had to deal with a case—*Hansard*—that was somewhat factually similar but came to a different outcome than the objective writer's prediction. Look at this excerpt from the Analysis in the objective memo:

> Distinct from the employee in *Hansard*, who did not satisfy the first element of his religious discrimination claim because his representations and actions surrounding his religious belief were inconsistent, Mr. Saint will likely establish that his religious belief was bona fide. *Hansard*, 1973 WL 129, at *2. While the facts in *Hansard* and Mr. Saint's case may appear alike because both employees have a common history of prior church membership and deactivated membership because of their dissatisfaction with the church, the *Hansard* holding turned on the fact that the employee was contradictory and inconsistent in his beliefs—which is unlike Mr. Saint. *See id.*; Ex. 2; Ex. 5 at 2; Ex. 6; Ex. 7 at 3; Ex. 10; Ex. 13. Unlike *Hansard*, where the employee asserted on select occasions that he could not work Sundays due to his religious belief against working for profit on Sundays, Mr. Saint was steadfast in his communications to his employer that he could not use the biometric scanner because of his religious belief in the "Mark of the Beast." 1973 WL 129, at *1; Ex. 5 at 2; Ex. 8. Although the employee in *Hansard* claimed that his religious belief against working on Sundays was "lifelong," he admitted to not always following his represented belief. 1973 WL 129, at *2. Despite the employee's attempt to justify his inconsistency by explaining that his belief reemerged following a "miraculous" event, he admitted to still working some Sundays even after his belief's renewal. *Id.* Unlike these inconsistent actions that the *Hansard* employee displayed surrounding his represented belief, Mr. Saint's actions reflect consistency because he never once used the scanner, he requested continuous exemptions from UI's new scanning policy, and he ultimately resigned rather than succumbing to use of the scanner. Ex. 2; Ex. 4; Ex. 5 at 2; Ex. 8; Ex. 12 at 5:14–15; Ex. 13. Thus, unlike *Hansard*, Mr. Saint's belief could hardly be argued to be based on "convenience rather than conviction" because Mr. Saint's made clear his religious belief forbade him from using the scanning technology, which he consistently refused to use, even though it inconveniently cost him his job. *See Hansard*, 1973 WL 129, at *2.

You can see that to support her prediction that element one was satisfied, the objective writer needed to show the reader why and how *Hansard* could be distinguished or overcome. This is a form of counter-analysis because the objective writer is addressing and overcoming an obstacle or counterargument that could be seen to potentially weigh against her prediction.

Now, of course, this type of objective counter-analysis is different from persuasive counter-analysis. The objective writer is not advocating for a certain outcome but is, instead, predicting the outcome that is most likely after a neutral analysis of the law. In persuasive writing, in your Analysis as discussed above, you are advocating for a specific outcome in favor of your client. You are illustrating case(s) in your Rule that are similar to the facts of your case and arguing that your case is like the illustrated case(s) such that the same outcome is warranted. However, there may be cases out there that are arguably similar to the facts of your case but come to the outcome opposite of the one you want. It is likely that the other side will rely on those cases and bring them to the court's attention. If the other side brings to the court's attention cases that are arguably factually similar to your case but that reach an outcome that is the opposite of the one you want for your client, then you must deal with those cases and the arguments that the other side makes regarding them. In persuasive writing, you do so in the Counter-analysis.

a. What is Counter-analysis?

The Counter-analysis (the new "C") will usually come in a new paragraph directly after your Analysis ("A") and before your final Conclusion (the last "C"). In your Counter-analysis, you will respond to the other side's strongest arguments and overcome potential weaknesses in your case that the other side has attempted to expose to the court.

The reason why the Counter-analysis is separate from the Analysis in persuasive writing is because you want to make your argument on the issue first (Analysis) and then separately deal with any weaknesses in your argument exposed by the other side (Counter-analysis). That is, you want to play offense before you play defense.

In objective writing, any counter-analysis (contrasting) is mixed with your Analysis because as an objective writer you are not trying to persuade. In objective writing, it does not matter that you use "prime real estate" in your memo to discuss a case that comes to the opposite conclusion of your prediction. However, in persuasive writing, you do not want to spend a lot of space—much less prominent space—in your motion or opposition on cases that are "bad" for your client. Instead, you want to first and foremost focus the court on the good: the strongest cases in favor of your position and arguments that highlight the strengths of your position. This is your Analysis. Then, separately, in your Counter-analysis, you briefly, but forcefully, address and overcome the bad.

You may be wondering why you need a Counter-analysis at all. Can you not just ignore the weaknesses of your case? It is important to include Counter-analysis because you do not make potential weaknesses "go away" by ignoring them. Instead, you make potential weaknesses in your case go away by addressing them head-on and overcoming them. But, while you want to address your weaknesses head-on, you also do not want to dwell on them or emphasize them. How do you address weaknesses without highlighting them? This Catch-22 (of sorts) is what makes Counter-analysis one of the most difficult persuasive-writing skills to master.

b. When do I need to include Counter-analysis?

You will notice that in the persuasive writing examples in this book, only the Plaintiff's MSJ Opposition has Counter-analysis in its CRACCs. Defendant's MSJ does not include Counter-analysis. Why is that? As you will recall, in trial court, a moving party files a motion, the non-moving party files an opposition, and then the moving party will usually get the opportunity to file a reply to the opposition. Thus, oftentimes, the motion does not have Counter-analysis because the Counter-analysis will be housed in the reply to the opposition. Indeed, at the time the motion is filed, the movant may not know what the other party's arguments will be or what weaknesses the other party will bring to the court's attention that need to be addressed. It will not be until the other party files his opposition that the movant will know, for example, which case(s) it needs to distinguish. Therefore, as a general rule, the motion will not contain Counter-analysis, but the movant will engage in Counter-analysis in the movant's reply. However, the opposition or response will contain Counter-analysis addressing the "best" legal authority and arguments in the movant's motion.

However, all rules have exceptions. Sometimes the movant will know exactly what the non-movant will argue. For example, in a post-trial motion, the movant may be able to predict the arguments the non-movant will make (and the legal authority she will rely on for such arguments) with respect to a particular issue because the same issue was briefed and argued at an earlier procedural stage. In this case, it can be powerful for the movant to include Counter-analysis in its motion so it can get out in front of and inoculate itself from the other party's arguments. This happens oftentimes in appellate briefs. Because the issues have been fully briefed and argued at the trial court level, both sides already know what the other will argue and, thus, appellants often include Counter-analysis in their opening briefs.

c. Counter-analysis structure and formulas

In your Counter-analysis, you will argue why the other side's analysis of the law and facts is wrong or, at least, less persuasive than the other side suggests. In order to draft Counter-analysis follow, these steps.

Step one: Critically analyze the other side's arguments and figure out what you need to address in your Counter-analysis.

Before you can write your Counter-analysis, you need to figure out which of the other side's legal authority needs to be addressed. That is, you must determine which of the other side's arguments with respect to their legal authority appear "bad" for your position such that they need to be addressed head-on. You will find the other side's arguments with respect to the law and the facts in the other side's Analysis of each issue. Therefore, before writing your Counter-analysis, you should closely re-read the opposing side's Analysis of the same issue and figure out which, if any, of the other side's cases need to be distinguished. The cases (and corresponding arguments) you will need to distinguish will likely be the ones that are most prominently referred to in the other side's Analysis of the issue. Often, the cases you need to address in your Counter-analysis are the same ones that the other side illustrated in its Rule.

Let's say that you represent Plaintiff EEOC and you want to draft a Counter-analysis for the reasonable accommodation element. First, you should read Defendant UI's Analysis for this element, which is set forth below. As you are reading it, ask yourself which of Defendant's cases you need to distinguish and which of Defendant's arguments you need to address.

> This Court should follow *Brener* and find that that UI offered Mr. Saint a reasonable accommodation that he refused to explore. Like the employer in *Brener*, who took "active steps" to accommodate the employee by going so far as deviating from its standard scheduling to accommodate the employee's religion, here, UI deviated from its retina scanner time keeping system applicable to all UI employees (with the exception of a single employee who lost his eye) to accommodate Mr. Saint. 671 F.2d at 145; Ex. 12, Edwards Dep. 5:3–14. Yet, like the employee in *Brener*, Mr. Saint "did not cooperate with the [employer's] efforts to satisfy his needs within the established . . . system" but instead, like the employee in *Brener*, categorically refused to sign in and out of work per company policy and resigned. 671 F.2d at 145; Ex. 14, Saint Dep. 5:9–19. *Brener* makes clear that Mr. Saint's failure to "fully explore" possible accommodations before casting off UI's good faith accommodation defeats his Title VII claim. 671 F.2d at 145.
>
> This Court should also find *Bruff* persuasive because the evidence proves that UI offered Mr. Saint a reasonable accommodation and actively worked to accommodate him, even if it was not his preferred accommodation. Like the employer in *Bruff*, who worked with the employee to find her a new position that would not conflict with her beliefs, here UI actively worked with Mr. Saint to find a new way for him to clock in and out that would not conflict with his beliefs. 244 F.3d at 501–02; Ex. 5 at 2. After learning of Mr. Saint's objection to having his retina scanned, UI immediately contacted Palmvein for more information, and Palmvein ensured UI that the "Mark of the Beast" could not be assigned through use of the scanner and that it "does not interfere with a person's body in any way." Ex. 5 at 1–2. Despite the fact that the scanner could not in any way impart a "Mark of the Beast," UI still offered Mr. Saint the reasonable accommodation of scanning his left thumb—an accommodation made in good faith based on the biblical passage Mr. Saint provided, which only referenced the "Mark of

> the Beast" on the forehead and right hand. *Id.*; Ex. 3. UI took Mr. Saint at his word when it interpreted the nature of his purported belief in attempting to accommodate him. Ex. 5 at 1. However, like the employee in *Bruff* who "displayed almost no such cooperation or flexibility," Mr. Saint never so much as responded to UI and, instead, maintained that he would not use the scanner "under any type of conditions." 244 F.3d at 503; Ex. 2. Mr. Saint insisted he would only accept signing in and out with his supervisor, however, as held in *Bruff*, "Title VII does not restrict an employer to only those means of accommodation that are preferred by the employee." 244 F.3d at 501, 503; Ex. 2. This Court should follow both *Bruff* and *Brener* because Mr. Saint was offered a reasonable accommodation that he refused to explore because it was not his single preferred accommodation.
>
> The law is clear that as long as UI offered "any reasonable" accommodation, it "has satisfied its obligation under Title VII as a matter of law." *Horvath*, 946 F.3d at 791. The undisputed evidence establishes that UI offered a reasonable accommodation by permitting Mr. Saint to scan in with his left thumb, which was the extent of its burden. Ex. 5 at 1. Accordingly, this Court should grant summary judgment because there is no genuine issue of material fact as to whether UI offered Mr. Saint a reasonable accommodation.

From reading Defendant's Analysis, you should recognize that the legal authority and corresponding arguments you need to address in your Counter-analysis are comprised of *Brener* and *Bruff*. The bulk of Defendant's Analysis is spent comparing the facts of Mr. Saint's case to these two cases and arguing that, like these two cases, Defendant offered Mr. Saint a reasonable accommodation. Therefore, in your Counter-analysis, you will need to address and overcome these cases head-on.

Step two: Carefully read the legal authority you need to distinguish and ask yourself five questions.

After you have identified the legal authority you need to distinguish and overcome, you should read that legal authority closely. You cannot rely on what the other side represents the legal authority to stand for in its motion; instead, you must read it yourself. For example, you cannot "trust" Defendant's case illustrations of *Brener* and *Bruff*. You must read both cases yourself.

While you are reading the cases, you are trying to identify how you are going to distinguish and overcome them in your Counter-analysis. To figure this out, ask yourself the following five questions when reading the opposing side's cases:

1. **Is the case relied upon by the opposing side no longer "good law"?** If the answer to this question is "yes," then it is your lucky day. If a case cited by the other side is no longer good law—meaning that it has been overturned or superseded—then you will present this in your Counter-analysis and can quickly move on. If

the case is no longer good law, it need not be distinguished any further because the court will not follow a case that is no longer good law. Usually the other side will not cite cases that have been overturned or superseded; therefore, oftentimes the answer to this question is "no" and you will have to work a bit harder in your Counter-analysis to distinguish the case in a different way.

2. **Did the opposing side misstate or misrepresent a holding from the case?** If, after reading the case, you find that the other side misstated or misrepresented the court's holding on the issue, you should state this in your Counter-analysis.

3. **Did the opposing side misstate or mispresent the reasoning from the case?** Sometimes the other side will misrepresent the reasoning of an illustrated case—how the court got from the trigger facts to the holding. For example, let's say the court granted a motion for summary judgment (holding), and the facts were similar to your case, but the reason the court granted it was in large part based on the fact that the other side did not file an opposition to the motion for summary judgment. If the other side omitted this reason, you would present this omission in your Counter-analysis to argue the case is less persuasive and should not be followed.

4. **Did the opposing side omit or misstate trigger facts from the illustrated case to make it seem more like your case?** After reading the case, you may note that the other side's illustration of the case is not complete. Rather, the other side omitted facts or misstated facts that were important to the court's holding and that make the illustrated case less like the facts of your client's case. Importantly, you are looking for omitted trigger facts—facts that affected the court's analysis—not simply omitted facts. No case illustration is going to include every fact, but if the other side omitted trigger facts or misstated trigger facts, you should present this in your Counter-analysis as a way to argue to the court that the case is less persuasive than presented by the other side.

5. **When comparing the illustrated case to your case, did the opposing side omit or misstate trigger facts from your case to make it seem more like the illustrated case than it actually is?** Sometimes the other side will perfectly illustrate a case but will then, in its Analysis, misrepresent the facts of your case to make it seem more like the illustrated case than it actually is. If this is the case, you should present in your Counter-analysis how the actual facts of your case (not those misrepresented by the other side) differ from the illustrated case.

Step three: Write your Counter-analysis using the formula.

Now that you know how you are going to distinguish and overcome the opposing side's case(s), you can write your Counter-analysis. In your Counter-analysis you are going to have to acknowledge this unfavorable legal authority, but you want to be careful not to emphasize or repeat the other side's legal arguments. First, you do not want to inadvertently restate the other side's position in a better or clearer way than it was stated in the other side's motion. Second, you do not want to waste the precious real estate of your motion or opposition restating the other side's arguments such that the court gets to read the other side's argument twice: for example, once in the other side's motion and once in your opposition.

As previously noted, addressing the other side's arguments and legal authority without emphasizing them is difficult. Striking that balance takes practice and experience. To help you get started, consider using the following formula.

COUNTER-ANALYSIS FORMULA

First sentence: Identify the legal authority relied on by the other side that you are addressing in your Counter-analysis.

- Defendant's reliance on [precedent case] is misplaced/misguided/not persuasive.

Middle sentences: Show why the legal authority is distinguishable and/or not as persuasive as represented by the other side. This is where your answers to the five questions in step two above come in handy. Repeat and mix these sample sentences as needed.

- The [legal authority] Defendant relied on is [no longer good law] because ______.
- In [its] motion, Defendant [omits/misstates] key facts that were important to the court's holding _______.
- Unlike [precedent case], where [trigger fact from precedent case], here [different trigger fact from our case].
- Defendant [misstates/misrepresents/omits] the court's holding because ________.
- Defendant [misstates/misrepresents/omits] the court's reasoning because ________.

Last sentence: Bring it all together and state why the middle sentences (distinguishing the legal authority) should matter to the court's decision.

- Accordingly, this Court should [not follow/not find persuasive/find distinguishable] [precedent case].

Note that the formula may **(read: will)** need to be tweaked as you tailor it to the particular case(s) you are distinguishing, and, as such, it should not be followed exactly. However, this formula will provide you with a starting-off point as you begin writing your Counter-analysis.

The example below is written using the Counter-analysis formula. Notice that because there are two cases that need to be distinguished, the Counter-analysis is in two paragraphs. Sometimes, you can distinguish multiple cases in a single paragraph, but, to begin, it is smart to separate it out so that you ensure that you fully address and distinguish each case.

As you read through this example, do a few things:

- First, highlight the first and last sentences of each of these paragraphs. Notice how Plaintiff signals to the court that it is turning to Counter-analysis in these first sentences and how Plaintiff tells the court why the cases relied upon by Defendant are not persuasive in the last sentences in a way that matters to the court's decision.
- Second, in the middle sentences of the paragraph, annotate how Plaintiff is distinguishing the cases. For example, for *Brener*, Plaintiff points out both that Defendant's illustration of *Brener* misstated the facts of *Brener* and misstated the reasoning of *Brener*. However, Plaintiff does not simply state that in a conclusory way without more; Plaintiff goes on to show this to the court in the middle sentences (i.e., plaintiff proves this to the court).
- Third, circle the citations in the Counter-analysis. For example, you will see that in the first sentence Plaintiff cites to Defendant's MSJ and where in Defendant's MSJ it discusses *Bruff*. Also, note that *Bruff* is a full cite in that first sentence. Why is that? It's because Plaintiff has not cited *Bruff* anywhere else in its Opposition (likely because *Bruff* isn't a great case for Plaintiff). In the middle sentences, you see that the citation depends on what is in the sentence. When citing to Defendant's argument, Plaintiff cites Defendant's MSJ. When citing to the facts of the present case, Plaintiff cites to the record. When citing to the facts, holding, or reasoning of *Bruff*, Plaintiff cites that case (which is now a short cite because it is cited in full in the first sentence). The last sentences (where Plaintiff tells the court why the middle sentences matter to its decision) do not include citations because these sentences are pure argument.

EXAMPLE COUNTERANALYSIS

Defendant's reliance on *Bruff v. North Mississippi Health Service, Inc.*, is misplaced. Def's Mot. Summ. J. 12–14; 244 F.3d 495 (5th Cir. 2001). Defendant's sparse application of *Bruff* to the present case fails to mention that unlike in *Bruff*, where the plaintiff's requested accommodation would have excused her from performing key aspects of her position as a counselor, here, Mr. Saint required an accommodation from the clocking-in and -out process, not an exemption from his primary duties as a general laborer. Def.'s Mot. Summ. J. 12–14; 244 F.3d at 500; Ex. 8. Defendant argues that *Bruff*'s holding applies here because "Mr. Saint's stubborn insistence on his sole requested accommodation does not require UI to offer it." Def.'s Mot. Summ. J. 14. However, Mr. Saint provided a suggestion for a possible accommodation—"to continue to sign in and out by checking in with Ms. Edwards." Ex. 8 at 1. He did not insist on that accommodation alone, he simply responded to Defendant's request to provide "suggestions for possible accommodations"; he was willing to sign in and out of work using an alternative method. Ex. 2; Ex. 8. Further, the plaintiff in *Bruff* was aware of the potential conflicts with her religious beliefs before she applied for the position, unlike Mr. Saint, who required an accommodation as a result of a policy change years into his employment with UI. 244 F.3d at 500; Ex. 1; Ex. 12, Anderson Dep. 3:2–3. Unlike the employer in *Bruff*, who made substantial efforts to accommodate its employee to eliminate the conflict between the employee's religious beliefs and her job duties (such as by facilitating the employee's transfer to another position or department in which she would be less likely to be confronted with subject matter she found objectionable based on her religious beliefs), here, Defendant mandated a single "accommodation" proposal that did not fully address Mr. Saint's religious needs. 244 F.3d at 498; Ex. 5 at 1–2. Therefore, this Court should not find *Bruff* persuasive.

Similarly, Defendant's reliance on *Brener* is unpersuasive because Defendant omits key facts that were important to the court's reasoning and holding. Def.'s Mot. Summ. J. 12–14 (citing *Brener*, 671 F.2d at 143). In *Brener*, the plaintiff's employer had a flexible scheduling system that allowed employees to trade shifts with their coworkers. 671 F.2d at 143–44. Further, the hospital deviated from established practice by directing employees to trade schedules with the plaintiff, and thus made a considerable effort to accommodate the plaintiff's needs. *Id.* at 144. Unlike the employer in *Brener*, Defendant did not make a considerable effort to accommodate Mr. Saint's religious needs. Ex. 5 at 1–2. Instead, Defendant offered Mr. Saint a single accommodation option that would have required him to use scanning technology in spite of his religious objections to it. Ex. 5 at 1–2.

Further, Defendant's reliance on *Brener* is also not persuasive because Defendant misapplies the court's reasoning. Def.'s Mot. Summ. J. 12–14. The *Brener* court reasoned there was inadequate cooperation by the employee to try to satisfy his religious needs because the plaintiff did not fully avail himself of the flexibility of the scheduling system when he only made "haphazard efforts" to trade schedules with his coworkers. 671 F.2d at 144–46. Unlike the employee in *Brener*, Mr. Saint was not responsible for the failure of the accommodation because Mr. Saint requested a total exemption from using the biometric scanner on any part of his body, and Defendant refused to excuse Mr. Saint from using the biometric scanner. Ex. 8; Ex. 5 at 1–2. Unlike in *Brener*, where the plaintiff had the ability to resolve his religious conflicts by trading shifts with his coworkers, here, Defendant did not offer Mr. Saint an alternative to using the biometric scanner. 671 F.2d 143–44; Ex. 5 at 1–2. Rather, Mr. Saint requested to continue signing in manually with his supervisor, and although that request was denied, Defendant did not offer him any alternative to the biometric scanner. Ex. 5 at 1–4; Ex. 12, Edwards Dep. 5:12–14. There was no dialogue with Mr. Saint past the original decision denying his accommodation request, leaving no opportunity for cooperation. Ex. 5 at 1. Because Mr. Saint was not responsible for the failure of the selective "accommodation" Defendant offered that did not fully address his religious objection, this Court should not follow *Bruff* or *Brener*.

H. Overall conclusion and signature block

The overall conclusion will be the last heading or section in your motion or opposition. And, here is the good news: it is the easiest part of your motion or opposition to write. While it is labeled a "conclusion," it is more of a prayer for relief asking the court to take a specific action. Normally, the conclusion in a motion or opposition is only one or two sentences long.

VIII. CONCLUSION

UI respectfully requests that this Court grant summary judgment as to Plaintiff's Title VII religious discrimination claim.

After your overall conclusion, you will include a signature block with the information required by your jurisdiction (normally, your name, bar number, law firm, and contact information, such as address, phone number, fax number, and email). Before your signature, you should include "Respectfully submitted." A sample of what a typical signature block might look like is below:

Respectfully submitted,

/s/ Dominique Baker
Dominique Baker
State Bar No.1234567
dbaker@lawfirm.com
Juan Jones
State Bar No. 2345678
jjones@lawfirm.com
Baker & Jones LLP
106 S. Harwood, Suite 400
Dallas, Texas 75201
214-555-0000 (office)
214-555-0001 (facsimile)
Attorneys for Defendant UI

Part 4 | Editing and Polishing

Editing and polishing do not mean the same thing, nor do they take place at the same point in time. However, both are essential to all writing, including legal writing. After you have finished writing, you may think you are finished, but your work is not complete. Instead, you must begin the editing and polishing process. Editing is where you review what you have written for organization, content, flow, and overall readability. Editing can be a bit of a misnomer because, during the editing phase, you are still writing. For example, you are making additions, deletions, and changes to your paper. After you complete editing, once again you may think you are finished, but again your work is not complete. Instead, you must begin the polishing or proofreading process. Polishing or proofreading is the final step in the writing process. Unlike editing, where you are reviewing the content of what you have written and making any necessary changes, when you begin the polishing phase of writing, the content should be finalized. That is, you should be polishing a final draft. In the polishing phase, you are working to make the content of your paper error free. You are proofreading for typos, misspellings, and grammar mistakes.

Chapter 11 | **Editing Process**

"There is no such thing as good writing. There is only good rewriting."[1] After you have finished writing the first draft of your paper (whether it be an e-mail, an objective memo, a motion, or a brief), you will begin editing what you have written for organization, content, flow, and overall readability. The term "editing" can be seen as synonymous with rewriting because, in the editing phase, you will often be rewriting portions of what you have already written.

One of the hardest parts about editing can be the fact that you are editing your own work. Often it can be difficult to look at what you have written and ascertain what needs to be rewritten or edited. That is, it is easier to rewrite others' work than your own. Therefore, it is necessary to approach editing your paper in a systematic way.

Step one: Zoom out and edit on a macro level

After you have finished writing the first draft of your paper, the first thing you should do is ensure that what you have written is complete and correctly organized on a macro level. In other words, check to make sure you have all the right parts in the right places. To complete this macro-level editing, you must make sure your paper follows procedural and substantive instructions.

Following procedural instructions sounds easy, but it is important because failure to do so can have dire consequences. In law school, the cost

---

1. Richard K. Neumann Jr., Legal Reasoning and Legal Writing: Structure, Strategy, and Style 61 (4th ed. 2001) (quoting Justice Louis Brandeis, Associate Justice of the U.S. Supreme Court).

of failure to follow assignment instructions is lost points. In real life, the failure to follow instructions can result in a court not accepting your non-conforming motion or brief. As a student in a first-year legal writing class, it is likely that your professor has given you assignment instructions that specify how your paper should be formatted. If you are practicing before a court, local rules will specify how your motion or brief should be formatted. You must follow these instructions and rules. To ensure you have followed your law school's formatting instructions, consider using the following formatting instruction checklist:

FORMATTING INSTRUCTION EDITING CHECKLIST

- ☐ Are you within the page limit?
- ☐ Are you using the correct font and font size?
- ☐ Are your margins correct?
- ☐ Do you need page numbers?
- ☐ Are your headings and subheadings correctly formatted and numbered?
- ☐ Are you abiding by any special instructions? (For example, we instruct our students that they should not put their names on their papers, but should, instead, use their anonymous exam IDs.)

Making sure your paper follows substantive instructions is also critical. This stage of the macro edit is where you will check to make sure that your paper has all the required parts in the correct places (macro organization) and addresses all the issues. What parts are required will depend on what you are writing and the instructions given to you, but you must make sure that you have them all. You should be able to do this by scanning your headings. For example, for an objective memo, do you have a question(s) presented, brief answer(s), statement of facts, discussion section, and overall conclusion? You also must look to see if you have addressed all required issues and if you have done a CRAC for each of those issues. At this point, you should also make sure that you have addressed the issues in the correct sequence and have included a proper heading for each. You are checking for "holes" in your paper. If you have any holes, you will need to fill them. To ensure that you have followed your law school's substantive formatting instructions, consider using the following substantive instruction checklist:

SUBSTANTIVE INSTRUCTION EDITING CHECKLIST

- ☐ Do you have all the formal parts of your paper and corresponding headings?
- ☐ Have you addressed all required issues?
- ☐ Do the number of issues = the number of CRACs?
- ☐ Do issues include subheadings where needed?

Step two: Zoom in and edit on a micro level

Now that you have ensured that you followed instructions (both the formatting and substantive instructions) and have all the required parts of your paper, you need to zoom in and edit each part. You should begin your micro-editing with the heart of your paper: the issues and their CRACs located in the discussion section of the objective memo and argument and authorities section of the motion. Then, you should move to the other formal parts of the objective memo (i.e., question(s) presented, brief answer(s), statement of facts, and conclusion) or motion (i.e., introduction, statement of facts, summary judgment evidence, standard of review, and conclusion). The reason for starting with your CRACs is that other parts of your paper are dependent on them. For example, your statement of facts is derived by the facts used in the Analysis section of your CRACs for each issue.

Each issue should have a CRAC (objective) or CRACC (persuasive) and that CRA(C)C should be a complete argument for that issue. To make sure that your CRA(C)Cs are complete and strong, we recommend going through the following CRA(C)C checklist.

CRA(C)C EDITING CHECKLIST

Conclusion sentences <u>C</u>RA(C)<u>C</u>

- ☐ Highlight your conclusion sentences in blue.
  - ☐ Does each CRA(C)C begin and end with your conclusion on the specific issue?

Rule C<u>R</u>A(C)C

- ☐ Highlight your general rules in green.
  - ☐ After your beginning <u>C</u>onclusion for the issue, do you include your general rule with a citation to the leading authority for that rule?
  - ☐ For persuasive writing, is the general rule stated in a way that is favorable to your client? Either positively and broadly or negatively and narrowly?
- ☐ Highlight your subrules in purple.
  - ☐ After your general rule, do you include subrules that explain the general rule?
  - ☐ Do you include a citation to the law after each subrule?
  - ☐ Do your subrules bridge to one another?
- ☐ Highlight your case illustrations in pink.
  - ☐ For each case illustration, do you have all four parts?

- ☐ Do you start with the topic sentence stating why the case is important?
- ☐ Do you next state the holding for the specific issue?
- ☐ Do you next include only the trigger facts that go to that issue?
- ☐ Do you include the reasoning (how the court got from the facts to the holding)?
- ☐ Do you avoid proper names in case illustrations and instead refer to the parties in case illustrations by using plaintiff, defendant, and/or another consistent and generic term (i.e., testator, establishment, employer, etc.)?
- ☐ Do you cite after all parts of your case illustrations with the exception of the topic sentence?

Analysis CRA(C)C

☐ Highlight your Analysis in yellow. Within your analysis, underline in red facts from your case and underline in blue parts of your rule you are using in your analysis. You should see significant amounts of both red and blue intermixed in your analysis.

- ☐ Do you start your Analysis with your Part One sentence?
- ☐ Does the Rule for the issue (CRA(C)C) and the facts for the issue from your Statement of Facts match with the Analysis for the issue (CRA(C)C)?
    - ☐ Are you doing rule-language bridging by incorporating "sound-bites" from your general rules and subrules into your Analysis?
    - ☐ Are you doing analogical reasoning for your illustrated case or cases for the issue? Are you comparing the facts of your case side by side with the similar facts from the precedent case? Are you making sure you explain in your Analysis why that comparison/contrast with the illustrated case matters? That is, are you giving the "so what"?
    - ☐ If your Rule and Analysis for the issue do not match, do you need to trim your Rule, beef up your Analysis, or do both in order to make them match?
    - ☐ In your Analysis, do you make sure you do not introduce any "new" law that was not included in your Rule for the issue?
    - ☐ Are you incorporating all of your client's facts that go to the issue in your Analysis? Put another way, are there any facts that you need to add for the issue?
- ☐ In your Analysis, do you include citations to the law and/or the record depending on the content of the Analysis sentence?

Counter-Analysis CRA(C)C (in persuasive writing only)

- ☐ Highlight your Counter-analysis for the issue in orange.
  - ☐ Do you include a Counter-analysis for the opposing side's best authority on the issue?
  - ☐ Do you begin your Counter-analysis by identifying the legal authority relied on by the other side that you are addressing (and address the opposing side's best authority on the issue)?
  - ☐ Next, do you show why the legal authority is distinguishable and/or not as persuasive as represented by the other side?
  - ☐ Do you end your Counter-analysis by stating why the way you have distinguished the opposing side's best authority should affect the court's decision?
  - ☐ Do you include citations to the case you are distinguishing, the record, and/or the other side's paper in your Counter-analysis?

Make sure the other formal parts of your paper are complete—after you have checked each CRA(C)C, you need to examine the other parts of your paper. Below are checklists for an objective memo's formal parts and a motion's formal parts:

OBJECTIVE MEMO EDITING CHECKLIST

Question(s) Presented

- ☐ Do you use either under/does/when or the multi-sentence approach?
- ☐ Do you incorporate the relevant law and trigger facts that go to the legal question at issue?

Brief Answer(s)

- ☐ Do you begin with your brief one- to two-word answer?
- ☐ Do you explain your answer concisely and without repeating what is in the question presented?

Statement of Facts

- ☐ Is your statement of facts in chronological order?
- ☐ Do the facts in your statement of facts match the facts used in your Analysis of the issue(s)?
- ☐ Do you state facts objectively?
- ☐ Do you include citations to the record throughout?

Discussion Roadmaps

- ☐ Do you begin your discussion section with an introductory roadmap?
- ☐ Does the first sentence of your roadmap state your overall conclusion?

- ☐ Do you next set forth the overarching rule for the cause(s) of action or issues?
- ☐ Do you set forth any overarching subrules that apply to all elements of the cause(s) of action or issues?
- ☐ Do you list your conclusions for each element or issue in the order they will be discussed?
- ☐ If there are multiple distinct issues or multiple causes of action, do you include mini-roadmaps for each distinct issue or cause of action that (1) states your overall conclusion for that distinct issue or cause of action and (2) lists the elements or issues in the order they will be discussed for that distinct issue or cause of action?

Conclusion

- ☐ Do you include an overall conclusion paragraph to end your memo that restates your predicted outcome?

MOTION EDITING CHECKLIST

Introduction

- ☐ Do you start by stating the overall relief you want the court to grant or deny?
- ☐ Do you, incorporating the legal standard for the motion, argue the conclusion you want the court to reach on each issue?
- ☐ For each issue, do you persuasively set forth the overarching rule and cite to the governing law?
- ☐ For each issue, do you preview the arguments to come in the order they will be addressed?
- ☐ Do you dispose of any issues that will not be addressed (for the non-movant)?

Statement of facts

- ☐ Is your statement of facts in chronological order?
- ☐ Do the facts in your statement of facts match the facts used in your Analysis (CRACC) of the issue(s)?
- ☐ Do you state facts persuasively by emphasizing favorable facts and de-emphasizing unfavorable facts?
- ☐ Do you include citations to the record throughout?

Legal standard

- ☐ Do you include the governing legal standard with a citation to the governing law?
- ☐ Is the governing legal standard stated persuasively for your client (either positively and broadly or narrowly and negatively)?
- ☐ Do you include favorable subrules for your client to explain the legal standard?

Argument roadmaps

- ☐ Under the argument and authorities heading, do you include an overall roadmap that (1) argues the overall conclusion you want the court to reach; (2) outlines the arguments you will make in the order you will make them; and (3) if applicable, disposes of any issues that will not be addressed?
- ☐ If there are multiple distinct issues or multiple causes of action, do you include mini-roadmaps for each distinct issue or cause of action that (1) states your overall conclusion for that distinct issue or cause of action and (2) lists your arguments in the order they will be discussed for that distinct issue or cause of action?

Conclusion

- ☐ Do you include a simple conclusion sentence restating the overall relief you want the court to grant?

Step three: Zoom in more and edit on a sentence level

Through the macro and micro editing steps one and two, you have edited for organization and content. Now, you will edit on a sentence level for flow and readability. Here is a checklist to help you edit on a sentence level:

SENTENCE-LEVEL EDITING CHECKLIST

- ☐ Do you use transition words (first, second, then, next, last, etc.) to explain the relationship between ideas?
- ☐ Do you include topic sentences before your case illustration paragraphs? (If you use the formulas in this book, topic sentences are sometimes "built in" to the other parts of CRA(C)C.)
- ☐ Do you use mostly active voice? Any time you use passive voice, do you make sure it is a conscious choice? To help find passive voice, you can do a search for the word "by." This search will not catch every instance of passive voice, but it will catch many.
- ☐ Do you minimize your use of adjectives and adverbs? If you use an adjective or adverb, can you eliminate it by using a stronger noun or verb instead?
- ☐ Do you use the correct dash each time you use an en dash, em dash, or hyphen?
- ☐ Look for any sentences that are longer than 25 words. Are these sentences, when read aloud, confusing or bulky because they contain too many ideas? If so, separate the sentence or add clarifying punctuation.
- ☐ Do you employ parallelism when "listing" things?

Step four: Check your citations to the law and factual record

The last items on your editing checklist are your citations to the law and to the factual record. It is helpful to check citations separately from the content of your paper. To edit citations, you should use the following checklist:

CITATION EDITING CHECKLIST

- ☐ Print a fresh copy of your objective memo, motion, or brief. Highlight all your long citations in one color and your short citations in another color.
- ☐ Do your citations conform to *The Bluebook* or your state's local citation manual?
- ☐ Do your citations include pincites throughout?
- ☐ Do you include the full citation the first time you cite an authority? Thereafter, do you use the short citation form or *id.*?
- ☐ Do you include citations after almost every sentence in your CRA(C)Cs (excluding your Conclusions and topic sentences)?

Chapter 12 | **Polishing Process**

After you have completed editing you should have a "final draft." It is from this "final draft" that you will begin polishing. The reason the words "final draft" are in quotations is because this final draft that you are polishing is not actually your end work product. Instead, only after you finish polishing, will you have your end work product—that is your "final, final draft" or the error-free version of your "final draft."

In the polishing phase, you are not rewriting. Rather, you are catching errors such as typos, misplaced commas, inconsistent spacing, etc. As you are polishing your work, it is important to know that catching your own errors—as opposed to the errors of others—is objectively difficult. The reason for this difficulty is that, when you read your own work product, your brain "autocorrects" or "generalizes" the small parts (individual words) so that it can focus on the complex parts (combining sentences to make ideas). When it comes to your own work product, your brain is so familiar with and aware of the ultimate content that your brain becomes blind to the errors in front of it: "The reason we don't see our own typos is because what we see on the screen is competing with the version that exists in our heads."[1] To fix this annoying (and amazing) autocorrect function that your brain performs when reading your own work, you must "trick" your brain into thinking that what it is proofreading is not something that it has seen hundreds of times, but is something that is brand new.[2] With this in mind, to catch errors, we recommend

1. Nick Stockton, *What's Up With That: Why It's So Hard to Catch Your Own Typos*, Wired Magazine (Aug. 12, 2014, 11:21 AM), https://www.wired.com/2014/08/wuwt-typos/.
2. *Id.*

that you do the following when polishing to "trick" your brain into thinking it is reading your paper for the first time.

1. **Sleep on it:** Try to polish on a different day than you edit and, ideally, after a full night's sleep. You want to approach polishing with "fresh eyes."

2. **Change the look of the paper:** When polishing, use a hard copy that is in a different font type and font size from what you are used to seeing. For example, if you typed your paper in Times New Roman, size 12 font, when you print out your paper to polish, change your font to Ariel, size 28 font. Notice how much easier it is to spot errors in the below example when you change the font. (Hint: you should see six errors.)

   > Like *Primera*, where the evidence showed the a establishment trained its employees to be "vigilant' against serving intoxicated patrons, here, the evidence show that "Chip-Home takes training very seriously." *Primera*, 349 S.W.3d at 169.; Ex. 4, Morgan Dep. 2:14-18..

   > Like *Primera*, where the evidence showed the a establishment trained its employees to be "vigilant' against serving intoxicated patrons, here, the evidence show that "Chip-Home takes training very seriously." *Primera*, 349 S.W.3d at 169.; Ex. 4, Morgan Dep. 2:14-18..[3]

3. **Focus on small sections:** Proofread in small sections and out of order. We recommend using a colored piece of paper or a ruler to isolate what you are proofreading line-by-line. Alternatively, you can use a highlighter to proofread words one-by-one as you go down the page. You can also proofread out

---

3. The sentence with errors fixed should read as follows:

Like *Primera*, where the evidence showed the establishment trained its employees to be "vigilant" against serving intoxicated patrons, here, the evidence shows that "Chip-Home takes training very seriously." *Primera*, 349 S.W.3d at 169; Ex. 4., Morgan Dep. 2:14–18.

of order by starting at the end and reading to the beginning or randomly reading paragraphs out of order.

4. **Set the mood:** Proofread while listening to classical music, chewing gum, and sitting under non-florescent lighting. All of these things have been shown to potentially help make your brain focus.

5. **Read it aloud:** Proofread by reading the document aloud or use the text-to-speech function on Google Docs or Microsoft Word or the like to read your document aloud to you.

Finally, before giving your edited and polished document to your professor, opposing counsel, boss, client, or a court, make sure to run a final, full grammar and spell check on the document. You can use the review function in Word or Google Docs or you can use a paid-for service, such as Grammarly, BriefCatch, Hemmingway, or PerfectIt to do this final check for grammar, usage, and syntax errors. If you are a student who tends to struggle with either attention to detail or grammar rules, we *highly recommend* you invest in one of the paid-for grammar programs early in your legal writing career. (And, no we do not get any kickbacks from the programs for making that suggestion.) Lawyers are notorious for judging each other (and—wait for it—job applicants) based on their grammar and citation skills almost as much as the substance of what is written. So, producing a clean and accurate document is especially important for lawyers. As an added benefit, many of the paid-for grammar programs also include access to plug-ins that provide grammar review functionality on e-mails and text messages.

Part 5 | Oral Presentations and Hearings

In this section of the book, we discuss how to present your written arguments in oral form. In many legal writing classes, your second semester will culminate in an in-class oral argument, where you will orally argue your persuasive work product (whether that be a motion, opposition, or brief) before a panel of "judges" (your professors, members of your school's mock trial or moot court teams, lawyers, or judges from the community). As a practicing lawyer, you will also have the opportunity to orally argue your written work product to the court.

The skills needed to be a successful oral advocate are somewhat different from the skills needed to be a successful legal writer, although not wholly unrelated. In this section, you will learn how to present a persuasive oral argument, how to prepare for an oral argument, and, specifically, how to transform your written arguments into an oral argument.

Chapter 13 | Purpose of Oral Presentations and Hearings

After submitting a written motion or brief, you may be given the opportunity to orally argue your position before the court. At the trial court level, orally arguing your case is often simply called an oral hearing, whereas at the appellate level orally arguing your case is called an oral argument. For purposes of this book, we will use the terms interchangeably. An oral hearing or an oral argument provides you with an additional opportunity to persuade the court of your position and, most importantly, to answer any questions or address any doubts the deciding judge or judges have about your case. An oral argument, unlike a written motion or brief, is interactive and allows you to clarify issues in real-time, to highlight your most important points, to eliminate any misconceptions held by the judge or judges, and to respond to the other side's arguments.

At the appellate level, most judges and lawyers agree that the oral argument is important, but they also argue that it is of secondary importance to a well-written brief. As explained by the late Justice Ruth Bader Ginsburg, "As between briefing and argument, there is a near-universal agreement among federal appellate judges that the brief is more important—certainly it is more enduring."[1] As explained by another judge, "Appellate advocacy comes in two parts, briefs and oral arguments, and its sole object is the persuasion of appellate judges. The brief is the more important part of ap-

1. Ruth Bader Ginsburg, *Remarks on Appellate Advocacy*, 50 S.C. L. Rev. 567, 567–68 (1999).

pellate advocacy, because judges have it in hand both before and after oral argument. It is physically with us long after the argument evaporates and is forgotten."[2] Although not as significant as the written brief, an oral argument is important and can make a difference in the outcome of the issue or the entire case. In their book *Making Your Case*, the late Justice Antonin Scalia and Bryan Garner note that while an oral argument "rarely" will change a well-prepared judge's mind, oral argument can make a difference when the judge, after reading the briefs, is still undecided.[3] At the trial court level, where judges are busier and have less time to read the motions or briefs, an oral argument may have an even greater impact on a judge's decision.[4]

You should note that an oral argument is not guaranteed at either the trial or appellate level. While the rules vary, as a general matter, at the appellate level, oral argument must be requested. Often, as an appellant (the party bringing the appeal), it is in your best interest to request an oral argument, especially if the legal issue before the court is complex. However, data suggests that the frequency with which federal courts of appeals grant oral arguments is declining. According to a 2019 report, oral arguments were held in only 20 percent of federal courts of appeals cases decided on the merits at the end of the 2017 fiscal year.[5] Likewise, at the federal district court level, the rarity of oral arguments is also a chief complaint among some lawyers.[6]

Thus, while oral argument is certainly important, the opportunity for oral argument is not guaranteed, and, even when granted, it is of secondary importance to your written motion or brief. Regardless, oral advocacy is an important skill for law students to learn. Often, as noted above, in the first-year legal writing program, students will present an oral argument based on their persuasive motion or brief.

---

2. Roger J. Miner, *Froessel Award Acceptance Address Confronting the Communication Crisis in the Legal Profession*, 34 N.Y.L. SCH. L. REV. 1, 8–9 (1989).

3. ANTONIN SCALIA & BRYAN A. GARNER, MAKING YOUR CASE: THE ART OF PERSUADING JUDGES 139 (2008).

4. DAVID C. FREDRICK, THE ART OF ORAL ADVOCACY 4 (2019).

5. Todd Ross, *Quiet Time? Oral Arguments Disappear in Federal Appeals Courts*, NAT'L L.J., June 1, 2018, at 16.

6. Mark R. Kravitz, *Written and Oral Persuasion in the United States Courts: A District Judge's Perspective on Their History, Function, and Future*, 10 J. APP. PRAC. & PROCESS 247, 255 (2009) ("Of course, oral argument in many federal district courts is even more rare than in the federal courts of appeals. Indeed, at a recent hearing of the Judicial Conference's Civil Rules Advisory Committee on proposals to amend Rule 56, which governs summary judgment, a chief complaint of practitioners—plaintiffs' and defendants' lawyers alike—was that district court judges rarely, if ever, provide an opportunity for oral argument on summary judgment motions. There appears to be a widespread belief among both court of appeals and district court judges that oral argument is inefficient and consumes too much court time, without attendant benefit. This rejection of oral argument has also been accompanied by a movement away from oral judgments and opinions."); Suzanne Ehrenberg, *Embracing the Writing-Centered Legal Process*, 89 IOWA L. REV. 1159, 1162 (2004) ("Over the past 150 years, appellate courts [and more recently, trial courts] have increasingly limited the role of oral argument, and have relied more heavily on written briefs in their decision-making processes.").

Chapter 14 | Structure and Content of an Oral Argument

The general structure and content of an oral argument will depend on your audience, specifically, whether that audience is a trial court judge or an appellate court panel of judges. For example, you can imagine that arguing a motion before a state trial court judge is very different than arguing before the nine justices of the U.S. Supreme Court.

Generally, in an oral argument, the moving party (the party asking for relief) argues first, next the responding party argues, and last the moving party argues a short rebuttal. At the appellate level, the moving party who argues first is the appellant, and the responding party is the appellee. At the trial court level, the party who argues first is the moving party (whichever party filed the motion), and the party that goes second is the responding party (whichever party filed the response/opposition to the motion).

At the outset, it is important to discuss the main differences between trial court hearings and appellate court oral arguments. First, unlike trial court hearings, which are done before a single judge, appellate court oral arguments are done before a panel of judges, ranging from three at the Circuit Courts of Appeals to nine at the U.S. Supreme Court. Second, appellate court judges are generally more prepared than trial court judges. At the appellate court level, judges will have carefully read your briefing and will be very familiar with the issues. At the trial court level, judges have busier dockets and, as a result, may or may not have had enough time to carefully read and digest the issues in your motion.

Third, appellate court oral arguments are generally more formal than trial court hearings. At an oral argument before an appellate court, you will be strictly timed, argue standing behind a lectern, and begin with the phrase "May it please the court." At a trial court hearing, the format of the oral argument will vary greatly depending on the court before which you are arguing. A trial court argument may be done sitting or standing. It may be done in open court or in the judges' chambers. The argument may be timed, with each side getting a certain number of minutes like in an appellate court, or it may be an untimed back-and-forth discussion between you, opposing counsel, and the judge. Thus, before arguing before a trial court judge, it is especially important to talk with a lawyer who has previously argued before that judge so that you know what to expect.

Regardless of whether you are arguing at the trial court or appellate level or whether you are representing the moving party or the responding party, generally speaking, your oral argument can be broken into five "parts": **(1) the opening; (2) the statement of facts; (3) the body of the argument; (4) responding to questions; and (5) the closing.**

If your argument is in an appellate court or in a more formal trial court, the argument will be timed (often 20 minutes total per side) and proceed in the following order:

- Moving party/appellant argument;
- Responding party/appellee argument; and
- Rebuttal by moving party/appellant, if requested.

The moving party/appellant's time for rebuttal will be reserved at the start of the oral argument and will be subtracted from the total 20-minute time period allotted.

Because the focus of this book is writing at the trial level as opposed to the appellate level, the examples in this chapter will originate from an argument on a motion for summary judgment in a trial court. However, during first-year legal writing, whether the document being argued is a trial court document or an appellate court document, you should expect that the oral arguments will be conducted with the formality of an appellate oral argument. This means you will stand in front of a podium, you will be strictly timed, and you will likely argue in front of a panel of well-informed judges.

A. Opening

After the court gives you permission to proceed with your argument, you will begin your argument with an opening. Because your opening will be your first impression, you want to start with confidence. To do this, it is important that you script your opening, memorize it, and recite it with ease. Your opening can be broken into three subparts: (1) introduce yourself; (2) state your overall position or theme; and (3) give a roadmap or overview of what you will discuss during your oral argument.

1. Introduce yourself (and reserve time for rebuttal if movant or appellant)

At the appellate level, the first words out of your mouth at an oral argument are "May it please the court." At the trial court, these formal words are not required. Rather, you start by introducing yourself, your client, your client's position in the case (plaintiff or defendant), and your client's position on the issue (movant/respondent or appellant/appellee). In trial court, your introduction may look like this:

> Good morning, your Honor. My name is Julius Hernandez, and I represent the Plaintiff-Respondent the EEOC.

In the law school setting, student advocates will typically begin even a trial court oral argument with "May it please the court" even though that formal language is not required when arguing before a "real" trial court.

In appellate court, your introduction will be similar. However, if you are the appellant, you should, immediately after introducing yourself, reserve time for rebuttal. An example introduction for an appellant may look like this:

> May it please the court. My name is Dominique Baker, and I represent the appellant in this case Defendant-Appellant United Information. At this time, I would like to reserve two minutes for rebuttal.

If you are in a court that gives each side 20 minutes to argue, you will have 18 minutes for your argument and then two minutes for rebuttal. If your trial court is formal and the judge has given you a set amount of time, you should also, as movant, reserve time for rebuttal in a similar manner as above.

2. State your overall position or theme

After introducing yourself, you should state your overall position or theme. Figuring out your overall position or theme is simple. Just ask yourself: what do you want the outcome of the hearing to be? Using the problem in the Appendix of this book, if you represent Defendant/Movant United Information, what outcome do you want? You want your motion for summary judgment to be granted! How do you get the court to grant the motion? By showing that Plaintiff cannot establish a fact issue with respect to at least one element of his religious discrimination claim or by proving reasonable accommodation or undue hardship. Defendant/Movant might state its overall position/theme like this:

> This Court should grant summary judgment as to Plaintiff's Title VII claim for religious discrimination claim because Plaintiff cannot prove the essential element of bona fide religious belief. Alternatively, even if

> Plaintiff can create a fact question on its prima facie case, the undisputed evidence proves that: (1) UI offered a reasonable accommodation; and/or (2) the accommodation Mr. Saint requested would have caused undue hardship such that Plaintiff's religious discrimination claim should still be dismissed.

On the other hand, if you represent the EEOC what do you ultimately want from the court? You want Defendant United Information's motion for summary judgment to be denied. Why? Because there are, at a minimum, genuine disputes of material fact regarding the religious discrimination claim. Therefore, you could state your overall position like this:

> This Court should deny Defendant's Motion for Summary Judgment because Defendant fails to meet its burden of proof to show that there are no genuine disputes of material fact with respect to Mr. Saint's Title VII religious discrimination claim.

3. Give a brief roadmap or overview of what you will discuss

After stating your overall position or theme, you should briefly give the court an overview of what you will discuss in the order that you plan to discuss it. This should be similar to what your "roadmap" looks like in your written motion or brief. However, you may or may not hit all of the points made in your written motion or brief in your oral argument. If that is the case, you will need to adjust your oral argument roadmap to reflect only those issues you plan to cover during your oral argument. For example, let's say you represent Defendant/Movant United Information. In your motion, you discuss three reasons that the Court should grant sum-mary judgment. But, how many of these arguments do you need to win to have the court grant your motion for summary judgment? Just one! It may be that you make the strategic decision to argue only your strongest reason during oral argument as opposed to arguing all three. For example, your roadmap could look like this:

> In our motion, United Information provides three independent grounds on which this Court should grant summary judgment. However, Defendant will spend its limited time today showing this Court that it was unable to reasonably accommodate Mr. Saint's needs without undue hardship such that summary judgment should be granted.

If representing the EEOC, you need to rebut all three of Defendant's arguments to survive summary judgment. Accordingly, your planned roadmap or overview might sound like this:

> First, there is, at a minimum, a genuine dispute of material fact that Mr. Saint sincerely held a bona fide religious belief. Second, Defendant has failed to conclusively prove that it offered Mr. Saint a reasonable accommodation. Third, Defendant failed to conclusively establish that accommodating Mr. Saint's religious belief would impose an undue hardship on Defendant.

However, as the respondent, you must be flexible even in the "scripted" opening section of your argument. As respondent, you will have had the benefit of already hearing the movant's argument and the court's questions such that you have a better idea of the main issues that need to be confronted. For example, if the Defendant/Movant spent its entire oral argument time on undue hardship, it might be smart to rework your roadmap to start with that issue and then address the remaining two issues. In that case, your revisited roadmap or overview may look like this:

> First, because Defendant spent the bulk of its time on undue hardship, I will start with it and show that the evidence proves Defendant failed to conclusively establish that accommodating Mr. Saint's religious belief would impose an undue hardship on Defendant. Second, there is, at a minimum, a genuine dispute of material fact that Mr. Saint sincerely held a bona fide religious belief. Third, Defendant has failed to conclusively prove that it offered Mr. Saint a reasonable accommodation.

4. Pulling your opening together

Put together, your opening should take less than one minute. Here is an example of a complete opening, with all three parts, for the lawyer representing Plaintiff EEOC:

> Good morning, your Honor. My name is Julius Hernandez, and I represent the Plaintiff-Respondent the EEOC. This Court should deny Defendant's Motion for Summary Judgment because Defendant fails to meet its burden of proof to show that there are no genuine disputes of material fact with respect to Mr. Saint's Title VII religious discrimination claim. First, there is, at a minimum, a genuine dispute of material fact that Mr. Saint sincerely held a bona fide religious belief. Second, Defendant has failed to conclusively prove that it offered Mr. Saint a reasonable accommodation. Third, Defendant failed to conclusively establish that accommodating Mr. Saint's religious belief would impose an undue hardship on Defendant.

Remember, you should have your opening down cold. When you get up to argue, your nerves will be high. Being extremely comfortable and confident in your opening will help calm you.

B. Statement of facts

The statement of facts portion of an oral argument will differ for the movant and the non-movant or respondent. This difference makes sense if you think about the timing and order for an oral argument. The movant is the first to speak and, thus, the one to introduce the case to the court. As such, the movant has to give the court factual context for its decision. The respondent, on the other hand, speaks only after the movant has argued. It would be inefficient for the respondent to spend limited argument time reiterating the facts that the movant already covered. Instead, the factual recitation part of a respondent's argument will likely be more limited in nature. Below we provide more detail into how each side should approach the statement of facts.

1. Movant

After your opening, the movant should be prepared to provide the court with a brief overview of the facts of your case that pertain to the issues before the court. Often, if the court is familiar with the facts, it will interrupt your recitation of the facts and say something like "Counsel, move on. I am familiar with the facts." However, sometimes the court will allow you to give a brief overview of the facts before diving into the bulk of your argument. Note, given that you only have a limited amount of time, your recitation of the facts should be brief. Some lawyers, especially those arguing before appellate courts that are likely familiar with the parties' briefs, skip over the statement of facts and go straight to the argument. In a trial court, a brief overview of the facts may be helpful, especially if you think the judge may not be familiar with the facts underlying your motion.

Here is an example of what the lawyer representing Defendant United Information's statement of facts could look like during oral argument:

> Before working at United Information, Mr. Saint ceased attending church and denounced his Christianity. However, when United Information informed employees that it would use a new retina scanning system for employees to clock in and out of work, Mr. Saint objected to new system based on his alleged religious belief that it would impose the "Mark of the Beast." Upon receiving Mr. Saint's objection, United Information offered him the accommodation of using his left thumb, instead of his retina, to clock in and out of work. Mr. Saint did not respond to the accommodation and resigned from his position at United Information. Mr. Saint then contacted the EEOC to pursue his claim of religious discrimination pursuant to Title VII.

2. Respondent

The respondent's statement of facts largely depends on what the movant did or did not do. If the movant began by giving a statement of facts and the court indicated to the movant that it was familiar with the facts, then respondent should not give a statement of facts. Why? The court just said it was familiar with the facts so move on! If the movant omitted a statement of facts, you should also probably omit a statement of facts and simply incorporate the important facts in the body of your argument.

On the other hand, if the movant gave a statement of facts, the respondent may also want to give a short statement of facts. However, the respondent should be careful not to waste the court's time repeating the facts of the case, but instead limit its facts to correcting only important omissions, misstatements, or mischaracterizations of the facts presented by the movant. In their book *Making Your Case*, the late Justice Scalia and Bryan Garner recommend that the respondent when providing a statement of facts use an approach like the following:

> The EEOC's description of the facts is obviously quite different from those stated by Defendant United Information. But, for the sake of time, I will rest on the facts in our written opposition and make the following corrections to Defendant's statement....[1]

C. Body of planned argument

The bulk of your oral argument time will be spent in the body of your planned argument. The body of your argument is where you will set forth the points you need to make in the order provided in the roadmap you gave during your opening. In the body of your argument, you should not read from or recite your motion or brief. Not only would this be boring and redundant, there is simply not time to cover everything in your motion or brief in an oral argument. Instead, you will argue the main points or, put another way, the highlights of your argument. As a general matter, you should limit yourself to no more than three points for your oral argument, even if there are more than three points in your written motion or brief.

For each point, you will do an oral version of "CRACC." The oral version of "CRACC" is, however, quite a bit different than the written version. So instead of calling it "CRACC," we prefer to call it "C-R/A-C." For each point, you will start with your "C" or <u>C</u>onclusion and then state why the conclusion is supported by both the law ("R" or <u>R</u>ule) and facts as applied to the law ("A" or Analysis). However, unlike a written motion or brief, where you fully explain the law (<u>R</u>ule) before applying it (<u>A</u>nalysis), in an oral argument, presumably the court has read your motion or brief and, as such, you can mix the <u>R</u>ule and <u>A</u>nalysis. Moreover, depending on the issue, and, especially if you are in trial court, you may spend significantly more time on the facts than on the law. Why? Often the judge is painfully familiar with the law, but the facts of your case are unique.

---

1. Scalia & Garner, at 168–69.

For example, if you have a negligence case, you do not need to waste time explaining the definition of causation in great detail to the judge. Instead, you need to focus on the topic with which the judge is less familiar: why causation is or is not established in your case. Why causation is or is not established in your case will be a mix of the law with the facts, but the bigger focus will be on the facts of your case. This is especially true with a motion for summary judgment because the governing legal standard is whether there is a genuine dispute of material fact.

If you have time, after your "R/A," you will briefly restate your "C" or Conclusion for the issue and simultaneously transition to the next issue. If you are running short on time, it is okay to skip the last "C" or Conclusion and simply transition to the next issue. Note that transitions are especially important in oral arguments because it is imperative that at all times the court knows what point you are addressing and can recognize when you are moving on from one issue to another. Therefore, use words like "first," "second," or "third" and phrases like "moving to the second issue" to signpost your argument.

To understand what the body of a planned argument looks like in C-R/A-C form, it is most helpful to take it out of the abstract and use an example. For the undue hardship issue, Defendant/Movant United Information's planned argument might look like the below if Defendant is starting with this issue. The "C" or Conclusion sentences are underlined and what is in the middle is the "R/A."

Conclusion

> First, this Court should grant summary judgment because the undisputed evidence establishes that the only accommodation Mr. Saint proposed—to personally check in and out with his supervisor—would have imposed an undue hardship on United Information. If an accommodation results in "more than a de minimis cost," it constitutes an undue hardship to the employer and excuses the employer from providing the accommodation. The Fifth Circuit explained that the "mere possibility of an adverse impact on co-workers... is sufficient to constitute an undue hardship." Mr. Saint's only deemed acceptable accommodation of checking in and out his supervisor would do just that. The evidence establishes that allowing Mr. Saint to continue to sign in and out with his supervisor would cause her to do extra work that would take away from her ability to do innovative projects and trainings. The very reason that United Information implemented the scanning system was to, one, capture savings of more than $4,000 previously stemming from the inefficiency of checking employees in and out manually and, two, to eliminate "costly positions" for addressing timekeeping fraud. Similar to the Fifth Circuit case *Tagore*, where the court reasoned that the asking the employer's security officers, on a daily basis, to ascertain the dullness of the blade would be "time-consuming" and "impractical," here, too, requiring Mr. Saint's supervisor to keep track of Mr. Saint's time every day by hand would be "time-consuming" and "impractical."

RULE/ ANALYSIS

Additionally, similar to the Fifth Circuit case *Weber*, where the court held the requested accommodation of not being paired with a female driver in overnight drives would force co-worker schedule changes and alter neutral procedures, requiring Mr. Saint's supervisor to unwillingly assume additional duties to accommodate Mr. Saint would force a change in her schedule and alter the "neutral" procedure of using the scanner for all employees. Thus, like *Weber* and *Tagore*, this Court should hold United Information easily proves that allowing Mr. Saint to clock in and out with his supervisor, would involve far "more than a de minimis cost" on United Information.

Conclusion Accordingly, because Defendant proves undue hardship, United Information was excused from providing the accommodation and summary judgment should be granted.

Compare what is written above to this portion of Defendant United Information's Motion for Summary Judgment in the Appendix. What is different? For one, the argument is much shorter than the motion. There simply is not time to read what you have written in your motion. Plus, a listener simply cannot absorb the same quantity of information (or the same complexity of information) that a reader can absorb.

Second, you will notice that the legal rules (Rule) is *combined* with the facts of the case. By doing this, you are always persuading, and you are moving forward more efficiently (i.e., covering more material in less time). This efficiency is important because, in oral argument, time is of the essence, especially when you are "interrupted" with questions by the court, which you will be (as we will discuss in the next section). Third, you will notice that there are no citations and, instead, only a few references to case names. You do not need to cite the law or the record in your oral argument. If asked during oral argument by a judge for a citation or case name, you should be familiar enough with the case law and the record to provide such information, but, as a general matter, you do not need to "cite" in oral argument. Repeatedly "citing" the law, even just by case name, can be distracting and will slow down your argument. As put by one judge, "[I]t is almost certain that not a single case cited in argument by either name or volume and page will have been remembered."[2]

1. Remain flexible in the body of your planned argument

The body of your argument is where you will spend the bulk of your time. The most important rule to live by as you prepare and deliver the body of your argument is: be flexible. In most instances, you will not be able to present a "canned" argument, and, as a result, writing and memorizing a detailed script is useless. Rather than a script, you need an outline of points you plan to make in the body of your argument, in the order

2. BRYAN A. GARNER, THE WINNING ORAL ARGUMENT 138 (2009) (quoting Judge George R. Currie, who was on the Washington Supreme Court).

you plan to make them. However, you must be mindful that "plans change," and you must be prepared for the reality that your plans **will** change. The reason is that you will be interrupted with questions. The questions may move your argument on the issue forward or they may move you to a totally a different issue. The questions may take so much time that you do not have time for your planned argument or only have time for a small portion of it. While arguing an issue, you may realize that the judges agree with you on that issue; therefore, your time will be better spent on other issues. Or, it may be that you realize that the judges disagree with you on an issue and are unlikely to change their minds so you should move on to an issue you can win.

If you are the responding party or appellee (the party that goes second), you must be especially flexible. You will have the benefit of having heard the other side's argument and the judges' questions to the other side. Therefore, you know where the judges' concerns lie, and you need to address those or use those concerns in your argument.

As the responding party, you cannot give your planned argument in a vacuum. Instead, you must give your argument in the context of what has already happened—namely, what the other side argued and how the judges questioned the other side. If possible, you should incorporate the judges' comments or questions into your own argument. For example, you might say something like the following: "As commented by Judge Smith, all five factors need not be present to establish the first element ...." Also, in your argument as the responding party, you should respond to specific points raised by the other side in its oral argument. This is not to say that your oral argument should be "Defendant argued that .... Plaintiff responds that ...." No, instead, the responding party should incorporate its response to the other side's arguments within the responding party's own planned structure. For example, Plaintiff EEOC (responding party) might respond to United Information's oral argument by incorporating the following within Plaintiff's *own* discussion of undue hardship: "Defendant argued that Mr. Saint's request accommodation would alter a neutral procedure, however, Defendant omits the crucial fact that Mr. Saint's supervisor was already manually keeping time for another employee."

2. *Keep calm by being prepared*

In addition to being flexible, you must keep calm. The best way to keep calm is to be prepared. It is easy to get flustered when you planned to address three issues, but with three minutes left, you are still on issue one. To combat the feeling of panic you might have, you need to prepare yourself for any scenario that could be thrown at you. You should go into the argument expecting anything and everything. You should go in expecting to hit all of your points with minimal questions, expecting to change the order of your issues, expecting to devote most of your time to one issue to the exclusion of the others, expecting to be interrupted with so many questions that you do not reach any of your planned argument, and so forth.

For example, if you only have three minutes left for your remaining two issues, what would you say? You need to have a plan for this. It may be that you have a short version of the argument for both issues that you are ready to present. It may be that you skip to the third issue for your remaining three minutes and rest on your briefing for the second issue. Being prepared for whatever scenario is thrown your way will keep you calm.

D. Responding to questions from the bench

The most important part of any oral argument is the questions asked by the judge or judges and the answers given by the lawyers. Questions allow you to understand and respond to the judges' concerns about your case, clarify issues, and persuade the judges of your position. You may initially think, "I hope I am not interrupted with too many questions." However, questions should not be looked at as a burden but rather as a welcomed opportunity. A question, though an interruption to your planned argument, is not an interruption as we usually think of the word. To answer a judge's question is ultimately why you are there. The more questions, the better. Questions also give you insight into what the court is thinking. Thus, a question asked may not only be a question, but a "cue" to counsel. As put by the late Justice Ruther Bader Ginsburg:

> [I]t seems to me, a waste of a lawyer's precious opportunity to use oral argument or attempt to use it just to recapitulate the briefing instead of trying to uncover what is in the decisionmaker's mind. Questions from the bench can give counsel a chance to satisfy the court on matters the questioner at least thinks significant and might resolve less satisfactorily without counsel's aid. Sometimes it is true, a question will be asked with persuasion of a colleague in mind, and the lawyer may sense at those times that she is being talked through, not to. Other times, the questioner may be trying to cue counsel, that an argument, pursued with gusto, is a loser and that counsel would be well advised to move on. A counsel too intent on a prepared script may miss that kind of cue.[3]

You should hope for, plan for, and expect to have multiple questions during your argument. These questions can come at any time (opening, body, or closing) and can be about anything (the issue you are currently discussing, a totally different issue you planned to discuss later, or an issue you did not plan to discuss at all). Answering questions from the bench is both a skill and an art.

1. How to respond to questions

When asked a question from a judge, it is important to know not only the answer, but generally how to respond. Questions can come at any point during the oral argument. You might not so much as state your name before a judge interrupts you with a

---

3. Hon. Ruth Bader Ginsberg, *Remarks for American Law Institute Annual Dinner (May 19, 1994)*, 38. St. Louis L.J. 881, 885 (1994).

question. Below are some guidelines to follow when answering questions during oral argument.

Step one: Stop talking and immediately listen.

As soon as the judge starts asking a question, you should immediately stop talking, even if you are mid-sentence, or even if you are mid-syllable. As soon as the judge starts to speak, you stop speaking. No matter what. Stop. Talking over a judge is a mistake and a sign of disrespect to the court. As the judge is asking the question, you should be intently listening. This means you should be making eye contact with the judge. You should not be looking down at your notes or looking away.

Step two: Pause.

After the judge asks the question, you should pause for a moment. The purpose of the pause is three-fold. First, a pause allows you to make sure the judge is finished asking the question. You do not want to accidentally interrupt the judge by beginning to answer a question before the judge has finished speaking. Second, a pause gives you time to make sure you understand the question. Importantly, if you do not understand the question, you should ask the judge to clarify, rephrase, or repeat the question. You might say, "Your Honor, I apologize, but would you mind repeating your question?" Or, you may ask, "Your Honor, if I understand your question, you are asking whether credibility issues should solely be left to the jury?" This will allow the judge to clarify or rephrase the question if you do not understand it. Note that asking for clarification on a question is one of the only times you (the lawyer arguing) ever get to ask the court a question. Simply put, your job is to answer questions, not to ask them. Finally, a pause allows you to take a moment to formulate your answer.

Step three: Answer the question directly and then explain.

After you have paused, you should answer the question directly and then explain your answer. This is similar to what you learned previously in this book regarding writing your brief answer in an objective memo. You begin with your direct answer (yes or no), and then you explain.

If the judge asks a yes or no question, you should begin with a direct and short answer: "Yes, Your Honor" or "No, Your Honor." Some variation of "yes" or "no" is also okay as long as you begin by directly answering the question. For example, "Absolutely, Your Honor" or "Definitely not, Your Honor." After you respond with a clear version of "yes" or "no," then, and only then, do you explain why. For example:

Judge: Counsel, is it true that you are arguing that, as a matter of law, a court should always find an employee's purposed religious belief, however wacky it may be, to be bona fide based on that employee's word alone?

Counsel for Defendant United Information: No, not exactly, Your Honor. What the law says is that an employee's belief is bona fide as long it is sincerely held and determining that sincerity is largely a matter of individual credibility. Therefore, a court should—exercising judicial shyness—look at the employee's testimony regarding his belief and determine whether the employee sincerely believed it to be religious in his own scheme of things.

Even if the judge does not ask a yes/no question, you should still begin with your direct and short answer before explaining your reasoning. For example:

Judge: Counsel, how can you say that Mr. Saint's proposed accommodation of clocking in and out with his supervisor would not impose an undue hardship when it would force additional duties on a co-worker?

Counsel for United Information: Because, Your Honor, other than the unsubstantiated statement Mr. Saint's supervisor, Defendant fails to provide any evidence of undue hardship. For example, while Defendant claims the biometric scanning system was implemented to avoid losses associated with suspected fraudulent time-keeping and employees forgetting their codes, Defendant fails to provide evidence indicating that Mr. Saint ever falsified his time records or forgot his code. Additionally, Defendant has provided no evidence as to whether other methods of accommodation were explored besides clocking in and out with the supervisor.

By beginning with a short and direct answer to the judge's question and then explaining your answer, you do not leave the judge guessing or waiting for an answer. We all find it annoying when we ask a direct question, and, in response, we get a rambling, long-winded answer that is not responsive to our question or leaves us in suspense for a while before getting an answer to the question that we asked.

Imagine this exchange with your friend:

You: Are you going to travel home for Thanksgiving?

(Annoying) Friend: I have so many finals to study for and feel like I am really falling behind. Also, I am short on money. Law school is expensive. I told my mom that I could not come home for Thanksgiving break, and she was sad about it. The next day, my dad called me and said that he would pay for my flights. He also said that, if I come home, he would set up a quiet room with a desk for me at the house so that I could study in peace and not be disturbed by family. So, I am now traveling home for Thanksgiving.

That's super irritating, right? You would rather your friend start with, "Yes, I am traveling home for Thanksgiving." Then, she can explain the details behind why. At this point, you will have your answer and be free to listen (or maybe not listen) to the explanation. Judges are the same way. Judges want the direct answer to their question to come first and then the explanation for that answer.

Step four: After answering the question, transition back to your planned argument.

After you have answered the question asked, you must transition back to your planned argument. Arguably the hardest part about answering questions is not the actual answer, but, rather, it is the transition from answering a question back to your planned argument.

Think of telling a story. Your friend "interrupts" your story with a question or series of questions. If your friend only asks one question and the question relates to the part of the story you were just telling, it is easier to answer the question and get back to the rest of your story. However, if your friend asks you numerous questions in a row and the questions are not at all related to the part of the story you were previously telling, getting back to your story will be harder. After answering all your friend's questions and detouring from your story, you might have forgotten where you left off. You may think or say aloud, "Now, what was I saying before?"

A similar scenario can happen when answering a judge's question or questions, especially if the question is not related to the argument you are making at that time. However, you cannot ask a judge, "Now, what was I saying before?" Instead, you must know how to answer any question (or series of questions) and get back to your argument. This is difficult and takes practice.

Being able to transition back to your argument goes hand in hand with being flexible. You may not transition back to exactly where you left off. For example, if you were just starting your discussion of your first issue and were asked back-to-back questions on that issue, it may be that, after answering those questions, you feel like issue one has been sufficiently addressed. In that case, you would not return to your planned argument on issue one, but, instead, you would make the choice to transition to issue two. As you can imagine, this requires quite a bit of quick thinking on your feet. The best way to practice transitioning back to your argument is by practicing your agument with friends or colleagues and asking them to interrupt you with questions as you practice.

2. *Additional guidelines for responding to questions*

Below are a few additional guidelines to follow when answering questions.

- Do not call a judge "sir," "ma'am," "you," "Mrs.," "Mr.," or the like. Call the judge "Your Honor."
- Do not patronize the judge by saying "Great question," "I am so glad you asked that," "I thought you'd never ask." Such comments can be interpreted as disrespectful.

- Do not put off a question until later. When asked a question, you must answer it. You cannot say, "Your Honor, I will get to that question in a moment when I discuss the third issue." Rather, you must answer whatever question is asked at that moment, even if the question is wholly unrelated to what you are currently discussing.
- Do not answer a hypothetical question by saying, "That's not our case." Duh! It is a hypothetical, which necessarily means it is a different set of facts than the facts of your case. You may get hypothetical questions designed to test your position, and you should answer them.
- Do not ask a judge questions. Besides asking for clarification of a question that a judge asked or asking to speak after your time has expired, you should never ask the judge a question.
- Do not argue with a judge or take a combative tone. Some judges will seem difficult. It is important that you maintain respect. For example, let's say that a judge misstates your position. The judge could do this repeatedly. A good way to handle this would be to say, "Respectfully, Your Honor, that is not a correct characterization of my client's position. Our position is that ..." A bad way to handle this would be to say, "That's not what I said" or "You're wrong."
- Do not fight softball questions. Sometimes, a judge will ask you a question that seems too simple or too good to be true because it is so favorable to your position. For example, if you represented United Information, the court could give you the following softball question: "Counsel, is it correct that Mr. Saint did not respond to United Information's attempts at accommodation?" You should recognize this question as a softball, be internally grateful for it, answer it, and use it to move your argument forward: "That is precisely correct, Your Honor. United Information deviated from its standard retina scanner clocking in and out practice to accommodate Mr. Saint, but Mr. Saint did not respond and instead did not report his presence to anyone before resigning ...." Some lawyers make the (cringeworthy) mistake of fighting easy questions. Don't let that be you.
- Do not make up an answer. If you do not know the answer to a judge's question, the worst thing you can do is to invent an answer. You do not want to end up saying something that is incorrect and hurt your credibility. Instead, if you do not know the answer, you should state, "Your Honor, I apologize, but I do not know the answer to that question" and move on. Alternatively, if the question seems important to the court, offer to get the court the answer to the question by filing a post-hearing or post-oral argument letter brief. For example, you might say: "Your Honor, I do not know the answer to that question at this time, but I will provide an answer to the court by letter brief tomorrow."

E. Conclusion

Your argument will end either when (1) you have nothing left to say or (2) your time is up, whichever comes first.

1. *Concluding with some time left*

If time is remaining, but you have nothing left to say, you should conclude. You need not "run out the clock." After all, courts appreciate brevity. As noted by one Fifth Circuit judge, "There never has been a panel that resented an advocate's using less than all of his or her allotted time."[4]

How you conclude will depend on how much time is left on the clock. If you have plenty of time left after finishing the body of your argument, you may (1) give a brief summary of your main points; (2) restate the overall relief you want (e.g., deny summary judgment); and (3) end by saying something like, "Unless the Court has further questions [pause in case the court does], that concludes my remarks. Thank you." You would then sit down.

If you only have, say, 30 seconds remaining, you do not have time to give a brief summary. Instead, you may conclude by (1) restating the overall relief you want and (2) end by saying, "Unless the Court has further questions [pause in case the court does], that concludes my remarks. Thank you." You would then sit down.

If you have less than 30 seconds remaining, you may conclude by simply saying, "Unless the Court has further questions [pause in case court does], that concludes my remarks. Thank you." You would then sit down.

2. *Concluding when your time has expired*

If time runs out and you are in the middle of speaking, you should stop speaking when you are out of time, say thank you, and sit down. The only exception to this rule is if you are in the midst of answering a judge's question. If you are in the middle of answering a judge's question and your time expires, you may ask, "Your Honor, I see my time has concluded. May I briefly finish answering your question?" If the court agrees and grants you permission to finish answering the question, do not do anything else. You should answer the question or finish answering the question, say "thank you," and sit down. You should not "conclude" or make another point.

F. Rebuttal (Movant/Appellant)

If you are the movant or appellant (the party that argues first), you may have the opportunity for rebuttal. Recall that in the opening of your argument, you will need to reserve time for rebuttal if you wish to present a rebuttal. If you do not reserve the time,

---

4. Honorable Jacques L. Wiener, Jr., *Ruminations from the Bench: Brief Writing and Oral Argument in the Fifth Circuit*, 70 TUL. L. REV. 187, 204 (1995).

you waive rebuttal. For example, if your argument is 20 minutes long, you may choose to reserve two or three minutes for rebuttal.

Rebuttal can be a powerful tool because it is the last word of oral argument the court hears before making its decision. During rebuttal, you should not raise new points or re-argue points that you argued during your previous time. Rather, you should rebut the strongest points that the other side just argued to the court. While the respondent or appellee is arguing, you should be taking notes of the points you want to rebut. If by the court's questioning, you sense that the court is having doubts about your position on an issue after hearing oral argument from the other side, you should make sure to address these doubts head-on in your rebuttal. Rebuttal is usually very short. Most lawyers do not recommend reserving more than two or three minutes for rebuttal. Given the brevity of rebuttal, you must use your time judiciously and address only the most significant point or points you need to win.

Chapter 15 | Preparing for Your Argument

Now that you understand the structure of an oral argument and how challenging making an oral argument can be, how do you prepare for it? Preparing is two-fold: (1) you must be prepared substantively to argue the issues before the court by knowing the law, the record, and how to present your argument; and (2) you must be prepared to present as a public speaker before the audience of the court.

A. Preparing substantively for your oral argument

1. *Review the motions or briefs, the law cited therein, and the record or any exhibits*

The good news about preparing substantively for oral argument is that you have done most of the heavy preparation during the writing process. To be prepared for an oral argument, you must be intimately familiar with what you have written, as well as what the other side has written, the law cited therein, and the facts of the case as set forth in the exhibits or the record.

In reviewing the written papers at issue (the motion and opposition, or the briefs), you need to understand your argument and what the other side is arguing. You should assess your best points, as well as the best points the other side makes that you may need to address in oral argument. You also need to pull the law relied on by your side and the other side from the written papers. You need not memorize all of the legal authority, but you should read through it all. For the most important cases you rely on and the other side relies on, you should know some key details. It is helpful to create a case chart "cheat sheet" to help you jog your memory during oral argument. For the important cases relied upon by the other side, you may include on your cheat sheet ways to distinguish the cases.

Before oral argument, you should also do some quick research to make sure nothing changed between the time you submitted your papers and the date of the oral argument. You should make sure that none of the cases have been overturned or questioned by Shepardizing™ (LexisNexis®) or KeyCiting® (Westlaw®) the cases. You should also run a search to see if any new, relevant cases on the issue have been decided since you filed your motion or brief. A quick way to do this is to run the relevant search and then organize the search results by date so the newest cases are on the top of the search results.

In reviewing the record and exhibits, you need to become the expert on the facts of your case. Not knowing the facts of your own case or confusing the facts of your own case is especially damaging to your credibility.

2. *Next, prepare your oral argument content*

After you have reviewed the motions or briefs, the law, and the record and exhibits, you need to prepare the substance of your oral argument. Remember, you do not have time to cover the entire content of your motion or brief; you should not simply read from it. Instead, you need to list (in order of priority) your side's main points that you need to argue combined with the other side's strongest points that you need to address.

For example, if you represent United Information, in your Motion for Summary Judgment, you will have three issues. To win, you only need to succeed on one of them. In your oral argument, you may decide to omit the bona fide religious belief argument (arguably your weakest point) and spend your time arguing the other two issues because they are stronger. You also may decide to start with undue hardship, if you think that argument is your best chance of winning.

Once you have your main points, you will need to prepare your opening, your argument body, and your closing. Preparing the opening and closing is simple. To prepare your opening, you should write out a script and memorize it (as discussed in the previous chapter). To prepare your closing, you should write out and memorize different versions of it, so you are prepared to conclude with ample time, limited time, or no time (as discussed in the previous chapter).

To prepare your body, you should list the main points you need to make for your "C" or Conclusion and, underneath those points, list the "R/A"—the law and facts that support that main point (as discussed in the previous chapter). Unlike your opening and closing, it is not necessary to write out the body of your argument word for word because, unless you have a silent court, you cannot script an oral argument. Rather, as explained, you will be interrupted with questions, and, based on those questions, you may need to move parts of your argument around or change your argument. Additionally, if you are the respondent or appellee, you may need to change your argument based on what the other side argued or the questions asked to the other side. Because you must be flexible and because oral argument is a conversation, not a speech, an outline will be more helpful than a script.

a. Predict the questions you will be asked and prepare answers

The scariest part of preparing for anything is the unknown. The unknown in oral argument is the questions the court will ask you. To prepare for this "unknown," you need to do your best to anticipate and predict what questions you may be asked. It is very likely that a court will question you about weaknesses of your case and strengths of the other side. You should write out those possible questions and prepare answers to them.

b. Create an outline to bring with you to oral argument

After you have figured out the substance of your oral argument, you should create a short outline to bring with you to oral argument. You cannot bring to oral argument a stack of cases or a thick binder to flip through. The reason is because you will not have time to search through documents during oral argument, and, regardless, fumbling and flipping through papers is distracting to the court.

To prepare your outline, the best advice is to use the manila folder method. Yes, it is that simple. Use a regular manila folder. When you open the folder, it will lay flat like a book and have two sides. On each side, you will staple to each corner of (or otherwise affix) an 8.5x11 piece of paper that sets forth your outline material. The manila folder method allows you to see a two-page outline without having to flip anything or move papers around.

There is no one "right" way to create your two-page outline. However, we recommend putting your planned argument outline with your main points on the left side of the manila folder. For your main points, make them bold, and, under your main points, include a bullet-point list of law and facts that support each of your main points. On the right side of the manila folder, we recommend putting information you may need to answer anticipated questions and group the information by anticipated subjects. If you need a personal reminder (e.g., eye contact, speak louder, slow down, or stay still), we recommend writing those on your outline in your own handwriting and in a color that stands out. For example, if you are a fast-talker, you could write "slow down!!!" somewhere on your outline to remind yourself to speak slowly.

On the back of the folder (i.e., the back of the folder when it is closed), we will sometimes staple a one-page case chart. The hope is that you do not need to "flip" or "turn" to this, but it will be there just in case you get a question about a case and need to jog your memory.

Note that you should not include your scripted opening and closing in your outline. The reason for this omission is that, if they are written out, you may be tempted to look down and read them, instead of maintaining eye contact and delivering your opening and closing from memory. We have seen students in oral argument look down at their outline when saying "My name is ...." Obviously, these students know their names, but because they have brought with them a script of their opening, they are looking down and reading it instead of confidently stating it from memory.

c. Practice, practice, practice

The best way to prepare the content of your oral argument is to practice. It is meaningless if you have everything you need to say in your brain or written in your outline, but you are unable to communicate it orally. Therefore, you must practice communicating your argument orally numerous times.[1] You should also practice your oral argument under different conditions. For example, practice your argument without being interrupted with questions so you are prepared for the (unfortunate) situation where the bench is quiet or "cold." Practice making your points in different orders in case you are asked by a judge to address an issue in an order other than what you had planned. Ideally, during some of your practices, you should have someone (a friend, a colleague, or a family member) play judge and interrupt you with questions. The practice questions could be the questions that you have predicted and written out.

The benefits of practicing aloud are numerous. First, when you practice your argument orally, you will find that things that sounded one way in your head or on paper sound differently when spoken aloud and will need to be adjusted. Second, you will also figure out the timing and pace of your argument and whether you are spending too much or too little time on any point. Third, you will hear how your argument flows and how you are moving from point to point. It may be that your argument, while organized and logical on paper, becomes confusing when spoken such that you need to add more signposts or transitions. Fourth, practicing answering questions orally will allow you not only to refine the substance of your answer, but also to commit the art of answering questions to "muscle memory." Recall that when asked a question by the court, you should immediately stop talking, keep eye contact during the question, pause, give a direct answer, explain, and then—the hardest part—transition back to your argument. Finally, practicing orally will allow you to understand any weaknesses you have as a speaker, as discussed in the next section.

B. Refining your oral argument presentation skills

Becoming an expert on the content of your oral argument is half the battle. You must be able to deliver that content to the court in a persuasive, strong, non-distracting, credible way. For example, it does not matter how brilliant the point you are making is if the court cannot hear it because you speak too softly. Therefore, part of being a strong oral advocate is having strong oral presentation skills. Below are some general tips for presenting a strong oral argument.

---

1. Consider videotaping yourself practicing your oral argument. By watching yourself on video (as painful as it may be), you will be able to isolate substantive and presentation-based weaknesses in advance of your "real" argument.

PRESENTATION TIPS	
Keep eye contact	You should strive to make eye contact with the judge or judges of the court. While it is okay to briefly look down at your outline, for the majority of your time you should be maintaining eye contact with your audience—the court.
Speak to be heard	In order to best deliver your message, you should speak loudly, you should speak slowly, and you should enunciate your words. In order to ensure that you are speaking to be heard, either record your oral argument to review it yourself or have someone watch you to provide feedback.
Make your tone conversational, but respectful	You should not sound like you are reading off your notes or performing off a memorized script. Instead, your tone should be conversational. Conversational does not mean that you are informal; you should always address the court with respect. However, you should treat an oral argument like a conversation between you and the judge (or among you and the judges), rather than as a performance where you are on stage and the judges are idle audience members watching.
Stand straight and still	When giving your oral argument, you should stand. Normally, you will stand behind a podium or lectern. While standing to deliver your oral argument, you should maintain good posture by keeping your shoulders back and head up. You should stand still. Unlike arguing before a jury, when arguing before a court, you should not move around or make gestures with your arms. You should also take care to not be unintentionally distracting by, for example, nervously tapping the podium, shuffling your papers, or otherwise fiddling with something.
Limit filler words	Limiting filler words, such as "um," "like," "uh," "er," and "ah," is easier said than done. Recording yourself arguing is the best way to know if you use a filler word. If you use a particular filler word, stopping its use is not something that necessarily happens overnight or on command. This is because your use of a filler word is not a cognizant decision made by you, but it is a habit and something that you are doing without thinking. However, filler words can be distracting and can make you sound less confident in what you are saying. Filler words are used more when you are unprepared or under-prepared, which causes you to trip over your words or be unsure in what you are saying. The more prepared you are, the fewer words you will use. Additionally, to eliminate filler words or, at least to reduce them, you should slow down your speaking pace and practice replacing filler words with pauses.

Avoid first person pronouns	When presenting the substance of your argument, you should avoid the use of first-person pronouns such as "I think," "I feel," "I believe," or "I anticipate." Put bluntly, the court does not care what you personally think, feel, or believe. The court cares about what the law says and what the facts of the case are. Keep yourself out of it.
Dress professionally	It should go without saying that on the day of your oral argument, you should dress in formal, courtroom attire. You do not want the court to be distracted from what you are saying by what you are wearing.
Keep the nerves at bay	Some of you are terrified of public speaking and an oral argument, by definition, is public speaking. To help keep your anxiety to a minimum, in addition to being very prepared, you should arrive early to the court, and, if possible, you should watch other people argue before the same court before you go so you know exactly what to expect. If when you get to the podium or lectern you are shaking or otherwise nervous, try discreetly squeezing the edges of the podium or lectern to release that nervous energy. Then, take a deep breath.

Part 6 | Bar Preparation: Bar-Style Essays and PTs

The type of writing you are doing affects the structure, the substance, and the format of your writing. In other words, formal legal writing, such as motions, objective memos, or briefs, looks different and contains different content than the writing you will do on law school exams and on the bar exam. To make things even more exciting, as much of the country moves from the Uniform Bar Exam (UBE) to the NextGen Bar Exam (NextGen Exam) beginning in July 2026, the bar exam will begin testing examinees using short-answer and fill-in-the-blank questions in addition to the previous UBE testing formats, Performance-Test-style assessments, essays, and multiple-choice questions.

While the foundational legal writing, reading, and analysis skills you learn in your legal writing courses will help you with other forms of legal writing, bar-style exam writing (in particular, essays and Performance Tasks (PTs)) are different than traditional legal writing in several ways. The biggest difference is that bar-style essays and PTs are required to be written under strict time pressure. The chart below highlights some additional differences (and similarities) between the legal writing you will do in law school, on the bar, and in practice.

	OBJECTIVE MEMOS	LAW SCHOOL EXAM ESSAYS	BAR EXAM ESSAYS	PTS
Citation and use of cases	Correct form and placement of citations from appropriate jurisdiction	Limited use of citations. Correct form not required.	No citations.	Limited use of citations. Correct form not required.
Organization	CRAC for each issue (i.e., each element of multi-element cause of action or defense).	Same.	Same.	Same, but can use abbreviated. Most important part of PT organization is to explain law then apply the law (RA).
Facts	Separate statement of facts (SOF) and trigger facts weaved into Analysis ("A").	No separate SOF. Trigger facts weaved into Analysis ("A").	Same.	Same (unless instructions of task provide otherwise).
Headings, Conclusion sentences, and topic sentences	Use conclusion-based headings. After heading, the CRAC will begin with a Conclusion that is similar to the conclusion-based heading. Each paragraph under the heading should have a well-developed topic sentence.	Use conclusion-based headings. After heading, no need to start with a formal Conclusion. While paragraphs are divided topically, no topic sentence is required.	Same.	Same.
Rules	Lengthy description of rule and subrules for the issue, defense, or element being discussed. Rules include key language, terms, and often quotations from case law and/or statutes. Rule also includes full case illustrations.	Accurate rule statement and inclusion of key subrules related to the particular issue, defense, or element being discussed. No quotations are needed. Case illustrations are not usually necessary.	Same.	Same, but a modified version of a case illustration may be needed depending on the legal authority you are given and the task you are asked to complete.

	OBJECTIVE MEMOS	LAW SCHOOL EXAM ESSAYS	BAR EXAM ESSAYS	PTS
Analysis and Counter-analysis	Includes rule-based reasoning plus extensive analogical reasoning that focuses on comparing or contrasting precedent cases to fact pattern at issue (or arguing case is like or unlike precedent case in persuasive writing).	Limited analogical reasoning, instead engaging mostly in rule of reason analysis (applying the rule to the facts to predict outcome). Both sides are discussed.	No analogical reasoning. Instead, a more limited analysis focused on applying the facts to the rule to yield a conclusion. Counter-analysis/ counter-arguments are raised to provide a fully explained answer.	Includes mix of rule-based reasoning and analogical reasoning (if cases are illustrated). Counter-analysis not required unless instructed otherwise in assignment.

This part of the book will detail the process, format, and content for drafting law-school and bar-style essay exam answers and PTs.

Chapter 16 | Bar-Style and Law School Essay Questions

After reading the title for this chapter, many of you are probably thinking, "Yea, but what about the NextGen Bar Exam? That's the exam I'm taking." You are smart to be thinking about the NextGen exam. But, for others, you will take either the Unifrom Bar Exam (UBE) or a state-specific bar exam. Moreover, for all of you, before you take the bar exam, you have to get through law school and that really almost always requires completing essay exams. To help you with your essay writing, let's start by understanding what types of essays you might encounter.

The UBE. The UBE's essay-based exam section, called the Multistate Essay Exam ("MEE"), is drafted by the National Conference of Bar Examiners and administered as part of most states' bar exams. The MEE exam is designed to "test an examinee's ability to (1) identify legal issues raised by a hypothetical factual situation; (2) separate material which is relevant from that which is not; (3) present a reasoned analysis of the relevant issues in a clear, concise, and well-organized composition; and (4) demonstrate an understanding of the fundamental legal principles relevant to the probable solution of the issues raised by the factual situation."[1]

The NextGen Bar Exam. The NextGen Bar Exam forgoes the UBE's components—the Multistate Bar Exam, the Multistate Essay Exam, and the Multistate Performance Exam—in favor of mixed-format, "integrat-

1. National Conference of Bar Examiners, Multistate Essay Examination Purpose, http://www.ncbex.org/exams/mee/ (last visited June 21, 2019).

ed "itemsets,"[2] designed to test an examinee's knowledge of doctrine and skills through a combination of short-answer, multiple-choice, multiple-answer, fill-in-the-blank, and lawyering-task-based questions. By way of good news for students and for legal writing and skills professors like us, the NextGen Exam reduces doctrinal coverage[3] and increases the lawyering skills tested, adding in the testing of legal research, client counseling and advising, and client relationship management skills.[4] However, the NextGen Exam will no longer test content using bar-style essays, instead, opting to test in various other formats.

Law School Essay Exams. Regardless of what happens to the bar exam in your jurisdiction, it is unlikely law professors will wholly forgo the age-old law school essay exam. "Why is this?" you might wonder. It's because testing by essay exam requires students to communicate their knowledge of the law in an organized, written form under time pressure. In other words, essay questions test your knowledge of the law **and** your ability to communicate that knowledge like a lawyer. There is really no better way to do that!

This chapter will introduce you to bar-essay exams and bar-style law school essay exams. In addition, it will provide you with a basic construct for using your critical legal writing skills to excel in essay writing.

A. Format of a bar-style essay question

During the time of the Paper Chase[5] and still in many law schools across the country, law school professors pride themselves in drafting lengthy and challenging end-of-the-semester essay exams. Some of these seemingly impossible exams cover hundreds of potential issues (i.e., causes of action and defenses) between numerous litigants such that no student can realistically identify or fully analyze all of them within the time allotted. Bar-style law school essays, however, are different. Do not misunderstand: they are time pressured just like traditional issue-spotter exams. But, bar-style essay exams have a distinct question or set of questions and do not contain any extraneous facts. In other words, they are asking a specific question or set of questions and each fact in the

---

2. The NextGen Exam will be split into multiple hour to hour and a half integrated sets of question called itemsets. Judith Gundersen, *Evolution of the Bar Exam*, presented at AALS Annual Meeting (San Diego, California, Jan. 5 2023), https://am.aals.org/wp-content/uploads/sites/4/2022/12/final_ncbe_presentation_for_aals_121922_accessible.pdf. As the NCBE has explained, these itemsets "[d]emonstrate one or more legal skills in context of a scenario raising one or more substantive or procedural legal issues." *Id.*

3. The NextGen Exam reduces doctrinal coverage in two ways. First, it removes entire doctrinal subjects from the exam, including wills, trusts, and estates and secured transactions. *See Next Generation of the Bar Exam Content Scope Outlines*, NAT'L CONF. OF BAR EXAM'RS, https://nextgenbarexam.ncbex.org/csopc-register/. Second, for the subjects that remain, the NextGen Exam delineates between subjects for which the examinees need memorized, deep knowledge and others for which examinees only need issue-spotting familiarity. *Id.*

4. *Id.*

5. THE PAPER CHASE (Twentieth Century Fox 1973).

hypothetical presented is legally relevant and likely has an impact on one of the questions asked. Below is a sample bar-style essay exam question annotated to help you understand the different parts of this type of essay question.

> Jack and Annie were married in January 1998 and filed for divorce in October 2023. They lived in Texas throughout their marriage. Annie is a real estate investor, earning a good salary. Near the end of their marriage, Annie's business had grown enough that she received $500,000 bonuses each year in 2021 and 2022. Jack was a lawyer. He has worked and continues to work for Happy Lawyer, LLP and earns a good salary. Jack and Annie put all of their work-related income into a joint bank account.
>
> Both Jack and Annie had received property from their families. In 1997, Jack's father had given him a mineral estate in Oilygas Ranch. Oilygas yielded $10,000 in royalties each year. Annie's father died in 2010. As part of his will, he bequeathed Annie a 50% interest in Birchwood, their Wisconsin summer home. In 2011, Annie's brother (to whom her father had bequeathed the other 50% of Birchwood) hit hard financial times. Annie and Jack borrowed $1.5M from Saveabuck Bank to purchase her brother's 50% interest in Birchwood, and then titled the entire property in Jack's name so he could manage the property in his spare time.
>
> When their marriage hit rocky times, Jack attempted to woo Annie back to him by giving her a bronze statue of Donald Trump, her favorite President, for their back yard. Jack purchased the statue with funds from his retirement account, which he opened through Happy Lawyer after he and Annie married. The statue was valued at $120,000 because it was signed by President Trump himself—"the best signature ever." During 2022, their last year of marriage, the couple charged $50 per guest to visit the statue and earned $10,000 in cash related thereto.
>
> On the other hand, when faced with their marital strife, in early 2024, during the pendency of their divorce, Annie gifted Birchwood to their (she and Jack's) two children, Pip and Sancho.
>
> 1. To whom will the court award the following property: the joint bank account, Oilygas Ranch, the royalties from Oilygas Ranch, the bronze Trump statue, the income from the Trump statue, and Annie's 2022 bonus? Explain.
> 2. If Jack and Annie fail to pay the mortgage for Birchwood, from whom can Saveabuck collect? Explain.
> 3. Will the trial court void Annie's gift of Birchwood to Pip and Sancho? Explain.

B. How to format an answer to a bar-style essay question

Bar takers and law students alike struggle to understand what constitutes a bad, a better, and the best essay-exam answer. This age-old problem has resulted in speculation that professors grade by throwing papers down a staircase (the As traveled the farthest down the staircase, the Fs barely landed at the nearby top), that law school and even bar exam grading is arbitrary, and that all professors or bar-graders are looking for something different. It certainly is true that different graders or different professors have and value different styles in terms of writing, but all graders and all professors want and reward essay answers that are organized to mirror the way a lawyer reasons (CRAC) and that set forth precise and accurate rules.

Given these universal truths, below are two examples that illustrate acceptable formats for bar-style essay organization and a third example of what not to do—the "rule-dumping" organization that law professors warn against. There is no failsafe formula for how to identify issues and subdivide your answers properly, because, unfortunately, that is a question-specific struggle. Similarly, this short section of this book does not purport to instruct you on how to draft a thoughtful analysis that avoids the dreaded "fact dump" or "conclusory descriptions." Those lessons are for another day. Instead, the goal here is to provide you with a macro formula for drafting bar-style essay answers and to provide you with our top five tips for maximizing the points you receive on a bar-style essay exam.

1. The basic formula

An excellent essay response will subdivide the answer into bite-sized pieces—that is, into causes of actions and then further into elements or sub-issues. Each piece will then have its own CRAC.

GENERIC FORMULA

I. Conclusory Heading on Question I

a. Conclusory Heading Sub-Issue I	= C
GR.[6] SR[7] 1. SR2. SR3.	= R
A SR[8] 1. A SR2. A SR3.	= A
C	= C
b. Conclusory Heading Sub-Issue II	= C
GR. SR 1. SR2. SR3.	= R
A SR 1. A SR2. A SR3.	= A
C	= C

6. GR = general rule
7. SR = subrule
8. A SR = analysis of subrule

II. Conclusory Heading on Question II

a. Conclusory Heading Sub-Issue I = C
GR. SR 1. SR2. SR3. = R
A SR 1. A SR2. A SR3. = A
C = C

b. Conclusory Heading Sub-Issue II = C
GR. SR 1. SR2. SR3. = R
A SR 1. SR2. A SR3. = A
C = C

If you look back at the sample bar-style essay question, how many question headings will you have? There are three questions, so you will have three conclusory headings. But, if you read each question more carefully, you will discover that you need additional subheadings (and additional CRACs) under each large question heading. For example, look at the first question:

> To whom will the court award the following property: the joint bank account, Oilygas Ranch, the royalties from Oilygas Ranch, the bronze Trump statue, the income from the Trump statue, and Annie's 2022 bonus? Explain.

By carefully reading this question, you will notice that there are multiple questions within this single question. So, you will need a separate conclusory subheading and a separate CRAC for each piece of property included and asked about in the question. See below for the skeletal structure for a response to the first question presented by this bar-style essay.

I. The court will award [INSERT PROPERTY] to Annie and [INSERT PROPERTY] to Jack.

a. The court will award the joint back account to [INSERT].
b. The court will award Oilygas Ranch to [INSERT].
c. The court will award the royalties from Oilygas Ranch to [INSERT].
d. The court will award the bronze Trump statue to [INSERT].
e. The court will award the income from the bronze Trump statue to [INSERT].
f. The court will award Annie's 2022 bonus to [INSERT].

2. *Top five tips for maximizing points on your bar-style essay exam responses*

Tip # 1: **Read the call of the question first, and then *read the hypothetical.***

Tip #2: **Instead of highlighting and taking notes on the facts in the hypothetical, write out the rules on the side of the hypothetical that are triggered by each of the facts presented.** The facts are written down in the problem, and they will not disappear. But you need to pull the rules from your head that are triggered by the questions presented and then the particular facts included. Given the time pressure, it is most efficient if you note the rules that are triggered by the main facts as you navigate your way through the hypothetical.

Tip #3: **Do not forget CRAC.** Each question should have at least one CRAC. Most will have sub-issues or elements, in which case each sub-issue or element will also have its own CRAC.

Tip #4: **Answer the question or questions asked—not the question or questions you wish the essay had asked you.**

Tip #5: **Practice makes perfect.** When studying for bar-style essay exams, you must practice writing essays and then you must evaluate and rewrite your essays after reviewing a sample answer. What did you miss in terms of the legal rules? How did your organization compare to the organization of the sample answer? Did you include extraneous information or rules?

C. How bar-style essay questions are graded

Typically, professors and bar essay graders use detailed point sheets or rubrics to grade bar-style essays. But the intricacies of those grading sheets are not as important as understanding this: your professors and graders are grading quickly and always appreciate well-organized essays because, in many ways, organized essays grade themselves. The success of an essay response will turn on the following:

1. Is the essay well organized by issue?
2. Does the essay response address all the issues presented by the question?

3. Does the essay response follow CRAC?
4. Does the essay response correctly state the rules of law (and all the relevant elements)?
5. Does the essay response demonstrate that the student can engage in real analysis (that is, tie the relevant facts from the hypothetical to the identified rules of law to show how she reaches her conclusion)?
6. Does the essay response address all the legally relevant facts in the hypothetical?
7. Does the essay response reach the correct conclusion on each question presented?

These tell-tale measurements of essay excellence may seem "squishy" or unclear to you as a new law student. But, truthfully, they are easy for professors to identify and objectively measure. Given this reality, you need to focus on mastering the law and organizing your essay responses to answer the question(s) asked in the CRAC format.

Chapter 17 | The PT or MPT

Almost every bar exam tests an examinee's ability to conduct legal reasoning and analysis in a realistic setting (i.e., test of an examinee's ability to do what beginning lawyers are expected to do). The National Conference of Bar Examiners' NextGen Bar Exam has three Performance Tasks (PTs), which comprise a third of the exam. Likewise the Uniform Bar Exam includes two Multi-State Performance Tests (MPTs) that comprise 20 percent of the exam. Even states that do not administer the UBE often administer the MPT or a similar form of test that they independently draft (California, for example, drafts its own performance tests, which are very similar the NCBE's MPT). In other words, regardless of which bar exam you plan to take, read on!

Note that for simplicity's sake, in this chapter, we will refer to these bar questions designed to test examinee's lawyering skills in realistic scenarios as Performance Tasks (PTs). However, the NextGen's PT and the UBE's MPT are very similar. Both "require examinees to demonstrate their ability to use fundamental lawyering skills in realistic situations, completing tasks that a beginning lawyer should be able to accomplish."[1] The PTs main purpose is to "assess an examinee's skills in legal research and written legal analysis."[2]

That is, the PT is not testing your knowledge of the law, but whether you know how to do what lawyers do—solve a problem by applying the law to a set of facts. In fact, the PT problem is not even set in a "real"

1. National Conference of Bar Examiners, NextGen Bar Example Sample Questions, https://www.ncbex.org/exams/nextgen/sample-questions (last visited April 30, 2024).

2. *Id.*

jurisdiction but is set in the fictitious state of "Franklin." Thus, knowledge of the substantive law does not help you with the PT because the law used in the PT is fake Franklin law.

A. Format of a PT exam

For the NextGen Bar Exam, while all PT's will assess an examinee's legal writing and research skills, PTs that focus on written· legal analysis will require you to provide a written work product to the question you are presented.[3]

In a PT, the examinee is given (1) a "file," which consists of an "assigning memorandum" or "task memo" with a task you must complete from a supervising lawyer and the facts of the case (which can come from interviews, client documents, court documents, depositions, reports, articles, etc.); and (2) a "library," which consists of the legal authority (cases, statutes, rules, etc.) relevant to the task you are being asked to complete.

If this sounds familiar to something you have already done in first-year legal writing, it is because it is! A PT is similar to your closed-packet objective memo. In the first semester of legal writing, you are given a problem from a supervising lawyer (the "assigning memorandum"), the facts of the case (the "file"), and packet of law (the "library"). Moreover, for your first-semester legal writing assignment, you are not allowed to do any outside research, but, rather, everything that you will use to write your answer is given to you. A PT is similar—everything you will use to complete the task is provided to you. Just like when you did your closed-packet problem in legal writing, when doing a PT, even though you are provided a packet with the legal authority (the "library"), not all of the legal authority provided will necessarily be relevant or need to be used; and, with respect to the facts (the "file"), some will be relevant, some will not be, and some that would be helpful are missing.[4]

Importantly, in a PT you have everything you need to complete the task at hand and you are working in a closed universe where you are not to bring in your outside knowledge of the substantive law, although you will bring with you generally the analysis and legal writing and reading skills you learned in law school.[5]

What makes the PT difficult is not that the task you will be asked to complete is hard, but rather that you must read the materials and write your response in 60 minutes. (The MPT is similar but requires you to write the response in 90 minutes). It is up to you how to allocate your 60 minutes between reviewing the materials and writing. The 60 minutes goes by quickly and this time pressure is what makes the PT especially challenging.

---

3. *Id.* Note that the NextGen also has tasks that focus more on research skills, which will consist of multiple choice questions, short answer questions, and a long-response question. This chapter discusses the PTs that focus on written analysis skills and, therefore, the ones that require one long response.

4. *Id.*

5. *Id.*

B. How a PT is graded

While the actual rubrics and score sheets for how the PT is graded vary state by state, PT graders are looking for the following:

- **Answers that follow instructions.** For example, if you are told to be objective, your tone should be objective. If you are told to omit the statement of facts, you should omit it. If you are told to write a memorandum, your response should look like a memorandum.
- **Answers that are organized per the instructions and look organized.** Remember that people who grade the PT are grading dozens or maybe hundreds of exams. They need to be able to grade answers quickly and visually see that your answer is complete and organized. Therefore, the use of noticeable (bold, underlined, etc.) headings is especially important on the PT.
- **Answers that reach all issues such that it is evident the examinee allocated his/her time efficiently.** On the PT, if there are three issues, you must allocate your time such that you address all three issues.
- **Answers that include citation to legal authority.** On the PT, your citations need not be in correct form, but you should reference the relevant legal authority by name and make the references noticeable (italic, underlined) so they look like a citation to the grader.
- **Answers that conduct strong legal analysis (showing both a good grasp of the facts and law).** The PT is testing your ability to do what lawyers do. The most important skill that lawyers must have is the ability to analyze the facts, analyze the law, and apply the law to the facts. This is where "CRAC" comes in. For the PT exam, you will use a simplified version of CRAC.

C. How to tackle a PT

You have 60 minutes to understand the problem, read the facts and the law, and organize and write your answer. How do you tackle all of this in 60 minutes?

Step one: Read the assigning memo ("task memo") to understand what you are being asked to write.

When you open your PT exam, the very first thing you should do is go to the first document of the file, which is the assigning memorandum from the supervising lawyer that gives you the assignment or task you must complete. The assigning memorandum will give you some background on the problem, tell you what task you will complete (i.e., what you will write), and give you special instructions. Note that the task you will be given is meant to mimic something a lawyer would do in the real world. For example, the assigning memorandum may ask you to write a memorandum to a supervising lawyer, a portion of a persuasive brief, a statement of facts, or a letter.[6] The assigning memorandum may ask you to do something that is less familiar to you, like draft a contract or a will, write discovery, write a settlement proposal or agreement, outline a witness examination plan, or write a closing argument.[7] Regardless of what you are asked to do, whether it seems familiar or not, take peace in knowing that you will be given instructions on how to complete the assigned task. If you are asked to, for example, draft a letter to a client, you will be given detailed instructions as to what should be included in the letter.

After reading the task memo, ask yourself the following questions:

- What am I being asked to write?
- How will it be organized?
- Who is the audience?
- What will the tone be (objective vs. persuasive)?
- Are there any special instructions?

Step two: Create a shell document that follows the task memo's instructions.

After you understand what you are being asked to write, you should create a shell document that follows the instructions provided. A shell document is what you will type your response into, and it should include, based on the special instructions given to you, placeholders for the different parts of your response.

For example, let's say that you were asked to draft a letter to your client Sam Smith for the signature of your assigning lawyer Molly May, briefly discussing the facts and then analyzing three issues. What should your response look like? A letter! If your response is anything other than something that looks like a letter, you did not complete the task you were asked to complete. Your shell document might look like the example below.

> Dear Mr. Smith,
>
> [discuss facts]
>
> [issue 1]
>
> [issue 2]
>
> [issue 3]
>
> Sincerely,
>
> Molly May

---

6. National Conference of Bar Examiners, Multistate Performance Test http://www.ncbex.org/exams/mpt/ (last visited April 30, 2024).

7. *Id.*

If, given the time pressure, you do not create a shell document right away, you risk having an incomplete or unorganized response. Some students simply begin to type a response rather than drafting a shell and, in so doing, totally forget the response is supposed to be a letter to the client. This omission means they will lose points. Therefore, we recommend that before moving on from the task memo you create a shell document such that you ensure, at minimum, your response is organized correctly and follows instructions.

Please do not underestimate the importance of following instructions. On the one hand, following instructions is the easiest thing to do. On the other hand, experience in grading PTs demonstrates that following instructions is actually difficult. In fact, failure to follow instructions is, in our experience, the number one reason students fail the PT.

Step three: Read the file (facts) and the library (law), taking notes and pre-outlining as you go.

After reading the task memo and creating your shell response, you need to read the rest of the file and the library. Which one should you read first? It depends. Some people prefer reading the file first. They need to first grasp the facts of their client's case in order to appreciate the law that will apply. Other people prefer to read the library first. They need to understand the law, so that when they read the facts of the client's case they can understand which facts are important. We suggest that, as you take practice PTs, you switch off reading the file first and library first. After you complete several PTs, you will figure out which approach is most helpful to you.

Regardless of what you read first, as you read through the file and library, you should be taking notes. You really only have time to read through the packet one time. Therefore, you should annotate the documents with notes. For example, if a case in the library goes to the first issue, you may write "issue 1" on the top of the case in the library. You should also take notes in your shell document. For example, as you read the case that goes to issue one, you might type rules from that case in your shell document under the placeholder heading for that issue. If in the file you read from a deposition with testimony that goes to issue one, you might annotate that on the deposition testimony and add notes from that deposition in your shell under the placeholder heading for issue one. In this way, you are beginning a pre-outline of your response.

Step four: Organize your response.

After you have finished reading through the packet, you should have in your shell the beginnings of an outline, although it might be a bit messy. Spend some time cleaning it up and getting organized before you begin to write. Make sure that, before you write, you know which facts and which law go to each issue.

Step five: Write your response.

While the PT does not explicitly separate out reading time and writing time, generally speaking, you should spend about half of your 60 minutes of time doing each. Therefore, when the clock says you only have about 30 minutes left, you should begin writing.

Writing a PT response differs a bit from the writing you complete in legal writing courses in a few ways. First, you do not need to include properly formed citations to the law. Rather, in a PT, citing to the law can be done by simply referring to a case by name. Note that, as PT exam graders are sometimes grading hundreds of exams and are looking for you to use citations, it is worth spending time making sure your references to legal authority stand out by using boldface, italics, and/or underlining.

> In Franklin, courts use the substantial factor causation test. ***Jones***. The substantial fact test requires that . . .

Also, in a PT exam, unless instructed otherwise, you should not need to cite to the factual record (the "file").

Second, in a PT exam, organization is king. This means that you should spend time, as we have mentioned, getting your response organized according to the assignment instructions. You should also spend time doing things like bolding and underlining headings, so they are easily spotted and differentiated from the text.

Third, when doing legal analysis for a PT exam, it is not necessary to do a full-blown CRAC. Rather, time is limited, and it is okay to take short cuts. For example, if your heading for the issue is a conclusion, you need not waste time restating your conclusion under the heading as the first "C" of CRAC. In such a situation, you would draft a conclusory heading for the issue and then follow it with your rule and analysis for the issue. Additionally, in legal writing courses, the "R" or Rule of CRAC has three parts—the general rule, the subrules, and the case illustrations. In contrast, your Rules on a PT may be abbreviated. Oftentimes on a PT you will not have time to do complete case illustrations. That is okay. What is most important is that you explain the law (and cite/reference to it) and apply the law to the facts.

Therefore, when we counsel students on doing legal analysis for a PT, we say legal analysis is a two-step process: (1) explain the law; (2) apply the law. Do not worry too much about the breakdown of CRAC—simply make sure you explain the law then apply the law. Additionally, unless specifically instructed to do so, on a PT you do not need to do counter-analysis.

Finally, in writing your response, it is very important that you reach all of the issues. If, for example, there are three issues, it is much better to have completed "okay" analyses of all three issues than to have "perfect" analyses of only one issue. The PT graders are evaluating you based on your ability to efficiently manage your time. Failing to reach all of the issues presented shows a failure of time management.

Part 7 | **Appendix**

OBJECTIVE WRITING DOCUMENTS

A. Sample e-mail memo
B. Sample case brief
C. Objective memo assigning e-mail
D. Sample objective memo

PERSUASIVE WRITING DOCUMENTS

E. Motion and opposition record
F. Sample motion for summary judgment
G. Sample opposition to motion for summary judgment

OTHER

H. *Tagore v. United States*

APPENDIX A:
SAMPLE E-MAIL MEMO

From: Loiya, Neu <NeuLoiya@lawfirm.com>
Sent: Thursday, July 25, 2024, 8:15:32 AM
To: Baker, Dominique <dbaker@lawfirm.com>
Subject: United Information, Inc. (Client 30408.123): Title VII Religious Discrimination

Dear Ms. Baker

The purpose of this e-mail is to identify the legal requirements for Mr. Saint to establish a Title VII religious discrimination claim in the Fifth Circuit against United Information, Inc. (UI).

The Fifth Circuit employs a burden-shifting framework to analyze Title VII religious discrimination claims. *Davis v. Fort Bend Cnty.*, 765 F.3d 480, 485 (5th Cir. 2014). Under this framework, an employee has the initial burden to establish a prima facie case of religious discrimination. A prima facie case of religious discrimination requires the employee to prove the following four elements:

1. he had a bona fide religious belief;
2. his belief conflicted with an employment requirement;
3. his employer was informed of his belief; and
4. he suffered an adverse employment action for failing to comply with the conflicting employment requirement.

Id. Once the employee has satisfied his burden, the burden shifts to the employer to demonstrate that it reasonably accommodated the employee or could not reasonably accommodate the employee without undue hardship. *Id.*

For your convenience, I have attached the *Davis* case to this email and have highlighted the relevant language.

Please let me know if I can provide you with any additional help on this case or any future cases.

Best Regards,

Neu

Neu Loiya
Baker & Jones, LLP
106 S. Harwood, Suite 400
Dallas, Texas 75201
(214) 555–1234 (telephone)
(214) 555–6709 (facsimile)

PRIVILEGED AND CONFIDENTIAL: Communication Subject to the Attorney-Client Privilege and the Attorney-Work-Product Doctrine

APPENDIX B:
SAMPLE CASE BRIEF

ITEM	DESCRIPTION
Case Citation	*Davis v. Fort Bend Cnty.*, 765 F.3d 480 (5th Cir. 2014).
Parties	Plaintiff-Appellant is Louis M. Davis, an employee who filed suit against Defendant-Appellee Fort Bend County, her former employer
Procedural History	Davis sued Fort Bend for claims, including religious discrimination under Title VII. Fort Bend filed a motion for summary judgment on all claims, and the district court granted it. Davis is appealing the direct court's grant of summary judgment on her Title VII claim for religious discrimination.
Disposition	The Court of Appeals reversed the district court's grant of summary judgment as to Davis's claim for Title VII religious discrimination.
Issue(s) Presented (i.e., issue(s) for which you are using case)	Whether the district court properly granted summary judgment as to the plaintiff's Title VII claim of religious discrimination. Specifically: • (Issue 1) Did the plaintiff-employee present sufficient evidence demonstrating a genuine issue of material fact that she "sincerely felt that she was religiously compelled to attend and participate in a special service at church on Sunday, July 3" such that the first element of bona fide religious belief is satisfied? • (Issue 2) Did the defendant-employer present sufficient evidence of its affirmative defense of undue hardship?
Trigger Facts (i.e., the legally relevant facts for each issue)	The plaintiff's employer Fort Bend required all technical support employees, including plaintiff Davis, to be at work for an installation on the weekend of July 4, 2011. On June 28, 2011, Davis told her employer she could not work Sunday, July 3 "due to a previous religious commitment." Davis said she had to attend a "special church service" but that she could come in afterwards. Davis also arranged for a replacement to attend work in her absence. Fort Bend did not approve the absence, and, after Davis did not show up for work on July 3, she was fired.
Rule (i.e., the law applied by the court on each issue)	(Issue 1) The first element of a plaintiff's prima facie case for Title VII religious discrimination is proving that she held a bona fide religious belief. Bona fide religious beliefs include "moral or ethical beliefs as to what is right and wrong which are sincerely held with the strength of traditional religious views." A court focuses on the "individual's motivation" and decides when the individual's beliefs are "in his own scheme of things, religious." The court does not look at whether the belief is a "true religious tenant." The sincerity of a religious belief is a fact question and inquiry into it "must be handled with a light touch, or judicial shyness." (Issue 2) After a plaintiff proves its prima facie case, the burden shifts to the defendant to "demonstrate either that it reasonably accommodated the employee, or that it was unable to reasonably accommodate the employee's needs without undue hardship." Requiring an employee to substitute for another employee's absence may impose more than a de minimus cost and, thus, an undue hardship. Additionally, permitting an employee to be absent and leave the staff short-handed may prove an undue hardship. However, when there is another employee who is a "ready and willing volunteer to substitute" for the employee, no undue hardship exists.
Holding (i.e., the how the court ruled on each issue)	(Issue 1) "Davis's testimony about her own sincere belief regarding her religious need to attend a special service at church on Sunday sufficiently evidenced a genuine dispute of material fact whether she held a bona fide religious belief." (Issue 2) "Because Fort Bend does not argue that permitting Davis's arranged substitute to work in place of Davis would impose an undue hardship, there exists a genuine dispute of material fact whether Fort Bend would have suffered undue hardship in accommodating Davis's religious observance."
Reasoning (i.e., the how the court applied to rule to the trigger facts for each issue)	(Issue 1) The Court of Appeals relied on Davis's testimony that she was a devout member of her church who attended at least two to three services each weekend and volunteered at church. The Court of Appeals relied on Davis's testimony that she "needed" to attend the service on July 3, even though the pastor only "requested" members participate, noting that it must consider the evidence with "judicial shyness" and not make credibility determinations or weigh the evidence. The Court of Appeals explained that sincerity could be found on "little more than the plaintiff's credible assertions." (Issue 2) The Court of Appeals reasoned that there was no undue hardship because Davis arranged for a substitute on July 3 who voluntarily agreed to work her shift. Because there was at least one volunteer to work Davis's shift, Fort Bend did not have to incur any cost "requiring" an employee to work for Davis, and Fort Bend would not be left short-handed. The Court of Appeals distinguished precedent cases that held there was an undue hardship because in those cases the employers had no volunteers and would have had to require another employee to cover the shift of be left short-handed.
Take-Aways and Other Notes	This is a factually analogous case to illustrate for the bona fide religious belief and undue hardship CRACs. It also is a good case for general rules and subrules because it is binding.

APPENDIX C: OBJECTIVE MEMO ASSIGNING E-MAIL

From: Baker, Dominique <dbaker@lawfirm.com>
Sent: Tuesday, August 27, 2024 5:54 PM
To: Loiya, Neu <NeuLoiya@lawfirm.com>
Subject: United Information, Inc. (30408.123): Title VII Liability Analysis

Dear Neu:

A long-time firm client, United Information, Inc. (UI), which is based in Texas, contacted me earlier this week and would like our firm's help in assessing an area of potential liability for the company. One of UI's employees, Mr. Saint, has accused the company of discriminating against him on the basis of his religious beliefs in violation of Title VII of the Civil Rights Act of 1964.

I am hoping you have some time to help me on this matter by drafting a formal memorandum that I can forward to UI in which you assess the likelihood UI will be held liable for violating Title VII. To do this analysis, you will need to analyze two issues: (1) whether Mr. Saint will likely establish a prima facie case of Title VII religious discrimination; and (2) whether, if Mr. Saint is successful establishing a prima facie case, UI can avoid liability by proving one of the affirmative defenses available under Title VII.

To get you started, I have attached a file containing factual documents UI provided to me, transcripts from interviews we did at UI, and preliminary research a summer associate completed last week before she left to return to law school. As a cost-conscious law firm that places our client's interests first, I would like you to rely on the preliminary research that has already been completed to draft your initial memo. If Mr. Saint ends up filing a claim, we will update the research at that time.

The case, as you can tell, is in the Fifth Circuit and would likely be filed in the U.S. District Court for the Northern District of Texas.

Dominique Baker
Baker & Jones, LLP
106 S. Harwood, Suite 400
Dallas, Texas 75201

APPENDIX D: SAMPLE OBJECTIVE MEMO

MEMORANDUM

TO:	Ms. Dominique Baker
FROM:	Neu Loiya
DATE:	September 16, 2024
SUBJECT:	United Information, Inc. (30408.123): Title VII Liability Analysis

QUESTIONS PRESENTED

1. Under Title VII of the Civil Rights Act of 1964, as interpreted by the Fifth Circuit, can Mr. Saint establish a prima facie case of religious discrimination against United Information, Inc. (UI) when Mr. Saint refused to use the required biometric-scanner timekeeping system but asserted that his belief in the Mark of the Beast supported his refusal and elements two, three, and four are uncontested?

2. Under Title VII of the Civil Rights Act of 1964, as interpreted by the Fifth Circuit, can UI avoid liability for a religious discrimination claim by showing it reasonably accommodated Mr. Saint's religious belief when it gave him the options to scan his right hand or left thumbprint instead of his retinas?

3. Under Title VII of the Civil Rights Act of 1964, as interpreted by the Fifth Circuit, can UI avoid liability for a religious discrimination claim by showing that reasonably accommodating Mr. Saint's religious belief would cause UI undue hardship when UI's implementation of the new biometric-scanner timekeeping system increased a UI supervisor's efficiency and saved UI an estimated $4,000 annually?

BRIEF ANSWERS

1. Very likely, yes. Mr. Saint is very likely to establish the four elements of a religious discrimination prima facie case under Title VII because Mr. Saint consistently asserted his Evangelical Christian belief against using biometric-scanning technology to UI, and the remaining elements of Mr. Saint's prima facie case remain uncontested. Accordingly, a court will likely find Mr. Saint met his burden to prove his religious discrimination claim.

2. Very unlikely, no. UI is very unlikely to establish that it offered Mr. Saint a reasonable accommodation because it only offered to allow Mr. Saint to scan his right hand or left thumb rather than his retinas. Accordingly, UI likely cannot avoid liability for Title VII religious discrimination using this affirmative defense because it did not

offer Mr. Saint an accomodation that reconciled his religious belief in the Mark of the Beast and the company's biometric-scanning requirement.

3. Likely, yes. UI will likely establish that reasonably accommodating Mr. Saint would cause the company undue hardship because it would impose more than a de minimis cost on its finances, efficiency, and other employees. Accordingly, because it can likely establish the affirmative defense of undue hardship, a court will likely not find UI liable for Title VII religious discrimination.

STATEMENT OF FACTS

Our client, UI, seeks the firm's assistance in assessing the likelihood that its former employee, Mr. Abraham Saint, can hold UI liable for Title VII religious discrimination.

A. Mr. Saint claims to be an Evangelical Christian and previously participated in organized religion.

Mr. Saint asserts that he is an Evangelical Christian and that, as part of his religiosity, he believes in the Mark of the Beast and antichrist. Ex. 2. Mr. Saint was an active member of the St. Jaguar Community Church from his childhood years until 2016, his attendance rapidly decreased from 2016 to 2018, and he stopped attending that church altogether in 2018. Ex. 6. Between 2016 and 2018, Mr. Saint documented his movement away from his former church—and organized religion generally—on Facebook. *See* Ex. 7. Mr. Saint's UI colleague, Mr. Jonathan Anderson, who had worked with Mr. Saint since 2016 and remains close with him, did not know that Mr. Saint was religious and did not believe Mr. Saint attended church. Ex. 11 at 3:7–10.

B. Mr. Saint's employer, UI, moved from using a manual system to a retina-based biometric-scanning system for employees to clock in and out of work.

Mr. Saint began working at UI in 2016. *Id.* at 3:2–3. Since he started at UI, UI used a manual timekeeping system that required employees to sign in and out of work using their identification codes with their supervisor. Ex. 12 at 3:23–5:2. When using the original timekeeping system, UI employees "frequently forg[ot] their codes," "sen[t] constant emails to management asking . . . to be manually clocked in and out," and "clock[ed] in and out for their friends." *Id.* at 4:16–5:2. In July 2023, UI announced a new policy, effective August 1, 2023, mandating that employees use a new retina-based biometric-scanning system manufactured by PalmVein to clock in and out of work. Ex. 4; *see* Ex. 5. UI switched from its original, manual timekeeping system to the new, biometric-scanning system for two reasons: (1) to further its mission to streamline operations, advance technology, and "embark on innovative projects" and (2) to counteract the inefficiencies and susceptibility to fraud raised by UI's previous timekeeping system. Ex. 4; Ex. 1; Ex. 5 at 3; Ex. 12 at 4:16–5:2; Ex. 9.

Unlike the original timekeeping system, which required a supervisor to manage the time and attendance records for fifteen employees, UI's new biometric-timekeeping system lessened supervisors' timekeeping and attendance responsibilities—giving supervisors more time to "embark on innovative projects" and to lead recruitment and training efforts. Ex. 9; Ex. 5 at 3; Ex. 12 at 4:16–5:2. Moreover, UI's new biometric-timekeeping system allowed UI to eliminate the "costly position" at UI that dealt with fraudulent timekeeping and was estimated to save the company $4,000 annually after expenditure for the new technology. Ex. 12 at 4:16–5:2. Given these realities, UI stated that the cost of running both the new and the old timekeeping software systems "would be insane." Ex. 5 at 2.

C. Mr. Saint asserted his religious belief against using the biometric scanner.

After UI announced its new biometric scanning policy in July 2023, Mr. Saint sent a letter, e-mails, and a Religious Accommodation Request form to UI through Mr. Saint's supervisor, Ms. Kathy Edwards, and UI's Human Resources Manager, Mr. Sean Farmor, asserting his religious belief that use of biometric scanners could "mark" him and citing a Bible verse regarding the "Mark of the Beast." Ex. 2; Ex. 5 at 2; Ex. 8; Ex. 3. As such, Mr. Saint requested an exemption from UI's new policy. Ex. 2; Ex. 5 at 2; Ex. 8. When Mr. Saint informed UI of his religious belief against using biometric scanners "under any type of conditions," he expressed willingness to "sign in and out of work . . . using an alternative method." Ex. 2. In his religious accommodation request form, Mr. Saint indicated the duration of his accommodation as "permanent" and expressed his preference "to continue to sign in and out by checking in with Ms. Edwards." Ex. 8.

D. UI offered Mr. Saint the option of scanning his right hand instead of his retina, but Mr. Saint refused the accommodation.

From August 2, 2023, through August 10, 2023, UI allowed Mr. Saint to temporarily use its old system while investigating whether it could accommodate Mr. Saint's request. Ex. 13. During that period, UI gave Mr. Saint the option of scanning his right hand instead of his retinas. Ex. 5 at 3. When Mr. Saint refused to scan his right hand, UI gave him the option to scan his left thumbprint, believing it was acceptable because the Bible verse Mr. Saint cited only referenced the right hand and forehead. Ex. 5 at 1. Mr. Saint refused UI's offered accommodations. Ex. 13; Ex. 12 at 5:14–15. Another UI employee, Mr. Svelt, was permanently disabled after losing an eye, and temporarily disabled after breaking both arms. Ex. 12 at 5:7–14. Consequently, UI offered him the "temporary measure" of checking in with his supervisor until his arms healed, and he could then use the thumbprint scanner. *Id.*

E. Mr. Saint resigned after UI did not compensate him for the time he worked after the manual timekeeping system was deactivated.

After August 11, 2023, UI's original, manual timekeeping system was no longer available to Mr. Saint, but he continued working his usual hours through August 21, 2023, without clocking in or out. Ex. 5 at 1; Ex. 13. On August 22, 2023, Mr. Saint received a paycheck from UI without compensation for the hours he worked—but could not clock in—from August 11, 2023, through August 21, 2023. Ex. 13. The next day, Mr. Saint resigned, claiming that he had no other option because using the biometric scanner—now the only timekeeping option UI offered—under any circumstances conflicted with his religious belief. *Id.*; Ex. 2. Before Mr. Saint resigned, UI e-mailed PalmVein about the validity of Mr. Saint's claim that the biometric scanner could "mark" its users, to which PalmVein responded that it could not "assign any 'mark' to a person." Ex. 5. at 1–2.

DISCUSSION

Mr. Saint is unlikely to succeed in his attempt to hold UI liable for Title VII religious discrimination. Title VII prohibits an employer from discriminating against an employee based on the employee's religion. 42 U.S.C. § 2000e–2(a)(1). Religion "includes all aspects of religious observance and practice, as well as belief." 42 U.S.C. § 2000e(j). The Fifth Circuit employs a burden-shifting framework to analyze Title VII religious discrimination claims. *Davis v. Fort Bend Cnty.*, 765 F.3d 480, 485 (5th Cir. 2014). Under this framework, the plaintiff must first establish a prima facie case of religious discrimination. *Id.* If the plaintiff establishes a prima facie case, the burden shifts to the defendant to demonstrate that it reasonably accommodated the employee or could not reasonably accommodate the employee without undue hardship. *Id.* First, Mr. Saint is very likely to establish a prima facie case of religious discrimination against UI. To establish a prima facie case of religious discrimination under Title VII, a plaintiff must prove that (1) he had a bona fide religious belief; (2) his belief conflicted with an employment requirement; (3) his employer was informed of his belief; and (4) he suffered an adverse employment action for failing to comply with the conflicting employment requirement. *Tagore v. United States*, 735 F.3d 324, 329 (5th Cir. 2013). Because, at this point, UI does not contest elements two, three, and four, only the first element of Mr. Saint's prima facie Title VII case remains at issue. Second, UI is very unlikely to avoid liability by establishing that it offered Mr. Saint a reasonable accommodation. Third, however, UI will likely be able to avoid liability by establishing that it could not reasonably accommodate Mr. Saint without undue hardship. Therefore, Mr. Saint's Title VII claim will likely fail.

I. Mr. Saint will likely establish the first element of religious discrimination under Title VII and, because the remaining elements are uncontested, will likely establish a prima facie case of religious discrimination against UI.

Given Mr. Saint's consistent representations to UI and actions surrounding his religious belief against using UI's new biometric-scanning system, Mr. Saint will likely establish the first element required for religious discrimination and, as such, his prima facie case. To satisfy the first element of a religious discrimination claim, a plaintiff must prove that he had a "bona fide religious belief." *Id.* In other words, the first element requires a plaintiff to prove two things: first, that his belief is religious and, second, that his belief is bona fide. A bona fide religious belief includes "moral or ethical beliefs as to what is right and wrong [that] are sincerely held." *Davis*, 765 F.3d at 485. In determining whether a plaintiff's belief is a religious belief, a court must ask "whether [the individual's beliefs] are, in his own scheme of things, religious." *Id.* (citing *United States v. Seeger*, 380 U.S. 163, 185 (1965)). A plaintiff's belief may constitute a "religious belief" despite its incomprehensibility or imprecision. *Id.* at 487 (first quoting *Seeger*, 380 U.S. at 184; and then quoting *A.A. ex rel. Betenbaugh v. Needville Indep. Sch. Dist.*, 611 F.3d 248, 261 (5th Cir. 2010)). Put another way, "a belief is 'religious' if it is '[a] sincere and meaningful belief which occupies in the life of its possessor a place parallel to that filled by . . . God.'" *Id.* at 485 (citing *Seeger*, 380 U.S. at 176). Because the belief's trueness or centrality as a religious tenet is "not open to question," whether a belief is religious is ultimately a question of sincerity. *See id.* Courts hesitate to challenge a plaintiff's sincerity, inquiring with "a light touch" and "judicial shyness" and performing a limited assessment of a plaintiff's credibility based on his representations and actions relating to his asserted belief. *Tagore*, 735 F.3d at 328 (citing *Moussazadeh v. Tex. Dep't of Crim. Just.*, 703 F.3d 781, 792 (5th Cir. 2012)). To be sincere, an employee's reliance on a religious belief must stem from conviction and not convenience. *Hansard v. Johns-Manville Prods. Corp.*, No. 1902, 1973 WL 129, at *2 (E.D. Tex. Feb. 16, 1973).

An employee's consistent representation that she holds a particular religious belief coupled with action consistent with that belief supports a finding of sincerity. In *Davis*, the Fifth Circuit held that the employee's representation and action evidenced sincerity such that she, at minimum, raised a genuine issue of material fact as to the sincerity of her belief. 765 F.3d at 485–86. In that case, the employee notified her employer that she could not work on a particular Sunday because she had a special church service to attend that involved breaking new ground and feeding the community. *Id.* at 486–87. The employee attended the church event, was fired for being absent from work without approval, and then sued her employer for religious discrimination under Title VII. *Id.* at 484. At trial, the employee testified about her devotion to the church, stating that she "believed strongly" that she "needed" to attend a "special church service." *Id.* at 486. The employee further testified about her active commitment to her church, referencing her frequent church attendance and participation. *Id.* at 487. The Fifth Circuit reasoned that the district court erred when it granted summary judgment because it improperly inquired into the nature of the activity and its status as "a true religious tenet," whereas it should have looked to the employee's credibility and asked whether the employee sincerely believed that the activity was religious "in her own scheme of things." *Id.* The Fifth Circuit further reasoned that the employee's representation and action surrounding her belief that she was religiously required to attend a special church service, through her testimony, sufficiently evidenced a genuine issue of material fact as to whether she sincerely believed the event to be religious. *Id.* at 487. Accordingly, the employee's prima facie case survived summary judgment for a trier of fact to later determine whether the employee held a bona fide religious belief. *Id.*

In contrast, an employee's consistent representation that he holds a particular religious belief coupled with action inconsistent with that belief negates a finding of sincerity. In *Hansard*, the court held that the employee failed to establish the requisite sincerity because his actions were inconsistent with his asserted religious belief. 1973 WL 129, at *2. In that case, the employee, a New Testament Christian, told his employer that he could not work on a particular Sunday because it conflicted with his religious belief against working for profit on Sundays. *Id.* at *1–2. The employee was fired after refusing to work that Sunday, and he then sued his employer for religious discrimination under Title VII. *Id.* at *1. The employee was raised in the Church of Christ but dropped his membership and claimed to be a New Testament Christian years later. *Id.* at *2. The employee had occasionally refused to work Sundays but admitted to not always following his "lifelong" belief against working for profit on Sundays. *Id.* at *1–2. The court reasoned that the employee's attempt to frame his action as consistent failed because although he attested to his belief's reemergence following a "miraculous" event, his testimony about when the alleged event occurred and his admission to working several Sundays following the event remained inconsistent. *Id.* at *2. The court explained that the employee's inconsistent action surrounding his religious belief against working Sundays suggested that his belief was grounded more in convenience than conviction, thus, negating a finding of sincerity. *Id.* Accordingly, the employee failed to prove that he held a bona fide religious belief. *Id.*

Mr. Saint will likely satisfy the first element of his religious discrimination claim because, like the employee in *Davis*, and distinct from the employee in *Hansard*, Mr. Saint was consistent in his representations and actions surrounding his religious belief, which weighs in favor of a court finding Mr. Saint's belief to be sincere. As an initial matter, Mr. Saint's belief about the scanner will be held to constitute a "religious belief" because, following *Davis*, the trueness of or centrality of the belief is "not open to question." *Davis*, 765 F.3d at 485 (citing *Seeger*, 380 U.S. at 185). Thus, a court is almost certain to reject any argument by UI that its own interpretation of the Bible led it to determine Mr. Saint's religious belief about the scanner was wrong because it is improper to focus on whether the activity was a "true religious tenant." *See id.* at 486; Ex. 5 at 1. Thus, in assessing the first element of Mr. Saint's religious discrimination claim, a court will likely focus on whether Mr. Saint's belief was sincere. *Davis*, 765 F3d at 485 (citing *Seeger*, 380 U.S. at 176). Like the employee in *Davis*, the consistency of Mr. Saint's representations and actions are likely sufficient to demonstrate the sincerity of his religious belief that biometric scanners are "Mark of the Beast" and of the "Antichrist." *See Davis*, 765 F.3d 487; Ex. 2; Ex. 5 at 1; Ex. 13. Like *Davis*, where the employee once informed her employer that she could not work on a particular Sunday because she strongly believed she needed to be at church for an event, Mr. Saint repeatedly told UI that he could not use the biometric scanner because of his Evangelical Christian belief that Revelation 13:16–18 indicates that the "Mark of the Beast" is a "symbolic mark" and that "technology will be used to carry out its implementation." 765 F.3d at 483; Ex. 2; Ex. 5 at 2; Ex. 8; Ex. 13. In *Davis*, the employee acted consistent with her representation when she missed work to attend the church event and testified at trial about her devotion to the church and frequent church attendance and participation. 765 F.3d. at 484, 487. Similarly, Mr. Saint acted consistent with his belief by being steadfast in his refusal to use the biometric scanner during the twenty days between when UI's new policy became effective and his resignation, by continuously seeking exemption from UI's new policy, and by resigning rather than use the biometric scanner. Ex. 5 at 2; Ex. 8; Ex. 13.

Unlike in *Davis*, where the employee's testimony about her devotion and active commitment to the church was uncontroverted, here, Mr. Anderson's disbelief that Mr. Saint was religious, and the letter from Reverend Connors and Mr. Saint's Facebook posts, indicating that he stopped attending St. Jaguar Community Church in 2016, raise concerns that Mr. Saint's devotion and active commitment to the church were inconsistent. Ex. 11 at 3:7–10; Ex. 6; Ex. 7 at 2–3. However, Mr. Saint's multiple representations about his belief as an Evangelical Christian and his actions reflect consistency, if not consistency beyond that of the employee in *Davis*. Ex. 2; Ex. 4; Ex. 5 at 2; Ex. 8; Ex. 13. Thus, following *Davis*, Mr. Saint's testimony about his own sincere belief regarding what was "religious in [his] own scheme of things" is sufficient to establish the first element, especially because a court will assess Mr. Saint's religious belief with "judicial shyness" and hold that the bona fide religious belief element is met "on little more than the plaintiff's credible assertions." 765 F.3d at 484, 487.

Distinct from the employee in *Hansard*, who did not satisfy the first element of his religious discrimination claim because his representations and actions surrounding his religious belief were inconsistent, Mr. Saint will likely establish that his religious belief was bona fide. *Hansard*, 1973 WL 129, at *2. While the facts in *Hansard* and Mr. Saint's case may appear alike because both employees have a common history of prior church membership and deactivated membership because of their dissatisfaction with the church, the *Hansard* holding turned on the fact that the employee was contradictory and inconsistent in his beliefs—which is unlike Mr. Saint. *See* 1973 WL 129, at *2; Ex. 2; Ex. 5 at 2; Ex. 6; Ex. 7 at 3; Ex. 10; Ex. 13. Unlike *Hansard*, where the employee asserted on select occasions that he could not work Sundays due to his religious belief against working for profit on Sundays, Mr. Saint was steadfast in his communications to his employer that he could not use the biometric scanner because of his religious belief in the "Mark of the Beast." 1973 WL 129, at *1; Ex. 5 at 2; Ex. 8. Although the employee in *Hansard* claimed that his religious belief against working on Sundays was "lifelong," he admitted to not always following his represented belief. 1973 WL 129, at *2. Despite the employee's attempt to justify his inconsistency by explaining that his belief reemerged following a "miraculous" event, he admitted to still working some Sundays even after his belief's renewal. *Id.* Unlike these inconsistent actions that the *Hansard* employee displayed surrounding his represented belief, Mr. Saint's actions reflect consistency because he never once used the scanner, he requested continuous exemptions from UI's new scanning policy, and he ultimately resigned rather than succumbing to use of the scanner. Ex. 2; Ex. 4; Ex. 5 at 2; Ex. 8; Ex. 12 at 5:14–15; Ex. 13. Thus, unlike *Hansard*, Mr. Saint's belief could hardly be argued to be based on "convenience rather than conviction" because Mr. Saint's made clear his religious belief forbade him from using the scanning technology, which he consistently refused to use, even though it inconveniently cost him his job. *See Hansard*, 1973 WL 129, at *2.

Consequently, a court will likely hold that Mr. Saint held a bona fide religious belief, thus, establishing the first element of a prima facie case of religious discrimination under Title VII. *Davis*, 765 F.3d at 485. Because Mr. Saint can likely establish the first element—and the remaining three elements are uncontested—Mr. Saint will likely establish a prima facie case of religious discrimination.

II. UI will likely avoid liability for Title VII religious discrimination based on an affirmative defense.

UI will likely be able to avoid liability for religious discrimination because it can establish an affirmative defense to the Title VII religious discrimination claim. An employer can avoid liability for Title VII religious discrimination by establishing one of two affirmative defenses: the employer can either show that it offered the employee a "reasonable" accommodation for his religious conflict or that it was "unable to reasonably accommodate [the] employee's . . . religious observance" because doing so would have imposed "undue hardship on the conduct of the employer's business." 42 USC §2000e(j); *see also Davis*, 765 F.3d at 487. Although UI will not likely be able to prove that it offered Mr. Saint a reasonable accommodation, UI likely can show it could not reasonably accommodate Mr. Saint's religious belief without undue hardship, and, thus, UI will likely avoid Title VII liability.

A. UI is unlikely to prove the affirmative defense of reasonable accommodation.

UI likely cannot establish that it offered Mr. Saint a reasonable accommodation. An employer can avoid liability for religious discrimination under Title VII if it can show it offered the employee any reasonable accommodation. 42 USC §2000(e)(j). An employer and employee must work together to identify a reasonable accommodation—that is, an accomodation that reconciles the employee's religious needs and the employer's business demands. *Brener v. Diagnostic Ctr. Hosp.*, 671 F.2d 141, 145–46 (5th Cir. 1982). Once an employer offers any reasonable accommodation, an employee has a corollary duty to make a good faith effort to act flexibly and cooperate with the offered measure, even if the employee prefers an different reasonable accommodation. *Id.* at 146; *Bruff v. N. Miss. Health Servs., Inc.*, 244 F.3d 495, 501, 503 (5th Cir. 2001); *Eversley v. MBank Dallas*, 843 F.2d 172, 176 (5th Cir. 1988). However, an employee need not modify his religious belief in his efforts to work with the employer's offered measure. *Brener*, 671 F.2d at 146 n.3. In the end, an accommodation is only "reasonable" if it "*eliminates* the employee's conflict between his religious practices and work requirements." *Favero v. Huntsville Indep. Sch. Dist.*, 939 F. Supp. 1281, 1287–88 (S.D. Tex. 1996) (emphasis in original).

Because the two accommodations UI offered Mr. Saint both continued to require him to use the biometric-scanning technology prohibited by his religious belief, UI probably will not be able to establish the first affirmative defense—that it offered Mr. Saint a reasonable accommodation for his religious conflict. After UI announced its new policy requiring the use of a biometric-scanning system, Mr. Saint told UI that in light of his religious belief he preferred to forgo use of the biometric scanner and either sign in and out using the old system or check in and out directly with Ms. Edwards. Ex. 5 at 2; Ex. 8; Ex. 2. UI did not offer Mr. Saint either of his requested accomodations. Ex. 5. In order for an accomodation to be "reasonable," however, it need not be the accomodation "preferred" by Mr. Saint; instead, UI was only obligated to work with Mr. Saint to arrive at any reasonable accomodation—that is, any accomodation that fully eliminates the conflict between the company's new timekeeping policy and Mr. Saint's religious belief. *Favero*, 939 F. Supp. at 1287–88. After some back and forth between UI, Mr. Saint, and others, UI offered to accommodate Mr. Saint's religious belief by allowing him to forgo retinal scanning and, instead, scan in to work using either his left thumb or his right hand. Ex. 5. Both of the accomodations offered by UI fall short of "reasonable" because they failed to "eliminate" the conflict between Mr. Saint's religious belief and the company's biometric-scanning policy; after all, both offered accomodations continued to require use of the biometric-scanning system, use of which is in conflict with Mr. Saint's religion. *Favero*, 939 F. Supp. at 1287–88; Ex. 2; Ex. 9. Because UI's two offered measures failed to fully eliminate Mr. Saint's religious conflict with the company's scanning policy, UI likely will not establish that it offered Mr. Saint a "reasonable" accommodation. *Favero*, 939 F. Supp. at 1287–88.

B. UI is likely to prove the affirmative defense of undue hardship.

UI can probably establish that offering Mr. Saint a "reasonable" accommodation would have imposed undue hardship on its business. An employer can avoid liability under Title VII if it can show it could not accomodate the employee's religious practice without undue hardship on the employer's business. 42 U.S.C. § 2000e(j). Undue hardship exists when an employer must "bear more than a de minimis cost" to reasonably accommodate its employee's religious belief. *Weber v. Roadway Exp., Inc.*, 199 F.3d 270, 273 (5th Cir. 2000). An employer need not wait to feel the accommodation's impact or attempt to accommodate the employee to establish an undue hardship; instead, an employer can establish undue hardship by showing evidence that the "mere possibility of an [accommodation's] adverse impact" could impose more than de minimis costs on the employer. *Id.* at 274–75. In the Fifth Circuit, courts have recognized the requisite undue hardship in a variety of circumstances:

- An employer can establish more than de minimis costs by showing that a religious accommodation is inflexible to the employer's business demands. *Id.* at 275.
- An employer can establish more than de minimis costs by showing that an accommodation could adversely impact its finances, employees, or efficiency. *Favero*, 939 F. Supp. at 1288; *Weber*, 199 F.3d at 273.
- An employer can establish more than de minimis financial costs through economic loss or an increase in wage expenditure. *Brener*, 671 F.2d at 146; *Favero*, 939 F. Supp. at 1288.
- An employer can demonstrate more than de minimis costs without quantifying the hardship in economic terms but by showing that providing a "reasonable" accommodation could "require coworkers to unfairly perform extra work" or decrease company efficiency. *Tagore*, 735 F.3d at 330; *Brener*, 671 F.2d at 146.

An accommodation that requires other employees to take on additional time-consuming work or to do their assigned work in a way that lessens their efficiency constitutes an undue burden. In *Tagore*, the Fifth Circuit held that the employer's failure to offer an employee her proposed accommodation did not violate Title VII, as a matter of law, because accommodating the employee *could* have imposed more than *de minimis* costs on its employees and efficiency. *Tagore*, 735 F.3d at 330. In that case, the employee's religious belief required her to wear a kirpan—an article resembling a knife—but a federal law prohibited possession of "dangerous weapon[s]" in the public office where she worked. *Id.* at 326–27. The employer denied the employee entry to her workplace when she wore the kirpan, refusing to offer the employee her proposed accommodation—wearing a dulled kirpan blade. *Id.* at 326. The Fifth Circuit, affirming the district court's grant of summary judgment, reasoned that the proposed accommodation would impose more than de minimis employee cost because it would require the employer's security guards to ascertain whether the kirpan blade was sharp or dull—a dangerous weapon or not—each time the employee entered the building, which constituted extra "time-consuming" work. *Id.* at 330. The Fifth Circuit also recognized that such an inquiry would impose more than de minimis efficiency costs on the employer because requiring security guards to determine whether the kirpan was a dangerous weapon every time the employee entered the building would be "impractical, and detrimental to the broad vigilance required at the entrance to public offices." *Id.* Accordingly, the employer avoided liability under Title VII, as a matter of law, by establishing that it was unable to reasonably accommodate the employee without undue hardship. *Id.*

On the other hand, unsubstantiated assertions that any reasonable accommodation would impact other employees or impact the employer financially are insufficient to establish undue hardship. In *Ford v. City of Dallas, Texas*, the court held that an employer failed to meet its burden of proving that offering *any* reasonable accommodation would be unduly burdensome. No. 3:05-CV-1676-D, 2007 WL 2051016, at *1 (N.D. Tex. July 12, 2007). In that case, the employee sued her employer for religious discrimination under Title VII for failing to accommodate her religious belief against working on the Sabbath. *Id.* The employer claimed that accommodating the employee would require it to create an entirely new position for the employee and hire additional employees—which it claimed were more than de minimis costs—but failed to offer supporting evidence. *Id.* at *5. The court reasoned that the employer's unsubstantiated assertion failed to establish that all conceivable accommodations would have imposed more than de minimis costs. *Id.* at *4–5. Accordingly, the employer did not avoid liability under Title VII, as a matter of law, because it failed to support its claimed inability to reasonably accommodate the employee without undue hardship. *Id.*

UI will likely establish the second affirmative defense because, like the employer *Tagore*, and distinct from the employer in *Ford*, UI will likely establish that letting Mr. Saint sign in and out without using the scanner would impose more than de minimis financial and efficiency-based costs on UI. In *Tagore*, the accommodation at issue—requiring security guards to ascertain the dullness of a kirpan blade when the employee entered the building—was time-consuming, impractical, and detrimental to the employer's broad safety efforts. *Tagore*, 735 F.3d at 330. Similarly, here, the accommodation at issue—manual time and attendance supervision—would impose a time burden on Ms. Edwards and would upend UI's broad fraud prevention efforts. Ex. 5 at 3; Ex. 12 at 4:16–5:2. Although requiring Ms. Edwards to manually timekeep for Mr. Saint may seem to require less effort than the *Tagore* requirement that security guards ascertain the kirpan blade's dullness each time the employee enters the building, both impose more than de minimis costs because they both require employees to "unfairly perform extra work." *Tagore*, 735 F.3d at 330. The court's willingness in *Tagore* to find the requirement of determining whether an article is a "dangerous weapon" unduly burdensome—a duty seemingly inherent to the role of a security guard—suggests that a court would be even more inclined to find the requirement that Ms. Edwards manually check Mr. Saint in and out—a duty that goes beyond her existing role—unduly burdensome. Ex. 5 at 3; Ex. 9. Therefore, following *Tagore*, a court here would likely also find that requiring Ms. Edwards to perform this extra work is time-consuming and impractical, as it would decrease her efficiency at spearheading recruitment and training efforts—duties that more aptly support UI's broader goals and purpose for adopting the new software policy in the first place. Ex. 9; Ex. 5 at 3; Ex. 12; Ex. 1; Ex. 4. As such, it would "require coworkers to unfairly perform extra work" and impose more than a de minimus cost. *See Tagore*, 735 F.3d at 330; *Favero*, 939 F. Supp. at 1288.

The broad fraud concern in Mr. Saint's case at first blush may seem less significant than the security concern in *Tagore* because the *Tagore* accommodation implicates safety risks and illegal conduct, arguably more serious matters than fraudulent timekeeping. *Tagore*, 735 F.3d at 326–27. However, the cases remain alike because the court's analysis in *Tagore* did not hinge on the nature of the impact—safety, legal, or fraud—but on the accommodation's adverse effect on the employer's goal of viligance. *Id.* at 330. Like how the court considered the employer's vigilance concerns in *Tagore*, here, a court would weigh other timekeeping systems' susceptibility to fraud—an issue tied to UI's financial and efficiency costs—against the overall effectiveness of its company-wide scanner requirement at alleviating its fraud concerns. *Id.*; Ex. 12 at 4:16–5:2; Ex. 5 at 3. Consequently, a court will likely hold that UI can avoid liability under Title VII by establishing that it could not reasonably accommodate Mr. Saint without undue hardship. *Id.*

Unlike in *Ford*, where the employer's unsubstantiated assertion—that making a particular accommodation would impose more than de minimis costs through the creation of a new position and hiring of additional employees—failed to support a court in finding undue hardship, UI's assertion—that it would be unduly burdensome to offer Mr. Saint an accommodation not requiring the use of the scanner—goes beyond a conclusory claim. 2007 WL 2051015, at *5. In contrast to the employer in *Ford* who offered only broad assertions of cost without any substantiation, UI can provide testimony and documentation that any accommodation not requiring the use of the scanner could impose more than de minimis costs to its finances, employees, and efficiency. Ex. 1; Ex. 4; Ex. 5; Ex. 9; Ex. 12 at 4:16–5:2. In addition, unlike in *Ford*, where the employer failed to prove that it had explored more than one accommodation, UI explored alternative accommodations when it e-mailed PalmVein asking for help resolving Mr. Saint's conflict and offered Mr. Saint the options to scan his right hand or left thumbprint instead of his retinas. Ex. 5; 2007 WL 2051015, at *5. Thus, unlike in *Ford*, UI did not establish that all conceivable accomodations would impose more than de minimus costs. *See Ford*, 2007 WL 2051015, at *5.

Because UI can provide evidence of the "mere possibility" that it could have experienced undue hardship—precisely what was missing in *Ford*—if forced to offer Mr. Saint an accommodation not requiring use of the scanner, it will likely establish the second affirmative defense under Title VII. *See Weber*, 199 F.3d at 274.

CONCLUSION

Mr. Saint can very likely establish a prima facie case of religious discrimination under Title VII because, he can show that he had a bona fide Evangelical Christian belief against using biometric scanners and the remaining elements of his prima facie claim are uncontested. However, because any permanent accommodation not involving the use of the scanner would impose undue hardship on UI, UI can likely avoid liability under Title VII by asserting that it could not reasonably accommodate Mr. Saint without undue hardship. Accordingly, Mr. Saint is unlikely to establish a Title VII religious discrimination claim against UI.

EXHIBIT I

From: **Sean Farmor** <sean_farmor@ui.com>
Date: June 2, 2023 at 8:06 AM
Subject: NOTICE: TIME AND ATTENDANCE POLICY CHANGE
To: "All_UI_Employees"

Dear valued employees,

In keeping with our mission to advance technology across the globe, we will be implementing a convenient and innovative new method for you to clock in and out of work. The new system is mandatory for all employees and will be ready to launch in early August.

Stay tuned for more information about this important policy change.

Sincerely,

Sean Farmor
Human Resources Manager

EXHIBIT 2

Ms. Edwards,

The purpose of this letter is to inform you, as my supervisor, that I cannot use the biometric scanner under any type of conditions. My religion as an Evangelical Christian, as well as The Bible, bars me from using eye scanning technology on my forehead because it is the Mark of the Beast and the antichrist. Therefore, because of my religious views and beliefs I should be exempt from taking part in this method.

The mark is symbolic and a true representation of the beast and his name. You should review Revelation 13:16-18, so that you too can be enlightened. These verses indicate a mark personally symbolic of the beast. Technology will be used to carry out its implementation. I am convinced that this could be done through an eye scanning device, like the one used to sign in and out of work at United Information. In fact, I fear for my colleagues who do and will pray for them.

I am willing to sign in and out of work at United Information using an alternative method and believe I should be exempt from using the PalmVein retina scanning device per my religious beliefs as an Evangelical Christian.

Regards,

Abraham Saint

cc: Mr. Sean Farmor

EXHIBIT 3

Revelation 13 King James Version (KJV)

13 And I stood upon the sand of the sea, and saw a beast rise up out of the sea, having seven heads and ten horns, and upon his horns ten crowns, and upon his heads the name of blasphemy.

2 And the beast which I saw was like unto a leopard, and his feet were as the feet of a bear, and his mouth as the mouth of a lion: and the dragon gave him his power, and his seat, and great authority.

3 And I saw one of his heads as it were wounded to death; and his deadly wound was healed: and all the world wondered after the beast.

4 And they worshipped the dragon which gave power unto the beast: and they worshipped the beast, saying, Who is like unto the beast? who is able to make war with him?

5 And there was given unto him a mouth speaking great things and blasphemies; and power was given unto him to continue forty and two months.

6 And he opened his mouth in blasphemy against God, to blaspheme his name, and his tabernacle, and them that dwell in heaven.

7 And it was given unto him to make war with the saints, and to overcome them: and power was given him over all kindreds, and tongues, and nations.

8 And all that dwell upon the earth shall worship him, whose names are not written in the book of life of the Lamb slain from the foundation of the world.

9 If any man have an ear, let him hear.

10 He that leadeth into captivity shall go into captivity: he that killeth with the sword must be killed with the sword. Here is the patience and the faith of the saints.

11 And I beheld another beast coming up out of the earth; and he had two horns like a lamb, and he spake as a dragon.

12 And he exerciseth all the power of the first beast before him, and causeth the earth and them which dwell therein to worship the first beast, whose deadly wound was healed.

13 And he doeth great wonders, so that he maketh fire come down from heaven on the earth in the sight of men,

14 And deceiveth them that dwell on the earth by the means of those miracles which he had power to do in the sight of the beast; saying to them that dwell on the earth, that they should make an image to the beast, which had the wound by a sword, and did live.

15 And he had power to give life unto the image of the beast, that the image of the beast should both speak, and cause that as many as would not worship the image of the beast should be killed.

16 And he causeth all, both small and great, rich and poor, free and bond, to receive a mark in their right hand, or in their foreheads:

17 And that no man might buy or sell, save he that had the mark, or the name of the beast, or the number of his name.

18 Here is wisdom. Let him that hath understanding count the number of the beast: for it is the number of a man; and his number is Six hundred threescore and six.

King James Version (KJV)

EXHIBIT 4

From: **Sean Farmor** <sean_farmor@ui.com>
Date: July 21, 2023 at 10:42 AM
Subject: NOTICE: TIME AND ATTENDANCE POLICY CHANGE
To: "All_UI_Employees"

Dear valued employees,

You received notice in June that we will be implementing a new method for you to clock in and out of work. The new system will be installed this week, and all employees will be required to switch to the new system.

Beginning August 1, you will "clock" in and out of work using a retina scanning device. The retina scanning device will replace the current timekeeping system. You will no longer have to remember your identification number as the retina scanner will identify you based on your personal biometrics.

Your supervisor will be giving you more details about the new system in your next team meeting. Again, all employees will "clock" in and out of work using the new retina scanning device instead of the current timekeeping system.

This revolutionary paperless system will be easy, convenient, and in keeping with our mission to streamline operations by using technology wherever possible.

Thank you for your continued hard work. If you have any questions, please direct them to your immediate supervisor.

Sincerely,
Sean Farmor
Human Resources Manager

EXHIBIT 5

From: **Sean Farmor** <sean_farmor@ui.com>
Date: Aug 11, 2023 at 9:08 AM
Subject: Fwd: RE: RE: I WILL NOT USE THE BIOMETRIC SCANNER
To: "ASaint@ui.com"

Mr. Saint,

After some considerable research we think we have found a reasonable accommodation that will work for everyone. As you had indicated in your email and prior letter, the Bible does in fact reference the "Mark of the Beast" and "antichrist."

Fortunately, Chapter 13, Verse 16 of the Book of Revelation notes that the "Mark of the Beast" and "antichrist" refer only to the right hand and forehead. While we understand that you believe that forehead includes eyes, we do have the ability to allow you to scan in by way of a thumb print on your left hand. We do not offer this to other employees because the eye scan is quicker and does not get smudged. However, we will make an exception for you.

Moving forward, please have your left thumb scanned for identification purposes in order to clock in and out.

Feel free to contact me with any questions.

Sincerely,

Sean Farmor
Human Resources Manager

---------- Replied message ----------
From: **Alexander Bell** <a.bell@palmvein.org>
Date: Aug 9, 2023 at 1:26 PM
Subject: Fwd: RE: I WILL NOT USE THE BIOMETRIC SCANNER
To: "sean_farmor@ui.com"

Mr. Farmor,

We appreciate your forwarding the recent concern regarding the Palmvein scanner as we are striving to make our product as accurate and user-friendly as possible.

Our team has looked into the "Mark of the Beast" issue raised by your employee and can assure you and your employee that the Palmvein scanner cannot assign any "mark" to a person. The Palmvein is a scanner only and functions to create a pattern of blood vessels in order to identify a person. Our tests have proven that the scanner does not interfere with a person's body in any way, it is a recognition device only.

Please let us know if we can be of any further assistance.

Best regards,

Mr. Alex Bell
Biometric Department Manager

---------- Forwarded message ----------
From: **Sean Farmor** <sean farmor@ui.com>
Date: Aug 1, 2023 at 4:22 PM
Subject: Fwd: I WILL NOT USE THE BIOMETRIC SCANNER
To: "a.bell@palmvein.org"

Hey Alex,

Have you ever seen anything like this? This guy is saying he can't use our brand new software? This system is so expensive, and the cost of running the old software along with this would be insane. Please let me know if you can help.

Best,

Sean Farmor
Human Resources Manager

---------- message ----------
From: **Abe Saint**<ASaint@ui.com>.
Date: Aug 1, 2023 at 4:05 PM
Subject: I WILL NOT USE THE BIOMETRIC SCANNER
To: "sean farmor@ui.com"

Mr. Sean Farmor,

On July 31, 2023, I delivered a letter to my supervisor Kathy Edwards notifying her that I cannot use the biometric scanner. As an Evangelical Christian, the bible tells me that retina scanning technology is the Mark of the Beast and of the antichrist.

Please tell Ms. Edwards that due to my religious belief I am exempt from taking part in this exercise. I would prefer to continue to sign in and out of work using the old system.

Kind Regards,

Abraham Saint

From: **Kat Edwards** <Kathy Edwards@ui.com>
Date: Aug 1, 2023 at 4:58 PM
Subject: RE: Saint's Refusal to Comply with New Policy
To: "sean farmor@ui.com"

Sean,

I've been praying about this Saint guy's situation with the retina scanner all day. When we discussed the new retina scanning system, I was informed that I would only have to continue manual timekeeping duties for Mr. Svelt. I understand that Svelt's unique situation makes it impossible for him to comply with the scanning requirements right now.

However, it is no longer in my job description to supervise time and attendance records for employees. As you know, I only agreed to take on new duties (spearheading recruitment and training new hires) because we agreed that I would no longer have to spend time supervising employee attendance records. When we first discussed this issue with Saint, we offered him a reasonable solution to accommodate his religion by offering him the option to scan his right hand instead of his retinas.

The purpose of retina scanning was to make things easier on us supervisors and to give us time to embark on innovative projects, such as training people on using the new aviation monitoring devices. But this extra work . . . ain't nobody got time for that! Work with me here, Sean.

Best,

Kathy Edwards
Supervisor IV
General Labor Division

EXHIBIT 6

St. Jaguar Community Church
1234 Royal Lane
Dallas, Texas 75203

Mx. Partner
106 S. Harwood, Suite 400
Dallas, Texas 75201

August 24, 2023

Dear Mx. Partner,

I received your letter asking for information about Mr. Saint's attendance at church.

Mr. Saint was a very active member of my congregation for years, since he was a small child. He constantly participated in church activities, including Bible studies and potlucks after services on Sundays. However, in recent years, this has changed significantly. Mr. Saint stopped attending church completely in 2018. Prior to that, his attendance rapidly decreased between 2016 and when he finally stopped coming. It was concerning to me, as there did not seem to be a reason why, and he was one of our most active members. I wish I knew more about his reasoning, and that there was a chance for me to help with his reentry back into church life.

Please let me know if there is more information that you need from me.

Have a blessed day

Sincerely,

Reverend Jim Connors
John 3:16

EXHIBIT 7

Abraham Saint
March 11, 2016 ·

Romans 12:2- Do not conform to the pattern of this world, but be transformed by the renewing of your mind. Then you will be able to test and approve what God's will is—his good, pleasing, and perfect will.

Like · Comment · Share

4 people like this.

Write a comment ...

Abraham Saint
July 18, 2017

Sermon today was so moving, so blessed to be a part of this church family
@St. Jaguar Community Church
Philippians 4:8

Like · Comment · Share

12 people like this.

Write a comment ...

Abraham Saint
May 21, 2015·

Having a rough week, where is god when you need him.

Like · Comment · Share

7 people like this.

Susan Rogers God is always listening, just keep your head up and pray.
Like · Reply · 2 · May 21, 2015

Write a comment ...

Abraham Saint
October 15, 2017 ·

Tired of praying to someone that doesn't change anything. #overit

Like · Comment · Share

17 people like this.

Write a comment ...

Abraham Saint
July 25, 2018 ·

When you run into people from your old church and they ask why you haven't been in a while. Awkward...

Like · Comment · Share

6 people like this.

Jonathan Anderson Didn't know u were a church guy.
Like · Reply · 1 · July 25, 2018

Abraham Saint Not anymore
Like · Reply · 2 · July 25, 2018

Write a comment ...

EXHIBIT 8

United Information Incorporated

United Information, Inc.
972-123-4567 (Phone)
972-123-0000 (Fax)
EEOconcerns@ui.com

APPENDIX I – RELIGIOUS ACCOMMODATIONS REQUEST FORM

United Information, Incorporated (UI) is committed to diversity and inclusiveness of all individuals. This form is to be used when an individual is seeking a religious accommodation because his or her sincerely held religious belief(s) or practice(s) conflict with the work environment. This form is NOT to be used for religious exceptions to the Mandatory Influenza Vaccination Policy HSE 048 or for requests not to engage in clinical or patient care activities.

Instructions: In order for your request to be processed properly, please fill out the sections below completely and use additional space if necessary (Page 3).

CONTACT INFORMATION	
Name: *Abraham S. Saint*	**Date of Request:** ***August 1, 2023***
Department/ Unit:	**Immediate Supervisor:** ***Kathy Edwards***
Mailing Address ***666 Heaven St.*** ***Dallas, TX 75228***	**Phone:** ***Cell: 972-666-0123***
Email Address: ***ASaint@ui.com***	

BELIEF AND ACCOMMODATON INFORMATION	
Identify requested accommodation (e.g., time to pray, leave for religious observance, or religious attire).	*Exemption from using the biometric scanner.*
Identify your religious beliefs or practices.	*As an Evangelical Christian, the Bible tells me that scanning technology is the Mark of the Beast and of the Anti-Christ.*
Provide suggestions for possible accommodations.	*I prefer to continue to sign in and out by checking in with Ms. Edwards.*
Identify duration of accommodation.	☐ **Temporary (i.e. seasonal) Explain:** ☑ **Permanent (e.g. annual religious event or daily religious requirement)**

United Information Incorporated

DISCLOSURE OF PREVIOUS ACCOMODATIONS If you previously received a religious accommodation from UI, complete the table below	
Description of Accommodation Previously Granted	*N/A*
Department/Unit	
Supervisor's Name	
Date Granted	

ADDITIONAL INFORMATION & SUPPLEMENTAL DOCUMENTS

In some cases UI will need to obtain additional information and/or documentation about your religious practice(s) or belief(s). This may include documentation from your religious or spiritual leader.

If requested, can you provide documentation to support your belief(s) and need for accommodation?

YES ☑ **NO** ☐

Are you attaching any supporting documentation to this request?

YES ☑ **NO** ☐

If yes, please list documents below:

1. ***Bible Verse – Revelations 13:16***
2. ***Letter from Pastor***
3. __________
4. __________
5. __________
6. __________

CERTIFICATION

I certify that the above information is complete and accurate to the best of my knowledge, and I understand that any intentional misrepresentation contained in this request may result in disciplinary action. I also understand that my request for an accommodation may not be granted if it is unreasonable and/or if it creates an undue hardship on my employer.

Signature: A Saint Date: *08/01/23*

Print Name: *Abraham S. Saint*

SUMMARY OF NEXT STEPS

1. This request will be reviewed by Organizational Equity.
2. You will be notified, in writing, of the decision regarding the request

United Information Incorporated

SPACE FOR SUPPLEMENTAL INFORMATION
Abraham S. Saint Employee Name *ASaint@UI.com - 972-666-0123* Employee's Preferred Contact Information [Email or Mailing Address]

EMPLOYER'S USE ONLY	
Date Received:	Initials of Recipient: Name of Recipient:

EXHIBIT 9

PAYROLL PRACTICES AND COMPENSATION POLICY

Administration of This Policy

The HUMAN RESOURCES Department is responsible for the administration of this policy. If you have any questions about this policy or UNITED INFORMATION INC.'s payroll procedures or overtime pay policy, please contact the HUMAN RESOURCES Department.

UNITED INFORMATION, INC. expressly reserves the right to change, modify, or delete the provisions of this Payroll Practices and Compensation Policy without notice.

Workweek and Business Hours

UNITED INFORMATION, INC.'s normal workweek is seven days, Monday through Friday, and our normal business hours are from 8 a.m. to 5 p.m. Full-time employees are expected to work eight hours per workday, five days per work week, exclusive of meal breaks and rest periods.

Employees may be required to come in early, work late, or work overtime from time to time, depending on various factors, such as workloads, staffing needs, and special projects. Employees will receive their specific work schedule from their direct supervisor. Nonexempt employees must have permission from their supervisor before working overtime.

Payday

Employees are paid twice a month on FRIDAY for the pay period that ends on the previous Friday. If a particular payday falls on a weekend or holiday, employees normally will be paid on the last business day before the weekend or holiday. Employees enrolled in direct deposit will have their pay deposited in their designated account on payday. For all other employees, pay checks will be mailed to the employee's home address on file with the HUMAN RESOURCES Department. If you do not receive your direct deposit or paycheck, notify the HUMAN RESOURCES Department immediately.

Employees should review their pay checks for errors. If you find an error, report it to the HUMAN RESOURCES Department immediately. If there has been an erroneous overpayment or underpayment, UNITED INFORMATION, INC. will correct it as soon as possible. For information on how to report errors, please see the Employee Complaints section below.

Timekeeping

To ensure that UNITED INFORMATION, INC. has accurate time records and that employees are paid for all hours worked in a timely manner, employees are required to accurately record all hours worked on UNITED INFORMATION, INC., PALMVEIN BIOMETRIC RETINA SCANNER. Employees should record all hours worked and breaks. Your supervisor will review your time records and ask you to verify them at the end of each pay period.

Exempt employees are required to accurately record all hours worked by a method prescribed by UNITED INFORMATION, INC.

Employees must ensure all time is recorded accurately. Off-the-clock work is strictly prohibited. Fraudulent timekeeping and falsification of time records are subject to discipline, up to and including termination of employment.

Employees are responsible for reporting any supervisor or manager who encourages or requires off-the-clock work to the HUMAN RESOURCES Department.

Employee Complaints

If you believe there are any errors in your pay, including that you have been overpaid or underpaid, that improper deductions have been taken from your pay or that your pay does not accurately reflect all hours worked, you must report your concerns to HUMAN RESOURCES DEPARTMENT MANAGER immediately. UNITED INFORMATION, INC. will promptly investigate all reported complaints and, if appropriate, take corrective action.

UNITED INFORMATION, INC. prohibits and will not tolerate retaliation against any employee because that employee filed a good faith complaint under this policy. Specifically, no one will be denied employment, promotion, or any other benefit of employment or be subjected to any adverse employment action based on their good faith complaint. In addition, no one will be disciplined, intimidated, or otherwise retaliated against because they exercised their rights under this policy or applicable law.

Administration of This Policy

The HUMAN RESOURCES Department is responsible for the administration of UNITED INFORMATION, INC.'s Payroll Practices and Compensation Policy. If you have any questions regarding this policy or if you have questions about payroll practices that are not addressed in this policy, please contact the HUMAN RESOURCES Department.

Any employee who abuses this policy will be subject to disciplinary action, up to and including termination of employment.

Acknowledgment of Receipt and Review

I,__________________________(employee name), acknowledge that on ________________________(date), I received and read a copy of the UNITED INFORMATION INC.'s PAYROLL PRACTICE AND COMPENSATION POLICY, and understand that it is my responsibility to be familiar with and abide by its terms. I understandthat the information in this Policy is intended to help UNITED INFORMATION, INC.'s employees to work together effectively on assigned job responsibilities. This Policy is not promissory and does not set terms or conditions of employment or create an employment contract.

[SIGNATURE PAGE FOLLOWS]

____

Signature

____

Printed Name

____

[Date]

EXHIBIT 10

St. Jaguar Community Church
1234 Royal Lane
Dallas, Texas 75203

January 4, 2016

Dear Mr. Saint,

I want to thank you for being an active member of St. Jaguar Community Church. I have personally enjoyed watching you grow up and bask in the light of Jesus Christ.

The purpose of this letter is to confirm your membership with the church and to thank you for your regular financial and temporal contributions to the congregation.

Have a blessed day.

Sincerely,

Reverend Jim Connors

John 3:16

EXHIBIT 11

Case 4:2024CV00970 Filed 01/03/24

IN THE UNITED STATES DISTRICT COURT
NORTHERN DISTRICT OF TEXAS
DALLAS DIVISION

United States Equal Employment	§	
Opportunity Commission	§	
Plaintiff,	§	
	§	4:2024CV00970
vs.	§	CIVIL ACTION NO.
	§	
United Information, Incorporated	§	
Defendant.	§	
	§	
	§	

DEPOSITION OF JONATHAN ANDERSON

The deposition of Jonathan Anderson, a witness in the above-listed cause, taken before Teresa Defarge, Notary Public in and for Dallas County, Texas, at 1818 Georgia Street, Dallas, Texas, on the 3rd day of March, 2024, commencing at 1:00 p.m.

In attendance: Dominique Baker, Baker & Jones LLP
Julius Hernandez, E.E.O.C
Teresa Defarge, Notary Public
Jonathan Anderson

Q: Good afternoon, Mr. Anderson.
A: Hello.
Q: My name is Dominique Baker. I'm an attorney, and I'm here representing United Information Incorporated, which is being sued by the U.S. Equal Employment Opportunity Commission. Do you understand that?
A: Yes.
Q: Okay, good. I'll be asking you some questions today about the incident with your colleague Abraham Saint's request for religious accommodation. You understand that

you're under oath today, and that you have to tell the truth just like you would if you were in court?
A: Yes.
Q: If I ask any questions that you do not understand, or if you can't hear me, let me know and I will ask the question again or ask it in a different way.
A: Yes.
Q: I need you to answer everything out loud, so that the reporter can take down your answers, okay?
A: Okay.
Q: And since the reporter will be taking down everything we say, we need to make sure we don't talk over each other.
A: Okay.
Q: Can you give me your full name please?
A: Jonathan Beast Anderson.
Q: And where do you live, Mr. Anderson?
A: I live at 405 Boxer Lane in Dallas.
Q: How long have you lived there?
A: Fifteen years.
Q: You are employed at United Information, Incorporated, is that correct?
A: Yes.
Q: And how long have you been employed there?
A: Since 2016.
Q: What is your title at the company?

A: I'm just a general inside laborer.

Q: How long have you known Mr. Saint?

A: Since I started at United Information, Incorporated in 2016. We started the same year.

Q: Would you say that you two are close?

A: I would say so. We have been close since I started, Abraham is like a big brother to me now.

Q: Are you aware if Mr. Saint is religious?

A: I don't believe so, as long as I've known him, he never said anything about it.

Q: Do you know if he ever attended church?

A: No, he never went as far as I know.

Q: Are you aware of the religious accommodation that Mr. Saint applied for?

A: I only heard something about it after he received a rejection and was told that he could use his thumb to scan in.

Q: What was Mr. Saint's reaction to that news?

A: He was pretty angry--he didn't think that it was fair that his religious beliefs were tossed aside so easily.

Q: Did Mr. Saint say that he was going to take any further action, or did he say that he would comply with the compromise that his supervisor suggested?

A: He did not believe that the compromise was a real compromise, so he said he was taking it to the EEOC and that's the last I heard until you called me.

Q: Those are all of the questions that I have for you today, Mr. Anderson. Thank you for your time and cooperation.

A: You're welcome.

Case 4:2024CV00970 Filed 01/03/24

CERTIFICATION

I hereby certify that the foregoing answers of Jonathan Anderson, the witness forenamed, were signed and sworn to before me on the 3rd day of March, 2024, by said witness.

Notary Public's Signature

EXHIBIT 12

Case 4:2024CV00970 Filed 01/03/24

IN THE UNITED STATES DISTRICT COURT
NORTHERN DISTRICT OF TEXAS
DALLAS DIVISION

United States Equal Employment	§	
Opportunity Commission	§	
Plaintiff,	§	
	§	4:2024CV00970
vs.	§	CIVIL ACTION NO.
	§	
United Information Incorporated	§	
Defendant.	§	
	§	
	§	

DEPOSITION OF KATHY EDWARDS

The deposition of Kathy Edwards, a witness in the above-listed cause, taken before Teresa Defarge, Notary Public in and for Dallas County, Texas, at 1818 Georgia Street, Dallas, Texas, on the 3rd day of March, 2024, commencing at 11:00 a.m.

In attendance: Dominique Baker, Baker & Jones LLP
Julius Hernandez, E.E.O.C
Teresa Defarge, Notary Public
Kathy Edwards

Q: Good morning, Ms. Edwards.
A: Good morning.
Q: My name is Dominique Baker. I am here representing United Information, Incorporated, which is being sued by the U.S. Equal Employment Opportunity Commission. Do you understand that?
A: Yes, I do.

Q: Okay good. I'll be asking you questions about the company's policies and regarding Mr. Saint's request for religious accommodation. You understand that you're under oath today, and that you have to tell the truth just like you would if you were in court?

A: Yes.

Q: If I ask any questions that you don't understand, or if you can't hear me, let me know that and I'll ask the question again or ask it in a different way.

A: Sure.

Q: And I need you to answer everything out loud, so that the reporter can take down your answers. Okay?

A: Okay.

Q: And since the reporter will be taking down everything we say, we need to make sure we don't talk over each other.

A: Okay.

Q: Can you give me your full name, please?

A: Kathy Lynn Edwards.

Q: And where do you live, Ms. Edwards?

A: I live at 106 Water Creek Drive, apartment number 210 in Dallas.

Q: How long have you lived there?

A: About ten years.

Q: How long have you been working at United Information Incorporated?

A: Three years.

Q: What is your title at the company?

Case 4:2024CV00970 Filed 01/03/24

A. I am a supervisor.
Q: How long have you been a supervisor?
A: About two years.
Q: Who do you supervise?
A: All of the general inside laborers.
Q: About how many general inside laborers does United Information Incorporated employ?
A: At least fifteen people.
Q: Does that include Mr. Saint?
A: Yes. Well, it did.
Q: Do you have knowledge of the company's policies?
A: Generally.
Q: Are you familiar with the company's Title VII policies, such as equal employment, antidiscrimination, anti-harassment, and anti-retaliation policies?
A: Yes, I am.
Q: How do employees learn about the company's policies?
A: They are briefed on the policies at the outset of their employment, policies are also clearly stated in the employee handbook. This is how United Information, Incorporated publicizes and distributes its policies.
Q: Have any of the policies been revised?
A: The only policy that has changed is the manner in which all employees are required to sign-in and out of work, to now using the PalmVein biometric retina scanner.
Q: How did employees sign out before the scanner?

A: By hand, with an employee in charge of signing folks in and out.

Q: Who was responsible for revising the policy?

A: Head management, of course.

Q: How did United Information Incorporated publicize or distribute the revised version?

A: All employees were informed about this policy change through an email, as well as a meeting that was called to brief all employees on the new retina scanning device that would be used by all employees employed by United Information, Incorporated.

Q: When did you implement the use of the PalmVein biometric retina scanner?

A: Oh, don't hold me to this, but I think it was in early August 2023.

Q: How could I find out the exact date?

A: Look at the emails we sent the employees about the change in policy.

Q: The emails set forth a timeline?

A: Yes.

Q: And that timeline is accurate?

A: Yes.

Q: What is the purpose of the retina scanning technology?

A: This scanning system not only streamlines the clocking in and out process, it has allowed us to eliminate a costly position within the organization for dealing with fraudulent time keeping. Before the scanner, we used software where an employee could punch in his or her identification code. Unfortunately, people were clocking in and out for their friends. Additionally, we found that people would frequently forget their codes, and send constant emails to management asking for them to be manually clocked in and out. Now because of the new scanner, you cannot fake someone else's retina scan, and failure to remember a code is no longer an excuse. We estimate a savings of over $4,000 annually even after the expenditure for the new technology.

Q: Who has to use this technology?

A: This is the pet project of our CEO, everyone scans in with their eyes.

Q: Everyone?

A: Yes.

Q: Isn't it true that Marvin Svelt doesn't scan in, and hasn't used the scanner since this new process was implemented?

A: I'm sorry, yes, you are correct, but that was a temporary measure related to his disability. Mr. Svelt wears an eye patch unfortunately. He got in a bar fight. Lost one eye and broke both arms. We allowed Mr. Svelt to check in with his supervisor for a bit. However, his arms are now healed, and he uses a thumb print add-on for the scanner. I understand the same was offered to Mr. Saint. However, he refused. Unlike Mr. Svelt, Mr. Saint did not want to use the scanner at all under any circumstances.

Q: When did you become aware that Mr. Saint did not want to use the device?

A: When he sent a letter directly to me informing me about his religious beliefs as an Evangelical Christian and requested an exemption from using the scanning process due to his religious beliefs.

Q: When did you receive the letter?

A: I am pretty sure it was the day before the scanner went into effect.

Q: Did he also send the letter to Mr. Sean Farmor?

A: Yes, I think the letter was sent to him too.

Q: Who is Mr. Farmor?

A: An HR manager at U.I.

Q: So both of you were aware of his strong religious beliefs?

A: Yes.

Q: Does United Information Incorporated have a policy for disciplining employees?

A: Yes, disciplinary action of employees is clearly stated in the employee handbook. Mostly dependent on the type of action that was taken by the specific employee.

Q: Does United Information, Incorporated have a policy for terminating employees?

A: Yes, that policy is also stated in the employee handbook. An employee will not be terminated unless he fails to correct a course of action that he had previously been reprimanded on.

Q: Is it true that Mr. Saint was not paid for work between August 11 and August 21, 2023?

A. Yes, pursuant to our policy on payroll, an employee who fails to keep his time properly will not be paid.

Case 4:2024 CV00970 Filed 01/03/24

CERTIFICATION

I hereby certify that the foregoing answers of Kathy Edwards, the witness forenamed, were signed and sworn to before me on the 3rd day of March, 2024, by said witness.

Notary Public's Signature

EXHIBIT 13

August 22, 2023

Dear Mr. Sean Farmor:

The purpose of this letter is to submit my formal resignation to United Information, Incorporated. As you know, the implementation of the company's new policy requiring employees to clock into work using the PalmVein scanner is in conflict with my religious beliefs. The alternative mechanism that the company provided for clocking in did not resolve this conflict.

I love my job, but the company's failure to find a reasonable alternative (such as allowing me to manually clock in and out) makes it impossible for me to continue to work. Moreover, I am hesitant to work for a company that would allow someone—me—to knowingly work hard for ten days and refuse to compensate them for hours served simply because of a religious belief.

What am I talking about? Between August 2, 2023, and August 10, 2023, you allowed me to use the old clock-in method, so I signed into and out of work every day. On August 11, however, this old clock-in method was no longer available and the only methods available for signing in were the retinal or thumb scanning methods. Both of these methods are in conflict with my beliefs and to avoid being Marked I opted not to use either method. However, I love my job and my colleagues, so I continued to work full days even though I could not clock in from August 11 through August 21—as you and your superiors are well aware. On August 21, 2023, I received my paycheck and to my surprise it was only a partial paycheck and did not provide compensation for any of the work I did after August 10. It was as if I was not there!

I am so sad this has happened and pray that you will treat others better in the future.

In prayer,
A. Saint

EXHIBIT 14

Case 4:2024CV00970 Filed 01/03/24

IN THE UNITED STATES DISTRICT COURT
NORTHERN DISTRICT OF TEXAS
DALLAS DIVISION

United States Equal Employment Opportunity Commission Plaintiff,	§	
	§	4:2024CV00970
vs.	§	CIVIL ACTION NO.
United Information, Incorporated Defendant.	§	

DEPOSITION OF ABRAHAM SAINT

The deposition of Abraham Saint, a defendant in the above-listed cause, taken before Teresa Defarge, Notary Public in and for Dallas County, Texas, at 1818 Georgia Street, Dallas, Texas, on the 8th day of March, 2024, commencing at 1:00 p.m.

In attendance: Dominique Baker, Baker & Jones LLP
Julius Hernandez, E.E.O.C
Teresa Defarge, Notary Public
Abraham Saint

Q: Good afternoon, Mr. Saint.

A: Hello.

Q: My name is Dominique Baker. I'm an attorney, and I'm here representing United Information, Incorporated, which is being sued by the U.S. Equal Employment Opportunity Commission. Do you understand that?

A: Yes.

Q: Okay, good. I'll be asking you some questions today about the incidents that occurred at work and your religious beliefs. You understand that you have to tell the truth just like you would if you were in court?

A: Yes.

Q: If I ask any questions that you do not understand, or if you can't hear me, let me know and I will ask the question again or ask it in a different way.

A: Okay.

Q: I need you to answer everything out loud, so that the reporter can take down your answers, okay?

A: Okay.

Q: And since the reporter will be taking down everything we say, we need to make sure we don't talk over each other. Okay?

A: Okay.

Q: Can you give me your full name please?

A: Abraham Samuel Saint.

Q: And where do you live, Mr. Saint?

A: I live at 666 Heaven Street.

Q: How long have you lived there?

A: Since 1994.

Q: Are you a member of a church?

A: Yes, St. Jaguar Community Church.

Q: How long have you been a member?

A: Since I was a child.

Q: Do you attend services regularly?

A: I haven't lately.

Q: Are you religious?

A: I am an Evangelical Christian.

Q: But you have not attended church "lately?"

A: I don't get to attend church as often as I would like. But church is just a building, right?

Q: When was the last time you attended church?

A: Maybe 2016. But, I am still a Christian. You don't have to go into a building to attend church. Surely we all learned that in 2020.

Q: Please describe the events and circumstances that you claim were discriminatory.

A: UI implemented a new system to clock in and out of work. It is some sort of weird eye scanner. I refused to scan in. I believe that machine issues the Mark of the Beast! I refused to scan my eyes because of my religious beliefs.

Q: What did you do when you learned that UI was going to start using a scanner?

A: I directly contacted Ms. Edwards, my supervisor, and Sean Farmor, HR Manager, and let them know of my concerns.

Q: What was Ms. Edward's role?

A: She is my direct supervisor.

Q: Why did you contact Ms. Edwards and Mr. Farmor specifically?

A: According to policy, I am to contact her and Sean Farmor if I need accommodations. Which is what I did.

Q: What did Ms. Edwards say or do when you contacted her?

A: Ms. Edwards advised me that she would look into the situation and would see what she could do.

Q: Then what happened?
A: Well, I told her again. I told her that I was not going to use that machine. I told her that I couldn't be clocking in using it because I was worried about the Mark.
Q: Did you object?
A: Heck yeah I did. I mean, I don't care what way they spin it, I refuse to use that machine!
Q: To your knowledge were you the only employee that voiced concern about the scanning device?
A: No. Well, I was the only one I know of who was smart enough to object to avoid the Mark.
Q: Who else objected for other reasons?
A: Marvin Svelt.
Q: Why did Mr. Svelt object to the technology?
A: Poor guy, lost an eye in a drunken accident.
Q: Do you know how he scans in given his situation?
A: The company lets him clock in by simply checking in with Ms. Edwards. How unfair right? I know I did not lose an eye, but I wonder why didn't they let me do that? Maybe they do not like God. I would have gladly checked in every day.
Q: Does United Information have a policy on how they discipline employees?
A: Yes.
Q: Tell me your understanding of that policy.
A: I remember signing a lot of documents when I first started working here. I think the policy mentions that UI disciplines based on whether or not an employee misses work

Case 4:2024CV00970 Filed 01/03/24

and when an employee fraudulently clocks into work. I think they were trying to keep people from clocking in for others.

Q: Why did you quit your employment with United Information?

A: They forced me out.

Q. What do you mean?

A: What other option did I have other than to quit? I couldn't clock in, and eventually I learned that if I couldn't clock in, they would not pay me.

Q: They didn't pay you?

A: I thought they were joking. I didn't think they could refuse to pay me. So, I came to work every day and did my job, but of course did not clock in. No Mark for me, no way, no how. But they knew I was there. They acknowledged that I was there. They allowed me to do my job. So I went about my work. I worked my full days without scanning in after they offered for me to scan my left thumb. I did this until August 21st. I got my paycheck and it was just a partial paycheck. They did in fact count me absent for the days after August 11 when I did not clock in and they refused to compensate me for my work. I didn't know what else to do. I felt like I had no other option. Working for free? Who would do that?

Q: So after you received the partial paycheck, you quit?

A: Exactly. Quit next day. Didn't show up. That was that.

Q: Then you contacted the EEOC?

A: Yes, in August, late August. I was done with communicating with UI. Told the EEOC they discriminated against me because of my religion, and here I am.

CERTIFICATION

I hereby certify that the foregoing answers of Abraham Saint, the witness forenamed, were signed and sworn to before me on the 8th day of March, 2024, by said witness.

Notary Public's Signature

UNITED STATES DISTRICT COURT
NORTHERN DISTRICT OF TEXAS
DALLAS DIVISION

U.s. Equal Employment Opportunity Commission, Plaintiff	§ § § §	
vs.	§	CIVIL ACTION NO. 4:2024-CV-00970
United Information, Inc., Defendant	§ § §	

DEFENDANT UNITED INFORMATION, INC.'S MEMORANDUM OF LAW IN SUPPORT OF ITS MOTION FOR SUMMARY JUDGMENT

Defendant United Information, Inc. (UI) moves for summary judgment pursuant to Federal Rule of Civil Procedure 56 as to Plaintiff's Title VII claim for religious discrimination.

TABLE OF CONTENTS

I. TABLE OF AUTHORITIES

Cases

Anderson v. Liberty Lobby, Inc., 477 U.S. 242 (1986)
Antoine v. First Student, Inc., 713 F.3d 824 (5th Cir. 2013)
Brener v. Diagnostic Ctr. Hosp., 671 F.2d 141 (5th Cir. 1982)
Bruff v. N. Miss. Health Servs., Inc., 244 F.3d 495 (5th Cir. 2001)
Davis v. Fort Bend Cnty., 765 F.3d 480 (5th Cir. 2014)
DIRECTV Inc. v. Robson, 420 F.3d 532 (5th Cir. 2005)
Duffy v. Leading Edge Prods., Inc., 44 F.3d 308 (5th Cir. 1995)
Hansard v. Johns-Manville Prods. Corp., No. 1902, 1973 WL 129 (E.D. Tex. Feb. 16, 1973)
Horvath v. City of Leander, 946 F.3d 787 (5th Cir. 2020), as revised (Jan. 13, 2020)
Little v. Liquid Air Corp., 37 F.3d 1069 (5th Cir. 1994)
Lujan v. Nat'l Wildlife Fed'n, 497 U.S. 871, 885 (1990)
Tagore v. United States, 735 F.3d 324 (5th Cir. 2013)
Trans World Airlines, Inc. v. Hardison, 432 U.S. 63 (1977)
Weber v. Roadway Express, Inc., 199 F.3d 270 (5th Cir. 2000)

Statutes

42 U.S.C. §§ 2000e(j), 2000e–2(a)(1)

Rules

Fed. R. Civ. P. 56

II. INTRODUCTION

This Court should grant summary judgment as to Plaintiff U.S. Equal Employment Opportunity Commission's Title VII claim for religious discrimination. Title VII prohibits an employer from discriminating against an employee on the basis of his religion. 42 U.S.C. §§ 2000e(j), 2000e–2(a)(1). To establish a prima facie case of religious discrimination, Plaintiff has the burden to prove four elements: (1) employee Abraham Saint "held a bona fide religious belief"; (2) the "belief conflicted with a requirement of [his] employment"; (3) the "employer was informed" of the belief; and (4) Mr. Saint "suffered an adverse employment action for failing to comply with the conflicting employment requirement." *Davis v. Fort Bend Cnty.*, 765 F.3d 480, 485 (5th Cir. 2014). First, UI proves Plaintiff cannot establish a prima facie case because there is no genuine issue of material fact as to the first essential element. The summary judgment evidence proves that Mr. Saint's professed evangelical Christian belief in the "Mark of the Beast" arose more than five years after departing his church and after an open and public disavowal of religion on Facebook. This Court should grant summary judgment because Mr. Saint's belief was grounded in convenience rather than conviction such that Plaintiff cannot prove the essential element of a "bona fide religious belief."

Second, even if this Court were to hold that summary judgment is not warranted because Plaintiff can establish a genuine issue of material fact regarding its prima facie case of Title VII religious discrimination, this Court should still grant summary judgment because UI can prove one of the following: (1) it "reasonably accommodated the employee"; or (2) "it was unable to reasonably accommodate the employee's needs without undue hardship." *Antoine v. First Student, Inc.*, 713 F.3d 824, 831 (5th Cir. 2013). First, UI proves that it reasonably accommodated Mr. Saint. Within hours of receiving notice of Mr. Saint's alleged religious conflict, UI began seeking a solution. Ten days after learning of Mr. Saint's religious belief, UI offered Mr. Saint the reasonable accommodation of scanning his left thumb instead of his retina—thereby avoiding the forehead and right hand referenced in Revelation 13:16–18. After UI offered Mr. Saint this reasonable accommodation, Mr. Saint did not object in any way that UI's offered accommodation would violate his religious beliefs. Despite UI's attempts to find a reasonable solution with Mr. Saint, he failed to communicate or cooperate and, instead, resigned without notice. UI's accommodation was reasonable, and, therefore, this Court should grant summary judgment.

Last, in the alternative, UI shows that Mr. Saint's specific accommodation request—continuing to clock in and out directly with his supervisor—would cause UI undue hardship. It is undisputed that Mr. Saint's accommodation request would put at risk the more than $4,000 in savings UI associated with the implementation of the scanning system and require UI to reallocate other employees and resources to accommodate Mr. Saint. Accordingly, this Court should also grant summary judgment because Mr. Saint's requested accommodation would cause undue hardship.

III. STATEMENT OF FACTS

A. Mr. Saint ceased attending church or publicly associating with religion before he started working at UI.

Since 1994, Abraham Saint has resided at ***666*** Heaven Street. Ex. 14, Saint Dep. 2:14–17. He maintains a phone number of 972-***666***-0123. Ex. 8. Revelation 13:16–18 provides that the number 666 is associated with the "Mark of the Beast." Ex. 3. While Mr. Saint grew up in St. Jaguar Community Church, his attendance at church "rapidly decreased" beginning in 2016. Ex. 6; Ex. 14, Saint Dep. 3:4–8. In 2017, Mr. Saint posted to his Facebook page that he was "[t]ired of praying to someone that doesn't change anything #overit." Ex. 7. In 2018, he posted to his Facebook page: "When you run into people from your old church and they ask why you have [sic] been in a while. Awkward." *Id.* He clarified in response to a comment on his 2018 post that he was not a "church guy" anymore. *Id.* While Mr. Saint claims to still be an evangelical Christian and a member of St. Jaguar Community Church, he "stopped attending church completely in 2016." Ex. 14, Saint Dep. 3:2–8.

Mr. Saint started working for UI as a general laborer in 2016. Ex. 11, Anderson Dep. 6:9–12. Jonathan Anderson, who started working at UI at the same time and classified Mr. Saint as "like a big brother," was not aware Mr. Saint was religious. *Id.* at 3:2–4. Mr. Anderson said Mr. Saint "never said anything about [religion]" and that Mr. Saint never mentioned going to church. *Id.* at 3:7–10.

B. UI implemented a new, uniform system for employees to clock in and out at work entirely.

When Mr. Saint started working at UI, employees clocked in and out of work by hand, and one of UI's employees was charged with overseeing the sign-in and sign-out processes. Ex. 12, Edwards Dep. 3:21–4:1. The system was "costly" and lead to "fraudulent time keeping." *Id.* at 4:16–23. Employees were clocking in and out for their friends and would often forget their employee codes for clocking in and out. *Id.* On June 2, 2023, and again on July 21, 2023, UI notified all employees that beginning on August 1, 2023, it would commence use of a new system for employees to clock in and out of work. Ex. 1; Ex. 4. This new system involved the use of the Palmvein biometric retina scanner and required employees to clock in and out of work by scanning their eyes. Ex. 4. The purpose of implementing the new scanning system was to: (1) eliminate the need for manual timekeeping; and (2) prevent fraud associated with the manual timekeeping system. Ex. 12, Edwards Dep. 4:17–5:2. The scanner was estimated to save UI $4,000 and eliminated "costly positions" for handling timekeeping fraud. *Id.*

C. Mr. Saint objected to the new system based on his alleged religious belief that it would impose the "Mark of the Beast."

On July 31, 2023, Mr. Saint delivered a letter to his supervisor, Kathy Edwards, stating that he would not use the scanner "under any type of conditions" because his "religion as an Evangelical Christian, as well as The Bible, bar [him] from using eye scanning technology on [his] forehead because it is the Mark of the Beast and the antichrist." Ex. 2. Mr. Saint cited Revelation 13:16–18, explaining that the "verses indicate a mark personally symbolic of the beast" and that "[t]echnology will be used to carry out its implementation." *Id.* Revelation 13:16–18 provides:

> And he causeth all, both small and great, rich and poor, free and bond, to receive a mark in their right hand, or in their foreheads: And that no man might buy or sell, save he that had the mark, or the name of the beast, or the number of his name. Here is wisdom. Let him that hath understanding count the number of the beast: for it is the number of a man; and his number is Six hundred threescore and six.

Ex. 3. On August 1, 2023—the day the new scanning system went into place—Mr. Saint emailed Human Resources Manager, Sean Farmor, explaining his religious objection and noting that he would "prefer to continue to sign in and out of work using the old system." Ex. 5 at 5. That same day he filed a religious accommodation request for a "permanent" accommodation. Ex. 8.

D. UI quickly offered Mr. Saint an accommodation.

Within twenty minutes of receiving Mr. Saint's request, UI began investigating the best way to accommodate his religious beliefs. Ex. 5 at 3. UI contacted Palmvein for more information, and Palmvein ensured UI that no such "Mark of the Beast" could be assigned through use of the scanner and that it "does not interfere with a person's body in any way." *Id.* at 1–2. Nevertheless, on August 11, 2023, Mr. Farmor informed Mr. Saint that UI reviewed the Bible passage that formed the basis for Mr. Saint's request for a religious accommodation, and UI would accommodate Mr. Saint by allowing him to scan in and out of work using his left thumb, instead of his retina, via an attachment to the scanner. *Id.* at 1. Allowing Mr. Saint to continue to sign in and out with Ms. Edwards was not an option because it would cause her to perform extra work that would take away from her ability to do innovative projects and trainings. *Id.* at 3.

All employees used the retina scanner timekeeping system. Ex. 12, Edwards Dep. 5:4–6. An exception was permitted only once on a temporary basis when an employee lost an eye and broke both arms. *Id.* at 5:7–14. During the time his arms were broken, UI permitted the employee to clock in and out with his supervisor; however, once the employee's arms healed, he was required to use same the left thumb scan offered to Mr. Saint. *Id.*

E. Mr. Saint never responded to UI's offered accommodation.

Mr. Saint never responded to UI's August 11, 2023, email nor did he inform UI that its offered accommodation was insufficient. Between August 1, 2023, and August 22, 2023, Mr. Saint did not communicate with anyone at the company regarding his religious belief or the status of his accommodation. Ex. 13; Ex. 14, Saint Dep. 5:13–17. Nevertheless, without permission, Mr. Saint continued attending work after August 11,

2023, without scanning in or officially reporting his presence to anyone. *Id.* Pursuant to UI's payroll policies, because Mr. Saint did not scan in, he did not receive pay for attending work from August 11 (the offered accommodation date) through August 21. Ex. 5 at 1; Ex. 9; Ex. 14, Saint Dep. 5:8–16.

Mr. Saint resigned from UI on August 22, 2023, after he received only a partial paycheck for that month. Ex. 14, Saint Dep. 5:8–16. Mr. Saint never lodged a complaint regarding his final paycheck, as is required by UI's payroll policies. Ex. 9; Ex. 14, Saint Dep. 5:18–19. Shortly after voluntarily resigning, Mr. Saint contacted the EEOC to pursue his claim of religious discrimination pursuant to Title VII against UI. Ex. 14, Saint Dep. 5:20–22.

IV. SUMMARY JUDGMENT EVIDENCE

UI files the following summary judgment evidence concurrently with the Motion and incorporates it in full:

1. Email from Sean Farmor to UI Employees, dated June 2, 2023, attached as Exhibit 1.
2. Letter from Abraham Saint to Kathy Edwards, dated July 31, 2023, attached as Exhibit 2.
3. Revelation 13:16–18 (King James), attached as Exhibit 3.
4. Email from Sean Farmor to all UI Employees, dated July 21, 2023, attached as Exhibit 4.
5. Email chain, dated August 1, 9, & 11, 2023, attached as Exhibit 5.
6. Letter from Reverend Jim Connors to Mx. Partner, dated August 24, 2023, attached as Exhibit 6.
7. Abraham Saint Facebook posts, attached as Exhibit 7.
8. Abraham Saint's Religious Accommodation Request Form, dated August 1, 2023, attached as Exhibit 8.
9. UI's Payroll Practices and Compensation Policies, attached as Exhibit 9.
10. Letter from Reverend Jim Connors to Abraham Saint, dated January 4, 2016, attached as Exhibit 10.
11. Deposition of Jonathan Anderson, dated March 3, 2024, attached as Exhibit 11.
12. Deposition of Kathy Edwards, dated March 3, 2024, attached as Exhibit 12.
13. Letter from Abraham Saint to Sean Farmor, dated August 22, 2023, attached as Exhibit 13.
14. Deposition of Abraham Saint, dated March 8, 2024, attached as Exhibit 14.

V. STANDARD OF REVIEW

Summary judgment is proper when the evidence presented does not establish a genuine dispute of material fact, and the moving party is entitled to judgment as a matter of law. Fed. R. Civ. P. 56(c). To succeed on a motion for summary judgment, the moving party need not negate the elements of the nonmoving party's case; rather, summary judgment should "be granted so long as whatever is before the district court demonstrates that the standard for the entry of summary judgment, as set forth in Rule 56(c), is satisfied." *Lujan v. Nat'l Wildlife Fed'n*, 497 U.S. 871, 885 (1990) (citations omitted). To meet its initial burden, the moving party need only establish that there is no genuine dispute of material fact. *Duffy v. Leading Edge Prods., Inc.*, 44 F.3d 308, 312 (5th Cir. 1995) (citation omitted). The moving party "may do so by pointing out 'the absence of evidence supporting the nonmoving party's case.'" *Id.* Once the moving party meets its initial burden, the nonmoving party must come forward with admissible evidence establishing the existence of a genuine dispute of material fact. *Id.* A material fact is limited to those facts whose "resolution could affect the outcome of the action." *DIRECTV Inc. v. Robson*, 420 F.3d 532, 536 (5th Cir. 2005) (citations omitted). There is no genuine dispute of material fact "unless there is sufficient evidence favoring the nonmoving party for a jury to return a verdict for that party." *Anderson v. Liberty Lobby, Inc.*, 477 U.S. 242, 249 (1986). Evidence that is "merely colorable" or "not significantly probative" is insufficient to defeat summary judgment. *Id.*

For a Title VII religious discrimination claim, there are two ways in which this Court could grant summary judgment. First, this Court should grant summary judgment because UI proves there is no genuine issue of material fact as to at least one of the four elements of Plaintiff's prima facie case. *See Tagore v. United States*, 735 F.3d 324, 329 (5th Cir. 2013). Second, even if UI fails to prove there is no genuine issue of material fact as to a least one of the four elements of Plaintiff's prima facie case, summary judgment is still warranted if UI can prove there is no genuine issue of material fact that either it "reasonably accommodated the employee, or that it was unable to reasonably accommodate the employee's needs without undue hardship." *Davis*, 765 F.3d at 487.

VI. ARGUMENT AND AUTHORITIES

This Court should grant summary judgment on Plaintiff's religious discrimination claim. First, the undisputed evidence proves that Mr. Saint did not hold a "bona fide religious belief," one of the essential elements of its prima facie case. Second, even if Plaintiff can create a fact question on its prima facie case, the undisputed evidence proves that (1) UI offered a *reasonable* accommodation and/or (2) the accommodation Mr. Saint requested would have caused undue hardship.

A. This Court should grant summary judgment because no fact issue exists as to whether Mr. Saint's religious belief was sincerely held when Mr. Saint was okay with some marks of the beast but not others.

First, this Court should grant summary judgment because the undisputed evidence proves that Mr. Saint did not hold a bona fide religious belief. A plaintiff cannot succeed in a Title VII religious discrimination claim unless it meets the burden to prove that the employee sincerely held a bona fide religious belief. *Davis*, 765 F.3d at 485. A belief is not bona fide unless it is "sincerely held with the strength of traditional religious views." *Id.*

While the correctness of an employee's religious belief cannot be questioned, the sincerity of the employee's belief may (and must) be scrutinized. *Hansard v. Johns-Manville Prods. Corp.*, No. 1902, 1973 WL 129, at *2 (E.D. Tex. Feb. 16, 1973). Even where a foundation is laid for an employee's religious belief, "the court must determine the individual plaintiff's sincerity in relying on those religious beliefs." *Id.* Further, an employee's reliance on a religious belief must stem from conviction and not convenience. *Id.*

A religious belief based in convenience will not satisfy the first element of a religious discrimination claim. In *Hansard*, the court held that the employee's "religious conviction against working for profit on Sundays" was not sincerely held. *Id.* at *3. In that case, the employee refused to work on Sundays because of his Christian religion. *Id.* at *1. The employee, while claiming his belief was "lifelong," admitted he did not always follow it. *Id.* The employee dropped out of the Church of Christ he attended because of "the hypocrisy within the organized church," which caused him to become a "New Testament Christian." *Id.* In addition, although the employee claimed to have experienced a "revival" of his religious conviction after his infant son purportedly "miraculously" recovered after a difficult birth, the employee "worked several Sundays after the alleged miraculous recovery." *Id.* The court, while not questioning the correctness of the employee's belief, reasoned that the employee's reliance on the belief "appears to be grounded more in convenience than conviction" because he worked some Sundays but not others. *Id.* at *2.

Here, this Court should reach the same conclusion as *Hansard* and hold Plaintiff fails to prove the first element of its claim because the undisputed evidence demonstrates that Mr. Saint's purported religious belief, which prevented him from scanning his retina, was not sincere. Like the employee in *Hansard*, who claimed to have a "lifelong" belief but dropped out of church, Mr. Saint claims to be an evangelical Christian, but has not attended church regularly since 2016—before he started working at UI. *Hansard*, 1973 WL 129, at *2; Ex. 14, Saint Dep. 3:2–8; Ex. 6. Mr. Saint's pastor said Mr. Saint "stopped attending church completely in 2018." Ex. 6. Additionally, like the employee in *Hansard*, who criticized the hypocrisy in the church, Mr. Saint posted to his Facebook page that he was "[t]ired of praying to someone that doesn't change anything #overit." *Hansard*, 1973 WL 129, at *2; Ex. 7. In 2018, he posted the following on his Facebook page: "When you run into people from your old church and they ask why you have [sic] been in a while. Awkward." *Id.* He clarified in response to a comment on his 2018 post that he was not a "church guy" anymore. *Id.* Furthermore, Jonathan Anderson, who started working at UI at the same time and classified Mr. Saint as "like a big brother," was not aware Mr. Saint was religious. Ex. 11, Anderson Dep. 3:8–10. Mr. Anderson said Mr. Saint "never said anything about [religion]" and that Mr. Saint never mentioned going to church. *Id.* at 3:7–10. Accordingly, given Mr. Saint's public separation from religion, Mr. Saint's beliefs were not "sincerely held with the strength of traditional religious views." *See Davis*, 765 F.3d at 485.

Moreover, like the employee in *Hansard*, who worked some Sundays but not others such that his alleged beliefs were inconsistent, Mr. Saint's beliefs are likewise inconsistent in that he is okay with some "marks of the beast" but not others. *Hansard*, 1973 WL 129, at *2. The biblical passage on which Mr. Saint relies for his religious belief—Revelation 13:16–18—defines the number of the beast to be 666. Ex. 13. Mr. Saint's address and cell phone number both include the number of the beast: ***666*** Heaven St. and 972-***666***-0123. Ex. 8; Ex. 14, Saint Dep. 2:14–17. Mr. Saint refused to clock in using the retina scanner, fearing the "Mark of the Beast," yet he admitted that he is "over religion" and lives in a house and used a cell phone both bearing the number of the beast. Ex. 8; Ex. 14, Saint Dep. 2:14–17. This evidence proves that, like the employee in *Hansard*, Mr. Saint's belief was one of "convenience rather than conviction" and was not "sincerely held with the strength of traditional religious views." *See Hansard*, 1973 WL 129, at *2; *Davis*, 765 F.3d at 485.

Accordingly, because the undisputed evidence establishes that Mr. Saint does not have a sincere bona fide religious belief—an essential element of Plaintiff's prima facie case—the Court should grant summary judgment.

B. This Court should grant summary judgment because the undisputed evidence proves that UI offered Mr. Saint a reasonable accommodation and/or that the accommodation Mr. Saint requested would have caused UI an undue hardship.

Regardless of whether there is a fact issue regarding Plaintiff's prima facie case of religious discrimination, UI is still entitled to summary judgment as a matter of law because undisputed evidence proves that (1) UI offered Mr. Saint a reasonable accommodation and/or (2) the accommodation Mr. Saint requested would have caused undue hardship. *See Antoine*, 713 F.3d at 831.

1. <u>UI proves that it offered Mr. Saint a reasonable accommodation when it allowed him the alternative of scanning his left thumb.</u>

This Court should grant summary judgment because UI offered Mr. Saint a reasonable accommodation. A plaintiff's Title VII claim for religious discrimination fails whenever the defendant can prove that it offered the employee a reasonable accommodation. *Antoine*, 713 F.3d at 831. "Any reasonable" accommodation is sufficient, and, when "the employer has already reasonably accommodated the employee's religious needs, the statutory inquiry is at an end." *Id.* Furthermore, when presented with a reasonable accommodation, "the employee has a correlative duty to make a good faith attempt to satisfy his needs through means offered by the employer." *Brener v. Diagnostic Ctr. Hosp.*, 671 F.2d 141, 146–47 (5th Cir. 1982). The employee must completely explore the possibilities within the employer's proposed accommodation before asking for a different accommodation. *See id.* In accommodating an employee under Title VII, the employer is not restricted to "only those means of accommodation that are preferred by the employee." *Bruff v. N. Miss. Health Servs., Inc.*, 244 F.3d 495, 501 (5th Cir. 2001). If the employee is offered a reasonable accommodation—even if it is not the accommodation preferred by the employee—the employer "has satisfied its obligation under Title VII as a matter of law." *Horvath v. City of Leander*, 946 F.3d 787, 791 (5th Cir. 2020), as revised (Jan. 13, 2020). When presented with a reasonable accommodation, an employee has an obligation to "fully explore" it. *Brener*, 671 F.2d at 145.

An accommodation is reasonable when the employer took active steps to try to accomodate the employee while the employee refused to explore the accommodation offered. In *Brener*, the Fifth Circuit held that the employer had taken sufficient steps such that the accommodation offered was reasonable. 671 F.2d at 145–46. In that case, the employee pharmacist advised his employer that his faith prohibited him from working on the Sabbath. *Id.* at 143. The employer agreed to exchange his shifts so that he would not be scheduled to work on that day. *Id.* Thereafter, the employee asked not to work Jewish holidays as well, and, in response, the employer asked the employee to arrange his own shift exchanges with other pharmacists. *Id.* at 143–44. When the employee failed to secure an exchange in shifts, he did not show up for work and resigned. *Id.* at 144. The court reasoned that the employer reasonably accommodated the employee by offering the employee an opportunity to work more typical religious days in exchange for his days of religious observance and that it even deviated from its established practices by directing other employees to trade schedules. *Id.* at 145. The court rejected the employee's argument that the pharmacy's scheduling system was inflexible because other employees were not always willing to trade and reasoned that the employee "did not cooperate with the [employer's] efforts to satisfy his needs within the established scheduling system." *Id.* The court explained that an employee must "fully explore the possibilities for accommodation" offered by his employer before rejecting them as inadequate and demanding some other form of accommodation. *Id.*

Once an employer establishes that it offered the employee a reasonable accommodation, even if that alternative was not the employee's preference, the employer has, as a matter of law, satisfied its obligation under Title VII. In *Bruff*, the court held that the employer fulfilled its obligation under Title VII to provide a "reasonable accommodation" through its attempts to assist the employee. 244 F.3d at 501–02. In that case, the employee was a Christian counselor who refused to work with homosexuals or with individuals having extramarital affairs. *Id.* at 497–98. The employer offered her a reasonable accommodation by "giv[ing] [her] 30 days, and the assistance of its in-house employment counselor, to find another position at the Center where the likelihood of encountering further conflicts with her religious beliefs would be reduced." *Id.* at 501. The employee refused to apply for any non-counselor positions; applied for one counselor position that came open but was not selected; and "declined to even consider" a transfer to a pastoral counseling department. *Id.* at 498–99, 502. When the 30-day window lapsed, she was terminated. *Id.* at 499. The court, holding that the employer fulfilled its obligations to provide a reasonable accommodation as a matter of law, reasoned that "Title VII does not restrict an employer to only those means of accommodation that are preferred by the employee"; rather, an employee has a "duty to cooperate in achieving accommodation of his or her religious beliefs, and must be flexible in achieving that end." *Id.* at 501, 503. The court further reasoned that the employee "displayed almost no such cooperation or flexibility." *Id.* at 503.

This Court should follow *Brener* and find that that UI offered Mr. Saint a reasonable accommodation that he refused to explore. Like the employer in *Brener*, who took "active steps" to accommodate the employee by going so far as deviating from its standard scheduling to accommodate the employee's religion, here, UI deviated from its retina scanner time keeping system applicable to all UI employees (with the exception of a single employee who lost his eye) to accommodate Mr. Saint. 671 F.2d at 145; Ex. 12, Edwards Dep. 5:3–14. Yet, like the employee in *Brener*, Mr. Saint "did not cooperate with the [employer's] efforts to satisfy his needs within the established . . . system" but instead, like the employee in *Brener*, categorically refused to sign in and out of work per company policy and resigned. 671 F.2d at 145; Ex. 14, Saint Dep. 5:9–19. *Brener* makes clear that Mr. Saint's failure to "fully explore" possible accommodations before casting off UI's good faith accommodation defeats his Title VII claim. 671 F.2d at 145.

This Court should also find *Bruff* persuasive because the evidence proves that UI offered Mr. Saint a reasonable accommodation and actively worked to accommodate him, even if it was not his preferred accommodation. Like the employer in *Bruff*, who worked with the employee to find her a new position that would not conflict with her beliefs, here UI actively worked with Mr. Saint to find a new way for him to clock in and out that would not conflict with his beliefs. 244 F.3d at 501–02; Ex. 5 at 2. After learning of Mr. Saint's objection to having his retina scanned, UI immediately contacted Palmvein for more information, and Palmvein ensured UI that the "Mark of the Beast" could not be assigned through use of the scanner and that it "does not interfere with a person's body in any way." Ex. 5 at 1–2. Despite the fact that the scanner could not in any way impart a "Mark of the Beast," UI still offered Mr. Saint the reasonable accommodation of scanning his left thumb—an accommodation made in good faith based on the biblical passage Mr. Saint provided, which only referenced the "Mark of the Beast" on the forehead and right hand. *Id.*; Ex. 3. UI took Mr. Saint at his word when it interpreted the nature of his purported belief in attempting to accommodate him. Ex. 5 at 1. However, like the employee in *Bruff* who "displayed almost no such cooperation or flexibility," Mr. Saint never so much as responded to UI and, instead, maintained that he would not use the scanner "under any type of conditions." 244 F.3d at 503; Ex. 2. Mr. Saint insisted he would only accept signing in and out with his supervisor, however, as held in *Bruff*, "Title VII does not restrict an employer to only those means of accommodation that are preferred by the employee." 244 F.3d at 501, 503; Ex. 2. This Court should follow both *Bruff* and *Brener* because Mr. Saint was offered a reasonable accommodation that he refused to explore because it was not his single preferred accommodation.

The law is clear that as long as UI offered "any reasonable" accommodation, it "has satisfied its obligation under Title VII as a matter of law." *Horvath*, 946 F.3d at 791. The undisputed evidence establishes that UI offered a reasonable accommodation by permitting Mr. Saint to scan in with his left thumb, which was the extent of its burden. Ex. 5 at 1. Accordingly, this Court should grant summary judgment because there is no genuine issue of material fact as to whether UI offered Mr. Saint a reasonable accommodation.

2. Alternatively, accommodating Mr. Saint would cause undue hardship in the form of extra work for another employee and additional cost.

This Court should also grant summary judgment because the undisputed evidence establishes that the only accommodation Mr. Saint proposed would have imposed an undue hardship on UI. A plaintiff's Title VII claim for religious discrimination also fails whenever the defendant can prove that it cannot reasonably accommodate the employee's needs without undue hardship. *Davis*, 765 F.3d at 487. Under Title VII, an accommodation that results in "more than a de minimis cost" constitutes an undue hardship to the employer and excuses the employer from providing the accommodation. *Trans World Airlines, Inc. v. Hardison*, 432 U.S. 63, 84 (1977). If an accommodation imposes an adverse impact on other employees, including "lost efficiency in other jobs," it imposes an undue hardship. *Id.*

An accommodation constitutes an "undue hardship" if it would place the employee in a more favorable position than her co-workers at the employer's expense. In *Tagore*, the Fifth Circuit held that the employee's requested accommodation would cause an undue hardship. 735 F.3d at 330. In that case, the employee said that she held a sincere religious belief that her Sikh faith required her to wear a "kirpan," a Sikh article that "resembles a knife or sword." *Id.* at 326. Her employer's security protocols permitted knives with blades up to 2.5 inches long, but the employee insisted on wearing a dulled kirpan at least three inches long. *Id.* at 328, 331. The court reasoned the plaintiff's requested accommodation would pose an undue hardship because asking the employer's security officers, on a daily basis, to ascertain the dullness of the blade would be "time-consuming" and "impractical." *Id.* As such, it was "more than [a] de minimus adjustment that require[d] coworkers unfairly to perform extra work to accommodate the plaintiff." *Id.* at 330.

An undue hardship may consist of an adverse impact on other workers. In *Weber v. Roadway Express, Inc.*, the Fifth Circuit held the accomodation caused an undue hardship because "the mere possibility of an adverse impact on co-workers . . . is sufficient to constitute an undue hardship." 199 F.3d 270, 274 (5th Cir. 2000). In that case, the employee asked that he not be paired with a female driver on overnight drives in order to accommodate his religious beliefs. *Id.* The court reasoned that the employee's "only suggested accommodation, that of skipping over assignments involving women . . . would impose more than a de minimis cost." *Id.* at 275. The fact that a requested accommodation "may adversely affect" other employees was enough. *Id.* at 274. Rejecting the employee's arguments that the employer's concerns were "too speculative," the court reasoned that the employer was not required to "wait until it felt the effects" of the employee's proposal to prove an undue burden. *Id.* at 275. Instead, the court explained that "an undue burden is present if the proposed accommodation would force changes in the schedules of other employees and alter the employer's otherwise neutral procedure." *Id.* (citing *Hardison*, 432 U.S. at 84).

Here, the Court should follow *Tagore* and find that Mr. Saint's requested accommodation to check in with his supervisor would pose an undue hardship on UI. Like the employee in *Tagore*, who insisted on wearing a kirpan at least three inches long in violation of the employer's policy and causing additional work on the security officers, Mr. Saint deemed only one accommodation acceptable—checking in and out his supervisor. 735 F.3d at 330; Ex.8. Just like the accomodation in *Tagore*, here, the proposed accomodation would require Mr. Saint's supervisor "unfairly to perform extra work to accommodate" Mr. Saint such that it would cause an undue hardship. 735 F.3d at 330; Ex. 5 at 3; Ex. 8. Specifically, allowing Mr. Saint to continue to sign in and out with Ms. Edwards would cause her to do extra work that would take away from her ability to do innovative projects and trainings. Ex. 5 at 3. Thus, like *Tagore*, where the court reasoned that the requested accommodation would pose an undue hardship because asking the employer's security officers, on a daily basis, to ascertain the dullness of the blade would be "time-consuming" and "impractical," here, too, requiring Ms. Edwards to keep track of Mr. Saint's time every day by hand would be "time-consuming" and "impractical." 735 F.3d at 331; Ex. 5 at 3; Ex. 8.

This Court should also find *Weber* persuasive because of the burden Mr. Saint's request would have put on a co-worker. Like *Weber*, where the court reasoned that the employee's "only suggested accommodation, that of skipping over assignments involving women . . . would impose more than a de minimis cost," here, Mr. Saint's only proposed accommodation of clocking in and out with his supervisor would impose significant costs. 199 F.3d at 275; Ex. 12, Edwards Dep. 4:17–5:2. The very reason that UI implemented the scanning system was to capture savings of more than $4,000 previously stemming from the inefficiency of checking employees in and out manually (e.g., Mr. Saint's requested accommodation) and to eliminate "costly positions" for addressing timekeeping fraud. Ex. 12, Edwards Dep. 4:17–5:2. Therefore, allowing Mr. Saint to clock in and out manually with his supervisor, would involve far "more than a de minimis cost" on UI and, therefore, impose an undue hardship such that UI is excused from providing the accommodation. *See Hardison*, 432 U.S. at 84. Additionally, like in *Weber*, where the court reasoned an undue hardship is present if "the proposed accommodation would force changes in the schedules of other employees and alter the employer's otherwise neutral procedure," forcing Ms. Edwards to unwillingly assume additional duties to accommodate Mr. Saint would force a change in her schedule and alter the "neutral" procedure of using the scanner for all employees. 199 F.3d at 275; Ex. 12, Edwards Dep. 5:4–6.While Mr. Saint suggests that his request was reasonable because his supervisor already kept time for another employee, that arrangement was temporary and expired after that employee recovered from his arm injuries. Ex. 12, Edwards Dep. 5:7–14. Here, like the employees in both *Tagore* and *Weber*, Mr. Saint requested a "permanent" accommodation. *Weber*, 199 F.3d at 275; *Tagore*, 735 F.3d at 330; Ex. 8. To accommodate Mr. Saint in his preferred manner would force UI to create permanent, additional duties for Mr. Saint's supervisor, reducing her efficiency—the opposite of what the costly scanner system was designed to do. Ex. 12, Edwards Dep. 4:16–23.

Accordingly, there are no genuine issues of material fact as to whether Mr. Saint's preferred accommodation would have imposed an undue hardship and "more than a de minimis cost" on UI such that this Court should grant summary judgment. *See Hardison*, 432 U.S. at 84.

VII. CONCLUSION

UI respectfully requests that this Court grant summary judgment as to Plaintiff's Title VII religious discrimination claim.

Respectfully submitted,

/s/ Dominique Baker
Dominique Baker
State Bar No. 1234567
dbaker@lawfirm.com
Juan Jones
State Bar No. 2345678
jjones@lawfirm.com
Baker & Jones LLP
106 S. Harwood, Suite 400
Dallas, Texas 75201
214-555-0000 (office)
214-555-0001 (facsimile)
Attorneys for Defendant UI

CERTIFICATE OF SERVICE

This is to certify that on the 9th day of June 2024, I electronically filed the foregoing document with the clerk of the Court for the United States District Court, Northern District of Texas, using the electronic case filing system of the Court, and served this document on all attorneys of record in accordance with Rule 5 of the Federal Rules of Civil Procedure.

<u>/s/ Dominique Baker</u>

UNITED STATES DISTRICT COURT
NORTHERN DISTRICT OF TEXAS
DALLAS DIVISION

U.S. Equal Employment Opportunity Commission, Plaintiff,	§ § § §	
v.	§	CIVIL ACTION NO. 4:2024-CV-00970
United Information, Inc., Defendant.	§ § §	

PLAINTIFF U.S. EQUAL EMPLOYMENT OPPORTUNITY COMMISSION'S MEMORANDUM OF LAW IN SUPPORT OF ITS OPPOSITION TO DEFENDANT UNITED INSTRUMENTS, INC.'S MOTION FOR SUMMARY JUDGMENT

Plaintiff the U.S. Equal Employment Opportunity Commission (EEOC) opposes Defendant United Information, Inc.'s (UI) Motion for Summary Judgment brought pursuant to Federal Rule of Civil Procedure 56 as to Plaintiff's Title VII claim for religious discrimination.

TABLE OF CONTENTS

I. TABLE OF AUTHORITIES

Cases

Statutes

Rules

II. INTRODUCTION

This Court should deny Defendant's Motion for Summary Judgment because there is, at a minimum, a genuine issue of material fact as to the one disputed element of the EEOC's Title VII religious discrimination claim and Defendant fails to conclusively prove either of its affirmative defenses. Title VII "prohibits an employer from discriminating against an employee on the basis of his religion." 42 U.S.C. § 2000e–2(a)(1), 2000e(j). To prove religious discrimination under Title VII, four prima facie elements must be established: (1) the employee Abraham Saint "held a bona fide religious belief"; (2) the "belief conflicted with a requirement of Mr. Saint's employment"; (3) the "employer was informed" of the belief; and (4) Mr. Saint "suffered an adverse employment action for failing to comply with the conflicting employment requirement." *Davis v. Fort Bend Cnty.*, 765 F.3d 480, 485 (5th Cir. 2014). Once the prima facie elements have been established, the burden shifts to Defendant to prove either that (1) Defendant "reasonably accommodated" Mr. Saint or (2) Defendant was unable to reasonably accommodate Mr. Saint "without undue hardship." *Antoine v. First Student, Inc.*, 713 F.3d 824, 831 (5th Cir. 2013).

Defendant does not dispute and, therefore, concedes fact issues exist as to the second, third, and fourth elements of the EEOC's prima facie case. Def.'s Mot. Summ. J. 1. With respect to the first element of the EEOC's prima facie case, Defendant fails to meet its burden to prove the absence of a genuine issue of material fact and as a matter of law that Mr. Saint's religious belief was not bona fide. Mr. Saint—an Evangelical Christian—testified that his religious belief pursuant to Revelation 13:16–18 prohibits the use of a biometric scanner because the device imposes the "Mark of the Beast." Because the Fifth Circuit has instructed that the bona fide religious belief element is met "on little more than the plaintiff's credible assertions," summary judgment should be denied as to the EEOC's Title VII religious discrimination prima facie case. *Davis*, 765 F.3d at 484, 489.

Because the Defendant cannot conclusively disprove the only element of EEOC's prima facie case that is the subject of its motion, the burden shifted to Defendant to demonstrate either that it reasonably accommodated the employee or that it was unable to reasonably accommodate the employee's needs without undue hardship. *Antoine*, 713 F.3d at 831. First, Defendant failed to meet its burden to prove the absence of a genuine issue of material fact that it offered a reasonable accommodation because Defendant failed to offer any accommodation that eliminated the conflict between Mr. Saint's religious beliefs and the Defendant's time-keeping policies. Despite Mr. Saint objecting to the use of the biometric scanner based on his religious belief that it would impose the "Mark of the Beast" through technology, the only "accommodation" Defendant offered required Mr. Saint to use the objectionable biometric scanner on a different part of his body. The Defendant did not explore, discuss, or evaluate any other alternatives and did not seek any accommodation that would avoid Mr. Saint using the objectionable scanner. Accordingly, Defendant failed to reasonably accommodate Mr. Saint.

Second, Defendant failed to meet its burden to prove the absence of a genuine issue of material fact that providing a reasonable accommodation would cause undue hardship. Other than the unsubstantiated claim of Mr. Saint's supervisor, Defendant offered no evidence to prove as a matter of law that Mr. Saint's accommodation request—continuing to clock in and out directly with his supervisor as he had done for the prior six years—would somehow cause more than de minimis cost. Rather, the evidence proves that Defendant had already implemented this identical accommodation request for another employee. Even if one were to assume allowing Mr. Saint to clock in and out with his supervisor would cause undue hardship, Defendant failed to prove "that all conceivable accommodations" would have imposed an undue hardship because Defendant merely rejected Mr. Saint's proposed accommodation and failed to explore any others. *Ford v. City of Dallas*, No. 3:05-CV-1676, 2007 WL 2051016, at *2 (N.D. Tex. July 12, 2007).

Therefore, this Court should deny summary judgment because there remains, at a minimum, a genuine issue of material fact with respect to the one disputed element of the EEOC's Title VII cause of action, and Defendant cannot definitively prove its purported defenses with competent summary judgment evidence.

III. STATEMENT OF FACTS

A. Mr. Saint is a lifelong Evangelical Christian who believes technology will assign the "Mark of the Beast."

Abraham Saint is an Evangelical Christian. Ex. 14, Saint Dep. 3:1–2. He is a member of St. Jaguar Community Church, which he has attended since he was a child. *Id.* at 2:18–21, Ex. 7. Growing up in the church, he was a "very active member" and "constantly participated in church activities." Ex. 8, Ex. 6. While Mr. Saint has recently attended church less often than he would like, he is "still a Christian." Ex. 14, Saint Dep. 3:4–8. He believes a physical "church is just a building" and that "you don't have to go into a building to attend church." *Id.* As an Evangelical Christian, Mr. Saint believes that Revelation 13:16–18 indicates that the "Mark of the Beast" is a "symbolic mark" and that "technology will be used to carry out its implementation." Ex. 2; Ex. 8; Ex. 3.

B. Defendant implemented a new policy requiring employees to clock in and out of work using a biometric scanner.

Mr. Saint started working for Defendant UI as a general laborer in 2016. Ex. 11, Anderson Dep. 3:1–3. During the entire tenure of Mr. Saint's employment until 2021, UI required employees to clock in and out of work manually. Ex. 12, Edwards Dep. 3:21–22 & 4:16–23. Mr. Saint's supervisor, Ms. Edwards, was responsible for the time-keeping of fifteen general laborers. *Id.* at 2:4–10. However, because employees were clocking in and out for their friends and would forget their codes, UI decided to implement a new time-keeping system to address potential fraudulent time-keeping. *Id.* at 4:20–22.

On June 2, 2023 and July 21, 2023, Defendant notified all employees that beginning on August 1, 2023, it would commence use of a new system for employees to clock in and out of work "in keeping with [Defendant's] mission to advance technology." Ex. 4, Ex. 1. This new system involved the use of the Palmvein biometric retina scanner and required employees to clock in and out of work by scanning their eyes. Ex. 5.

C. Mr. Saint promptly objected to using the biometric scanner based on his sincerely held religious belief that the scanner would impose the "Mark of the Beast."

Promptly after learning of Defendant's new biometric scanning device, Mr. Saint wrote to his supervisor, Kathy Edwards, and Defendant's Human Resources Manager, Sean Farmor, to voice his objections. Ex. 14, Saint Dep. 3:13–15; Ex. 2. On July 31, 2023, Mr. Saint notified Ms. Edwards by letter, and Mr. Farmor via e-mail, that he could not use the scanner "under any type of conditions" because, as an Evangelical Christian, he believes the Bible states that the scanning technology is the "Mark of the Beast." Ex. 14, Saint Dep. 3:10–12; Ex. 2. On August 1, 2023, Mr. Saint officially requested a religious accommodation, noting his belief that as "[a]n Evangelical Christian, the Bible tells me that scanning technology is the Mark of the Beast and of the Anti-Christ." Ex. 8. He supported his request with a letter from his pastor and a copy of Revelation 13. Ex. 8; Ex. 10; Ex. 13. Specifically, Mr. Saint cited Revelation 13:16–18, which refers to a "symbolic mark" and that "technology will be used to carry out its implementation." Ex. 8; Ex. 2; Ex. 13. While Mr. Saint's home address and phone number contain a reference to the so-called number of the beast, "666," his fear is related to the use of scanning technology as a means to impose upon him the "Mark of the Beast." Ex. 8.

D. Mr. Saint proposed a reasonable accommodation of continuing to sign in and out with his supervisor—as he had done his entire tenure working for Defendant.

Mr. Saint told Defendant that he was willing to sign in and out of work using an alternative method but requested exemption from the Palmvein biometric scanning device because of his religious beliefs as an Evangelical Christian. Ex. 12. He also filed a religious accommodation request form supported by certain verses from the Bible and a letter from his pastor. Ex. 8; Ex. 6; Ex. 3. His requested accommodation was an "exemption from using the biometric scanner" on the basis that "as an Evangelical Christian, the Bible tells me that scanning technology is the Mark of the Beast and the Anti-Christ." Ex. 8.

E. Defendant ignored Mr. Saint's request to be exempt from using the scanner and, instead, claimed it would only accommodate him by forcing him to use the objectionable scanner on another body part.

Ten days after the policy for the new biometric scanner took effect, on August 11, 2023, Mr. Farmor e-mailed Mr. Saint requiring that he use his left hand to scan in from then on because Farmor's interpretation of the Bible associates the right hand or forehead as receiving the "Mark." Ex. 5 at 1. Defendant insisted that using the scanner on his left thumb as opposed to retina was a "reasonable accommodation," based on its own interpretation of the Bible and assurances from the scanner's manufacturer that the scanner did not physically assign a "Mark." Ex. 5 at 1–2.

F. The accommodation Mr. Saint proposed had already been implemented for another employee—however, Defendant refused to offer it to Mr. Saint.

Mr. Saint proposed the accommodation of continuing to sign in and out with Ms. Edwards as he had been doing his entire time at UI and did not request any change in his job duties. Ex. 5 at 2. This accommodation was already offered to another employee, Marvin Svelt, who was permitted to "clock in by simply checking [in] with Ms. Edwards." Ex. 14, Saint Dep. 4:12–16. Indeed, Edwards, Saint's supervisor, was keeping Mr. Svelt's time manually. Ex. 5 at 3. Ms. Edwards—in allowing Mr. Svelt to "continue manual time-keeping" because he lost an eye and had broken arms—noted that she "understood that Svelt's unique situation makes it impossible for him to comply with the scanning requirements right now." Ex. 5 at 3; Ex 12, Edwards Dep. 5:7–11. Defendant did not offer any evidence of the cost associated with accommodating Mr. Svelt with manual time-keeping instead of using the left-hand scanner Defendant requested that Mr. Saint use. Ex. 12, Edwards Dep. 5:5–13; Ex. 14, Saint Dep. 4:16–18; Ex. 8. While Defendant admitted that it was aware of Mr. Saint's "strong religious beliefs" that made it impossible for him to use the scanner, Ms. Edwards refused to perform "extra work" to manually keep Mr. Saint's time as she did to accommodate Mr. Svelt, even though Defendant's new payroll policy still required Ms. Edwards to manually review and verify employee time records. Ex. 5 at 3; Ex 12, Edwards Dep. 6:2–3; Ex. 9.

G. Mr. Saint was forced to resign in lieu of receiving the "Mark of the Beast."

While Mr. Saint did not reply to Mr. Farmor's e-mail suggesting that he scan his thumb, Mr. Saint made clear that he could not clock in using the scanner because he was "worried about the Mark" and "refuse[d] to use that machine." Ex. 14, Saint Dep. 4:2–6. Moreover, UI's accommodation form makes it clear that the company's decision regarding the requested accommodation would be communicated to the employee in writing. Ex. 8 at 2. The only writing following the accommodation request was a proposal that Mr. Saint still use the scanner. Ex. 5 at 1.

After the implementation of the new scanner, Mr. Saint "came to work every day and did his job." Ex. 14, Saint Dep. 5:6–16. Defendant acknowledged that he was there and allowed him to work, but Defendant then refused to pay Mr. Saint for any time worked after August 11. *Id.* On August 21, 2023, Mr. Saint discovered that his paycheck was short and that he had been counted absent for the days he did not use the scanner after August 11. *Id.* at 5:8–16. UI's payroll policy reads that it will "correct as soon as possible" underpayments. Ex. 9. Nevertheless, it refused to compensate Mr. Saint for his work. Ex. 14, Saint Dep. 5:14–16. Faced with the option of using the scanner or working without pay, he "had no other option" than to resign in lieu of receiving the "Mark." *Id.* at 5:9–19.

IV. SUMMARY JUDGMENT EVIDENCE

The EEOC files the following summary judgment evidence concurrently with the Opposition and incorporates it in full:

1. Email from Sean Farmor to UI Employees, dated June 2, 2023, attached as Exhibit 1.
2. Letter from Abraham Saint to Kathy Edwards, dated July 31, 2023, attached as Exhibit 2.
3. *Revelation* 13:16–18 (King James), attached as Exhibit 3.
4. Email from Sean Farmor to all UI Employees, dated July 21, 2023, attached as Exhibit 4.
5. Email chain, dated August 1, 9, & 11, 2023, attached as Exhibit 5.
6. Letter from Reverend Jim Connors to Mx. Partner, dated August 24, 2023, attached as Exhibit 6.
7. Abraham Saint Facebook posts, attached as Exhibit 7.
8. Abraham Saint's Religious Accommodation Request Form, dated August 1, 2023, attached as Exhibit 8.
9. UI's Payroll Practices and Compensation Policies, attached as Exhibit 9.
10. Letter from Reverend Jim Connors to Abraham Saint, dated January 4, 2016, attached as Exhibit 10.
11. Deposition of Jonathan Anderson, dated March 3, 2024, attached as Exhibit 11.
12. Deposition of Kathy Edwards, dated March 3, 2024, attached as Exhibit 12.
13. Letter from Abraham Saint to Sean Farmor, dated August 22, 2023, attached as Exhibit 13.
14. Deposition of Abraham S. Saint, dated March 8, 2024, attached as Exhibit 14.

V. STANDARD OF REVIEW

Under Federal Rule of Civil Procedure 56(a), summary judgment is not appropriate unless the movant meets its burden to prove that there is no genuine dispute as to any material fact and that it is entitled to judgment as a matter of law. Fed. R. Civ. P. 56(a); *Matsushita Elec. Indus. Co. v. Zenith Radio Corp.*, 475 U.S. 574, 587 (1986). Under the "stringent criteria for summary judgment," the movant has the burden of proof, and "a court can only enter a summary judgment if everything in the record pleadings, depositions, interrogatories, affidavits, etc. demonstrates that no genuine issue of material fact exists." *Keiser v. Coliseum Props., Inc.*, 614 F.2d 406, 411 (5th Cir. 1980). The movant must prove "beyond peradventure all of the essential elements of the claim or defense." *Bank One, Tex., N.A. v. Prudential Ins. Co. of Am.*, 878 F. Supp. 943, 962 (N.D. Tex. 1995) (citing *Fontenot v. Upjohn Co.*, 780 F.2d 1190, 1194 (5th Cir. 1986)). In reviewing the motion, "the court must view the facts in the light most favorable to the non-moving party" and "any doubt as to the existence of a genuine issue of material fact must be resolved against the moving party." *Coury v. Moss*, 529 F.3d 579, 584 (5th Cir. 2008); *Keiser*, 614 F.2d at 411. While the court must review all the evidence in deciding a motion for summary judgment, it is not permitted to make credibility determinations or weigh evidence because those tasks, "along with the drawing of legitimate inferences from the facts, are for the jury, not the court." *Reeves v. Sanderson Plumbing Prods., Inc.*, 530 U.S. 133, 135 (2000). Summary judgment is "a lethal weapon, and courts must be mindful of its aims and targets and beware of overkill in its use." *Brunswick Corp. v. Vineberg*, 370 F.2d 605, 612 (5th Cir. 1967).

This Court should deny summary judgment because Defendant fails to negate the EEOC's prima facie case for recovery under Title VII, and the EEOC proves there is, at a minimum, a fact issue as to the sole element Defendant challenges—whether Mr. Saint held a bona fide religious belief. Because the Defendant cannot conclusively disprove EEOC's prima facie case, the burden shifts to Defendant to prove as a matter of law either a reasonable accommodation or that it was unable to reasonably accommodate Plaintiff without undue hardship. *Antoine*, 713 F.3d at 831. Defendant fails to meet its burden to prove either affirmative defense as a matter of law. Accordingly, this Court should deny summary judgment.

VI. ARGUMENT AND AUTHORITIES

This Court should deny summary judgment as to the EEOC's Title VII claim for religious discrimination. First, there is, at a minimum, a genuine issue of material fact that Mr. Saint sincerely held a bona fide religious belief. Second, Defendant has failed to conclusively prove that it offered Mr. Saint a reasonable accommodation. Third, Defendant has failed to conclusively prove that accommodating Mr. Saint's religious belief would impose an undue hardship on Defendant.

A. Defendant's Motion for Summary Judgment should be denied because there remain genuine issues of material fact as to whether Mr. Saint's religious belief was bona fide.

First, this Court should deny summary judgment because the evidence shows that a genuine issue of material fact exists as to whether Mr. Saint sincerely held a bona fide religious belief. An employee satisfies the first element of a Title VII claim for religious discrimination whenever he establishes that he holds a bona fide religious belief. *Davis*, 765 F.3d at 485. A court will hold an employee's belief is bona fide as long as the belief is sincerely held, and plaintiff's sincerity in espousing his belief is in the Fifth Circuit largely a matter of "individual credibility." *Tagore v. United States*, 735 F.3d 324, 328 (5th Cir.2013). Indeed, courts hold the first element is met "on little more than the plaintiff's credible assertions." *Id.* The sincerity of a plaintiff's engagement in a particular religious practice is "rarely challenged" and, when it is, the court must analyze the issue "with a light touch, or 'judicial shyness.'" *Id.* (citing *Moussazadeh v. Tex. Dep't. of Criminal Just.*, 703 F.3d 781, 791–92 (5th Cir. 2012)). Furthermore, in deciding whether a belief is bona fide, the court "is limited to focusing upon the individual's motivation," and a court's task is merely to decide whether the individual's beliefs are, "in his own scheme of things, religious.'" *Davis*, 765 F.3d at 485 (citing *United States v. Seeger*, 380 U.S. 163, 185 (1965)).

An employee's testimony as to his sincere religious belief is sufficient to defeat summary judgment. In *Davis*, the Fifth Circuit, overturning the district court's grant of summary judgment, held that the employee's testimony that she sincerely felt she was religiously compelled to attend a church event created a genuine dispute of material fact whether she held a bona fide religious belief. 765 F.3d at 485–86. In that case, the employee told her employer she could not work on a certain Sunday because she had a special church service to attend that involved breaking new ground and feeding the community. *Id.* at 486–87. The employee testified that she was a devout member of her church and "strongly believed" she "needed" to be there for the event. *Id.* at 486. In finding that the employee's belief was sincere, and, therefore, bona fide, the Fifth Circuit reasoned that the district court erred by improperly focusing on the nature of the activity itself. *Id.* at 486–87. The Fifth Circuit explained that the focus was properly not on whether the "church event was in itself a true religious tenet," but only whether the employee "sincerely believed it to be religious in her own scheme of things." *Id.* The Fifth Circuit further reasoned that "drawing all reasonable inferences in favor of [the employee] as the nonmoving party, and considering the 'light touch' and 'judicial shyness' that must be exercised," the employee's "testimony about her own sincere belief regarding her religious need to attend a special service at church on Sunday sufficiently evidenced a genuine dispute of material fact whether she held a bona fide religious belief." *Id.* at 487.

Here, like *Davis*, Mr. Saint establishes a genuine issue of material fact exists as to the sincerity of his bona fide religious belief in the "Mark of the Beast." Like *Davis*, where the employee provided evidence that she was a devout member of her church and that she "strongly believed" she "needed" to be there for a church event, here, Mr. Saint testified that as an Evangelical Christian, he strongly believed that Revelation 13:16–18 indicates that the "Mark of the Beast" is a "symbolic mark" and that "technology will be used to carry out its implementation." *Davis*, 765 F.3d at 486; Ex. 2; Ex. 3; Ex.8; Ex. 14, Saint Dep. 4:2–10. Like *Davis*, where the court held it was improper to focus on whether the activity was a "true religious tenant," here, it was improper for Defendant to interject its own interpretation of the Bible to determine whether Mr. Saint's religious belief about the scanner was somehow wrong. *Davis*, 765 F.3d at 486; Ex. 5 at 1–2. Similar to *Davis*, where the employee informed her employer that she would not be able to attend one of the required days for installation due to her prior religious commitment, here, Mr. Saint immediately informed his supervisor and the Human Resources manager that he could not use the new biometric scanning technology because of his belief in the "Mark of the Beast" being assigned through that exact type of technology. *Davis*, 765 F.3d at 484; Ex. 1; Ex. 2; Ex. 3; Ex 14, Saint Dep. 3:13–15. Following *Davis*, which is binding on this Court, Mr. Saint's testimony about his own sincere belief regarding what was "religious in [his] own scheme of things" is sufficient to create a genuine issue of material fact on summary judgment without more. *Davis*, 765 F.3d at 487. Accordingly, it is proper for this Court to assess Mr. Saint's religious belief with "judicial shyness" and hold that the bona fide religious belief element is met, for the purpose of establishing a genuine issue of fact, "on little more than the plaintiff's credible assertions." *Id.* at 484, 487.

Defendant's reliance on *Hansard v. Johns-Manville* is misplaced because Defendant misstates key facts that were central to the court's holding. Def.'s Mot. Summ. J. 8–10; No. 1902, 1973 WL 129, at *1 (E.D. Tex. Feb. 16, 1973). In *Hansard*, the plaintiff's claim of religious discrimination was rooted in his conviction against working for profit on Sundays. 1973 WL 129, at *1. The plaintiff's testimony in that case about the sincerity of his religious belief was contradictory and inconsistent, and the court determined the contradictions demonstrated a lack of reliance on the religious belief underlying the employee's requested accommodation. *Id.* at *2. However, unlike *Hansard*, where the plaintiff contradicted his professed belief by working "several Sundays after his . . . renewed conviction against working on Sundays," here, no evidence exists that Mr. Saint ever used a scanning device in the past that would contradict his belief that using scanning devices assigns the "Mark of the Beast." *Hansard*, 1973 WL 129, at *5; Ex. 14, Saint Dep. 3:11–12.

Similarly, although Revelation 13:16 defines the "number of the beast" to be 666, which is part of Mr. Saint's address and cell phone number, his association with certain numbers is not related to his argument against clocking in and out of work by using scanning technology. Ex. 2; Ex. 3; Ex. 14, Saint Dep. 2:14–15. Mr. Saint's reliance on his sincere fear about the "Mark of the Beast" comes from the assignment of the "Mark" through scanning technology, such as the Palmvein biometric scanning device, which is the root of his belief and his claim of religious discrimination through forced use. Ex. 14, Saint Dep. 3:10–12. Accordingly, because there is no evidence that Mr. Saint contradicted his sincere religious belief by using biometric scanning technology, this Court should not find *Hansard* persuasive.

Accordingly, this Court should deny summary judgment because there is at a minimum, a genuine issue of material fact as to whether Mr. Saint's belief in the "Mark of the Beast" is so sincerely held as to establish a bona fide religious belief.

B. Defendant's Motion for Summary Judgment should be denied because Defendant has not proven that, as a matter of law, it offered Mr. Saint a reasonable accommodation.

Second, this Court should deny summary judgment because the evidence shows that a genuine issue of material fact exists as to whether Defendant offered a reasonable accommodation to Mr. Saint. An employer fails to defeat a Title VII religious discrimination claim when it cannot prove it reasonably accommodated the employee. *Antoine*, 713 F.3d at 831. Though an employer does not have a duty to provide the specific accommodation requested by its employee, it must nevertheless offer an accommodation that is reasonable. *Brener v. Diagnostic Ctr. Hosp.*, 671 F.2d 141, 146–47 (5th Cir. 1982). What constitutes "reasonable" is a question ordinarily left to the fact finder. *E.E.O.C. v. Universal Mfg. Corp.*, 914 F.2d 71, 73 (5th Cir. 1990). "Selectively accommodating" an employee's beliefs is not reasonable. *Id.* Similarly, an offered accommodation is unreasonable if it does not allow the employee to completely fulfill his religious belief or practice. *Favero v. Huntsville Ind. Sch. Dist.*, 939 F. Supp. 1281, 1288 (S.D. Tex. 1996). Only when an employer offers a reasonable accommodation is the employee then obligated to make a good faith attempt to satisfy his religious needs in the manner offered. *Brener*, 671 F.2d at 146–47. All "forms and aspects of [an employee's] religion," no matter how unconventional, must be accommodated by an employer "except those that cannot be, in practice and with honest effort, reconciled with a businesslike operation." *Cooper v. Gen. Dynamics*, 533 F.2d 163, 168–69 (5th Cir. 1976).

An employer's offered accommodation is not reasonable if it only partially ameliorates the religious practice's conflict with an employee's job duties. In *Universal*, the court held that the accommodation offered by the employer did not constitute a "reasonable accommodation" under Title VII. 914 F.2d at 72. In that case, the employee requested that her employer allow her to take a seven-day period of unpaid leave so that she could attend a religious festival. *Id.* The employer denied the employee's request and told the employee she could either: (1) have five days of unpaid leave; or (2) take seven days of unpaid leave provided she worked at least one shift within that seven-day period. *Id.* The court found that the employee's request presented two religious conflicts and requests for accommodation: that she be excused from her normal working shift to attend the festival and that she be excused from any work whatsoever during the week of the festival. *Id.* at 73. The court reasoned that since two distinct accommodation requests were made by the employee, the employer's accommodation of one request but lack of any attempt to accommodate the other constituted "selective 'accommodation'" and was therefore unreasonable. *Id.*

Similarly, an employer's offered accommodation is unreasonable if it does not allow the employee to completely fulfill his religious belief or practice. In *Favero*, the court held that the employer failed to conclusively prove that it had provided a reasonable accommodation to the employee as a matter of law. 939 F. Supp. at 1288. In that case, the employee was a bus driver who requested an eight-day leave of absence to attend a religious gathering. *Id.* at 1285. Just a few days before the employee was scheduled to leave for the religious gathering, the employer informed him that his request for leave was being denied due to a shortage of other drivers. *Id.* The employer told the employee that he could take the first five days of his requested leave, but that he would need to return to work two days earlier than originally requested. *Id.* Because the employee would be unable to attend the entirety of the religious celebration if he were to return on the date demanded by his employer, the employee did not return to work as directed and was later terminated. *Id.* The court reasoned that the employer did not offer a reasonable accommodation because offering the employee five days of leave, rather than the eight days the employee requested, would not allow the employee "to fully satisfy [his] religious observance" by attending the religious gathering in its entirety. *Id.* at 1288.

Here, as in *Universal* and *Favero*, Defendant cannot demonstrate the lack of a genuine issue of material fact as to whether it offered Mr. Saint a reasonable accommodation. Like in *Universal*, where the employer made no attempt to accommodate an employee's inability to work during a seven-day religious festival, here, Defendant made no attempt to accommodate Mr. Saint's inability to use the biometric scanner on any part of his body. 914 F.2d at 73–74; Ex. 5 at 4; Ex 2, Edwards Dep. 5:23–6:1. More than *Universal*, where the employer at least attempted to accommodate one of the employee's religious needs, here, Defendant did not attempt to eliminate the conflict between Mr. Saint's religious need to avoid using the biometric scanning technology *at all* and Defendant's employment requirements. 914 F.2d at 73–74; Ex. 5 at 4; Ex. 2, Edwards Dep. 5:23–6:1. In *Universal*, the plaintiff needed to: (1) attend the seven-day festival; and (2) not work during the seven-day festival. 914 F.2d at 72. Her employer attempted to accommodate her attendance at the festival but did not attempt to accommodate her second religious conflict. *Id.* at 73–74. Here, Mr. Saint requested an exemption from using the biometric scanner "under any type of conditions" because pursuant to his Evangelical Christian beliefs, "scanning technology is the Mark of the Beast." Ex. 2; Ex. 8. However, Defendant's only offered accommodation would still require Mr. Saint to "scan in by way of a thumb print on [his] left hand." Ex. 5 at 1. Worse than the employer in *Universal*, Defendant did not even make a "selective accommodation," but merely assigned its perceived meaning to the Biblical verse central to Mr. Saint's religious belief, and then suggested he scan his left hand instead. Ex. 5 at 1–2. Beyond the single proposed accommodation, Defendant disengaged with Mr. Saint and offered no other options. *Id.* Accordingly, like in *Universal*, this Court should hold that Defendant's proposed accommodation was acting "selectively" by offering an alternative that effectively did not fully address Mr. Saint's religious needs and thus was patently unreasonable such that this Court should deny the motion for summary judgement. *See Brener*, 671 F.2d at 146–47; *Universal*, 914 F.2d at 73.

This Court should follow *Favero* and find that Defendant's selective accommodation would not have allowed Mr. Saint to "fully satisfy" his religious beliefs. *Favero*, 939 F. Supp. at 1288. Like the employee in that case, who asked that he be completely exempted from work for the entirety of the religious celebration he planned to attend, here, Mr. Saint asked that he be completely exempted from using the scanner system. *Id.*; Ex. 8. Like the employer in *Favero*, who only granted its employee enough leave to attend a portion of his religious celebration, here, Defendant only offered to allow Mr. Saint to refrain from scanning his retina but not the rest of his body. Ex. 5 at 1. Therefore, like the employees in *Favero*, Mr. Saint was not able to "fully satisfy" his religious practice through use of the selective accommodation of using the hand scanner on his thumb. *See* 939 F.Supp at 1288. Therefore, Defendant did not offer a reasonable accommodation to Mr. Saint.

Defendant's reliance on *Bruff v. North Mississippi Health Service, Inc.*, is misplaced. Def's Mot. Summ. J. 12–14; 244 F.3d 495 (5th Cir. 2001). Defendant's sparse application of *Bruff* to the present case fails to mention that unlike in *Bruff*, where the plaintiff's requested accommodation would have excused her from performing key aspects of her position as a counselor, here, Mr. Saint required an accommodation from the clocking-in and -out process, not an exemption from his primary duties as a general laborer. Def.'s Mot. Summ. J. 12–14; 244 F.3d at 500; Ex. 8. Defendant argues that *Bruff*'s holding applies here because "Mr. Saint's stubborn insistence on his sole requested accommodation does not require UI to offer it." Def.'s Mot. Summ. J. 14. However, Mr. Saint provided a suggestion for a possible accommodation—"to continue to sign in and out by checking in with Ms. Edwards." Ex. 8 at 1. He did not insist on that accommodation alone, he simply responded to Defendant's request to provide "suggestions for possible accommodations"; he was willing to sign in and out of work using an alternative method. Ex. 2; Ex. 8. Further, the plaintiff in *Bruff* was aware of the potential conflicts with her religious beliefs before she applied for the position, unlike Mr. Saint, who required an accommodation as a result of a policy change years into his employment with UI. 244 F.3d at 500; Ex. 1; Ex. 12, Anderson Dep. 3:2–3. Unlike the employer in *Bruff*, who made substantial efforts to accommodate its employee to eliminate the conflict between the employee's religious beliefs and her job duties (such as by facilitating the employee's transfer to another position or department in which she would be less likely to be confronted with subject matter she found objectionable based on her religious beliefs), here, Defendant mandated a single "accommodation" proposal that did not fully address Mr. Saint's religious needs. 244 F.3d at 498; Ex. 5 at 1–2. Therefore, this Court should not find *Bruff* persuasive.

Similarly, Defendant's reliance on *Brener* is unpersuasive because Defendant omits key facts that were important to the court's reasoning and holding. Def.'s Mot. Summ. J. 12–14 (citing *Brener*, 671 F.2d at 143). In *Brener*, the plaintiff's employer had a flexible scheduling system that allowed employees to trade shifts with their coworkers. 671 F.2d at 143–44. Further, the hospital deviated from established practice by directing employees to trade schedules with the plaintiff, and thus made a considerable effort to accommodate the plaintiff's needs. *Id.* at 144. Unlike the employer in *Brener*, Defendant did not make a considerable effort to accommodate Mr. Saint's religious needs. Ex. 5 at 1–2. Instead, Defendant offered Mr. Saint a single accommodation option that would have required him to use scanning technology in spite of his religious objections to it. Ex. 5 at 1–2.

Further, Defendant's reliance on *Brener* is also not persuasive because Defendant misapplies the court's reasoning. Def.'s Mot. Summ. J. 12–14. The *Brener* court reasoned there was inadequate cooperation by the employee to try to satisfy his religious needs because the plaintiff did not fully avail himself of the flexibility of the scheduling system when he only made "haphazard efforts" to trade schedules with his coworkers. 671 F.2d at 144–46. Unlike the employee in *Brener*, Mr. Saint was not responsible for the failure of the accommodation because Mr. Saint requested a total exemption from using the biometric scanner on any part of his body, and Defendant refused to excuse Mr. Saint from using the biometric scanner. Ex. 8; Ex. 5 at 1–2. Unlike in *Brener*, where the plaintiff had the ability to resolve his religious conflicts by trading shifts with his coworkers, here, Defendant did not offer Mr. Saint an alternative to using the biometric scanner. 671 F.2d 143–44; Ex. 5 at 1–2. Rather, Mr. Saint requested to continue signing in manually with his supervisor, and although that request was denied, Defendant did not offer him any alternative to the biometric scanner. Ex. 5 at 1–4; Ex. 12, Edwards Dep. 5:12–14. There was no dialogue with Mr. Saint past the original decision denying his accommodation request, leaving no opportunity for cooperation. Ex. 5 at 1. Because Mr. Saint was not responsible for the failure of the selective "accommodation" Defendant offered that did not fully address his religious objection, this Court should not follow *Bruff* or *Brener*.

This Court should deny summary judgment because there is at a minimum, a genuine issue of material fact as to whether Defendant offered Mr. Saint a reasonable accommodation when it still required him to use the biometric scanning technology Mr. Saint found objectionable on religious grounds and failed to engage in any further accommodation discussion.

C. Defendant's Motion for Summary Judgment should be denied because Defendant has not proven that, as a matter of law, accommodating Mr. Saint's religious belief would impose an undue hardship.

Third, this Court should deny Defendant's Motion for Summary Judgment because a genuine issue of material fact exists as to whether providing a reasonable accommodation to Mr. Saint would have imposed an undue hardship on Defendant. An employer fails to defeat a Title VII religious discrimination claim when it cannot prove that providing a reasonable accommodation would cause undue hardship. *Antoine*, 713 F.3d at 831. An "undue hardship" only exists when an employer would be forced to bear more than a de minimis cost to accommodate an employee's religious practice or belief. *Weber v. Roadway Express*, 199 F.3d 270, 273 (5th Cir. 2000). An employer bears more than a de minimis cost if the employer proves that the accommodation would cause changes in the schedule of other employees and alter the employer's otherwise neutral procedure. *Antoine*, 713 F.3d at 839. In other words, Title VII does not require "unequal treatment" such as denying the shift and job preference of some employees, as well as depriving them of their contractual rights, in order to accommodate or prefer the religious needs of others. *Trans World Airlines, Inc. v. Hardison*, 432 U.S. 63, 81 (1977).

An employer's "unsubstantiated assertion[s]" of the nature of alleged burden are insufficient to support the granting of summary judgment on the issue of undue hardship. *Ford*, 2007 WL 2051016, at *2. Furthermore, the extent of undue hardship on the employer's business is at issue only where the employer claims that it is unable to offer any reasonable accommodation without such hardship. *Ansonia Bd. of Educ. v. Philbrook*, 479 U.S. 60, 68–69 (1986) (emphasis added). An employer's assertion alone that it would be an undue hardship to allow an employee to continue to use a historically utilized business practice is insufficient to warrant summary judgment. *Alderman v. Great Atl. & Pac. Tea Co., Inc.*, 332 F. Supp. 2d 932, 937 (E.D. La. 2004).

An employer must provide more than "unsubstantiated assertion[s]" in order to prove that, as a matter of law, accommodating an employee's religious belief would constitute an undue hardship. In *Ford*, the court held that the employer did not meet its burden of proving that accommodating its employee's religious belief would have constituted an undue hardship. 2007 WL 2051016, at *1. In that case, the employee's religious beliefs precluded her from working on Sundays, and she asked that her employer accommodate her belief. *Id.* The employer claimed that accommodating the employee's belief would constitute an undue hardship by requiring the creation of a new, salaried position. *Id.* at *2. However, the employer only offered one unsubstantiated assertion to support its position. *Id.* The court reasoned that although the creation of a new position was "likely to impose more than a de minimis cost in many cases," the defendant failed to "to adduce any evidence that creating a new position for [the plaintiff] would have involved more than a *de minimis* cost" and failed to meet its burden to show "that all conceivable accommodations" would have imposed an undue hardship. *Id.*

Likewise, summary judgment is inappropriate when an employer merely claims it would be an undue hardship to allow the employee to continue to use a historically utilized business practice. In *Alderman*, the court denied summary judgment and held there was a genuine issue of material fact as to undue hardship. 332 F. Supp. 2d at 937. In that case, the employee notified his employer upon hiring that his religious beliefs and role as his church's pastor prevented him from working on Sundays. *Id.* at 935. The employee was not required to work a single Sunday in the first fourteen months of his employment; however, upon a change in supervising personnel, the employee was informed that he would need to begin working Sundays. *Id.* at 935. The employer claimed that accommodating the employee's request to refrain from working on Sundays would impose an undue hardship in that it would adversely affect the employee's coworkers. *Id.* at 937. Conversely, the employee argued that the employer was not subjected to any undue hardship in the fourteen months during which the employee was off on Sundays, and that the employer had not presented any evidence that a future undue hardship existed. *Id.* The court reasoned that "the obvious dominance of material fact issues" in the situation necessitated a denial of the employer's summary judgment motion. *Id.*

Here, like in *Ford* and *Alderman*, Defendant cannot demonstrate a genuine issue of material fact as to undue hardship. As in *Ford*, where the employer offered only one unsubstantiated assertion as the basis for its claim that providing a reasonable accommodation would constitute an undue hardship, here the only support Defendant offers as to its claim of undue hardship is the unsubstantiated statement of one employee, Mr. Saint's supervisor, who testified she refused to perform "extra work" to manually keep Mr. Saint's time. 2007 WL 2051016, at *2; Ex. 5, at 3. Moreover, while Defendant claims the biometric scanning system was implemented to avoid losses associated with suspected fraudulent time-keeping and employees forgetting their codes, Defendant fails to provide evidence indicating that Mr. Saint ever falsified his time records or forgot his code. Ex. 12, Edwards Dep. 4:17– 23, 5:1–2. Accordingly, like *Ford*, Defendant has failed to "to adduce any evidence" that allowing Mr. Saint to manually clock in and out "would have involved more than a *de minimis* cost." 2007 WL 2051016, at *2.

Furthermore, even if the Court were to accept that conclusory testimony alone is sufficient to show that allowing Mr. Saint to check in and out with his supervisor would have constituted an undue hardship, Defendant failed to prove that Mr. Saint's religious belief could not have been accommodated in some other manner without undue hardship or that such accommodation would constitute "unequal treatment." *See Hardison*, 432 U.S. at 81. While Mr. Saint's *preferred* accommodation was clocking in and out with his supervisor, he informed Defendant he was willing to sign in and out of work "using an alternative method." Ex. 2. Like *Ford*, Defendant has provided no evidence as to whether other methods of accommodation were explored such that Defendant fails to meet its burden to show "that all conceivable accommodations" would have imposed an undue hardship. 2007 WL 2051016, at *2. Defendant cannot "claim that it is unable to offer *any* reasonable accommodation without such hardship" because it did not explore any other accommodations whatsoever—rather, it simply denied Mr. Saint's proposed accommodation and forced him to use the objectionable scanner. *See Philbrook*, 479 U.S. at 68–69; Ex. 5 at 1–2. Moreover, Defendant cannot demonstrate that manually keeping Mr. Saint's time would result in "unequal treatment;" indeed, the opposite is true. *See Hardison*, 432 U.S. at 81. Defendant implemented manual time-keeping for another employee on non-religious grounds and its own policy requires a manual component for employee time-keeping. Ex. 12, Edwards Dep. 5:7–11; 6:2–3; Ex. 9.

Similarly, this Court should follow *Alderman* because it is not an undue hardship per se to allow an employee to continue to use a historically utilized business practice. *Alderman*, 332 F. Supp. 2d at 935. Like in *Alderman*, where the employee had a 14-month history of refraining from working on Sundays, here, Mr. Saint clocked in and out of work using the previously used manual time-keeping system for years before the new system was implemented. 332 F. Supp. 2d at 935; Ex. 12, Edwards Dep. 2:21–22. Further, as in *Alderman*, where the employer alleged that allowing the employee to continue being off on Sundays—as he always had been—would constitute an undue hardship, here, Defendant alleges that allowing Mr. Saint to continue clocking in with the manual system—the one used by all of Defendant's employees for years—would be an undue hardship. 332 F. Supp. 2d at 935; Ex. 5, at 3. However, like the employer in *Alderman*, Defendant has offered no evidence that Mr. Saint's practice of using the manual clock-in system placed an undue hardship on Defendant in the years prior to implementation of the biometric scanning system, nor that it would constitute a future undue hardship. Rather, another employee, Marvin Svelt, was permitted—after the implementation of the scanner—to "clock in by simply checking with Ms. Edwards." Ex. 14, Saint Dep. 4:16–18. Defendant—in allowing Mr. Svelt to "continue manual time-keeping" because he lost an eye and had broken arms—noted that it "understood that Svelt's unique situation makes it impossible for him to comply with the scanning requirements right now." Ex. 5 at 3; Ex. 12, Edwards Dep. 5:9–12. While Defendant admitted that it was aware of Mr. Saint's "strong religious beliefs" that made it impossible for him to use the scanner, Ms. Edwards said allowing Mr. Saint to do the same would be "extra work." Ex. 5 at 3; Ex. 12, Edwards Dep. 5:16–6:3. If allowing an employee to clock in and out manually did, in fact, impose an undue hardship, Defendant would have not allowed Mr. Svelt to do it. Maintaining a manual component to its time-keeping process is also inconsistent with Defendant's bald claim of undue hardship due to manual time-keeping. At the very least, as in *Alderman*, there is an "obvious dominance of material fact issues" and a lack of evidence that any accommodation of Mr. Saint's religious beliefs would cause Defendant undue hardship. 332 F. Supp. 2d at 937.

Defendant's reliance on *Tagore* is misplaced. Def's Mot. Summ. J. 15–16 (citing *Tagore*, 735 F.3d at 330). Central to the court's reasoning in *Tagore* was the fact that the employee's requested accommodation would impose unfair and impractical extra duties on security personnel that would "be detrimental to the broad vigilance required at the entrance to public offices." 735 F.3d at 330. Unlike the plaintiff in *Tagore*, who worked for a federal entity, inside a federal building, and wished to wear a religious blade long enough to be considered a "dangerous weapon" under federal law, here, Mr. Saint's requested accommodation to clock in manually poses no analogous threat to public safety as it does not involve weapons, would not require unfair and impractical extra duties on personnel since the duties were already being performed and must continue to be performed per Defendant's time-keeping policy. *Id.*; Ex. 12, Edwards Dep. 6:2–3; Ex. 9. Therefore, *Tagore* does not support Defendant's argument that accommodating Ms. Saint's request would constitute undue hardship.

Additionally, Defendant's reliance on *Weber* is unavailing. Def's Mot. Summ. J. 15–16 (citing *Weber*, 199 F.3d at 272). Unlike the employee in *Weber*, whose requested accommodation was exemption from certain job duties that were integral to his position and necessary for the basic functioning of the employer's business, here, Mr. Saint did not ask that his job duties be modified in any way—he merely requested that he be allowed to clock in and out by another method so that he could continue performing his job duties as normal. 199 F.3d at 272; Ex. 8. The court's reasoning in *Weber* centered around its concern that accommodating the employee would affect the work schedule, time off, and compensation of other employees who would be charged with performing the job duties that would otherwise be relegated to the employee. 199 F.3d at 274. Defendant has provided no evidence indicating that the *Weber* court's concerns would be applicable in this case and, as noted above, Defendant has already allowed another employee to clock in using an alternative, manual method. Ex. 5 at 3; Ex. 12, Edwards Dep. 5:7–14. Because Defendant offers no substantiated evidence to support that Ms. Edwards would be adversely affected by being forced to spend time manually clocking in Mr. Saint—a task that she already performs for another employee—this Court should not follow *Weber*. *Id.*

This Court should deny summary judgment because there is, at a minimum, a genuine issue of fact as to whether Defendant would incur an undue hardship by accommodating Mr. Saint's bona fide religious belief with an alternative method for clocking in and out of work.

VII. CONCLUSION

Plaintiff respectfully requests that this Court deny Defendant's Motion for Summary Judgment as to Plaintiff's claim of religious discrimination.

Respectfully submitted,

/s/ Julius Hernandez
Julius Hernandez
State Bar No. 888996
jhernandez@EEOC.com
Dallas District Office EEOC
207 S. Houston St.
Dallas, Texas 75202
214-555-5555 (office)
214-555-5556 (facsimile)
Attorney for Plaintiff

CERTIFICATE OF SERVICE

This is to certify that on the 7th day of July 2024, I electronically filed the foregoing document with the clerk of the Court for the United States District Court, Northern

District of Texas, using the electronic case filing system of the Court, and served this document on all attorneys of record in accordance with Rule 5 of the Federal Rules of Civil Procedure.

/s/ Julius Hernandez

these Plaintiffs of "modest means," would have been unjust. Furthermore, the court reasoned that four Plaintiffs had voluntarily elected to avoid monetary sanctions in favor of dismissal, and thus should not be straddled with both dismissal of their claims and additional costs.

Accordingly, I would affirm the district court's reduced cost award, and dissent from the majority's contrary opinion.

Kawaljeet K. TAGORE, Plaintiff–Appellant

v.

UNITED STATES of America; United States Department of Homeland Security; Federal Protective Service; United States of America Department of the Treasury–Internal Revenue Service, Defendants–Appellees.

No. 12–20214.

United States Court of Appeals, Fifth Circuit.

Nov. 13, 2013.

Background: Sikh employee for Internal Revenue Service (IRS) brought action against United States and various federal agencies, alleging violations of her religious rights under Title VII and Religious Freedom Restoration Act (RFRA). The United States District Court for the Southern District of Texas entered summary judgment for government. Employee appealed.

Holdings: The Court of Appeals, Edith H. Jones, Circuit Judge, held that:

(1) IRS did not engage in religious discrimination against employee under Title VII, and

(2) Court of Appeals would remand RFRA claim for further analysis.

Affirmed in part, reversed in part, and remanded.

1. Federal Courts 🔑776

The Court of Appeals reviews a district court's summary judgment de novo, applying the same standard as the district court.

2. Civil Rights 🔑1032, 1154

The sincerity of a plaintiff's belief in a particular religious practice is an essential part of the plaintiff's prima facie case under either Title VII or Religious Freedom Restoration Act (RFRA). Religious Freedom Restoration Act of 1993, § 2, 42 U.S.C.A. § 2000bb; Civil Rights Act of 1964, § 701, 42 U.S.C.A. § 2000e.

3. Federal Civil Procedure 🔑2497.1

Genuine issue of material fact existed as to sincerity of Sikh employee's religious practice of wearing kirpan with 3-inch blade, precluding summary judgment on grounds that employee lacked sincerity in religious belief in action against federal employer alleging violation of rights under Title VII and Religious Freedom Restoration Act (RFRA). Religious Freedom Restoration Act of 1993, § 2, 42 U.S.C.A. § 2000bb; Civil Rights Act of 1964, § 701, 42 U.S.C.A. § 2000e.

4. Civil Rights 🔑1153

To establish a prima facie case of religious discrimination under Title VII, the plaintiff must present evidence that (1) she held a bona fide religious belief, (2) her belief conflicted with a requirement of her employment, (3) her employer was informed of her belief, and (4) she suffered an adverse employment action for failing to comply with the conflicting employment requirement. Civil Rights Act of 1964, §§ 701(j), 703(a)(1), 42 U.S.C.A. §§ 2000e(j), 2000e–2(a)(1).

5. Civil Rights ⚷1157, 1162(2)

Internal Revenue Service (IRS) did not engage in religious discrimination against Sikh employee, even though employee was terminated after she refused to stop wearing kirpan with 3-inch blade into federal building, in violation of statutory ban on weapons with blades exceeding 2.5 inches; although employee claimed her religion mandated that she wear kirpan, IRS was not authorized to determine security requirements of federal buildings, requiring IRS to override agencies authorized to determine requirements would have placed IRS in position of violating federal law, and accommodations that employee proposed, including working from home, amounted to more than de minimus costs on IRS. 18 U.S.C.A. § 930(a), (g)(2); Civil Rights Act of 1964, §§ 701(j), 703(a)(1), 42 U.S.C.A. §§ 2000e(j), 2000e–2(a)(1).

6. Civil Rights ⚷1162(1)

Title VII does not require religious accommodations that impose more than de minimis costs on an employer. Civil Rights Act of 1964, §§ 701(j), 703(a)(1), 42 U.S.C.A. §§ 2000e(j), 2000e–2(a)(1).

7. Federal Courts ⚷932.1, 947

Court of Appeals would reverse district court's finding that federal agency's enforcement of statute banning weapons with blades exceeding 2.5 inches in federal buildings against Sikh employee did not substantially burden her religious practice and remand for further analysis in action under Religious Freedom Restoration Act (RFRA), where agency adopted new policy which contradicted arguments previously advanced by government for denying employee an exception or exemption for wearing of her kirpan to federal building. 18 U.S.C.A. § 930(a), (g)(2); Religious Freedom Restoration Act of 1993, § 2, 42 U.S.C.A. § 2000bb.

Scott David Newar, Houston, TX, for Plaintiff–Appellant.

Lowell V. Sturgill, Jr., Vesper Mei, U.S. Department of Justice, Washington, DC, for Defendant–Appellee.

Julia Fields Pendery, Dallas, TX, Hansdeep Singh, Jaspreet K. Singh, International Center for Advocates Against Discrimination New York, NY, for Amicus Curiae.

Appeal from the United States District Court for the Southern District of Texas.

Before JONES, DENNIS, and HIGGINSON, Circuit Judges.

EDITH H. JONES, Circuit Judge:

Kawaljeet Tagore ("Tagore") was refused permission to wear a kirpan (a Sikh ceremonial sword) with a blade long enough to be considered a "dangerous weapon" under federal law inside the federal building where she worked for the Internal Revenue Service ("IRS"). She lost her job by failing to comply with the applicable regulations or receive an appropriate waiver. Tagore sued the United States and various federal agencies and employees, alleging violations of her religious rights protected by Title VII, 42 U.S.C. §§ 2000e *et seq.*, and the Religious Freedom Restoration Act ("RFRA"), 42 U.S.C. §§ 2000bb *et seq.* The district court granted summary judgment in favor of the government defendants on both claims. We affirm summary judgment on Tagore's Title VII claim. We reverse and remand her RFRA claim for further development of evidence concerning the government's compelling interest in enforcing against *this plaintiff* the statutory ban on weapons with blades exceeding 2.5 inches. 18 U.S.C. § 930(a), (g)(2).

I. BACKGROUND

In 2004, Tagore was hired as a revenue agent for the IRS in the George "Mickey" Leland federal building ("Leland building") in Houston, Texas. In April 2005, she participated in an *Amrit Sanskar* ceremony, pursuant to which she was formally initiated into the Sikh faith. Following the ceremony, Tagore began wearing the five articles of the Sikh faith, including an approximately 9-inch kirpan, a Sikh article that "resembles a knife or sword but, unlike those objects, often has an edge that is curved or blunted."

On her first day back at work after taking *Amrit,* Tagore passed through security without setting off the metal detector and proceeded to her office. After Tagore informed her supervisor, Nieves Narvaez ("Narvaez"), that she was wearing her kirpan, Narvaez instructed her to request a security waiver. He told Tagore to explain that she had recently been baptized into Sikhism and needed to carry the five articles of faith, including the kirpan, on her person at all times. Thereafter, Tagore began wearing a shorter kirpan with a blade approximately 3 inches long in hopes that it would alleviate the security concerns.

Two days later, Tagore provided Narvaez a letter from Amardeep Singh Bhalla ("Bhalla"), Legal Director for the Sikh Coalition, which explained that wearing the kirpan is a mandatory article of the Sikh faith. The letter asserted that kirpans are less dangerous than scissors, box cutters, or other objects that are regularly brought into federal buildings. Narvaez forwarded Tagore's request for a security waiver to Micralyn Baker-Jones ("Baker-Jones"), an IRS labor specialist. After discussing the issue with Baker-Jones, Narvaez placed Tagore on an interim Flexiplace arrangement so she could work at home until the matter was resolved.

The Federal Protective Service ("FPS") advised Baker-Jones that 18 U.S.C. § 930(a) proscribes the knowing possession of "a firearm or other dangerous weapon in a Federal facility," and that the term "dangerous weapon" is defined by § 930(g)(2) as "a weapon, device, instrument, material, or substance, animate or inanimate, that is used for, or is readily capable of, causing death or serious bodily injury, except that such term does not include a pocket knife with a blade of less than 2½ inches in length." FPS determined that Tagore's kirpan qualified as a "dangerous weapon" due to its 3-inch blade. The FPS also decided that Tagore's kirpan did not fall within any of the statutory exemptions. *See* § 930(d)(1)-(3) (providing exemptions for (1) government officers acting in "lawful performance of official duties," (2) federal and military officials, "if such possession is authorized by law," and (3) other persons, if possession is "incident to hunting or other lawful purposes"). The FPS denied Tagore's request for a security waiver.

The IRS then convened a working group to determine whether Tagore's religious exercise of wearing a kirpan could be accommodated in a way that would not violate federal law. To assist in that process, Narvaez emailed Tagore to inquire whether she would consider (1) wearing a kirpan with a blade shorter than 2.5 inches, (2) wearing a dulled blade, (3) wearing a dulled blade sewn in its sheath, (4) wearing a 'symbolic kirpan' encased in plastic or lucite, or (5) leaving her kirpan at home or in her car while she was in a federal building. Sikh Coalition attorney Bhalla responded on Tagore's behalf. He noted that Tagore's kirpan already contained a dull blade and that the remaining accommodations would violate her conscience or religious mandates.

The IRS working group considered whether Tagore could work from home or be reassigned to a federal building without on-site security. Both ideas were rejected, however, because § 930(a) applies to nonsecure federal buildings and a permanent Flexiplace arrangement was not compatible with Tagore's job responsibilities. Seeing no other feasible option, the IRS directed Tagore to report to work at the Leland building without her kirpan by January 30, 2006, or be charged Absent Without Leave ("AWOL"). On January 24, Bhalla responded that "[i]n order to accommodate the IRS, the 'bladed' part of Ms. Tagore's kirpan is now three and one half inches long" and expressed that Tagore "sincerely believe[d] that any further reduction in the size of her kirpan ... would violate[ ] her sincerely held Sikh religious beliefs." When Tagore attempted to report to work at the Leland building with her kirpan, she was denied entry. The IRS declared her AWOL and stopped paying her salary. In March 2006, after an unsuccessful mediation, Tagore filed a Title VII charge with the United States Treasury Department. She alleged that the IRS had discriminated against her on the basis of religion by not allowing her to enter the Leland building while wearing her kirpan and declaring her AWOL. On May 4, the IRS issued Tagore a "Notice of Proposed Adverse Action," informing her of its intent to terminate her employment. She was formally terminated on July 11, 2006.[1]

Tagore then filed suit in district court against the United States and several federal agencies and employees,[2] alleging that the defendants violated her rights under Title VII and RFRA. The district court dismissed several of Tagore's claims.[3] These rulings left two live claims: the Title VII religious discrimination claim against Treasury Secretary Jacob Lew ("Lew"),[4] and the RFRA claim against the FPS, Department of Homeland Security ("DHS"), the DHS Secretary, William Carmody III, David Hiebert, and 25 unidentified defendants. After discovery, the parties filed cross-motions for summary judgment. The district court, writing comprehensive opinions, granted summary judgment in favor of the defendants on both claims, denied Tagore's motion for reconsideration, and dismissed the case with prejudice. Tagore timely appealed.

STANDARD OF REVIEW

[1] We review a district court's summary judgment *de novo*, applying the same standard as the district court. *Moss v. BMC Software, Inc.*, 610 F.3d 917, 922 (5th

1. Tagore exhausted internal administrative EEOC remedies.

2. The Complaint names as defendants the United States; four federal agencies (the Department of the Treasury ("DOT"), Department of Homeland Security ("DHS"), FPS, and IRS); two cabinet secretaries; and several federal employees (William A. Carmody, III, David Hiebert, Christina Navarete–Wasson, Sergio Arellano, James K. Ellis, Nieves Narvaez, and 25 unidentified persons referred to as the "Doe defendants").

3. The district court dismissed Tagore's Title VII retaliation claim, individual-capacity claims, Title VII religious discrimination claim against all defendants except the Treasury Secretary, and RFRA claims against the IRS and DOT. Tagore does not challenge any of these dismissals in this appeal.

4. Lew replaced Timothy Geithner during the pendency of this appeal.

Cir.2010). Summary judgment is warranted if, viewing all evidence in the light most favorable to the non-moving party, the record demonstrates that there is no genuine issue of material fact and that the moving party is entitled to judgment as a matter of law. *Id.* (citing Fed.R.Civ.P. 56). A fact is material if it "might affect the outcome of the suit under the governing law," and a dispute is genuine if "the evidence is such that a reasonable jury could return a verdict for the nonmoving party." *Anderson v. Liberty Lobby, Inc.*, 477 U.S. 242, 248, 106 S.Ct. 2505, 91 L.Ed.2d 202 (1986).

DISCUSSION

1. Sincerely held religious belief.

[2] On appeal, Tagore asserts that her evidence creates a genuine issue of material fact concerning the sincerity of her religious practice of wearing a kirpan with a blade longer than 2.5 inches. The sincerity of a plaintiff's belief in a particular religious practice is an essential part of the plaintiff's prima facie case under either Title VII or RFRA. *See Weber v. Roadway Express, Inc.*, 199 F.3d 270, 273 (5th Cir. 2000) (Title VII); *Gonzales v. O Centro Espirita Beneficente Uniao do Vegetal*, 546 U.S. 418, 428, 126 S.Ct. 1211, 163 L.Ed.2d 1017 (2006) (RFRA). After reviewing hundreds of pages of deposition testimony and exhibits, the district court concluded that Tagore did not create a triable issue of fact that her sincere religious beliefs require her to wear a kirpan with a 3-inch, rather than the statutorily permitted 2.5-inch, blade. With due respect to the able court, this is slicing too thin.

This court recently explored the threshold inquiry into a person's beliefs when discussing a prisoner's claim under the related Religious Land Use and Institutionalized Persons Act ("RLUIPA"). *Moussazadeh v. Tex. Dept. of Criminal Justice*, 703 F.3d 781, 790–92 (5th Cir. 2012). Briefly, each case turns on its particular facts. *Id.* at 791. The specific religious practice must be examined rather than the general scope of applicable religious tenets, and the plaintiff's "sincerity" in espousing that practice is largely a matter of individual credibility. *Id.* at 792. In fact, the sincerity of a plaintiff's engagement in a particular religious practice is rarely challenged. *Id.* at 791. As *Moussazadeh* explains, "[t]hough the sincerity inquiry is important, it must be handled with a light touch, or 'judicial shyness.' " *Id.* at 792 (quoting *A.A. ex rel. Betenbaugh v. Needville Indep. Sch. Dist.*, 611 F.3d 248, 262 (5th Cir.2010)). "[E]xamin[ing] religious convictions any more deeply would stray into the realm of religious inquiry, an area into which we are forbidden to tread." *Id.* (fn. omitted). Both before and following *Moussazadeh*, claims of sincere religious belief in a particular practice have been accepted on little more than the plaintiff's credible assertions. *See, e.g., Garner v. Kennedy*, 713 F.3d 237, 241 (5th Cir.2013) (Muslim prisoner's desire to wear a beard not challenged by TDCJ); *Betenbaugh*, 611 F.3d at 261–62 (Native American schoolboy wearing long hair a sincere religious belief; Texas RFRA parallels RFRA); *Mayfield v. Tex. Dept. of Criminal Justice*, 529 F.3d 599 (5th Cir.2008) (Odin worshiper's religious need for runestones and rune literature not challenged by TDCJ).

[3] There was ample evidence to create a genuine issue of material fact on the sincerity of Tagore's practice of wearing a kirpan with a 3-inch blade. The court's contrary decision focused on close questioning of Tagore in her deposition, which exhibited some ambiguity about whether her sincere beliefs require the kirpan blade, or the entire dagger, to exceed 3

inches. *Cf. Moussazadeh,* 703 F.3d at 792 ("stray[ing] from the path of perfect adherence" does not eviscerate claim of sincerity). She adduced voluminous evidence from the Sikh community, however, that kirpans are mandated to be worn by the religion's adherents and although there are no detailed regulations for the kirpans' appearance, most Sikhs wear kirpans with blades longer than 2.5 inches. As the government acknowledged during the pendency of this appeal:

> There is no prescribed blade length for the *Kirpan;* its size varies based on personal choice. The majority of *Kirpan* blades range in size from 3 to 6 inches, but blades may be as small as 2 inches.... *Kirpan* are always sheathed.... [S]ome Sikhs ... believe a *Kirpan* must be worn at all times....

Federal Protective Service, Policy Directive 15.9.3.1, Prohibited Items Program, Attachment 5 (2012) [hereafter, "Policy Statement"]. Tagore has worn her kirpan 24 hours a day after taking Amrit, with one exception when she travelled in an airplane. Tagore was willing to sacrifice her government employment for the sake of wearing a religiously significant symbolic kirpan. Tagore's actions, the independent evidence of Sikh practices, and the government's acknowledgement create a genuine issue of material fact as to her sincere belief in wearing a 3-inch bladed kirpan.

2. Title VII.

[4] Title VII prohibits an employer from discriminating against an employee on the basis of her religion, unless the employer is unable to reasonably accommodate the employee's religious exercise without undue hardship to its business. 42 U.S.C. §§ 2000e–2(a)(1), 2000e(j). To establish a prima facie case of religious discrimination under Title VII, the plaintiff must present evidence that (1) she held a bona fide religious belief, (2) her belief conflicted with a requirement of her employment, (3) her employer was informed of her belief, and (4) she suffered an adverse employment action for failing to comply with the conflicting employment requirement. *Bruff v. N. Miss. Health Servs., Inc.,* 244 F.3d 495, 499 n. 9 (5th Cir.2001).

[5] Assuming Tagore held a sincere religious belief in wearing a kirpan with a blade exceeding 2.5 inches, a prima facie case of Title VII religious discrimination exists because she lost her job as a result of her religious practice. The district court found this claim inadequate as a matter of law, however, on two additional grounds: the DHS and FPS, not the IRS, control decisions concerning federal building security and the application of Section 930(a); and the IRS proved the affirmative defense that it could not accommodate Tagore's wearing of the kirpan without undue hardship. Both of these holdings must be sustained. First, because the IRS is not authorized to determine the security requirements of federal buildings, it cannot be deemed legally responsible for discriminating against Tagore. Requiring IRS to override the DHS/FPS would place the revenue agency in the position of violating federal law concerning the introduction of "dangerous weapons" into federal buildings. An employer need not accommodate an employee's religious practice by violating other laws. *See Seaworth v. Pearson,* 203 F.3d 1056, 1057 (8th Cir.2000) (defendant need not accommodate plaintiff's religious beliefs when doing so would require defendant to violate federal law, which creates an undue hardship); *Sutton v. Providence St. Joseph Med. Ctr.,* 192 F.3d 826, 830–31 (9th Cir.1999) ("[C]ourts agree that an employer is not liable under Title VII when accommodating an employee's religious beliefs would require the employer to violate federal or state law."); *United States v. Bd. of Educ.*, 911 F.2d 882, 890–91 (3d Cir.1990) (holding that allowing a Muslim teacher to wear religious garb while teaching, thereby violating a state criminal statute, would impose undue hardship on defendant school district).

[6] Even if these defenses were not definitive, the FPS and DHS demonstrated that the accommodations that Tagore proposed to allow her to continue to wear her kirpan amount to more than "de minimis" costs on the employer. Title VII does not require religious accommodations that impose more than "de minimis" costs on an employer. *Trans World Airlines, Inc. v. Hardison*, 432 U.S. 63, 84, 97 S.Ct. 2264, 53 L.Ed.2d 113 (1977); *Bruff*, 244 F.3d at 501. In part, this is because costly accommodations would place the religious practitioner in a more favorable position, at the employer's expense, than her coworkers. Further, more than de minimis adjustments could require coworkers unfairly to perform extra work to accommodate the plaintiff. Tagore suggested three potential accommodations: wearing a dulled kirpan blade; working from her home; or working at other federal buildings that might have fewer security requirements. As the district court held, none of these is a de minimus measure. Security officers cannot be asked to ascertain whether a blade is sharp or dull in order to determine whether it is a "dangerous weapon" within the purview of Section 930(a); this inquiry would be time-consuming, impractical and detrimental to the broad vigilance required at the entrance to public offices. The IRS also determined, and Tagore does not seriously challenge, that she could not effectively perform her duties while working from home. Moreover, the option of her working from other federal facilities is unavailable because Section 930(a) is an across-the-board prohibition of dangerous weapons; it is not facility-specific. For these reasons, the IRS's failure to accommodate Tagore did not violate Title VII as a matter of law.

3. RFRA.

Assuming, again, that Tagore succeeds in establishing a sincerely held religious belief that mandates her wearing a 3–inch kirpan blade, the remaining predicate to a prima facie RFRA case is whether the FPS's enforcement of Section 930(a) substantially burdened her religious practice. *See Gonzales*, 546 U.S. at 428, 126 S.Ct. at 1216. This is not a serious hurdle: she gave up her job rather than wear a shorter-bladed kirpan, *cf. Sherbert v. Verner*, 374 U.S. 398, 403–06, 83 S.Ct. 1790, 10 L.Ed.2d 965 (1963), and she risked violating federal law when she entered the Leland building while wearing it. 18 U.S.C. 930(a)(imposing a fine and up to 1 year imprisonment). Once a prima facie case is established, the government must show a compelling interest in enforcing that provision and that its means are the least restrictive to achieve its objectives. 42 U.S.C. § 2000bb–1(a)–(b)(1) and (2); *Gonzales*, 546 U.S. at 424, 126 S.Ct. 1211. RFRA thus applies strict scrutiny to government regulations that substantially burden a person's religious exercise.

Surely, the government has a compelling interest in protecting federal buildings and the people in and around them, and Congress's choice in defining "dangerous weapons" that cannot be introduced into the buildings to include bladed instruments exceeding 2.5 inches must be given significant deference. The Supreme Court emphasized in *Gonzales*, however, that RFRA requires the government to explain how applying the statutory burden "to the person" whose sincere exercise of religion is being seriously impaired furthers the compelling governmental interest. 546 U.S. at 430–31, 126 S.Ct. 1211. A "categorical approach" is insufficient, particularly if, as here, the statute includes exceptions to the prohibition,[5] *cf. id.* at 430–37, 126 S.Ct. 1211, and the government must produce evidence justifying its specific conclusion. The district court held that the government carried its burden as a matter of law with affidavit testimony that building security officers must apply Section 930(a) uniformly, consistently and rigorously; authorizing individualized case-by-case determinations would undermine security.

The district court also held that the need for uniformity of application satisfied the least restrictive means test. Although the Supreme Court did not reach the less restrictive means test in *Gonzales*, it is settled that the government's is to explain "why alternative policies would be unfeasible, or why they would be less effective in maintaining institutional security." *Spratt v. R.I. Dept. of Corr.*, 482 F.3d 33, 41 (1st Cir.2007). The district court rejected Tagore's citations to case law and instances in which Sikhs wearing kirpans have been granted permission to enter federal buildings, including the White House. Such examples, the court held, reflect isolated exceptions rather than the blanket individual exemption for which Tagore contends. The court also rejected Tagore's argument that she is covered by the exception in Section 930(g) that allows the bearing of "dangerous weapons" for "other lawful purposes." In this regard, it accepted the government's argument that this exception only extends to people like construction workers whose job-related duties require tools that might otherwise violate the statute.

[7] We recite very briefly the district court's reasoning as preface to the point that it has been practically undermined by FPS's decision to acknowledge kirpans as ceremonial weapons that may be allowed in a federal building either by exception or exemption from the statute. The December 2012 FPS Policy Statement, earlier noted, "establishes FPS policy for applying security force countermeasures to mitigate prohibited item entry at Federal properties." Policy Statement at 1. The statement repeatedly references processes that "include[ ] allowing exceptions and exemptions to prohibited items for ... religious exercise ... or other purposes as necessary or required by law." Attachment 2 to the statement prescribes "Procedures for Exceptions and Exemptions for Otherwise Prohibited Items," Policy Statement at 5, one of which is for "accommodations" under the Religious Freedom Restoration Act. Attachment 5 describes "Accommodations for Sikh Articles of Faith," and instructs FPS officers that kirpans with blades longer than 2.5 inches require an exception or exemption before being carried into a federal building. One must ask, why refer to "accommodations" and append this attachment to a document describing procedures for obtaining exceptions or exemptions if, as FPS contends against Tagore, case-by-case determinations are impractical or inconsistent with maintaining security? The fact that FPS promulgated this Policy Statement after the case concluded in the district court does not prevent our taking judicial notice

5. As has been noted, 18 U.S.C. § 930(a) does not apply to law enforcement officers, military personnel, and those lawfully carrying weapons incident to hunting or other lawful purposes. 18 U.S.C. § 930(d). We agree with the court's determination that Tagore's kirpan is not permitted under the exceptions to Section 930(a) for law enforcement officers, military personnel, and hunters. We express no opinion as to whether Tagore's kirpan would be permitted under the subsection for "other lawful purposes."

of its implication for the difficult and fact-sensitive inquiry that must accompany application of strict scrutiny under RFRA.

Because the new policy contradicts the arguments previously advanced by the government for denying Tagore an exception or exemption for the wearing of her kirpan to the Leland building, the district court's application of strict scrutiny must be reversed and remanded for further analysis.

In so doing, we emphasize that we express no opinion on the ultimate application of strict scrutiny because the government should be allowed to offer more evidence concerning its asserted need for uniform application of Section 930(a) and the impact of the new Policy Statement on this case. Precisely because kirpans may be dangerous weapons in the wrong hands or may fall into the hands of evildoers who are not Sikhs, there would seem to be support for certain limitations, *e.g.* on blade length, security clearance status of the bearer of the kirpan, the frequency of the bearer's visits to a particular federal facility, the degree or method of concealment, or degree of attachment to the person's body. All of these considerations, and more, may bear on the fact-intensive nature of the RFRA strict scrutiny test. Despite the importance of deferring to officials charged with maintaining domestic security, conclusional affidavits will be insufficient to overcome the policies and procedures embodied in RFRA.

CONCLUSION

For the foregoing reasons, the judgment of the district court is reversed in part and remanded in part; further proceedings are necessary to determine as a matter of fact whether Tagore holds a sincere religious belief in wearing a kirpan with a blade exceeding the federally prescribed maximum and, if so, whether the government has proven that application of Section 930(a) to Tagore furthers a compelling government interest with the least restrictive means.

AFFIRMED IN PART; REVERSED IN PART; REMANDED IN PART.

THE CITY OF COLLEGE STATION, TEXAS, Plaintiff–Appellant

v.

STAR INSURANCE COMPANY, Defendant–Appellee.

No. 12–20746.

United States Court of Appeals, Fifth Circuit.

Nov. 14, 2013.

Background: City brought action against its general commercial liability insurer, seeking to recover defense costs, indemnification, and statutory penalty interest, after insurer refused to defend or indemnify the city in an underlying lawsuit. The United States District Court for the Southern District of Texas, Kenneth M. Hoyt, J., 2012 WL 4867568, granted insurer's motion for summary judgment. City appealed.

Holding: The Court of Appeals, Patrick E. Higginbotham, Circuit Judge, held that allegations in underlying complaint against city did not fall within the scope of policy's "inverse condemnation" exclusion.

Reversed and remanded.

Index